THE KING'S DEBTS

THE KING'S DEBTS

*Finance and Politics
in France
1589–1661*

by
RICHARD BONNEY

CLARENDON PRESS · OXFORD
1981

Oxford University Press, Walton Street, Oxford OX2 6DP

London Glasgow New York Toronto
Delhi Bombay Calcutta Madras Karachi
Kuala Lumpur Singapore Hong Kong Tokyo
Nairobi Dar es Salaam Cape Town
Melbourne Auckland

and associate companies in
Beirut Berlin Ibadan Mexico City

Published in the United States by
Oxford University Press, New York

British Library Cataloguing in Publication Data
Bonney, Richard
    The King's debts.
    1. France – History – 16th century
    2. France – History – 17th century
    I. Title
    944'.03   DC110
    ISBN 0-19-822563-6

Typeset by Phoenix Photosetting, Chatham
Printed and bound at the University Press, Oxford
by Eric Buckley
Printer to the University

An immediate and great expense . . . will not wait
for the gradual and slow returns of . . . new taxes. In
this exigency government can have no other
resource but in borrowing.
(Adam Smith, *Wealth of Nations*, 1776).

Kings cannot be coerced . . . to repay debts to their
subjects.
(François Miron, 22 April 1605).

PREFACE

There is no modern study of financial policy in France as it evolved between 1589 and 1661. A recent study in English[1] has provided a valuable service by stimulating interest in the subject, but its structure precludes a sense of chronological development. Both the state of royal finances and the individuals involved in the system were very different in 1661 and sixty years earlier. The fundamental purpose of this book, therefore, is to restore a sense of the development of financial management as contemporaries in France would have understood it. Since this study encompasses the reigns of Henri IV, Louis XIII, and the minority of Louis XIV, in one sense it should be entitled *The Kings' Debts*. On the other hand, each king had to decide whether or not to renounce the debts of his predecessor. If he decided not to do so, those debts became his own, *The King's Debts*. In practice, with the exception of the war years of Henri IV's reign the king himself rarely intervened in the conduct of financial administration. A study of the king's debts therefore becomes a study which focuses on central government in general and the decisions taken by successive finance ministers in particular.

Finance is important not only in itself but also because of its broader political, economic, and social implications. Seventeenth-century politicians in France were in no doubt about the importance of sound finances to the conduct of good government. Richelieu considered them fundamental: 'on a toujours dit', Richelieu wrote, 'que les finances sont les nerfs de l'état et il est vrai que c'est le point d'Archimède, qui étant fermement établi, donne moyen de mouvoir tout le monde.'[2] Claude le Bouthillier, one of the two French finance ministers after 1632, agreed, and pointed out that without adequate financial support the great designs of the state could not be achieved.[3] To the historian,

---

[1] J. Dent, *Crisis in finance. Crown, financiers and society in seventeenth-century France* (Newton Abbot, 1973).

[2] A. J. du Plessis, Cardinal de Richelieu, *Testament politique*, ed. L. André (1947), pp. 427–8. Some historians have questioned the authenticity of this work.

[3] Bouthillier wrote to Richelieu concerning the office of *surintendant*: '. . . bien qu'elle ne traicte pas des haultes affaires de l'estat, elle traitte de celles sans lesquelles elles ne peuvent soustenir, non pas mesme commancer . . .' A.A.E. France 839, fo. 357, 19 Nov. 1641.

therefore, financial policy cannot be understood in isolation from the broader issues of foreign policy, domestic politics, and the development of the economy and society. For example, the sale of the last pieces of the royal demesne was a fiscal expedient forced on Henri IV by his war with the Catholic League. Yet it opened up much wider issues of political theory (such sales could be said to be against the fundamental laws of the French monarchy), the power of the crown (the sale of crown lands weakened Henri's direct clientage network and thus his military reserve), and social policy (royal lands were allegedly sold to men of low social origins).[1] Virtually every aspect of royal financial policy raised a hornet's nest of other issues and these wider ramifications are the real importance of a study of the debts of the early Bourbon kings.

There are basically four types of source material which can help the historian in this task. Firstly, there is the vast bulk of decrees issued by the council of finance, the main financial tribunal which increased in importance for much of the period and certainly until the 1650s. There are also other tribunals, whose evidence is less well preserved, and whose work was more circumscribed—the *Chambre des Comptes* of Paris being the most significant. A second source is ministerial correspondence. The system of government dominated by a chief minister had one great advantage from the historian's viewpoint in that it led the finance minister to write down his opinions on occasions when the chief minister was in a different location, or too busy or too ill to listen to him in person. We can thus gauge to a considerable extent the way in which decisions were reached and the arguments presented, though not, it must be said, on every single issue nor for the whole period. (There is much less evidence, qualitatively as well as quantitatively, before Richelieu became chief minister, much as one would expect.) The notarial archives represent an enormous, complex, and intractable third source. Too large to be exploited systematically (there were over a hundred *notaires* in Paris at this time, most of whom kept at least one volume of minutes per year), this source material can nevertheless provide selective insights about financiers and the financial system. The notarial sources lead one to the pessimistic conclusion that there are some questions which are unanswerable from the surviving evidence[2] – questions which contemporaries would not have been able to answer either, except

---

[1] P 2332, p. 197, 30 Mar. 1593.
[2] Cf. D. Dessert, 'Le "laquais-financier" au grand siècle; myth ou réalité?', *XVIIᵉ Siècle*, cxxii (1979), 25.

on an individual or conjectural basis. Here the absence of business records of financiers is greatly missed. Business papers would not have provided the complete picture, but to judge from allusions to them in probate records[1] and acts of the council of finance[2] they would have served to dispel much debate, conjecture, and misunderstanding.

The financial statistics are the most important sources because they have tended to influence the judgements in the text. The great fire at the *Chambre des Comptes* in 1737 ensured that the surviving records in France would be much less complete than the English Exchequer Books for the comparable period.[3] Nevertheless, J. R. Mallet, who was chief clerk of Nicholas Desmaretz,[4] had access to material subsequently burnt in the great fire, and his tables have the inestimable advantage of forming, with the exception of the years 1657–61, the only continuous set of financial statistics in France for the first half of the seventeenth century. It would be idle to claim that there are no difficulties about the details of Mallet's figures, quite apart from typographical mistakes and errors in addition. Mallet's figures are thus the best that exist, but the best is far from perfect. They have to be used to supplement evidence from other sources, not as a statistical series on which exclusive reliance is placed. While the text of this book was in its last stages of preparation, two articles have appeared in print which have the merit of rekindling debate on Mallet's figures, a debate which has been dormant since the publication of Clamagéran's *Histoire de l'impôt* over a hundred years ago.[5] A summary of this debate forms the introduction to the tables presented in Appendix II.

The figures in this book have been presented in *livres tournois*, the

---

[1] A good example are the probate records concerning the great financier Thomas Bonneau: Minutier Central XXX 61, 26 Jan. 1663.

[2] For example, E 392, fo. 5, 7 Oct. 1666. *Liquidation* concerning the heirs of the financier Jean Galland.

[3] Cf. R. Ashton, *The crown and the money market, 1603–1640* (Oxford, 1960). Id., 'Revenue farming under the early Stuarts', *Economic History Review*, 2nd ser. viii (1956), 310–22.

[4] Desmaretz was an *intendant des finances* between 1678 and 1708 and *contrôleur-général des finances* between 1708 and 1715. Part of Mallet's study was a careful analysis in detail of Desmaretz's ministry: J. R. Mallet, *Comptes rendus de l'administration des finances du royaume de France . . .* (London, 1789). Mallet's study was published posthumously.

[5] Professor Chaunu's recent account [*Histoire économique et sociale de la France. I. De 1450 à 1660. i. L'état et la ville*, ed. P. Chaunu and R. Gascon (1977), pp. 182–9] relies on figures drawn from J. J. Clamagéran, *Histoire de l'impôt en France* (3 vols., 1867–76). The recent articles are: A. Guéry, 'Les finances de la monarchie française sous l'ancien régime', *Annales, E.S.C.*, xxxiii (1978), 216–39; J. B. Collins, 'Sur l'histoire fiscale du xviie siècle: les impôts directs en Champagne entre 1595 et 1635', ibid., xxxiv (1979), 325–47.

unit of account after 1602. This presents certain problems in an age of rising prices and the declining value of money. If a satisfactory general index of prices existed, it would be desirable to index the rise in royal income and expenditure against the general level of prices. However, the weighting of a commodity index poses particular problems, as does its regional bias. No price series can be taken as representative of national trends in the price of the same commodity, let alone national trends in the prices of other commodities. An index of Parisian grain prices has been established precisely for the purpose of comparison,[1] but this is no substitute for a general index of prices for France as a whole. In the absence of an acceptable general index, it has been felt preferable to dispense with systematic price comparison. The *livre tournois* was not a money of exchange, the most important coin in circulation in France in 1602 being the gold *écu* or crown (the book value of the *écu de change* after 1602 was 3 *livres*; the real value of the *écu d'or* was 3 *livres* 4 *sols*). There is no doubt at all about the decline in the value of the *livre tournois* in the seventeenth century. For the first third of the century, there were just over 10 *livres* to the £ sterling, but from the 1630s its value declined rapidly. At a low point in 1654, there were 14 *livres* to the £ sterling.[2] Similarly, there was a fall in the value of the *livre tournois* as expressed in terms of its theoretical weight in silver. From a high point of 10.98 grams of silver in 1602 the *livre tournois* fell to 7.92 grams in December 1653, although it recovered its value to 8.33 grams thereafter.[3] These values are important to bear in mind in any consideration of French subsidies to foreign powers or payments made by the crown in cash. However, the theoretical silver equivalent has very little meaning in a period when half the revenues and expenses of the crown were paper rather than cash transactions. For this reason, elaborate conversions of the figures have been avoided.[4]

---

[1] M. Baulant, 'Le prix des grains à Paris de 1431 à 1788', ibid., xxiii (1968), 539.

[2] J. J. McCusker, *Money and exchange in Europe and America, 1600–1715* . . . (Chapel Hill, N. C., 1978), pp. 305–7.

[3] N. de Wailly, 'Mémoire sur les variations de la livre tournois . . .', *Mémoire de l'académie des inscriptions et belles-lettres*, xxi, pt. ii (1857), table iii, 350–1. Conveniently summarized in M. Baulant and J. Meuvret, *Prix des céréales extraits de la mercuriale de Paris, 1520–1698* (2 vols., 1960, 1962), ii. 157, table i.

[4] Guéry, art. cit., 227–8, has impressive-looking graphs which are based on a statistical foundation of shifting sand. The importance of paper transactions in the 1630s, 1650s and the period of the war of the Spanish Succession has been minimized by D. Dessert, 'Les groupes financiers et Colbert, 1661–1683', *Bulletin de la Société d'Histoire Moderne*, lxxx (1981), 19–29. At p. 26, Dessert comments 'dès que vous payez avec un papier cela veut dire que vous ne payez pas.' However, see *infra*, chapters IV–VI, and especially the discussion of *billets de l'Épargne* and the procedure known as *remise en d'autre Épargne*.

I am extremely grateful to the Twenty-Seven Foundation and the Research Board of the University of Reading, without whose generosity the research that went into this book could not have been undertaken. The comments of Mrs Menna Prestwich, who read the earlier drafts of the text for Oxford University Press, have been most patient and helpful. This book is dedicated to my wife, without whose support and careful reading of successive drafts it might never have been completed.

February 1980   R. J. B.

Contents

Abbreviations

A.A.E. France	Archives des Affaires Étrangères, Mémoires et Documents, France
A.D.	Archives Départementales
A.G.	Archives de la Guerre
Annales, E.S.C.	*Annales, Économies, Sociétés, Civilisations*
a.p.	archives privées (Archives Nationales, fonds privées)
B.A.	Bibliothèque de l'Arsenal
B.I.	Bibliothèque de l'Institut de France
B.L.	British Library
B.M.	Bibliothèque Municipale
B.N. MS. fr.	Bibliothèque Nationale, Manuscrits français
B.N. n.a.f.	Bibliothèque Nationale, nouvelles acquisitions françaises
B.N. p.o.	Bibliothèque Nationale, pièces originales
Chambre des Comptes, ed. Boislisle	*Histoire de la maison de Nicolay. Pièces justificatives. II. Chambre des Comptes*, ed. A. M. de Boislisle (Nogent-le-Rotrou, 1873)
Dr.	Dossier
Foucquet, *Défenses*	*Les oeuvres de Mʳ Foucquet, ministre d'estat, contenant son accusation, son procez et ses défenses contre Louis XIV, roy de France* (16 vols., 1696)
Les papiers de Richelieu, ed. Grillon	*Les papiers de Richelieu. Section politique intérieure. Correspondance et papiers d'état*, ed. P. Grillon (in progress; volume i, 1975)
Lettres . . . de Henri IV	*Recueil des lettres missives de Henri IV*, ed. M. Berger de Xivrey and J. Guadet, 9 vols. (1843–76)
Mallet	J. R. Mallet, *Comptes rendus de l'administration des finances du royaume de France. . . .* (London, 1789)
Richelieu, *Mémoires*	A. J. du Plessis, Cardinal de Richelieu, *Mémoires*, ed. R. Lavollée *et al.*, 10 vols. (1907–31)

Véron de Forbonnais, F. Véron de Forbonnais, *Recherches et con-*
Recherches   *sidérations sur les finances de France depuis 1595*
jusqu'à l'année 1721 (Basle, 1758)

N.B.: All manuscript references are to the Archives Nationales unless otherwise stated. All printed works in English are published at London unless otherwise stated. All printed works in French are published at Paris unless otherwise stated

Introduction

The French financial system, 1589–1661

The financial system of the early Bourbon kings was a good deal more flexible than some historians might lead us to believe.[1] In theory, the king could dispose of his finances as he saw fit. He could control them himself, as Louis XIV sought to do in the first years of his personal rule after 1661. Alternatively, he could delegate the supervision of finance to a chief minister, which was the norm for much of the period between 1616 and 1661, the consequences of which were particularly marked in the 1650s. (For a few days in 1659, Cardinal Mazarin, the chief minister, contemplated becoming joint finance minister with Foucquet.[2]) Another possibility was that the king could vest his financial powers in a committee of the council, as happened in 1594 and 1611. In most years, however, the financial system was controlled by a finance minister (*surintendant des finances*).[3] The finance minister might take his orders direct from the king, as did François d'O and Sully, or from the king via his chief minister, as did d'Effiat and Foucquet. By the 1650s there was no formal restraint on the power of the finance minister, who was given a free hand to take such action as he saw fit according to his conscience and was not obliged to render account to the *Chambre des Comptes*, the financial sovereign court responsible for accounting other royal officials, or to anyone else save the king.[4] Foucquet argued that finance ministers since the beginning of the seventeenth century had enjoyed similar powers.[5] This may have been the case, but the point is impossible to prove because no commission of a finance

[1] Dent, *Crisis in finance*, part one, 'the administration of finance', provides some genuine insights, but is heavily dependent for evidence on the 1650s, which in some ways was an untypical decade. For an earlier period, M. Wolfe, *The fiscal system of renaissance France* (New Haven and London, 1972) contains some interesting comments but is insecurely grounded in the manuscript sources.

[2] G. B. Depping, 'Un banquier protestant en France au xvii⁰ siècle. Barthélémy Herwarth', *Revue historique*, x (1879), 324. J. Lair, *Nicolas Foucquet. Procureur général, surintendant des finances, ministre d'état de Louis XIV* (2 vols., 1890), i. 476–7. C. Badalo-Dulong, *Banquier du roi. Barthélémé Hervart, 160[7]–76* (1951), p. 133.

[3] Appendix One, Table I.

[4] Cf. the commissions to Servien and Foucquet (8 Feb. 1653) and Foucquet (21 Feb. 1659) cited in Appendix One, Table I.

[5] 144 a.p. 69 Dr. 4, fos. 257ᵛ–258ʳ [156 mi. 21].

minister has been found before 1619 and if we believe one well-informed contemporary observer, none was issued before that date.[1]

The early history of the French finance minister's power is thus largely *terra incognita*.[2] There seems little reason to attribute the plenitude of power to Semblançay in the reign of François Ier: he was not called *surintendant* and seems to have had a much weaker power base than that of his sucessors. Little is known about the financial administration of Artus de Cossé in 1564 or Pomponne de Bellièvre, who was apparently appointed finance minister by the council ruling of 10 September 1574. It is not until the appointment of François d'O in 1578 that a politician of the first importance became finance minister. There can be little doubt about d'O's power, which was recognized by Sully, by Sancy who tried to succeed to his position but failed,[3] and by the ruling of 25 November 1594 which abolished the position of finance minister and vested its powers in a committee of the council. Further reactions against the growth of the *surintendance* took place in 1611 and 1624; but by 1630 Cardin Le Bret could describe this post as 'maintenant une des plus importantes du Royaume',[4] which implied that this had not always been the case. With some vicissitudes, the power of the finance minister remained unchecked until abolished by the ruling of 15 September 1661. Some finance ministers bought their positions—perhaps the most celebrated example is La Vieuville, who paid Mazarin 400,000 *livres* for the post in 1651[5] – but this did not alter the fact that it was a political

[1] The well-informed observer was Robert Arnauld d'Andilly: *Journal inédit d'Arnauld d'Andilly, 1614–1620*, ed. A. Halphen (1857), pp. 448–9. Cf. A. M. de Boislisle, 'Semblançay et la surintendance des finances', *Annuaire-Bulletin de la Société de l'Histoire de France*, xviii (1881), 266 n. 4 at p. 267. However, the evidence is not clear-cut in the case of Sully. On 25 May 1599, Sully claimed that 'il estoit fondé d'une commission du roy' which had been granted by Henri IV at the time of the siege of Amiens two years earlier: *Histoire de la maison de Nicolay. Pièces justificatives. II. Chambre des Comptes*, ed. A. M. de Boislisle (Nogent-le-Rotrou, 1873), pp. 251, 253. This evidence is not quoted by Barbiche and Buisseret in their joint article cited below.

[2] Though there are two important guides: R. É. Mousnier, 'Sully et le conseil d'état et des finances', *Revue Historique*, cxcii (1941), 68–86. B. Barbiche and D. J. Buisseret, 'Sully et la surintendance des finances', *Bibliothèque de l'École des Chartes*, cxxiii (1965), 538–43.

[3] Sancy was regarded as *surintendant* by one memorialist (B.N. MS. fr. 16626 fo. 150^v) but the evidence is after 1594–8, when he would have held the position. It is probably more accurate to say that Sancy 'prenoit grande auctorité en ce conseil [the finance commission of 1594] comme s'il en eust esté le chef et seul surintendant': B.N. MS. fr. 4589, fo. 26^v.

[4] C. Le Bret, *De la souveraineté du roy* (1632), p. 172. Le Bret was given permission to publish this work on 10 Dec. 1630. His observation probably rests on the ruling of 18 Jan. 1630, which made the finance minister a minister of state.

[5] A.A.E. France 876, fo. 182, 28 July 1651.

appointment. The commission of the *surintendant* could be revoked because of financial incompetence or for political reasons, as all who held the post were well aware.

The next in order of command below the finance minister was the controller-general (*contrôleur-général des finances*).[1] After 1665, under Colbert and his successors, the controller-general became a true finance minister, replacing the *surintendant* whose position had been abolished.[2] In the years between 1589 and 1661, however, the controller-general was rarely more than a passive certifier and authenticator of the financial decisions taken by the *surintendant*. There were exceptions, particularly in the years 1616–17 and 1643–7 when the controller-general exercised more real power than the finance minister, but the exceptions do not disprove the rule.[3] There were several reasons for the weakness of the *contrôleur-général* in most years in comparison with the power of the finance minister. His function was narrowly circumscribed, having its origin in a royal ordinance of 12 April 1547.[4] Perhaps successive royal ordinances and rulings regulating the function of the controller-general were not fully implemented;[5] but no attempt was made in this way to define the functions of finance minister. Moreover, the powers of controller-general were frequently vested in more than one individual. On occasion, there were two finance ministers: but never four, as there could be controllers-general. Before 1665 the position of controller-general was bought and sold much more openly that that of finance minister, and an incumbent could not be dismissed without compensation. Thus in 1619 Pierre Castille bought Gilles Maupeou's office for 90,000 *livres*;[6] Jean Bochart sold his office for 100,000 *livres* in 1625–6, when there were 18 bidders;[7] in 1657 Barthélémé

---

[1] Appendix One, Table II.

[2] Colbert made the office important, not *vice versa*. When Colbert was still only an *intendant des finances*, Foucquet claimed that he was 'en possession de la surintendance des finances, qu'il exerce sous un autre titre . . .': 144 a.p. 68, Dr. 2, fo. 219 [156 mi. 19].

[3] Dent, *Crisis in finance*, p. 12, criticizes Marion's contention, made in 1923, that the controller-general before Colbert was usually a secondary figure. However, Dent's evidence rests on the exceptional period 1643–7; after 1648, as he points out (ibid., p. 96), the situation returned to normal with the appointment of a controller-general with little power.

[4] H. de Jouvencel, *Le contrôleur-général des finances sous l'ancien régime* (1901), pp. 22–3.

[5] Dent, op. cit., pp. 94–6, makes this point in reference to the rulings of 7 Oct. 1645. It is certain that the *Code Michaud* of Jan. 1629 was not fully carried out with regard to this office, and that subsequently many *billets de l'Épargne* had been issued which had not been 'sujets au controlle général des finances': cf. E 1734, no. 8, 9 Jan. 1666.

[6] A.A.E. France 779, fo. 87.

[7] R. d'Arnauld d'Andilly, *Mémoires*, ed. J. F. Michaud and J. J. F. Poujoulat, 2nd ser. ix (1838), p. 448. R. É. Mousnier, *La vénalité des offices sous Henri IV et Louis XIII*, 2nd ed. (1971), pp. 340, 343.

Hervart and Le Tonnelier de Breteuil jointly paid 1.3 million.[1] Particularly between 1649 and 1657 the government sought to exploit the sale of new offices for fiscal purposes, and there were similar threats at other times. It is scarcely surprising that few controllers-general took their tasks as seriously as Simon Marion, who had his house extended in 1627 to provide extra space for his archives.[2] Michel de Marillac, the Keeper of the Seals, encouraged this concern for improved record keeping. State papers were to be kept in one great collection, the *trésor des chartes*; financial papers were to be kept in another, at the *contrôle général des finances*.[3] However, this reforming zeal did not last long. Marion died in December 1628 and Marillac was arrested on 12 November 1630. The later controllers-general seem to have been much less efficient. Barthélémé Hervart seems to have had no clear idea of his function, kept no formal register, and the only record of his transactions were separate account sheets (*feuilles volantes*) which obviously could be misfiled or lost.[4]

From the time of Colbert, the position of controller-general became important because it was held as a commission, not an office that was bought and sold. A change from office to commission was the aim of the government regarding the two offices of *intendant des finances* after 12 October 1660, but before that date these subordinate offices were sold by the crown and the number increased as its financial position dictated. Thus there were eight intendants of finance between January 1594 and 1596–7, reflecting Henri IV's grave financial difficulties. They each bought their positions for 36,000 *livres* and had to be reimbursed when their offices were abolished after Sully became finance minister.[5] Two intendants remained: Jean Vienne, who was kept in office through

---

[1] *Arrêts du conseil du roi. Règne de Louis XIV. Inventaire analytique des arrêts en commandement. I. 20 mai 1643–8 mars 1661*, ed. M. Le Pesant (1976), no. 2595.

[2] E 93a, fo. 317, 24 July 1627.

[3] Respectively by decrees of 23 Sept. and 13 Sept. 1628: *Les papiers de Richelieu. Section politique intérieure. Correspondance et papiers d'état . . .*, ed. P. Grillon (in progress since 1975), iii. 498–500 (who attributes the decree erroneously to Richelieu). R. É. Mousnier, 'Les règlements du conseil du roi sous Louis XIII', *Annuaire-Bulletin de la Société de l'Histoire de France* (1948), 177–81. Marillac's role in drawing up these decrees is stressed by his apologist: B.N. MS. fr. 17486, fos. 91ᵛ–92ʳ.

[4] *Journal d'Olivier Lefèvre d'Ormesson et extrait des mémoires d'André Lefèvre d'Ormesson*, ed. P. A. Chéruel (2 vols., 1860–1), ii. 95.

[5] The offices were abolished in Jan. 1596, but reinstated the following month because of the king's need 'pour avoir de l'argent': *Mémoires-Journaux de Pierre L'Estoile*, ed. G. Brunet, A. Champollion, E. Halphen *et al.* (12 vols., 1875–96), vii. 52. The date of their abolition is complicated by the doubt concerning Sully's date of appointment as finance minister. The figure cited was that 'lent' by Louis Gilbert Gombaud: cf. E 38b, fo. 161, 15 Dec. 1612.

the influence of Gabrielle d'Estrées, the king's mistress, and Gilles Maupeou, who was appointed by 1600.[1] Thereafter, Sully kept the number of intendants of finance at two or three, but under the influence of Concini and his wife, the favourites of Marie de Médicis, a fourth office was established in 1615. The ostensible reason for the new office was the growth of business at the king's council.[2] One suspects that the real reason was that the royal favourites wanted to strengthen their control over royal patronage by placing their clients in the office of intendant of finance. The office took on a political character in this period: Dollé and Duret de Chevry were the clients of Concini and his wife; Déageant was the client of Luynes, the all-powerful favourite after 1617.[3] The value of the office had risen dramatically since 1594: when Déageant sold his office to Desportes-Baudouyn in 1618, it fetched 150,000 *livres*.[4] From 1615 until 1649 the usual number of intendants of finance was four.[5] Richelieu was no friend of these officials, and when in 1640 it was suggested that the number be increased to twelve for fiscal reasons, he rejected the idea. If the new intendants performed any function at all, Richelieu implied, it would be to rob the king.[6]

However, during the Fronde Mazarin threw such caution to the winds. In 1649 the number of intendants was increased to eight and in 1654 to twelve. Almost one million *livres* were raised from the four sales in 1649, and another 800,000 *livres* five years later.[7] By 1657 the intendants of finance were on the way to gaining heredity of office. A royal declaration of 24 October allowed their

---

[1] F. Mosser, *Les intendants des finances au xviiie siècle. Les Lefèvre d'Ormesson et le 'département des impositions', 1715–1777* (Geneva-Paris, 1978), p. 38. B.N. MS. fr. 4589, fos. 28, 96. Mosser, p. 291, gives 1596 as the date of Maupeou's appointment, but as late as 1598–9 he was a *maître des comptes* serving as royal commissioner 'à la direction des finances' in Brittany. For a more accurate list see Appendix One, Table III.

[2] O1 9, fo. 124^v–125^r, n.d. [1615]. Cf. E 51, fo. 144, 17 Oct. 1615.

[3] See below, Chapter II.

[4] *Journal inédit d'Arnauld d'Andilly*, ed. Halphen, p. 372.

[5] Thus the *brevet* of Sublet in 1629 mentioned two vacancies through death and two intendants in office: A.A.E. France 794, fo. 18 and O1 7, fo. 49^r, 14 July 1629. Bouthillier and Richelieu decided not to fill the fourth office after the death of Mallier du Houssay in 1641 [O. A. Ranum, *Richelieu and the councillors of Louis XIII. A study of the secretaries of state and superintendents of finance in the ministry of Richelieu, 1635–1642* (Oxford, 1963), pp. 177–8] but it was filled on 3 July 1643 when Mallier's son was appointed: O1 9, fo. 143.

[6] B.N. MS. fr. 16218, fo. 418^v, Jan. 1640. Richelieu called them 'douze argentiers, faisant cognoistre par ce discours qu'il tenoit les intendants pour des volleurs ...'

[7] Foullé paid 240,000 *livres* for his office on 18 June 1649 'pour estre employées aux dépenses les plus urgentes de la guerre': A.G. A1 112, no. 237. In 1654, the new intendants each paid 200,000 *livres*: A.A.E. France 893/1, fos. 56^v–57^r, 11 July 1654. A.A.E. France 893/2, fo. 240^v, 12 Aug. 1654.

heirs to take up *survivances* and some, such as Michel Foullé, did so. However, the ruling of 5 October 1658 stopped this process and reduced the number of intendants to four in an attempt to facilitate secret and prompt decision-making. The four intendants who remained in office were each required to lend the crown 400,000 *livres* at 7 per cent interest to reimburse their eight colleagues whose offices were abolished.[1] On 12 October 1660 the number was further reduced to two: Bordier and Bordeaux, whose offices were abolished, were each to be reimbursed 600,000 *livres*. The remaining two intendants, Le Tillier and Marin, henceforth were to hold their positions by royal commission. A third commission was issued for Colbert in March 1661, but after 1665, when he became controller-general, the number of commissions returned to two. This remained the position until February 1690, when four new offices were established and sold by the crown.[2]

In the years between 1649 and 1658, the new intendants of finance obtained their offices because they were rich. There was little investigation of the qualities of the new appointees. In theory, the double function of financier and intendant of finance was incompatible: an act renouncing former financial associates had to be signed and handed over to the Chancellor.[3] But was this measure effective? In the case of Claude Boylesve, who was appointed in 1654 because he was Mazarin's client,[4] apparently not. It seems that Mazarin wanted rich clients to hold the office of intendant both to raise an immediate revenue and later to obtain loans from a pliant inner group of officials.[5] Yet there was nothing new in financiers obtaining the post of intendant of finance and using their position for the purposes of financial gain. Claude

---

[1] B.N. MS. fr. 4589, fos. 96ᵛ–99, 5 Oct. 1658, which revoked the declaration of 24 Oct. 1657. The intendants were retained in order of seniority. Mauroy was named in the royal declaration, but asked for his office to be revoked. Le Tillier and Bordier had been appointed on 10 June 1649; Bordeaux on 18 June 1649 and Marin only in 1650. Étienne Foullé, who had been appointed on 18 June 1649, was unlucky in that Marin was preferred to him because he was a relative of Colbert. Cf. the protests of Foullé that 'aucuns desd[its] sieurs qui le suivent en réception s'efforcent par des voyes extraordinaires d'usurper sa charge': B.N. Morel de Thoisy 148, fos. 1–2, 7 Oct. 1658.

[2] Mosser, op. cit., pp. 40, 255–6. *Arrêts du conseil du roi*, ed. Le Pesant, nos. 3135, 3140.

[3] B.N. MS. fr. 18510, fo. 297, 22 July 1654. Act of renunciation by Claude Boylesve, who disavowed future association with Guillaume Languet, Marchant, Desbordes and François Jacquier, his former associates.

[4] J. Dent, 'The role of *clientèles* in the financial élite of France under Cardinal Mazarin', *French government and society, 1500–1850. Essays in memory of Alfred Cobban*, ed. J. F. Bosher (1973), p. 56. A.A.E. France 893/2, fo. 168, 19 July 1654.

[5] For example, loan of 113,336 *livres* by Paget (26 June 1655) and loan of 111,235 *livres* by Brisacier (1 July 1655): E 278c, fo. 407. E 279a, fo. 162.

Cornuel was an earlier example of a financier who became secretary of the council (a useful post because the secretary obtained information on royal policy before other financiers, which enabled him to prepare bids ahead of competitors)[1] and later intendant of finance in 1634. With the connivance of Bullion, the finance minister, Cornuel continued to participate in financial consortia after he became intendant, despite an explicit oath to the contrary in 1635. Cornuel's perjury only came to light after 1641, when Bullion's protection was removed. A fine of 200,000 *livres* was levied on the considerable fortune of 1.8 million Cornuel had left to his heirs on his death three years earlier.[2]

The intendant of finance was often appointed by a decree of the council of finance to examine new financial proposals (*avis*) submitted there; a favourable report would offer a corrupt intendant the prospect of a bribe from the successful consortium. Some of the intendants may have taken, on their own initiative, decisions of great importance.[3] It is therefore logical to deduce that more was worse: the greater the number of intendants of finance, the worse the abuses in financial administration.[4] Yet it is clear that in periods when there were a large number of intendants, they were not all given financial tasks at the same time. In 1594 only four of the eight intendants participated in the finance committee; the others presented requests to the council or served in the royal armies.[5] In 1656, when there were twelve intendants, Foucquet made it clear to Mazarin that there were only four who did the real work—Hervart, Marin, Le Tillier and Gargan. Others, such as Housset and Boylesve, were regarded as men who would pay over

---

[1] Dent, *Crisis in finance*, p. 146. Many great financiers held the office, such as Jean Galland, François Bossuet, and François Catelan. The secretaries of course transcribed many important financial documents. Cf. E 1702 fo. 1 and E 274b, fo. 267, 20 Feb. 1655.

[2] The oath was taken when Cornuel bought the office of *président* in the *Chambre des Comptes* of Paris: P 2363, pp. 285, 673, 14 Mar. and 5 May 1635. Though the fine was small, it amounted to half the proceeds of the sale of this office: E 161b, fo. 1, 15 May 1641. E 162c, fo. 167, 4 July 1641. E 163c, fo. 396, 28 Aug. 1641. The fortune would be reduced to one million if allowance is made for debts. However, the office of intendant of finance was not included among the assets: Dent, op. cit., p. 167. Minutier Central LI 191, 15 Dec. 1638.

[3] For example, Cornuel's decision to burn the minutes of the cash payments (*comptants*), which greatly hindered subsequent financial investigations. However, Bullion almost certainly connived in the abandonment of this elementary check. See Chapter IV.

[4] This view is stressed by Dent, *Crisis in finance*, pp. 99–100 and Dent, 'An aspect of the crisis of the seventeenth century. The collapse of the financial administration of the French monarchy, 1653–1661', *Economic History Review*, 2nd ser., xx (1967), 241–56.

[5] 120 a.p. 29, fo. 1, 25 Nov. 1594. Mazarin assumed in 1654 that the additional intendants of finance would be sent into the provinces and that the number serving in the council would not be increased. However, this does not seem to have happened: A.A.E. France 893/1, fo. 57, 11 July 1654. A.A.E. France 893/2, fo. 223, 9 Aug. 1654.

the odds simply to retain their offices. If the number of intendants were to be reduced, Foucquet saw no difficulty in employing the redundant officials as councillors of state or provincial intendants.[1] A resolute finance minister could prevent abuse of power by an intendant of finance; indeed the character of a regime was determined as much by the choice of trusted subordinates as by other, more general, financial decisions. There is no more eloquent contrast between the administration of d'Effiat and that of Bullion than the former's distrust of Claude Cornuel, while the latter promoted him and made him his chief adviser between 1634 and 1638. It was regarded as one of Sully's great achievements to have presided over a drastic reduction in the number of intendants and to have made a wise choice of those who were allowed to remain in office.[2]

The finance minister, the controller-general and the intendants of finance were all broadly speaking directors[3] (*ordonnateurs*). They could operate within the framework of the council of state (*conseil d'en haut*) to which all finance ministers were summoned as a matter of course after 1630.[4] They all sat, together with the Chancellor and other councillors of state, in the council of finance (*conseil d'état et des finances*), which issued its financial decisions in the form of decrees or rulings. In a sense, the council of finance, too, was an *ordonnateur*.[5] Thus, for example, no loan contract was legal—at least in theory—unless it had been sanctioned by a decree of the council.[6] Much preparatory work for the council of finance took place in a specialist committee, the *grande direction*; there was an even smaller inner group, the *petite direction*, which prepared financial questions with no political or legal overtones; on occasion there were also specialist commissions of the council. Clearly the functioning of the two *directions* evolved with the passing of time, but their precise role at a given moment in time is difficult to determine, and cannot be ascertained from the rulings which regulated the inner workings of the council. Had the rulings proved effective, they would not have been reissued or modified so

---

[1] A.A.E. France 900, fos. 255–6, 4 Aug. 1656.

[2] B.N. MS. fr. 16626, fo. 151. MS. fr. 4589, fos. 28, 96.

[3] In certain years, notably 1648–61, there were also officials called *directeurs des finances*, who were subordinate to the finance minister but superior to the intendants of finance.

[4] R. É. Mousnier, *La plume, la faucille et le marteau. Institutions et société en France du moyen âge à la Révolution* (1970) p. 150.

[5] Mousnier, *La vénalité*, p. 429.

[6] Whether Foucquet observed this rule after 1655 is unclear. Cf. the assertion that he did not: 144 a.p. 62, Dr. 60, fo. 4 [156 mi. 11].

frequently.[1] Moreover, a great deal of financial business was conducted by the finance minister on his own, or assisted by a trusted chief clerk or intendant of finance, who prepared the financial estimates in the greatest possible secrecy. Some finance ministers were much more concerned with detailed administration than others, and each chose his own method of work. Foucquet's reliance on his clerks was notorious,[2] but he may not have been altogether exceptional.

As *ordonnateur*, the finance minister supervised the numerous semi-autonomous accountants (*comptables*), financial office-holders who were accountable to one of the *Chambres des Comptes*[3] as a result of an oath sworn before it. There were two main types of accountant.[4] The first type were officials who did not themselves collect taxes, but simply received and redistributed funds collected by others: the most important official of this type was the chief treasurer (*trésorier de l'Épargne*), although there were numerous others, such as the *trésoriers de l'ordinaire* and *extraordinaire des guerres*, of the marine, artillery and so on. The second type were officials who collected taxes directly. One of the most important was the treasurer of 'occasional revenues' (*trésorier des parties casuelles*). The local receivers-general (*receveurs-généraux des finances*) were in a similar position. They all, however, had to submit their accounts in the first instance to the finance minister and the council of finance. When the accounts had been approved there[5] they were sent to the relevant *Chambre des Comptes*.

---

[1] Mousnier, 'Les règlements du conseil du roi sous Louis XIII', 113, is more optimistic. André Lefèvre d'Ormesson, however, thought 'les règlemens du conseil excitent tousjours beaucoup de bruict et peu de fruict'. The functioning of the *directions* is indicated in the ruling of 16 June 1644, and they were still operating at the end of Louis XIV's reign.

[2] '. . . qu'il n'en a point manié et que ses commis . . . ont fait des maniemens [et] ont dressé des estats des comptes des maniemens qu'ils ont faites': 144 a.p. 60, Dr. 2, fo. 39 [156 mi. 6].

[3] Some of the local accountants were answerable to the provincial *Chambres des Comptes*. In this book the *Chambre des Comptes* of Paris is referred to unless otherwise specified. This court consistently resisted the loss of jurisdiction to its provincial counterparts: *Chambre des Comptes*, ed. Boislisle, pp. 264–8 (remonstrances of 23 Jan. 1603). It received powerful backing from the third estate in 1614–15 which wanted 'tous les comptes . . . rendus en un seul lieu [et] non pas en tant de divers endroits': C. J. Mayer, *Des États Généraux et autres assemblées nationales* (18 vols., The Hague, 1788–9), xvii, pt. ii. 72. In 1628, the Queen Mother sided with the *Chambre des Comptes* of Paris in its struggle to prevent the establishment of a rival court with jurisdiction in Guyenne: *Les papiers de Richelieu*, ed. Grillon, iii. 380–1, 391–2.

[4] Cf. Dessert, 'Le "laquais-financier"', 25–6.

[5] The council verified Guénégaud's accounts of the *Épargne* for 1632 on 13 June 1633: B.I. Godefroy 144, fo. 259. The accounts of the *trésorier des ligues suisses* for 1647 were verified by the council on 9 May 1651: E 247a, fo. 118. The finance minister and the council of

The office of *trésorier de l'Épargne* illustrates the general position of the accountants. This office had been established in 1523; a second was added in the reign of Henri II; a third under Henri IV and Sully, by which time each *trésorier de l'Épargne* administered his fund (*caisse*) only one year in three.[1] In October 1645, the position was made more complicated by the establishment of a fourth office, which unlike the others was not sold to an individual purchaser, but exercised by one of the existing treasurers with the agreement of the other two. The first year in which this scheme came into operation was 1649, and it was still in effect in 1661–2, when Nicolas Jeannin held the fund in successive years.[2] The perquisites of office included charges of 3 *deniers* per *livre* (1.25 per cent) on money handled, which were not insubstantial fees bearing in mind the large quantities of coin of various types held by the *trésorier de l'Épargne*.[3] The office was a responsible one that brought rewards; it was correspondingly expensive. In July 1625 the great financiers Antoine Feydeau and Pierre Payen bought the offices formerly belonging to Morant and Beaumarchais for a million *livres* each.[4] These sales proved a disaster for the government, because Feydeau went bankrupt in January 1626 and Payen died unexpectedly the following April leaving debts. Their offices were resold to the highest bidders, but the disgrace of the bankruptcies undoubtedly affected the price. Gabriel Guénégaud paid only 730,000 *livres* for Payen's office.[5] The bankruptcies suggest the dangers of allowing formerly successful financiers, who retained their business connections, to purchase the office of *trésorier de l'Épargne*. On the other hand, Feydeau and Payen at least possessed technical expertise. If the office was transmitted within a family—as was the case with the Guénégaud family after 1626, and the Bertrand de la Bazinière family after 1628—then what guarantee was there of professional competence? On the death of

---

finance delegated some of the local accounting to the *trésoriers de France*, particularly the preliminary auditing of the accounts of the *receveurs-généraux des finances*. After 1642, some of this work was transferred to the provincial intendants.

[1] If the third estate had had its way in 1614–15 the senior *trésorier de l'Épargne* would have bought out the offices of his two junior colleagues: Mayer, op. cit., xvii, pt. ii. 99–100. The treasurers are listed in Appendix One, Table IV.

[2] *Arrêts du conseil du roi*, ed. Le Pesant, nos. 948, 3259. The second year of Jeannin's administration was interrupted by his arrest in May 1662. In late 1652 there had been a dispute over who should exercise the office in 1653: A.A.E. France 886, fo. 52.

[3] As revealed by the inventories of coin at the time of the monetary edict of 1636: E 129a, n.f., 5 Mar. 1636. E 131b, fo. 293, 26 June 1636.

[4] For Feydeau: Minutier Central LI 145, 28 July 1625. E 83b, fo. 112, 9 Aug. 1625. For Payen: E 82b, fos. 315ᵛ–316ʳ, 23 July 1625.

[5] E 91b, fo. 71, 20 Mar. 1627. E 96a, fo, 3, 5 Apr. 1628.

Macé I Bertrand, the government intervened to appoint Denis Gedoyn, his chief clerk, as acting *trésorier* in 1643.[1] Three years later, however, Macé II Bertrand was allowed to exercise the office although he had not reached the usual minimum age of twenty-five; his mother was required to stand surety, but this could not have provided any guarantee of his technical expertise.[2] Incompetence of some *trésoriers de l'Épargne* existed alongside corruption in others. Pierre Molan, who held the fund for much of the 1580s, was called an arch-robber ('cest archilarron'); in 1597 he was the first to buy letters of remission from the extraordinary financial tribunal (*chambre de justice*).[3] Sully made Étienne Puget one of the chief targets of his *chambres de justice*; yet in 1643 the accounts were reopened by d'Hémery and Puget's heirs had to pay a fine.[4]

There were two reasons why the *trésoriers de l'Épargne* were a principal target of the *chambre de justice*. One reason derived simply from their length of service: in 1624–5, they paid a fine proportionate to the number of years they had exercised the office. A second reason was that the finance minister required them to make loans to the state to cover the budgetary deficit in the years in which they administered the fund. These loans were very important before 1624. If they became relatively less important as time went on, this was due to the rapid growth of borrowing from financiers of a general type and the development of a credit market. Foucquet rejected the idea that the *trésoriers de l'Épargne* were the principal creditors of the state in the 1650s. They only lent sums that were specifically guaranteed on revenues, and rarely more than 2 or 3 million *livres*, whereas in some years the crown might need to borrow 50 or 60 million.[5] Their credit was

---

[1] *Arrêts du conseil du roi*, ed. Le Pesant, no. 538. E 186a, fo. 273, 13 Jan. 1644. Cf. E 176a, fo. 187, 10 Jan. 1643. B.N. Morel de Thoisy 157, fo. 12, 28 Dec. 1642.

[2] *Arrêts du conseil du roi*, ed, Le Pesant, nos. 458, 546. E 176a, fo. 7, 29 Nov. 1645 (misfiled in 1643).

[3] One of the judges of the *chambre*, La Grange Courtin, was horrified at the miscarriage of justice by Molan's obtaining an amnesty: A. Chamberland, *Le conflit de 1597 entre Henri IV et le Parlement de Paris* (1904), pp. 41–2. *Mémoires-Journaux de Pierre L'Estoile*, ed. Brunet *et al.*, iii. 254; vii. 95.

[4] E 183c, fo. 135, 23 Sept. 1643. E 185b, fo. 329, 19 Dec. 1643. E 217b, fo. 461, 28 Nov. 1646.

[5] 144 a.p. 66, Dr. 3, fo. 365ᵛ [156 mi. 16]. Foucquet seems to have minimized their role somewhat. On 9 Dec. 1651, the total debts of the crown to the three *trésoriers de l'Épargne* amounted to 11,198,996 *livres*. They were not fully reimbursed until 1659: B.N. Morel de Thoisy 156, fo. 77. In 1649, the crown's debts to Guénégaud amounted to 6.7 million; on 7 Mar. 1659, the debts to Jeannin amounted to 7,925,271 *livres*: *Arrêts du conseil du roi*, ed. Le Pesant, no. 1025. 144 a.p. 73, Dr. 4 [156 mi. 29], no. 2.

based on the value of their offices,[1] and thus very large sums were out of the question. The interrogations of Jeannin, Bertrand de la Bazinière and Guénégaud at the *chambre de justice* of 1661–5 reveal them as pliant instruments of the finance minister in other respects. Bertrand made it clear that in his view there was no 'règle dans les finances que l'usage', and that each finance minister made up the rules as he went along.[2] Guénégaud described how the finance minister went over his accounts, verifying each item. The original money order was then burnt. The summary accounts were approved by the full council of finance, and then sent to the *Chambre des Comptes*.[3] The accounting process took several years.[4] Once the *Chambre des Comptes* had approved the accounts of a particular year, the *trésorier de l'Épargne* burnt his own record.[5] Indeed the burning of money orders and accounts was so common that it carried risks: Guénégaud's house caught fire and the records of loan contracts for 1654 were burnt before the accounts had been finalized.[6] The systematic burning of records was no doubt partly inspired by the chief treasurer's desire to avoid the later reopening of his accounts once the long process had been completed. It was justified by the argument—which given the rudimentary expertise of some of the chief treasurers, may have had some validity—that the retention of vast numbers of papers would have led to 'une confusion horrible'.[7] It is clear that successive finance ministers tolerated this practice. Colbert regarded the *trésoriers de l'Épargne* as beyond reform, and their abolition to follow naturally from that of the *surintendance*. In April 1664, the offices of *trésorier de l'Épargne* and *trésorier des parties casuelles* were abolished. Since the hereditary nature of these positions was considered an important factor in causing the financial abuses of the 1650s, they were replaced by royal commissioners who could be removed from their functions without difficulty.[8]

---

[1] *Arrêts du conseil du roi*, ed. Le Pesant, no. 767. E 227c, fo. 105, 4 Dec. 1647.

[2] 144 a.p. 60, Dr. 9, fo. 5ᵛ [156 mi. 7].

[3] 144 a.p. 63, Dr. 1, nos. 3 and 4 [156 mi. 12].

[4] Gaspard Fieubet's accounts for 1636 were not finalized in the council until July 1639 and sent to the *Chambre des Comptes* only in Dec. 1639. They completed their verification in June 1642: Mousnier, *La vénalité*, p. 453. Further details from B.N. MS. fr. 10410 and n.a.f. 164.

[5] Jeannin claimed that he had no further need of his own record, and that this was a 'usage qu'il a trouvé estably dans l'espargne' when he entered in 1645: 144 a.p. 60, Dr. 5, fo. 14 [156 mi. 7].

[6] *Arrêts du conseil du roi*, ed. Le Pesant, nos. 2406, 3032, 3033.

[7] 144 a.p. 63, Dr. 1 no. 3, p. 20 [156 mi. 12].

[8] B. N. Morel de Thoisy 160, fo. 89, Apr. 1664.

However, the state of the king's finances precluded the systematic abolition and reimbursement of the offices of all the accountants.

French finance ministers were reluctant to change the basis of French taxation, which remained substantially the same from 1589 to 1661. There were three main types of revenue. The indirect taxes, of which there were several kinds, were leased or 'farmed' out to an individual or a financial consortium, which levied the tax for a set number of years and guaranteed the government—at least in theory—a fixed revenue.[1] The 'extraordinary' revenues (*affaires extraordinaires*), that is to say new fiscal expedients such as the sale of *rentes* or new offices, were administered as separate tax contracts (*traités*). The contractor (*traitant*) might be either a financial consortium or an individual financier; in both cases a fixed interest payment (*remise*) was specified at the time of the agreement.[2] A third type of revenue were the direct taxes, the most important of which was the *taille*, but to which were added certain military taxes, the *taillon*, the *crues* and after 1638 the *subsistances*. In the two-thirds of France with finance courts known as *élections* (the *pays d'élections*), the direct taxes were distributed and raised by office-holders; the *trésoriers de France* and *élus* were responsible for the allocation of taxes, the *receveurs particuliers* and *receveurs-généraux des finances* for their collection.[3] The relative importance of these types of revenue could vary from one period to another,[4] and these shifts of emphasis are important: but there was no fundamental reappraisal of the basic elements in the French revenue raising system between 1589 and 1661.

Why were successive finance ministers so cautious? Foucquet regarded the revenue system as a Pandora's box: once the lid was off, 'on ne [le] peut plus fermer'.[5] Unlike England, there was little public debate in France about the merits and defects of different types of taxation. Censorship of the press was reasonably effective, and it was a serious offence to suggest publicly that a tax ordered by the king's council was other than a good tax: if the tax was called undesirable, this might carry the implication that it

---

[1] Appendix One, Table V, A. Further details in R. J. Bonney, 'The failure of the French revenue farms, 1600–60', *Economic History Review*, 2nd ser., xxxii (1979), 11–32.

[2] Appendix One, Table V, B. Further details in A. Chauleur, 'Le rôle des traitants dans l'administration financière de la France de 1643 à 1653', *XVIIe Siècle*, lxv (1964), 16–49.

[3] Appendix One, Table V, C. Further details in R. J. Bonney, *Political change in France under Richelieu and Mazarin, 1624–1661* (Oxford, 1978), pp. 163–213.

[4] Appendix Two, Table V. These variations are discussed in more detail in the later chapters of this book.

[5] Lair, *Foucquet*, i. 505. A.A.E. France 910, fo. 152, 2 Apr. 1660.

should not be paid. The conservatism of French finance ministers must be viewed against the public hostility to the collection of all taxes, but particularly new taxes or taxes which had been recently increased. This public hostility was older than the Bourbon dynasty: it was evident in the 1540s, in the rebellions against the extension of the salt tax, the *gabelle*, into south-west France. It was brought home in the early years of the new dynasty, however, with the rebellion of the *Tard Avisés* of the Périgord in 1594–5, and comparable peasant risings in other provinces, and with the riots against the five per cent sales tax (the *sol pour livre* or *pancarte*) in the years 1597–1602. These examples were never forgotten, and of course there were many others in the first half of the seventeenth century.

The debate about taxation thus had to be conducted privately. Proposals for change tended to be presented as specific expedients (*avis*) to the king's council, inspired as much by the motive of gain as by the desire for reform. Thus in 1655, the sieur Imbert was promised 100,000 *livres* reward if the council decided to implement five memoranda he had presented to Anne of Austria. These included the sale of church property, the extension of the land tax from certain areas in the Midi throughout France, and the reform of the *gabelle*:[1] all were ignored. Such proposals were inspired by private, corporate, or regional financial considerations. One man's reform (and profit) was another man's tax burden, and thus Foucquet's scepticism about such schemes was justified.[2] On the other hand, it is not difficult to see why the administration of the revenue farms was criticized by 'ceux qui parlent de la liberté du commerce'. The three most important farms were the *gabelles de France*, the *aides* and the *cinq grosses fermes*, which produced between them about three-quarters of the total yield of the indirect taxes.[3] Yet these three farms operated in only part of the country—basically 12 *généralités* in northern France. Elsewhere, there were similar but distinct farms enjoying comparable but not necessarily identical taxes. The *gabelles*—whether of northern France (the so-called *gabelles de France*), or the Lyonnais and Languedoc, or of the Dauphiné and Provence—were basically taxes on the sale of salt, a vital commodity not especially burdened in England. Fiscal considerations had led with the passing of time to a distortion of the market. Artificial 'salt boundaries'

[1] *Arrêts du conseil du roi*, ed. Le Pesant, no. 2140.
[2] Lair, loc. cit.
[3] Bonney, 'The failure of the French revenue farms', p. 29 (Table 4, f).

had gradually evolved, and these were difficult to police. There was a basic inequity since the price of salt was much higher in some areas than in others—the revenue farmers had to import salt from areas in which they controlled production to fill the salt deposits (*greniers à sel*) in other areas of the tax farm, which might have been supplied more cheaply by direct trading across the artificial 'salt boundary'. The variation in the price of salt led to contraband in this staple commodity from one area of the kingdom to another. Contraband in turn led to high administrative costs:[1] the farmers had to employ *gardes des gabelles* to protect their rights. The monopolistic and distorting effect of the other indirect taxes was less marked, but each had its own defects. The taxes levied together in the farm of the *aides* were chiefly taxes on drink—especially wine, beer, cider and perry—levied when it arrived at the gates of the town. However, the great wine-producing area of south-west France had its own levy on the transportation of wines which formed part of the farm known as the *convoy et comptablie* of Bordeaux. There were local immunities from the *aides*, and the dues were heavier in some localities than others. The taxes levied together within the farm known as the *cinq grosses fermes* consisted chiefly of customs duties (*traites*), on exports between France and abroad, and between the area of the farm and the rest of the kingdom: the *traites* must have positively hindered commercial expansion by taxing home-based trade between provinces.

The French fiscal system had developed in a piecemeal way, and important political forces ensured the continuation of regional diversity. Certain provinces had been acquired relatively late by the French monarchy—Normandy, Guyenne, Burgundy, Provence and Brittany were gained only in the fifteenth century—and had retained some of their former customs and privileges. By the seventeenth century, the estates of Guyenne were in abeyance while those of Normandy and Provence were under threat or succumbed during Richelieu's ministry. Moreover, the provincial estates of one province acquired much earlier—Languedoc—were strongest of all. Nevertheless, all provinces with estates had a somewhat different fiscal regime from the rest of France, both in the nature of the taxes levied and the methods and officials by which they were collected. Where, as in Languedoc, Brittany, and Burgundy, the estates retained the

[1] Cf. the complaints of the farmers of the *gabelles de France* to Mazarin: A.A.E. France 902, fos. 235, 285, 8 and 22 Sept. 1657.

right to vote taxes, they secured effective control over the fiscal process. Perhaps understandably, French finance ministers tended to regard the privileges of the *pays d'états* as an obstacle to good financial management. As early as 1605 Sully declared his intention of having the *taille* collected in the same way throughout France,[1] which implied the reduction or abolition of the privileges of the *pays d'états*. The attack was resumed in the years 1628–32, under the inspiration of Marillac or d'Effiat. However, there was little permanent change in the direction of greater uniformity. As late as 1658, Foucquet rejected the idea of confronting the *pays d'états* in wartime, since with the army occupied elsewhere the king would have 'trop d'affaires à la fois'; he considered a province such as Burgundy capable of sinking its social and institutional differences in the common cause of opposing the government's fiscal demands.[2]

Finance ministers recognized the strength of regional institutions in France, committed to the twin causes of low taxation and fiscal conservatism, and this induced caution in their dealings with the *pays d'états*. This tendency to avoid fiscal experimentation was reinforced by other practical considerations. The proliferation of the sale of offices in the sixteenth century had had particularly serious consequences for financial administration. As has been seen, the numerous accountants (*comptables*) were effectively in charge of their funds, 'maîtres de leur maniement'. There were, moreover, numerous financial office-holders established in the local *bureaux des finances* and *élections*. Their offices could not be abolished, and the owners reimbursed, because this would be too heavy a burden on the king's already badly strained finances. The offices could not be abolished without compensation, because this would be tantamount to an attack on private property. On the other hand, the existence of a large number of semi-autonomous accountants and financial office-holders ruled out an efficient system of direct administration (*régie*), since the crown had no

---

[1] D. J. Buisseret, *Sully and the growth of centralized government in France, 1598–1610* (1968), p. 97. J. R. Major, 'Henry IV and Guyenne. A study concerning origins of royal absolutism', *French Historical Studies*, iv (1966), 376, reprinted in *State and society in seventeenth-century France*, ed. R. F. Kierstead (New York, 1975), p. 12. J. R. Major, *Representative government in early modern France* (New Haven and London, 1980), p. 284. R. G. Tait, 'The king's lieutenants in Guyenne, 1580–1610 . . .' (Oxford University D. Phil. 1977), 259–60. All use the evidence of Julien Cambefort, seigneur de Selves, the representative of the third estate of the Agenais, Condomois, and Armagnac, reporting back to the municipality of Agen on 11 Feb. 1605. While it would not be true to call this evidence hearsay, it is clearly secondhand.

[2] A.A.E. France 905, fo. 545, 23 Dec. 1658.

direct control over their activities.[1] If the king wanted a new and unpopular tax to be levied, it was by no means certain that his accountants or financial office-holders, men with property interests in the locality, would be co-operative. If the king wanted to borrow a significant amount of money as a matter of urgency, it was by no means certain that they would be able to help, since they had often invested much of their wealth in the purchase of office. Only entrepreneurs of a general type, who did not necessarily own a financial office, and whose business interests were of a scale and diversity greater than any single accountant or financial office-holder would normally contemplate, could respond to this demand. Such private financiers naturally placed greater emphasis on the security and profitability of their contracts than on the king's service: if they considered a new tax a risky venture, they charged appropriately high rates of interest.

Exactly what social groups provided financiers, the way in which they rose to business prominence, and the extent of their profits, has aroused considerable interest among historians and not all the studies have yet been completed.[2] Two conclusions may be hazarded at this stage with some degree of confidence. The first is the gradual decline in importance in the first quarter of the seventeenth century of Italian financiers, who had played an important role at the Lyon fairs under the last Valois kings. Investment abroad declined as the various Italian states experienced economic difficulties in the seventeenth century. The general importance of Lyon as a royal money market never recovered from its identification with the Catholic League between 1585 and 1594. Moreover, Paris rapidly developed as the main royal money market so that by 1636 Bullion could call it 'le seul lieu du royaume où l'on peult faire le service du Roy pour le recouvrement des deniers'.[3] A number of foreign, and especially Italian, financiers continued to participate in the financial system: but the overwhelming majority were now French and they held most of the market. A second conclusion is that the social origins of the French financiers were rather less humble than contemporaries

[1] D'Effiat's judgement was that 'les formes de l'Estat ne permett[e]nt point que le Roy touche ses deniers par luy-mesme, estant nécessité que ce soit par les officiers qui en donnent leurs quictances . . .': *Les papiers de Richelieu*, ed. Grillon, i. 347.

[2] Dent, *Crisis in finance*, part two, 'the world of the financiers'. Preliminary report by Dessert, 'Le "laquais-financier"'. Work on the Italians at Lyon and Paris by Mlle F. Bayard in progress. Cf. her study, 'Les Bonvisi, marchands banquiers à Lyon, 1575–1629', *Annales, E.S.C.*, xxvi (1971), 1234–69.

[3] A.A.E. France 820, fo. 228ᵛ, 26 Aug. 1636.

would have us believe. A recent study of 464 important financiers between 1653 and 1715 reveals the majority to have been office-holders, recently ennobled—often through the office of *secrétaire du roi*, which conferred immediate nobility on its purchaser—and not from particularly humble backgrounds. It is not difficult to appreciate why this should be the case. A financier had to be literate and numerate to understand the fiscal system and its complex legislation; moreover, an initial amount of capital was required to invest in an office for social status and for the first financial ventures. The seventeenth century was not the age of the self-made man; without the assistance of relatives and business associates, all of which implied a modicum of wealth and social status, a financier could never have made his way.[1] Although many financiers undoubtedly made considerable personal fortunes, popular opinion exaggerated both the extent of these fortunes and the speed at which they were made. Taxation was very unpopular and the taxpayers sought a clearly identifiable *ennemi du peuple*.[2]

Most, if not all, French finance ministers of the seventeenth century would have agreed with the judgement attributed to Richelieu that 'les financiers et les partisans[3] font une partie séparée, préjudiciable à l'État *mais pourtant nécessaire*'.[4] The difficulty was in knowing how to restrain profiteering by the financiers. Different finance ministers adopted different solutions,[5] but there were two main approaches to the problem. One approach would have been to reform and strengthen the sovereign court with responsibility for accounting, and thus the suppression of corruption and peculation—the *Chambre des Comptes*. However, by the seventeenth century the Parisian court and its counterparts in the provinces audited accounts only in the narrowest and most technical sense—they checked that the figures were accurate and balanced—but in normal years it was no part of their responsibility to decide whether funds had been usefully spent for the public benefit.[6] The council of finance encouraged this tendency, with-

---

[1] Dessert, 'Le "laquais-financier"', 33–4.

[2] Y. M. Bercé, *Histoire des croquants. Étude des soulèvements populaires au xviie siècle dans le sud-ouest de la France* (2 vols., Paris-Geneva, 1974), ii. 624–32. Bercé, 'La mobilité sociale, argument de révolte', *XVIIe Siècle*, cxxii (1979), 66–7.

[3] *Partisan* = contractor, someone who had entered a *parti* or *traité*.

[4] Richelieu, *Testament politique*, ed. André, p. 250. Author's italics.

[5] These are examined in the later chapters.

[6] For an earlier period (1574, 1584, and 1594), the work of the *Chambre des Comptes* of Paris is examined by J. F. Pernot, 'L'activité de la Chambre des Comptes de Paris à l'époque moderne . . .', *Revue d'histoire moderne et contemporaine*, xxvi (1979), 612–37.

holding details of much royal expenditure by the procedure of the *acquit de comptant*.[1] Details of loan and tax contracts were also outside its normal jurisdiction.[2] There were several reasons for keeping the *Chambre des Comptes* on a tight rein. If given the opportunity, it would seek to tie the hands of the finance minister on the question of interest rates. From 1594 to 1601, the legal rate of interest on new *rentes* was *denier* 12 (8.33 per cent); between 1601 and 1634 it was *denier* 16 (6.25 per cent); between 1634 and 1665 it was *denier* 18 (5.55 per cent). These rates of interest were established by royal ordinances which the *Chambre des Comptes* sought to enforce. However, the king never intended that these rates of interest should apply to his own financial transactions.[3] Any attempt to do so would make it impossible to obtain the services of financiers and would lead to the abandonment of existing contracts. The *Chambre des Comptes* also wanted tight budgetary control: it sought to restrict royal expenditure and income, with the aim of making an active foreign policy virtually impossible to sustain in financial terms. There were also fears that the courts, if allowed a free rein, would investigate ministerial profiteering. The interrelationship of public and private finance at the centre of government meant that there were matters which needed to be hidden from the public eye. The finance minister believed that without secret decision-making, his position would be vulnerable to public criticism and the financiers would be unco-operative: sound financial administration required conditions of political stability.[4] A thorough-going investigation of corruption would appeal greatly to the sovereign courts and the taxpayers; it might lead to a seizure of the political initiative by the courts and permit critics of royal policy to 'descrier le gouvernement de l'estat.'[5]

A second approach to the problem of restraining the financiers

---

[1] R. J. Bonney, 'The secret expenses of Richelieu and Mazarin, 1624–1661', *English Historical Review*, xci (1976), 825–36. For the figures, see Appendix Two, Table III.

[2] E 264b, fo. 613, 31 Mar. 1654: 'lad[ite] chambre ne doit cognoistre des prestz faitz à Sa Maté . . .' P 2682, fo. 98ᵛ, 12 Nov. 1641: 'il y avoit des traittez dont le Roy vouloit que l'on n'eust connoissance . . .'

[3] Article 151 of the *Code Michaud* of Jan. 1629 was quite explicit: 'n'entendons toutefois comprendre en cet article les traités que les nécessités de nos affaires nous obligent de faire, et les profits que nous accordons pour raison de ce à ceux avec lesquels nous faisons lesdits traités en notre conseil'. High interest rates were thus perfectly legal, and the financier Thomas Bonneau cited royal declarations of 4 Nov. 1624, Jan. 1629, and 3 July 1643 as public assurances of this: E 259a, fo. 336, 13 Aug. 1653. E 263b, fo. 621, 25 Feb. 1654.

[4] For the 'solide constance du temps et secure protection de ceux qui agissent': *Les papiers de Richelieu*, ed. Grillon, i. 349.

[5] As nearly happened with the meeting of the *Chambre St-Louis* in 1648: B.L. Harleian 4466, fo. 84ᵛ, 8 June 1648.

was to establish an extraordinary royal commission, the *chambre de justice*. More of these were held between 1584 and 1661 than in any other period of French history, with the possible exception of the reign of François Ier. What was needed was a sovereign tribunal which could judge anyone, and which could take precedence over the sovereign courts without arousing their wrath.[1] Unlike a reformed and strengthened *Chambre des Comptes*, the *chambre de justice* could never act as an effective check on the executive since the basis of its power was the royal commission which could be revoked at any moment. Effectively, this made the investigation dependent on the executive and protected ministerial relatives and clients. Moreover, whereas the government could not greatly influence the choice of members in the *Chambre des Comptes*, since membership there was gained by the private purchase of office, in the case of the *chambre de justice* it consistently defended its prerogative to make the choice. Ostensibly the the government packed the membership in this way to prevent the selection of relatives of the financiers, but there is little doubt that all appointments were of a political nature. Thus in 1648 Nicolas Foucquet was selected as *procureur-général* of the *chambre de justice*, an appointment which aroused such hostility because of his known support for the government that it had to be changed.[2] In other, more settled, times there is no reason to suppose that the ministers paid such heed to adverse comment on their appointments. The *chambre de justice* was a pliant instrument of royal control. It was also a breach of trust between the crown and its financiers, tantamount to an act of bankruptcy. By reneguing on previous contracts, and in effect taxing them retrospectively, it periodically threatened public confidence in the king's financial system. Not surprisingly, at the mere announcement of a *chambre de justice*, financiers went into hiding and sought to guard their money rather than invest in financial activities.[3] It was for each finance minister to determine whether the advantages of holding a *chambre de justice* outweighed the threat to financial confidence. There was no inevitability about the decision: it was certainly not the case that whenever one

---

[1] J. F. Bosher, '*Chambres de justice* in the French monarchy', *French government and society* . . ., ed. Bosher, p. 33.

[2] Finally, Savenières was appointed: Ormesson, *Journal*, ed. Chéruel, i. 576–7. Lair, *Foucquet*, i. 119. In 1650, Le Tellier considered Foucquet's 'attachement particulier à la cour' a possible obstacle to his appointment as *procureur-général* in the *Parlement* of Paris: A.A.E. France 872, fo. 213ᵛ, 12 Oct. 1650.

[3] E 8la, fo. 111, 23 Jan. 1625. E 82a, fo. 47, 6 Apr. 1625.

was summoned financial abuses were at their worst.[1] And on at least two occasions—La Vieuville in 1624 and Foucquet in 1661—the *chambre de justice* was held to conceal the crown's political purpose of removing a finance minister from office and restricting public sympathy for the victim. Finance was an integral part of politics, and it is only by viewing the political context that the development of royal financial policy may properly be understood.

---

[1] Bosher, '*Chambres de justice* in the French monarchy', 35–6. It is surprising that the most recent account of the *chambres de justice* in the first half of the seventeenth century [F. Bayard, 'Les chambres de justice de la première moitié du xviie siècle', *Cahiers d'histoire*, xix (1974), 121–40] scarcely alludes (except at pp. 121–2) to those held or threatened between 1624 and 1661.

Chapter I

A new dynasty, 1589–1610

I. THE WAR AGAINST THE CATHOLIC LEAGUE

When Jacques Clément's knife finished the life of Henri III on 1
August 1589, it ended also the Valois line of French kings which
had ruled since Philippe de Valois seized the throne in 1328. It
brought to the fore an issue which had been simmering below the
surface of French politics for five years: the right of Henri of
Navarre, the chief claimant of the new Bourbon dynasty, to
inherit. Henri III had no son, but until 10 June 1584 he had a
younger brother, Alençon,[1] under whom the Valois dynasty
might have survived. With Alençon's death, the heir presumptive
was a Huguenot, or, worse still to Catholic eyes, a lapsed
Catholic. Henri of Navarre had already changed his religion
twice. In 1572 he had been forced to abjure Protestantism and
marry Maguerite of Valois. Four years later, he had escaped from
captivity and returned to his earlier faith; the enforced marriage
proved to be a disaster and had to be annulled in 1599. The
majority of Catholics opposed Henri IV's accession from the
moment it became a probability rather than a possibility. On 31
December 1584, the leading members of the Catholic nobility
signed a subsidy treaty with Philip II of Spain – the so-called
secret treaty of Joinville, named after the country residence of
Henri de Lorraine, duc de Guise.[2] The League succeeded after
two rebellions (March–July 1585 and May –July 1588) in imposing its policies and its choice of successor on Henri III. The
League's candidate was an ageing political nonentity, Cardinal
Charles de Bourbon ('Charles X of the League'), who would have
been under the thumb of Guise, the effective leader of the movement.[3]

Henri III made solemn promises to the League, but, though a
deeply pious Catholic prince, he considered the legitimate heir

[1] The duc d'Alençon was renamed the duc d'Anjou on Henri III's accession in 1574.

[2] The barony of Joinville was established as a *principauté* for François duc de Guise,
Henri's father, by Henri II in Apr. 1551: B.N. MS. fr. 8182 fos. 21–5. My thanks to Dr M.
Greengrass for this reference.

[3] E. Saulnier, *Le rôle politique du Cardinal de Bourbon (Charles X), 1523–1590* (1912), pp.
110–11, 140.

presumptive to be Henri of Navarre, whom he sought to convert from Protestantism. The League suspected the king of seeking to engineer a Navarrist succession, and their views were made public in two manifestos of rebellion (31 March 1585 and 23 May 1588).[1] The threat to Catholicism posed by the probable change of dynasty was certainly stressed, but what was remarkable in the manifestos was the importance given to other aspects of Henri III's government where the religious significance was slight. The theory was expounded by the League that the king had been alienated from his true friends – that is to say, Catholic nobles such as Guise – by favourites who although Catholic had usurped power and authority against the true interests of the crown. In 1585 the favourites under attack were Joyeuse and d'Épernon, both raised to the status of duke and peer of the realm by Henri III,[2] and both enjoying offices and provincial governorships established to counterbalance the power of the Guises. Joyeuse had been rather less hostile to the League than d'Épernon and after his death in October 1587 was rehabilitated in Catholic opinion.[3] However, criticism of d'Épernon became fiercer with the passing of time, because instead of returning Joyeuse's offices and governorships to the Guises or their supporters, Henri III transferred them to his chief favourite on 7 November 1587.[4] By May 1588, the League focused its hostility on d'Épernon's influence and that of his younger brother, Bernard de la Valette. After the Day of the Barricades (12 May 1588), the conduct of François d'O—the governor of Paris and the Île-de-France, finance minister since 1578, and another of Henri III's favourites—was a secondary target for their criticism.[5] The propaganda

---

[1] *Archives curieuses de l'histoire de France* . . ., ed. L. Cimber and F. Danjou, 1st ser., xi (1836), 9–19. *Registres des délibérations du bureau de la ville de Paris* . . . *IX, 1586–1590*, ed. F. Bonnardot (1902), pp. 130–5. The manifesto of Péronne of March 1585 was apparently written by the Jesuit Claude Matthieu: A. L. Martin, *Henry III and the Jesuit politicians* (Geneva, 1973), pp. 134, 213.

[2] For the extraordinary nature of their elevation in 1581, both being given precedence over all other peers of the realm with the exception of the princes of the blood, and the king regarding them as his brothers-in-law: J. P. Labatut, *Les ducs et pairs de France au xviie siècle. Étude sociale* (1972), p. 348.

[3] G. Girard, *Histoire de la vie du duc d'Espernon* (1655), p. 29. D. Pallier, *Recherches sur l'imprimerie à Paris pendant la Ligue, 1585–1594* (Geneva, 1975), p. 66.

[4] Girard, op. cit., p. 62. One of these titles was the governorship of Normandy: R. R. Harding, *Anatomy of a power elite. The provincial governors of early modern France* (New Haven and London, 1978), p. 226 no. 106.

[5] For the criticism: *Registres . . . de la ville de Paris*, ed. Bonnardot, ix. 134. For the governorship: *Registres des délibérations du bureau de la ville de Paris. VIII. 1576–1586*, ed. P. Guérin (1896), pp. 589–91; Harding, op. cit., p. 224, no. 67. For d'O as favourite: P. Champion, 'La légende des mignons', *Humanisme et Renaissance*, vi (1939), 521–6. Cf. B.N.

campaign reached its height with the publication of *Gaveston* in July 1588, in which the fate of Piers Gaveston, Edward II's favourite who was executed by rebellious English nobles in 1312, was recalled as a dire warning to d'Épernon.[1]

The League insisted on the removal of the influence of the duc d'Épernon, whom they accused of preparing the way for a Navarrist and Protestant succession. Virtually all the evils of the body politic were blamed on Henri III's *mignon*, but two aspects of his influence were particularly singled out for criticism. It was said that d'Épernon was a friend of the mercenary troops who had invaded France in 1587 to support the cause of Henri of Navarre. The only evidence for this view was that d'Épernon had negotiated the 'treaties of capitulation' of 18 November and 8 December under which the Switzers and the German *reiter* and *landsknechts* had agreed on financial terms for their return home. Guise, who had won the victories of Vimory and Auneau, was humiliated that d'Épernan sought to gain all the credit from the campaign against the invasion force, which explains the criticism of the treaties. The second criticism of d'Épernon's influence contained more substance. It was said that he had gained spectacular wealth from the king's favour, and with his younger brother had 'ravy et mis en leurs coffres toutes les finances de France'. The League presented itself as the party of financial reform. It wanted to abolish the secret payments (*comptants*) by which the king had conferred gifts on his favourites; new financial practices such as the extensive use of tax contracts (*partis*) were also to be stopped. With the removal of d'Épernon's influence, the League contended that the war against the Huguenots could be paid for, yet the burden of taxation reduced. Perhaps d'Épernon's wealth was less great than the League suggested, not exceeding 3.9 million *livres*, a relatively small sum compared to the personal fortunes of the royal favourites of the seventeenth century.[2] On the other hand, it had been

---

MS. fr. 3645, fo. 18ᵛ, 15 Sept. 1591. D'O recalled to Henri IV the favours he had received from 'le feu Roy mon bon maître . . .' However, François d'O's hardline Catholic views were evident in 1585, when he sided with the League in its rebellion against Henri III. A contributory factor in his defection was his dismissal from the lieutenancy of Lower Normandy. He was reinstated on 13 Jan. 1586: *Lettres de Catherine de Médicis*, ed. H. de la Ferrière and G. Baguenault de la Puchesse, 11 vols. (1880–1909), viii. 463, 472, 474; ix. 6 n. 2. He had held the position on 6 Apr. 1580: B.N. p.o. 2133 (Dr. 48,464), no. 40.

[1] Pallier, op. cit., p. 261 (no. 191). P. Richard, *La papauté et la Ligue française. Pierre d'Épinac. Archevêque de Lyon, 1573–1599* (Paris and Lyon, 1901), p. 300. F. J. Baumgartner, *Radical reactionaries: the political thought of the French Catholic League* (Geneva, 1975), pp. 87–8.

[2] Girard, op. cit., p. 58. Cf. ibid., p. 11, for the first payment in 1577.

acquired in less than a decade during which time the secret payments of the king had undoubtedly grown.[1] Moreover, in view of the secret conduct of financial administration, and the use of nominees rather than the real beneficiaries in the letters patent conferring gifts, the public was not in a position to judge the true extent of the king's payments to his favourites. At the time of d'Épernon's marriage to Marguerite de Foix-Candalle, Henri III offered him a present of 1.2 million *livres* to be made by a secret cash payment, which the duke allegedly refused on the grounds that the king's finances were over-burdened and new taxes would be needed to pay for the gift.[2] He and his like had not always shown such moderation. Protestant propaganda alleged that between 1547 and 1580 the kings of France had spent 927 million livres yet levied 1,453 million in taxes. There ought to have been a budgetary surplus of 526 million, yet the king's coffers were empty. Either the king was lying and had a secret hoard of money, or else he had been robbed.[3] As in other respects, the League turned Protestant propaganda to its own purposes.[4]

From the time he was forced out of Paris on the Day of the Barricades until the assassination of the Guises (23 December 1588), Henri III came under increasing pressure from the League to reform his financial administration. The League was able to exploit the king's failure to honour the payment of salaries to office-holders and interest to the holders of annuities (*rentes*). By 1585, the office-holders were owed more than a year's salaries, while the arrears in the *rentes* amounted to over 4 million *livres*.[5] After the Day of the Barricades, Henri III diverted revenues normally assigned to meet these payments towards the cost of the war against the League. The remonstrances of the municipality of Paris were to no avail, although the aggrieved vested interests of *rentiers* and office-holders undoubtedly increased support for the League.[6] On 12 August 1588, opposition charges of maladministration were considerably reinforced by a wide-ranging indictment of the financial policies of Henri III and François d'O by the

---

[1] 715,538 *livres* in 1582, yet 1,894,928 *livres* in 1585, although the secret payments fell to 488,395 *livres* three years later: cf. B.N. MS. fr. 18510, fo. 248, 12 Dec. 1652.

[2] Girard, op. cit., p. 59.

[3] [N. Barnaud?], *Le secret des finances de France descouvert et départi en trois livres par N. Froumenteau* (1581), pp. 142–4.

[4] Baumgartner, *Radical reactionaries*, pp. 30–1, 109, 214.

[5] The arrears in the *rentes* were 1.4 million in 1576, 3.3 or 3.4 million in 1583, and over 4 million in 1585: *Registres . . . de la ville de Paris*, ed. Guérin, viii. 33, 318, 494.

[6] *Registres . . . de la ville de Paris*, ed. Bonnardot, ix. 169. Pallier, op. cit., p. 184.

Chambre des Comptes.[1] The chief accountancy court demanded the appointment of a new finance minister or ministers, who would conduct the king's financial business faithfully, competently, and without corruption. A distinction was proposed between the king's contractual obligations to pay salaries to office-holders and interest to *rentiers*, and other types of royal expenditure. The contractual obligations should be paid first before revenues were assigned to meet other expenses—critics of Henri IV's financial policies would later return to this proposal. The *Chambre des Comptes* emphasized that in its view royal ordinances on financial administration were not being enforced. The king was greatly in debt, yet many individuals enjoying royal favour expected preferential treatment and reimbursement on safe and secure royal revenues. It was argued that the procedure of secret payments (*comptants*) had introduced great abuses into financial administration. The *Chambre des Comptes* proposed a number of reforms: no royal debts were to be reimbursed before the claimant's title deeds had been verified; a list of royal pensioners was to be drawn up, and they were not to be paid until all other royal expenses had been met. An attempt was to be made to eradicate various abuses in the procedure whereby revenues were assigned to pay off royal creditors.

The departure of d'Épernon from the court in June 1588 had given Henri III the chance to recover some of his lost prestige, and he may have been genuinely attracted by ideas of financial reform some of which had been attempted in 1582–4 without lasting success.[2] Already on 20 May 1588, Henri III had responded to the criticism of the League by recognizing 'la confusion, abus et désordre' caused by the increase in secret expenditure and the excessive number of gifts, many of which were made under fictitious names. Henceforth gifts of more than 3000 *livres* were to be registered in the *Chambre des Comptes*, while the use of fictitious names to hide the real beneficiaries of royal patronage was declared illegal and to result in the loss of the grant.[3] Perhaps the king intended the meeting of the Estates-General forced on him by

---

[1] P 2330, pp. 355–75.

[2] A, Karcher, 'L'assemblée des notables de St-Germain-en-Laye (1583)', *Bibliothèque de l'École des Chartes*, cxiv (1956), 115–62. The three significant measures were the reform of the council of finance in 1582, the holding of the assembly of notables in 1583 and the *chambre de justice* of 1584.

[3] The concessions were made after the Day of the Barricades (12 May), but before the League had finalized its manifesto of 23 May: *Chambre des Comptes*, ed. Boislisle, p. 188. B.N. MS. fr. 16627, fo. 31. P 2330, pp. 237–40.

the League and the new ministers he appointed in September 1588 to achieve more permanent reforms. On the other hand, one of the new ministerial appointees—Revol—was a client of d'Épernon, which could not have reassured the opposition. Nor could the continuance in office of François d'O, the man who now above all personified the rule of financial corruption[1] and personal favour. If the king hoped to use the influence of Guise and his adviser, d'Épinac, the archbishop of Lyon, to control the Estates-General, which was packed with supporters of the League, the experiment failed disastrously. Despite the blandishments of Guise and d'Épinac, the Estates-General wanted war against the Huguenots yet refused to vote more than a derisory sum for this purpose. Moreover, on 19 December 1588, just four days before the *coup d'état* against the Guises, Henri III had to agree to the indignity of an extraordinary financial tribunal (*chambre de justice*) of twenty-four individuals drawn from a list of one hundred elected by the Estates. The assassination of Guise and his brother the Cardinal Louis de Lorraine may have been long premeditated by the king, but was precipitated by what Henri III considered to have been their duplicity in encouraging the resistance of the Estates-General.[2] Moreover, Henri was convinced that Guise had encouraged the duke of Savoy's invasion of the French-held marquisate of Saluzzo, which began in October 1588 and was defenceless because of the king's lack of funds.

To the extent that the *coup d'état* had been intended to rid Henri III of the Guises, it achieved its purpose. Apart from the two assassinations, the League's candidate for the throne was safely in royal custody, where he remained until his death on 8 May 1590. D'Épinac, the arch-conspirator of the League, was also arrested but later escaped. However, if Henri III had hoped to regain control of his kingdom, the *coup* misfired disastrously. The king had clearly underestimated the prestige of his victims and the

---

[1] He was severely criticized by Sully in his memoirs. Sully produced evidence of François d'O's *pot de vin* of 195,000 *livres* from the farmers of the *gabelles de France* under the name of Noel de Heere. François d'O was associated on 27 Oct. 1585 with Antoine Faschon for one-tenth of the lease. He is not mentioned in the association of 15 Dec. 1585 [120 a p. 33, fo. 1] which gave one-third of the lease to Faschon's associates Allemant, Aubéry and La Bistrade. Cf. Sully, *Mémoires des sages et royales oeconomies d'estat . . .*, ed. J. F. Michaud and J. J. F. Poujoulat, 2 vols. [2nd ser., ii and iii] (1837), ii. 16–17. Yet even Sully noted that François d'O was in debt by the time of his death in 1594, and indeed there were still creditors in 1611: Sully, *Les oeconomies royales . . .*, ed. B. Barbiche and D. J. Buisseret, i (1970), 530–1. E 29b, fo. 143, 5 Mar. 1611.

[2] Mayer, *Des États Généraux et autres assemblées nationales*, xv. 92. G. Picot, *Histoire des États Généraux . . .* (2nd ed., 5 vols., 1888), iii. 416–18. Richard, *La papauté et la ligue française*, pp. 325–8.

power exercised by the numerous oaths of association that had
followed his solemn undertakings to the League in July 1588.
Most of the towns and lawcourts north of the river Loire sided
with the League, while there were more isolated pockets of resistance further south, for example in Toulouse and Marseille. A
number of provincial governors sided with the movement, the
most important of whom was Charles de Lorraine, duc de
Mayenne, Guise's younger brother who had not attended the
Estates-General at Blois. Mayenne became the effective leader of
the aristocratic wing of the revolt, although he never completely
controlled the more radical urban movement.

Henri III's hopes of regaining control rested on the siege of
Paris, but the king was desperately short of money. Between
September and November 1588, when he had not been at war, the
king had spent 5.6 million *livres*. Between December 1588 and
May 1589 when he was at war, he was able to spend only 4.9
million.[1] The loss of political control over much of northern
France had resulted in a disastrous loss of revenues with which to
pay for the war effort. Henri III pawned the royal rubies,
diamonds, and pearls to the financiers,[2] and obtained an important loan of 1.2 million on 17 February from the d'Elbène
brothers;[3] but in the climate of political and religious insecurity,
the king lacked sufficient credit to attract more substantial loans.
Much of the royal borrowing was in quite small sums, as for
example the 18,564 *livres* obtained in twelve different contracts
from the *grand prévôt de France*.[4] In this situation, an alliance of the
king with Henri of Navarre, which was attractive from military
and political considerations, became a financial imperative. The
king may have assumed that the financial help to Henri of
Navarre from abroad was more substantial, his troops more
numerous and better paid, than was the case. Nevertheless, two
armies were better than one, although the blockade of the capital
had failed to achieve its purpose by the time of Henri III's
assassination.

In later French legal theory, Henri IV automatically became king

---

[1] Mlle H. Michaud, 'L'ordonnancement des dépenses et le budget de la monarchie,
1587–1589', *Annuaire-Bulletin de la Société de l'Histoire de France* [1970–1] (1972), 123.

[2] P 2330, p. 575, 25 Feb. 1589. Appendix Two, Table IX A iii. o.

[3] Appendix Two, Table IX A iii. e.

[4] François du Plessis was one of Henri III's most trusted confidants in his last year. He
was also, of course, the father of Cardinal de Richelieu. For his loans: Michaud, art. cit.,
140 n. 297.

on the death of his predecessor: 'the same instant that the dead king expires his last breath, his successor is perfect king . . .' The political reality was quite different. The League recognized Charles X, who was proclaimed king by the rebel *Parlement* of Paris on 7 August although he remained in the custody of his chief opponent. The Protestant army at Meudon may well have recognized Henri IV unconditionally.[1] The Catholic army of Henri III nearby at Saint-Cloud decidedly did not. There were heated debates between the royalist military commanders on 2–3 August. Among the Catholic hard-liners were two of the most loyal servants of Henri III, who had been with him at his deathbed,[2] d'Épernon and François d'O. Indeed, it was d'O who took to Henri of Navarre the first terms for recognition: the king must abjure immediately, prohibit the holding of Protestant services throughout France and reserve all offices in the kingdom for Catholics. The king rejected the terms out of hand; he would not change his religion at his subjects' whim.[3] The next day, however, he agreed to a more moderate proposal. He would protect the Catholic faith throughout France, and in six months' time would summon a national council from which he would receive religious instruction. The Protestants would be guaranteed rights which were less extensive than those enjoyed in 1577, but the best to be expected and whose final extent would be decided at the peace settlement. There would be no Protestant take-over during the war against the League, since control of towns and fortresses captured from the rebels would be given to Catholics. The new king promised to punish those who had plotted the assassination of Henri III, whose faithful servants he would protect. The terms were signed on 4 August 1589, and in return the Catholic military commanders recognized Henri IV as king by fundamental law. They requested him to summon a general meeting of his followers within two months to deliberate on affairs of state while awaiting a more favourable opportunity to summon a meeting of the Estates-General. They wanted an ambassador sent to the Pope to

---

[1] Sully quotes the maxim 'le mort saisit le vif': Sully, *Oeconomies royales*, ed. Barbiche and Buisseret, i. 219. For the theory: R. E. Giesey, *The royal funeral ceremony in Renaissance France* (Geneva, 1960), pp. 181–2. Giesey argues that the theory became accepted only after 1610–11; Sully wrote his account after this date.

[2] *Archives curieuses de l'histoire de France* . . ., ed. Cimber and Danjou, 1st ser., xi (1836), 375.

[3] Girard records words which ring true. The king would not change his religion 'à l'appetit de ses sujets et de recevoir la loy d'eux en la chose du monde qui devoit estre la plus libre . . .': Girard, *Histoire de la vie du duc d'Espernon*, p. 111. The fundamental account of the negotiations at Saint-Cloud is A. Poirson, *Histoire du règne de Henri IV* (2nd ed., 4 vols., 1862–7), i. 19–31.

explain their actions (Sixtus V would scarcely have been pleased: on 9 September 1585 he had declared Henri IV incapable of succeeding to the French throne).[1] Finally, they pledged their lives and 'moyens pour chasser et exterminer les rebelles et les ennemis qui veullent usurper cet estat'.[2]

By this agreement, Henri IV took the first step towards recognizing the fact that France was a Catholic country and a Protestant succession was impossible to achieve. It was a delicate compromise: the king wanted to retain the loyalty of both Protestants and Catholics by offering the hope of better things to come. Neither side was satisfied. Protestant zealots such as La Trémouille withdrew their troops from the camp at Meudon, while a number of Catholics at Saint-Cloud followed Vitry, refused to sign the agreement, and threw in their lot with the League. Other Catholics such as Nevers and d'Épernon refused to sign, but adopted a more neutral stance, returning with their troops to their estates or governorships and waiting on events: both rejoined Henri IV after his victory at Ivry the following year.[3] The defections were extremely serious. In a matter of days, the royal army was almost halved from 40,000 to 22,000. The importance of the mercenary contingent was dramatically increased: but the 12,000 Switzers and 2000 Germans had agreed to serve Henri III not Henri of Navarre, could not be paid, and were only kept on by a promise that they would receive satisfaction within two months.[4] François d'O continued in office as *surintendant des finances*. Henri IV could certainly have courted personal popularity by dismissing an unpopular minister with a reputation for corruption, and there were Protestants such as Philippe du Plessis-Mornay, his *surintendant* in Béarn and Basse-Navarre, and Nicolas Harlay de Sancy, who negotiated contracts with the mercenary troops, who could have taken his place. However, the dismissal of François d'O would have been a political disaster. By taking an extreme Catholic standpoint, refusing to sign the agreement of 4 August,

---

[1] *Archives curieuses de l'histoire de France* . . ., ed. Cimber and Danjou, 1st ser., xi (1836), 49–58.

[2] Poirson, op. cit., i. 647–8.

[3] D'Épernon's case is particularly interesting since his troops were a crack force. He considered that under the new king he would not enjoy the same favour as under Henri III, professed that the six months' delay before converting was simply a delaying tactic by Navarre, and probably feared that his reputation for wealth would lead the new king to ask him for loans: Girard, op. cit., pp. 110–11. L. Mouton, *Le duc et le roi. D'Épernon. Henri IV. Louis XIII* (1924), p. 6.

[4] Poirson, op. cit., i. 24, 39.

and threatening at any moment to defect,[1] François d'O had made himself extremely important to the new dynasty. As a soldier with financial expertise, d'O's services were needed in the campaigns against the League. He had personal ties with the financiers of Henri III and brought some of them to support the Navarrist succession.[2] Above all, his dismissal would have had damaging consequences on Henri IV's attempt to rally Catholic opinion which in the summer of 1589 had sided with the League or was neutral. If d'O was retained, disaffected former colleagues in office such as Cheverny and Villeroy, and fellow governors such as Nevers and d'Épernon, might return. From 1590 onwards, the policy began to pay dividends with the return to court of some of the servants of Henri III. The defections from the League came later.

In one of the aphorisms for which he later became famous, Henri IV described his position in 1589 as that of a king without a kingdom, a husband without a wife, and a warrior without money.[3] In 1596, emphasizing his commitment to reform, the king recalled the deplorable financial situation he had found on his accession.[4] Henri IV, who was a master of self-presentation, took care to disassociate himself from the previous financial regime. His expenses were not superfluous, but needed to pay for the war to regain his kingdom. The debts of the crown were not his

---

[1] Ibid., i. 51, 650. Though his brother, Jean d'O, seigneur de Manou, did sign on 4 Aug. For François d'O's hostility to the influence of du Plessis-Mornay: R. Patry, *Philippe du Plessis-Mornay. Un huguenot homme d'état, 1549–1623* (1933), p. 184 n. 53.

[2] D'O succeeded in bringing over, among the financial office-holders, Robert Miron de Chenailles, an *intendant des finances*, Baltazar Gobelin, a *trésorier de l'Épargne*, and François Hotman and Vincent Bouhier de Beaumarchais, *trésoriers ordinaires des guerres*. Miron and Hotman had lent money to Henri III: Michaud, art. cit., 130. Among the financiers, d'O brought over the consortium holding the lease on the *gabelles de France* under the name of Noel de Heere: *Recueil des lettres missives de Henri IV*, ed. M. Berger de Xivrey and J. Guadet (9 vols., 1843–76), iii. 230. The consortium originally had comprised Sebastien Zamet, Jérôme Gondy, Barthélémy Cénamy, Pierre le Grand and Charles Saldaigne, but Zamet at least defected to the League: 120 a.p. 33, fo. 1, 15 Dec. 1585. There were also defections from the League to Henri IV, although these seem to have come later. Philippe Castille, the *receveur du clergé*, lent money to Henri III, but sided with the League until Jan. 1594: *Registres des délibérations du bureau de la ville de Paris. X. 1590–1594*, ed. P. Guérin (1902), p. 405.

[3] *The letters and documents of Armand de Gontaut, baron de Biron . . .*, ed. J. W. Thompson (2 vols., Berkeley, 1936), i. xxxix. Henri's failure to secure annulment of the marriage to Marguerite de Valois could have had serious consequences for the succession had he died in battle or had the assassination attempt of Jean Châtel in Dec. 1594 succeeded. César, duc de Vendôme, Henri's bastard by Gabrielle d'Estrées, was born only in June 1594 and legitimized in Jan. 1595: A.A.E. France 762, fo. 251.

[4] *Lettres de Henri IV*, iv. 623–4. *Registres des délibérations du bureau de la ville de Paris. XI. 1594–8*, ed. A. Tuetey (1902), p. 286.

fault, but those of his predecessor.[1] How could the king's desire for financial reform—and even François d'O recognized the need for improvement[2]—be put into practice in the circumstances of 1589–94? The hopes of almost all proponents of reform had rested with the crown lands. The estimated capital value of these lands was 150 million *livres*, but they had mostly been sold off during the wars of religion in a land transfer much more significant than that affecting church lands.[3] In peacetime, it might have been possible to repurchase the alienated crown lands. However, a programme of repurchase required an initial capital investment, and it would be a long time before the scheme could be brought to fruition or a significant amount of revenue raised. Henri IV could not wait and hope. A desperate situation required desperate measures. Far from redeeming alienated crown lands, the new king sold off his patrimonial lands in Béarn and Navarre or mortgaged them to creditors.[4] In legal theory, the sale of crown lands was against the fundamental law of the kingdom, and indeed met with stiff opposition from the *Chambre des Comptes* in 1593. However, Henri IV forestalled some of the criticism by his refusal to link his lands in Béarn and Navarre with the crown of France: he could thus sell off his patrimonial lands without contravening the fundamental laws of the French monarchy.[5]

The royal lands could not be repurchased in wartime, indeed the last remnants had to be sold off to meet expenses on the army. Could Henri IV have improved his financial position by renounc-

---

[1] For Henri IV's comments: P 2332, pp. 215–16, 30 Mar. 1593. P 2335, p. 459, 22 Feb. 1595. U 23, fo. 200, 2 Oct. 1595. For Henri III's lavish *ballet* in 1581 (at a cost of 1.2 million *livres*) and Henri IV's much more austere court: R. M. Isherwood, *Music in the service of the king. France in the seventeenth century* (Ithaca and London, 1973), pp. 79, 88.

[2] After outlining his current tasks as *surintendant*, François d'O commented: 'ce me soit un extrême regret de la voir si mal servie et ses affaires maniées avec telle confusion comme elles sont . . .' B.N. MS. fr. 3645, fo. 72ᵛ, 3 Nov. 1591.

[3] The hopes of the reformers were illustrated by the emphasis placed on crown lands at the Estates-General of 1588–9: Picot, *Histoire des États Généraux . . .*, iv. 44. For the much better studied, but financially less significant, sales of clerical lands: I. Clouas, 'Les aliénations du temporel ecclésiastique sous Charles IX et Henri III (1563–1587). Résultats généraux des ventes', *Revue d'Histoire de l'Église de France*, xliv (1958), 5–56.

[4] H. A. Lloyd, *The Rouen campaign, 1590–1592. Politics, warfare and the early modern state* (Oxford, 1973), p. 19. B.N. Clairambault 654, p. 17, Oct. 1590. For the mortgaging of some of these lands to a royal creditor (the duke of Württemberg): *Lettres . . . de Henri IV*, iv. 463.

[5] Poirson, *Histoire du règne de Henri IV*, i. 49–50. The edict of 31 Dec. 1596 maintained the separation of Navarre and Béarn from France, but this was modified in July 1607: P. Tucoo-Chala, *La vicomté de Béarn et le problème de sa souveraineté des origines à 1620* (Bordeaux, 1961). The Estates-General of 1614–15 wanted the later edict strengthened to permit the repurchase of Navarrist lands 'aliéné depuis l'avènement du feu roi à la couronne': Mayer, *Des États Généraux et autres assemblées nationales*, xvii, pt. ii. 5.

ing the debts of his predecessor? Without the interest charge on Henri III's debts, and the commitment to repay the capital sum in full, his financial position would certainly have been improved: the debt amounted to 12 million *livres*.[1] It may have been Henri IV's intention at his accession to renounce the debts of the last Valois king, but circumstances forced the postponement of the decision until almost the end of the reign. The political risk of a premature renunciation of the debt was too great. Henri IV contrasted Habsburg unreliability with the loyalty of French kings to their foreign creditors.[2] Philip II of Spain, with whom he was at war—effectively from 1589,[3] although open war was not officially declared until 1595—declared bankruptcy three times. Henri IV's self-portrait as a king who kept his word was an illusion, but one that was reasonably convincing until 1592, when his foreign creditors began to have grave doubts about his willingness, or capacity, to repay: the illusion would have been shattered much earlier had the king bankrupted the creditors of Henri III.

The volatility of the mercenary troops was a further consideration. Any doubts concerning the 'foi et parole de roi' would risk inducing panic and the possible transfer of allegiance. François Dompmartin had entered the service of Henri of Navarre after the treaty of Fridelsheim in 1587.[4] On 14 August 1589, just a fortnight after his accession, Henri IV signed a new agreement with the mercenary captain. Dompmartin was to levy 1500 cavalry (*reitern*) for service by 25 October, and received an advance payment of 27,000 *livres*. The troops were not to be bought off by another prince offering higher wages. In return, Henri IV solemnly bound himself, his estate, and his heirs to pay the troops in monthly instalments with no more than a fortnight's delay. All arrears of pay were to be acquitted before the troops were disbanded and immediately after the king won a military victory.[5] The conditions

---

[1] Appendix Two, Table IX A ii. On 13 Dec. 1608, the council of finance concluded that many of the original loans to Henri III had been fictitious and renounced its obligation to repay them: *Inventaire des arrêts du conseil d'état. Règne de Henri IV*, ed. N. Valois (2 vols., 1886, 1893), no. 12910.

[2] *Lettres . . . de Henri IV*, iii. 658–60. In Sept. 1589, Henri IV offered to recognize all Henri III's debts to the Swiss: E. Rott, *Henri IV, les Suisses et la Haute Italie. La lutte pour les Alpes, 1598–1610 . . .* (1882), p. 166.

[3] *Lettres . . . de Henri IV*, iii. 260.

[4] A. Tuetey, *Les Allemands en France et l'invasion du comté de Montbéliard par les Lorrains, 1587–1588 . . .* (2 vols., Paris-Montbéliard, 1883), i. 47.

[5] L. Anquez, *Henri IV et l'Allemagne d'après les mémoires et la correspondance de Jacques Bongars* (1887), pp. 206–20.

of this, and comparable agreements (*capitulations*) with the mercenary captains were onerous. It was impossible to pay the troops in monthly instalments because the revenues did not arrive at regular or predictable intervals. Everything depended on the king's ability to retain the confidence of the mercenary captains. A declaration of bankruptcy would have left Henri IV without an army.

The German and Swiss mercenaries were reliable only as long as they were paid. As the king accumulated debt upon debt, so they became increasingly restless. In March 1590, a fortnight's opportunity to follow up the great victory at Ivry with the siege of Paris was wasted while François d'O negotiated with the Switzers who demanded the payment of arrears. In September, they were restless once more and threatened to return home. In June 1591, there were new difficulties and new negotiations. In July 1592 there was a new crisis after the failure of the siege of Rouen. Sublet d'Heudicourt, an *intendant des finances* acting on the king's orders, recognized debts of over 800,000 *livres* to Dompmartin, and over 3.2 million to Christian of Anhalt. The mercenary captains had to accept *rentes* and written promises as security for the arrears of pay. The solemn contracts undertaken when the troops were levied had not been fulfilled, and the king reluctantly had to accept the decision of the *reitern* and *landsknechts* to return home. However, Henri IV managed to retain the services of the Switzers in return for a new recognition of his debts to them and solemn assurances to assign repayment on secure revenues. As in most matters, the king's actions did not match his promises. In March 1593 the Switzers went to the *Chambre des Comptes* to protest at the size of the debts, which amounted to between 9 and 12 million *livres*: all they were offered was a sale of crown lands to the value of 1.5 million. In October 1595, there was a new crisis. The Switzers refused to cross the river Marne without first being paid their debts. The king admitted the justice of their demands and praised their great patience. He committed the crown to pay 900,000 *livres* per annum until the debt, both in principal and interest, was paid off.[1] In view of the difficulties in paying the mercenary troops, it is difficult to see how any coherent military strategy could have been put into effect. The duration of the war of succession resulted

---

[1] For the difficulties with the mercenaries: Sully, *Oeconomies royales*, ed. Barbiche and Buisseret, i. 251–2. *Lettres . . . de Henri IV*, iii. 254–5, 397, 401, 646, 655, 658–60. *The letters of Biron*, ed. Thompson, ii. 491–2. P 2331, p. 455, 14 Oct. 1591. P 2332, pp. 217–18, 30 Mar. 1593. P 2336, p. 167, 2 Oct. 1595. Appendix Two, Table IX A iii f and l.

almost as much from Henri IV's financial plight as the political obstacles posed by his religion.[1]

Henri IV's difficulties were compounded by the nature of warfare, with its emphasis on siegecraft. The great set-piece battles such as Ivry in 1590 and Fontaine-Française in 1595 were the exception, not the rule. Much of the time Henri IV spent fighting the Catholic League was consumed in two sieges of Paris, the siege of Rouen and a host of smaller-scale operations; the war against Spain saw the siege of La Fère in 1596 and that of Amiens the following year. As Philip II had found during his protracted war in the Netherlands, siege warfare tested the resources and logistics of the besieger to the full: it was much easier to defend than attack a fortified town. Of course, Henri IV was assisted in part by his alliances with England, the Dutch rebels, certain German princes and towns, and most of the Swiss cantons. Willoughby's expedition in 1589 had probably saved Henri's throne, but Essex's expedition in 1591–2 was little short of a disaster. Elizabeth I could not be expected to suffer a repetition of the intolerable wastage of men that had occurred partly because Henri refused to grant her a port or fortified town.[2] The support of the German princes also cooled with the passing of time. They were divided in their motives and the extent of their commitment to Henri IV: the death in 1592 of John Casimir, elector of the Rhine Palatinate, removed the most vigorous supporter of the Bourbon dynasty. Thus although former supporters of the League such as Villeroy could, as late as February 1594, contrast Philip II's apparent weakness with the strength of Henri IV's foreign alliances,[3] the Protestant counter-league was a good deal weaker than appeared at first sight. It could prevent defeat, but it was doubtful if it could secure a Bourbon victory. As the military stalemate became protracted, so the king's foreign allies became increasingly restless at his failure to repay their loans. Elizabeth I was later to call him the 'Antichrist of ingratitude'. However, the French attitude was that English support to the Bourbon dynasty had been self-interested in the first place and repayment of the debt in full was out of the

---

[1] Henri IV commented to the duke of Württemberg on 28 Dec. 1589 that 'rien ne me combat tant aujourd'hui que le défault d'argent, qui procède de la rébellion . . . en la meilleure part des bonnes villes . . .' *Lettres . . . de Henri IV*, iii. 107–8.

[2] For the financing of English intervention: L. Stone, *An Elizabethan: Sir Horatio Palavicino* (Oxford, 1956), pp. 135–79. For the logistics: Lloyd, *The Rouen campaign*.

[3] B.L. Add. MSS. 21, 512, fos. 19–22, 24 Feb. 1594.

question.[1] In the treaty of 25 June 1591 Henri IV agreed to mortgage the revenues of Normandy to help pay off the English debt. On 16 August 1594 he committed himself and his heirs to repay £14,173 (calculated as 141,730 *livres*). Yet the total English debt by 1596 was 3,343,550 *livres* (2,796,030 *livres* from military assistance; 547,520 *livres* from loans after 1589).[2] The English debt, moreover, was one of the smallest foreign debts of the Bourbon dynasty.

By March 1593, Henri IV was faced with a stark political and financial choice. In this month, the Navarrist *Chambre des Comptes*[3] openly criticized the conduct of financial administration. At a crucial moment in Henri's fortunes, when the Estates-General of the League was meeting in an attempt to elect an alternative king, the *Chambre des Comptes* linked the principles of the Salic Law and the inalienability of the royal demesne. Henri's claim to the throne rested chiefly on the Salic Law, which also served to rule out most if not all the alternative candidates. The linking of the two ideas was therefore acutely embarrassing. The *Comptes* argued that the king should not sell off the few remaining crown lands which would weaken the prestige, as well as the power, of the monarchy. They argued that the king's financial crisis was more apparent than real, and resulted from grave corruption in the administration of his finances. The burden of taxation was excessive yet the king had not honoured his contractual obligations to pay interest to *rentiers* and salaries to office-holders. Although they recognized the importance of the Swiss alliance, the *Comptes* refused to countenance a full repayment of this debt. The king listened to their remonstrances with 'une grande patience':[4] he had to choose between repaying his Protestant allies abroad, or buying off his Catholic supporters and opponents at home. The remark later attributed to Henri IV, that Paris was worth a mass, may well be apocryphal and form part of the later

[1] Stone, op. cit., p. 179. J. B. Black, *Elizabeth and Henry IV, being a short study in Anglo-French relations, 1589–1603* (Oxford, 1914), p. 155.

[2] P 2331, p. 375, 25 June 1591. P 2334, p. 1219, 7 Nov. 1594. B.N. MS. fr. 23026, pp. 117–20, 'estat des debtes demandées par le Roy de la Grande Bretagne et [des] payements qui ont esté faictz sur lesdictes debtes'. Sully's estimate of the debt in 1598 was considerably higher (7.4 million): Appendix Two, Table IX A ii.

[3] In the early 1590s most of the sovereign tribunals had divided loyalties, the majority of their members siding initially with the League while a smaller number left the seat of the court to establish a rival, Navarrist, tribunal. The *Chambre des Comptes* was no exception: the Navarrist tribunal resided at Blois and its members did not rejoin their colleagues at Paris until the collapse of the League in the capital in 1594.

[4] P 2332, pp. 197–220, 30 Mar. 1593.

legend of the *grand roi*.[1] On the other hand, there is little doubt that from about this time the king took a highly pragmatic view of his abjuration, which he virtually auctioned to the highest bidder. On 26 April, he promised Ferdinand of Medici, grand duke of Tuscany, that he would convert to Catholicism within two months of reaching an agreement with Mayenne. In return, the duke agreed to pay for the services of 4000 Switzers for a year and another 1000 troops for six months; in addition the king asked for a cash grant of 600,000 *livres*.[2] By May 1593, during the conference at Suresnes with representatives of the League, Henri was receiving religious instruction. The failure of the Estates-General of the League, and the six months' truce commencing on 31 July provided the ideal timing: Henri's symbolic mass at Saint-Denis preceded the truce by only five days.[3] According to one well-informed observer, François d'O played a crucial part in convincing the king to delay his conversion no longer.[4]

When the fighting recommenced in 1594, the prospects of a victory for the Catholic League had receded. Its cause now rested on the argument that the king's conversion was insincere: the Pope alone could determine the validity of the abjuration, and his views—favourable to Henri IV—were not known until November 1595.[5] The League's attitude was incomprehensible to some, and offended the Gallican sentiments of many. In addition, the internal divisions of the League (between aristocratic factions and radical parties in the towns, between those for and against the Spanish connection), the failure to elect an alternative king, and, most obviously, the self-interested policy of Spain made a revival of its fortunes unlikely. The credibility of Philip II had been gravely compromised by his attempt to press the claim of his daughter, the Infanta Isabella Clara Eugenia, to the throne of France. It is true that following Mayenne's appeal to Parma in July 1590[6] the Spanish army in the Netherlands had twice

---

[1] Cf. M. Reinhard, *La légende de Henri IV* (St-Brieuc, 1935), pp. 68–9.

[2] *Lettres . . . de Henri IV*, iii. 763–4.

[3] Ibid., iii. 822. When announcing his abjuration on 25 July, Henri noted his promise in 1589 that he would convert at a later date. The truce was originally for three months but was later extended.

[4] *Mémoires-Journaux de Pierre L'Estoile*, ed. Brunet *et al.*, vi. 73–4.

[5] The Papal dispensation was dated 17 Sept. 1595, but Henri IV did not announce it until 22 Nov.: ibid., iv. 458–60. D'Épinac regarded the abjuration as invalid until the Pope had pronounced his verdict: Richard, *La papauté et la ligue française*, pp. 521–2.

[6] A.A.E. France 762, fo. 10, 20 July 1590. Mayenne asked Parma to invade with 'une

invaded France to support the League and had helped save the beleaguered cities of Paris and Rouen. However, at the time when the maximum effort was required to prevent defections to Henri IV in 1594, no help at all from Spain was forthcoming because of mutinies in its army in the Netherlands. Not surprisingly, even supporters of the League began to doubt Philip II's sincerity: did he not perhaps seek to keep France divided and weak rather than win great victories for the cause of religion?[1]

The League had its own financial problems. Spain spent a substantial amount of money—perhaps 7.5 million *livres* between 1591 and 1595[2]—on intervention in France. The Papacy adopted a less consistent policy: no subsidy was paid under Sixtus V (1585–90), but Gregory XIV ordered considerable assistance in men and money after March 1591. The extent of the commitment to the Catholic League was gradually reduced under the succeeding Popes, Innocent IX and particularly Clement VIII after April 1592.[3] Yet foreign assistance was not enough. The League had to hire mercenary troops to support its cause, and by early 1593 Mayenne's debts reached 1.2 million, with over 904,000 *livres* owed to the comte de Collalto and his *landsknechts*.[4] Part of the initial appeal of the Catholic League had rested on its proposals for financial reform and a reduction in the burden of taxation. Sir George Carew, the English ambassador, later recalled that 'though religion was the first pretext, . . . adherence to the house of Guise grew . . . out of a desire of liberty . . . All the towns of France, like the bondmen of a galley, took the first occasion to abandon the cares of their duty and obedience . . .'[5] Supporters of

---

grande armée pour mettre en asseurance notre religion et le repoz en ce pauvre royaulme'. It is doubtful if Habsburg assistance achieved the first purpose; it manifestly had not achieved the second.

[1] The comment was made by Villeroy to the bishop of Rennes: B.L. Add. MSS. 21, 512, fos. 19–22, 24 Feb. 1594.

[2] N. G. Parker, *The Dutch revolt* (1977), p. 227 (who gives the figure of 2.5 million 'crowns').

[3] L. F. von Pastor, *The history of the Popes from the close of the Middle Ages . . .*, ed. F. I. Antrobus *et al.*, 40 vols. (1923–53), xxi. 347 (Sixtus V's criticism of the papal legate Caetani for paying 50,000 *scudi* to Mayenne); xxii. 373, 387, 424; xxiii. 59, 62. J. Delumeau, *Vie économique et sociale de Rome dans la seconde moitié du xvi* siècle, 2 vols. (1957, 1959), ii. 761–2. N. G. Parker, *Spain and the Netherlands, 1559–1659 . . .* (1979), p. 72.

[4] Richard, *La papauté et la ligue française*, pp. 518–19. A.A.E. France 763, fo. 44ᵛ, 4 Feb. 1593; debts to Collalto of 904, 670 *livres*.

[5] Sir George Carew, 'A relation of the state of France', *An historical view of the relations between the courts of England, France and Brussels, 1592–1617*, ed. T. Birch (1749), p. 466, *s.v.* 'names of exactions and the reasons'.

the League had packed the Estates-General at Blois in 1588–9, and the proposals of the third estate reflected the objectives of the movement. They proposed a full-scale resumption of crown lands and an attack on financial corruption by a *chambre de justice*, which should be repeated every five years. Individuals who had proposed the establishment of new offices or taxes since 1559 should be banished from the kingdom and their wealth confiscated. Foreigners were not to be allowed to participate in government or financial activities. Recent developments such as the consolidation of indirect taxes into large revenue farms (for example the *cinq grosses fermes* were established in 1584) were to be reversed: instead, small leases were to be negotiated in the localities. The most important indirect tax of all, that on salt (levied in the various farms of the *gabelles*) was to be abolished. The League wanted ultimately to reduce the burden of taxation to the level of 1515, although in the short-term it was prepared to accept the level of 1547–59.[1] The role of the Estates-General as keeper of the purse was boldly proclaimed: all new taxes were to receive its consent, and without it individuals ordering new taxes would be liable to punishment and local communities entitled to resist. Despite all these proposals, however, the League was committed to the war against the Huguenots and the principle of voluntary contributions by all classes to the war effort.[2]

It is difficult to see how the various elements in the financial programme of the Catholic League could be reconciled with a vigorous war against Henri of Navarre. Far from giving the Estates-General parliamentary control of the purse, Mayenne was reluctant to summon the assembly: when it met in 1593, he had deep misgivings about its prospects of success but saw no alternative. The financiers and financial officials of Henri III were not persecuted by the League. It is true that in the heady days of March 1589, before Mayenne was made lieutenant-general, the council of state of the League ordered the confiscation of 1,080,000 *livres* of assets belonging to Pierre Molan, the *trésorier de l'Épargne* known as the archrobber.[3] However, Benoît Milon de

[1] 1547 in the case of the *taille*; 1559 in the case of the *taillon*.

[2] Mayer, *Des États Généraux et autres assemblées nationales*, xv. 191–6. Picot, *Histoire des États Généraux*, iv. 44–53. Picot (iv. 52) quotes Pasquier's comment on the lack of realism of the proposals at a time of civil war.

[3] Lestoile describes the event on 4 Mar. 1589, while Mayenne did not take the oath as lieutenant-general until 13 Mar.: *Mémoires-Journaux de Pierre L'Estoile*, ed. Brunet *et al.*, iii. 253, 258. *Abrégé de l'histoire universelle de J. A. de Thou avec des remarques sur le texte de cet auteur . . .*, ed. P. Rémond de Sainte-Albine, 10 vols., (The Hague, 1759), vii. 433.

Videville, an equally corrupt *intendant des finances* who had thrown in his lot with the guises in 1584–5 as a result of his prosecution by Henri III's *chambre de justice*, was left in peace until his death in 1593.[1] Nor were foreign financiers exiled. The great Piedmontese financier Sébastien Zamet had recognized the unpopularity of the Italian *émigrés* at the time of the Day of the Barricades, made his peace with Guise, and offered him financial assistance.[2] He became the close confidant and adviser of Mayenne. The League was unable to make the great reductions in taxes envisaged by the third estate at Blois. In the aftermath of the assassination of the Guises, the muncipality of Paris ordered the levy of taxes at the rate of 1576 if this sufficed to pay the *rentes* and salaries to office-holders, or at two-thirds the rate of 1587 if not; but the reductions were more than offset by a general levy on all inhabitants to pay for the war.[3] This was the sign of things to come. Extraordinary levies for the war were added to the existing burden of taxes, and the *curés* were requested to preach diligence and prompt payment to the Catholic League.[4] Yet the old grievances remained: the League proved no better able than Henri III to pay the *rentes* and salaries of office-holders who had supported its cause. By the time of Henri IV's abjuration, the *rentiers* and office-holders in Paris and many other towns were ready to transfer their allegiance to the Bourbon claimant in the belief that he was the only candidate likely to secure civil peace and bring about an improvement in their lot.[5]

Similarly, in the provinces war-weariness was a trump card in Henri IV's hand. All the provincial governors were unpopular because they had been granted not just military but financial

---

[1] Milon's defection was recalled in 1624 as an argument for not pressing the *chambre de justice* too hard: *Les papiers de Richelieu*, ed. Grillon, i. 122. Milon was still wealthy at his death according to Lestoile, op. cit., vi. 48–9. Henri IV had appointed Adrien Petremol de Rosières to his office, but the *Chambre des Comptes* would not register his letters patent: P 2331, p. 209, 10 Apr. 1591.
[2] Lestoile reports Zamet as making his peace with Guise on 14 May 1588: ibid., iii. 148.
[3] *Registres . . . de la ville de Paris*, ed. Bonnardot, ix. 200.
[4] Ibid., ix. 342. On the increase in taxes as a cause of the loss of support: H. Drouot, *Mayenne et la Bourgogne, 1587–1596. Contribution à l'histoire des provinces françaises pendant la Ligue* (2 vols., 1937), ii. 112.
[5] On the issue of offices: Drouot, op. cit., ii. 333–9 and Mousnier, *La vénalité*, pp. 579–88. On 8 Oct. 1591, the Parisian municipality asked Mayenne to replace the funds he had diverted from the payment of *rentes* since for 'le petit peuple . . . il ne restoit que cela pour soustenir sa vye'. On 12 Mar. 1592 it argued that 'l'extrême misère et nécessité' of all inhabitants was likely to lead either to the abandonment of the capital or the collapse of resistance: *Registres . . . de la ville de Paris*, ed. Guérin, x. 172, 234.

control in their localities.[1] However, those supporting the League were even more unpopular than those who served Henri IV. They suffered more from the dashed hopes of reduced taxation, they were under acute military pressure from the king, and above all the control they had assumed over the League councils in the towns was contested: by 1594, the military and financial command of the League had disintegrated into faction-fighting.[2] In several provinces, moreover, there were peasant rebellions against heavy taxation, the lawless nobility and the depredations of the troops. It is significant that whereas the earlier peasant uprisings in Brittany and Normandy were aligned with the Catholic League, the later ones in Guyenne and Burgundy were non-partisan or else supported Henri IV. These uprisings may have posed a greater threat to the social order than is sometimes assumed,[3] and accelerated the transfer of allegiance among the propertied classes to the king. The great subsistence crisis of 1589–94, with rocketing food prices and a rapid decline in the value of money, had the same effect. There is not much doubt that areas supporting the League were worst hit: Henri IV's blockades and sieges of the League towns created shortages which forced up prices; the financial assistance from Spain brought with it much debased coin and inflation.[4]

There were thus many reasons why support for the League was beginning to drop off by 1594. Yet Henri IV exploited his opportunity with consummate skill. In a letter to Sully on 8 March, he

---

[1] François d'O denounced the conduct of the Navarrist governors in open council; if they exceeded their financial authority, they and their heirs were liable to repay excessive taxes levied or cash removed from the king's coffers: B. N. Clairambault 654, p. 291, 26 Jan. 1593. P 2332, p. 247, 20 Mar. 1593. For the powers accorded to the duc de Nevers in his governorship of Champagne: *Lettres . . . de Henri IV*, iii. 301–2, 405, 447, 614 ('sans vous arrester aux formes ordinaries ny à l'ordre des finances . . . pour un coup d'estat sy important . . .').

[2] H. Drouot, 'Les conseils provinciaux de la Sainte-Union, 1589–1595', *Annales du Midi*, lxv (1953), 433. Harding, *Anatomy of a power elite*, pp. 105–6. The duc de Nemours was arrested at Lyon on 18 Sept. 1593, and accused of levying excessive taxes and disposing of the League's finances 'beaucoup plus absolument que jamais n'avoient fait [nos rois]': *Mémoires-Journaux de Pierre L'Estoile*, ed. Brunet *et al.*, vi. 99.

[3] Drouot, *Mayenne et la Bourgogne*, ii. 288–93. J. H. M. Salmon, *Society in crisis. France in the sixteenth century* (1975), pp. 276–91. The picture of the *croquants* of Limousin and the Périgord given by Bercé, *Histoire des croquants*, i. 257–93 is effectively challenged by Tait, 'The king's lieutenants in Guyenne', 193–217, who uses local sources to supplement Bercé's account and stresses the real and potential social conflict.

[4] For the social crisis: J. Jacquart, *La crise rurale en Île-de-France, 1550–1670* (1974), pp. 179–87. For the debased coin: F. C. Spooner, *The international economy and monetary movements in France, 1493–1725* (Cambridge, Mass., 1972), pp. 166–7, 231–2. Spooner, 'Monetary disturbance and inflation, 1590–3: the case of Aix-en-Provence', *Mélanges en l'honneur de Fernand Braudel . . .* (Toulouse, 1973), 583–97.

recalled the method used by Louis XI to deal with his rebellious magnates during the war of the Public Weal (1465). This was to 'séparer par intérêtz particuliers tous ceux qui estoyent liguez contre luy soubz des prétextes généraux', and was highly successful: 'the public weal', Commynes wrote, 'had been turned into the private interest.' Henri IV's letter may have been subsequently rewritten by Sully,[1] but its tone illustrates his methods. Sir George Carew remarked acidly that 'those, who hazarded their lives and fortunes for settling the crown upon his head, [the king] neither rewardeth nor payeth; those, who were of the League against him, he hath bought to be his friends and giveth them preferments.'[2] 1594 was the year in which the French towns fell to the king, beginning with Méaux in January,[3] followed by Lyon in February and Paris and Rouen in March. These political gains were not bought cheaply by Henri IV. The 'treaties of capitulation' limited the king's freedom of action, since they contained clauses excluding Protestants from practising their faith within the town and securing the continuance in office of Mayenne's appointees. All office-holders were to receive letters patent from Henri IV, but Navarrists were to be compensated for their loss of office in favour of erstwhile supporters of the League. These treaties contained other financial arrangements, too, sometimes a guarantee that the king would acquit the debts of the town (even though these debts were incurred by fighting on the side of the League) or alternatively, remission of arrears of the *taille* owed by the town and its fiscal exemption for a number of years into the future.[4] Similar provisions were contained in the separate treaties later signed with the leading nobles who had commanded the forces of the

---

[1] *Lettres . . . de Henri IV*, iv. 110–1. Sully, *Oeconomies royales*, ed. Barbiche and Buisseret, i. 420–1. Cf. Philippe de Commynes, *Memoirs. The reign of Louis XI, 1461–1483*, trans. M. Jones (1972), p. 104. Maximilien de Béthune was known during the 1590s as the baron de Rosny. To avoid confusion, however, he is called throughout the duc de Sully, his title after Mar. 1606.

[2] Carew, op. cit., p. 478.

[3] The decision of Vitry, its commander, was regarded by both sides as crucial. In 1597, he was rewarded with an annuity on the *taille* of the *élection* of Méaux, but three years earlier, when he had led the defections, it was without certainty of recompense: *Mémoires-Journaux de Pierre L'Estoile*, ed. Brunet *et al.*, vi. 128–9. *Chambre des Comptes*, ed. Boislisle, pp. 235–6. Vitry published an important self-justification: A. Devyver, *Le sang épuré. Les préjugés de race chez les gentilhommes français de l'ancien régime, 1560–1720* (Brussels, 1973), p. 95.

[4] P 2333 contains *réductions* of Méaux, Bourges, Troyes, Saint-Florentin, Vézelay and Chablis. P 2334 contains *réductions* of Poitiers, Beauvais, Chaumont, Pontoise, Amiens and Reims—all in 1594. For a model on which the treaties were drawn up: A.A.E. France 762, fo. 193.

League.[1] François d'O had his doubts about the policy, and thought the price of reducing Paris to obedience too high.[2] The fears of the *surintendant* were well founded, though he did not live to see all the treaties completed and the full cost revealed. The gifts (*dons*) of Henri IV to private individuals reached the record figure for his reign of over 5 million *livres* in 1594. His secret expenses (*comptants*) reached almost thirteen million in the same year—the highest figure before 1626. According to Sully, Henri IV spent between 30 and 32 million in treaties 'for the recovery of the kingdom'—although whether all these debts were honoured is another matter.[3]

François d'O died on 24 October 1594. Contrary to expectations, and probably as a result of the influence of Gabrielle d'Estrées, his mistress, Henri IV did not appoint Sancy, his expert on dealings with the mercenary troops, as *surintendant*.[4] Instead, on 25 November, he established a finance commission in addition to the council of finance which continued to operate.[5] It remained to be seen whether a collegiate form of control with four nobles, the Chancellor, and four financial experts would prove sufficiently robust to find the revenues necessary to pay the king's outstanding debts[6] and the new ones he was contracting as he won over the

[1] Treaties with the sieur de Ballagny (Apr. 1594), the sieur de Bois-dauphin (Aug. 1595), the ducs de Mayenne, Nemours, and Joyeuse (all in Jan. 1596) and the duc de Mercoeur (Mar. 1598): P 2335, pp. 319, 1259. P 2336, pp. 389, 713. P 2337, p. 397. P 2338, p. 279.

[2] Sully, *Oeconomies royales*, ed. Barbiche and Buisseret, i. 432.

[3] Between 1589 and 1596 Henri IV spent 16,709,140 *livres* through the *dons* an average of nearly 2.1 million a year: 120 a.p. 12. Brissac's *don* of 360,000 *livres*, accorded for his part in the return of Paris to allegiance, had still not been paid in Dec. 1598: *Chambre des Comptes*, ed. Boislisle, p. 241. There are no continuous figures for the *comptants* between 1589 and 1593. For those in 1594 and after: Appendix Two, Table III. (The use of secret expenses by Henri IV is analysed in detail by F. Bayard, 'Étude des comptants ès mains du roi sous Henri IV', *Bulletin du centre d'histoire économique et sociale de la région lyonnaise*, iii (1974), 1–27.) François d'O was blamed by some for the growth of the *comptants*: B.N. MS. fr. 16626, fo. 150. A more realistic appraisal, however, was that of Dreux, the *procureur-général* of the *Chambre des Comptes*, who noted on 7 Feb. 1594 that the secret expenses would rise because those who made agreements with the king 'ne veulent pas estre nommés': *Chambre des Comptes*, ed. Boislisle, p. 209. For the estimated cost of the treaties: Appendix Two, Table IX A ii.

[4] Sully, *Oeconomies royales*, ed. Barbiche and Buisseret, i. 555. However, Sancy's influence remained considerable until Jan. 1598: Buisseret, *Sully*, p. 44. B. Barbiche, *Sully* (1978), pp. 40, 45.

[5] Appendix One, Table I. Valois distinguishes the commission from the council in his inventory of decrees. The earliest surviving records of the finance commission date from 2 Jan. 1595: *Inventaire des arrêts du conseil d'état*, ed. Valois, no. 1890.

[6] The four nobles were the ducs de Nevers, Retz, Montmorency-Damville and the comte de Schomberg, 'felt-maréchal des gens de guerre allemands de Sa Majesté'. The financial

supporters of the League. The difficulties of the finance commission were made worse by the declaration of open war on Spain (16 January 1595), followed up by the French invasion of Artois. Henri IV was gambling on the willingness of Frenchmen to sink their differences in the common cause,[1] but the extension of the conflict carried enormous risks. It assumed that increased war expenses could actually be paid for by the French peasantry in the form of higher taxes. It is true that as the provinces returned to allegiance so the king's revenues were bound to increase: this was an argument in favour of the campaign against Mercoeur in Brittany as late as 1598.[2] On the other hand, the taxable limit on the peasants, whether they paid the king or the League, had probably been reached in 1594: the countryside was exhausted.

In 1594, the provinces controlled by Henri IV were required to pay nearly 11.3 million *livres* in direct taxes.[3] This sum did not cover the additional levies of the governors to pay for the quartering of troops. The amount of these extraordinary levies varied greatly from province to province, but could add a colossal additional burden on the peasants. Thus the Treasury expected to receive only a tiny amount (less than 100,000 *livres*) from the Dauphiné, but the total levy between March 1594 and February 1595 was nearly 1.4 million, much of it ordered on the lieutenant-general's fiat. Of course, the total paid to the Treasury does not

---

experts were Bellièvre, who had been *surintendant* in 1574–8, Sancy, Jacques la Grange-le-Roy, a former *trésorier de l'Épargne*, and Pierre Forget de Fresnes. Bellièvre's letter of appointment specified the extent of the king's Swiss debts as one of the pressing concerns of the commission: *Lettres . . . de Henri IV*, iv. 266–7.

[1] Ibid., iv. 385: 'il faut estre françois ou espagnol'.

[2] Cf. Bellièvre's comment to the municipality of Paris on 23 Jan. 1598: *Registres . . . de la ville de Paris*, ed. Tuetey, xi. 473.

[3] More money was levied in taxes than was actually paid to the Treasury. There were three additional items, the assigned revenues paid directly to royal creditors (*assignations*), local payments (*charges*), and alienated taxes (*droits aliénés*): Collins, 'Sur l'histoire fiscale du xviiᵉ siècle', 327–34. The title of this article is misleading, since no figure for direct taxes in Champagne is provided for 1595. Moreover, the author's claim concerning the authority of his figures is weakened by the admission (p. 340 n. 39) that there is no allowance for arrears. Cf. ibid., p. 334: '. . . les non-valeurs rendent peu sûres les sommes mentionnées dans les budgets des guerres civiles . . .' The 1594 *état* distinguishes payments direct to the Treasury, to the *trésorier de l'extraordinaire des guerres*, the local *charges* and *assignations*. The net amounts paid to the Treasury were often tiny: in the case of Champagne, the *état* was 1,411,398 *livres*, but the net payment to the Treasury was only 36,000 *livres*. (N.B.: the figure of 1.4 million is higher than any of Collins's figures for Champagne before 1634.) The total of 11,283,627 *livres* is the total burden of taxation (given in the document in *écus*) not the payment to the Treasury. However, it may include some revenue from indirect taxes and the crown lands: B.N. MS. fr. 4680, fo. 15.

cover payments made by areas loyal to the League.[1] Not surprisingly, the rebellious peasants in the Périgord called themselves the *Tard-Avisés*, the late-comers in the queue for concessions and privileges.[2] Rebellious peasants lacked constitutional rights,[3] and the *Tard-Avisés* were defeated at the battle of St-Crépin d'Auberoche in August 1595. However, their basic claim, that there was no prospect of raising additional money from the *plat pays* 'duquel l'impuissance est tout manifeste' came to be accepted by 1596. The limit of direct taxes was nearer 11 million *livres* than the figure of 18 million suggested by the assembly of notables in 1596, and the arrears from previous years had to be remitted.[4]

If the peasant tax-payers had difficulty in making their voice heard, the office-holders—now greatly reinforced by the amalgamation of the rival tribunals for and against the League of the earlier 1590s—did not. By the spring of 1595 their condemnation of the king's financial policies had taken on a new sharpness and sense of purpose. As Henri IV failed to pay salaries to office-holders and interest to *rentiers*, so the suspicion grew that he was a prince who did not keep his word: payment of the *rentes* was nearly nine years in arrears.[5] On 22 February 1595, the *Chambre des Comptes* issued a blistering attack on the king's financial policies. 'Vos finances ont été si peu ménagées', Nicolay, the *premier président*, informed Henri IV, 'qu'elles semblent avoir esté mises à l'abandon.' He protested at the excessive level of expenditure since 1589, and claimed that 120,000 *livres* had been spent on gifts in the previous two months alone.[6] He argued that there were hordes of pensioners enjoying the fruits of the king's liberality. Moreover, the administration of the royal debts was open to the gravest suspicion: it was alleged that Henri III's creditors had

---

[1] L. S. Van Doren, 'Civil war taxation and the foundations of fiscal absolutism. The royal *taille* in the Dauphiné, 1560–1610', *Proceedings of the . . . Western Society for French History*, iii (1976), pp. 36, 48.

[2] Bercé, *Histoire des croquants*, i. 275. Tait, 'The king's lieutenants in Guyenne', p. 194.

[3] Henri IV accepted the justice of the peasants' grievances, but thought their method of presenting them 'd'une périlleuse conséquence': *Lettres . . . de Henri IV*, iv. 156.

[4] Of course, if the higher figure of 18 million could not be collected, this places Sully's reduction of direct taxes in a rather different perspective. For the 'faute de fonds' in the provinces in 1594–5: B.N. MS. fr. 4680, fo. 13 (only 7 months of *garnisons* could be paid for by Champagne and Brie instead of 9). P 2335, p. 447, 22 Feb. 1595. The levy of arrears was remitted in Dec. 1596. The levy of arrears from 1597 was suspended in Dec. 1599: Barbiche, *Sully*, p. 91.

[5] Nine years' arrears were claimed on 21 Nov. 1595: *Registres . . . de la ville de Paris*, ed. Tuetey, xi. 193. For the first doubts as to whether Henri IV was 'prince de parolle': U 23, fo. 152, 8 Mar. 1595.

[6] 2,734,119 *livres* were spent through the *dons* in 1595: 120 a.p. 12.

been reimbursed for loans that had never been made ('prests imaginaires').[1] Prompt reforming action was required by the finance commission to stop this and other financial malpractices. The excessive financial powers of the provincial governors, and the partisan use to which they were put, were also denounced.[2] The principal target for criticism, however, were the fiscal edicts by which the crown proposed to establish new offices as a source of revenue. The *Comptes* considered the proposed sales to be excessive. The sales would store up trouble for the future, since the offices were sold cheaply yet the crown was committed to pay inordinate sums in salaries to the office-holders which would become a permanent burden on the Treasury. Furthermore—and here they anticipated an argument that would later be used by Chancellor Bellièvre against Sully—they argued that the sale of offices encouraged the wrong sort of people to become office-holders: rather than merit, money became the most important qualification for office.[3] The *Parlement* of Paris proved equally obdurate in its refusal to register new fiscal edicts. On 26 April 1595, it demanded a special commission to investigate the alleged misappropriation of payment of the *rentes* (in fact most of the money had simply been diverted to pay for the war effort).[4] There were further difficulties in October, again over the issue of registration of fiscal edicts.[5]

By the summer of 1596 the administration of the finance commission had effectively collapsed. The Spanish army in the Netherlands had temporarily ceased to mutiny the previous year, and the Spanish offensive resulted in the capture of Doullens, Cambrai, Calais, and Ardres. Henri IV's counter-measures had not been a conspicuous success. The siege of La Fère was in the end successful, but it took seven months to achieve: the massive cost of this operation was stated openly by the king as the reason why he was unable to repay his Swiss creditors.[6] No further loans

---

[1] The fictitious nature of some of the loans was the official reason for the later renunciation of the debt: *Inventaire des arrêts du conseil d'état*, ed. Valois, no. 12910.

[2] That there had been financial malpractices by the governors is suggested by the fact that the crown amnestied the levies by Matignon (Jan. 1594), Ornano (Sept. 1595), the comte d'Auvergne (Apr. 1594), and d'Épernon (Feb. 1596): P 2333, p. 639; P 2336, pp. 507, 751, 795.

[3] *Chambre des Comptes*, ed. Boislisle, pp. 213–16. P 2335, pp. 447–59, 22 Feb. 1595.

[4] U 23, fo. 166ᵛ. It wanted an investigation of 'rentes mal constituées, mal acquises et mal payées'.

[5] *Lettres . . . de Henri IV*, iv. 414–16. U 23, fo. 200, 2 Oct. 1595.

[6] The decision to lay siege was taken on 6 Nov. 1595 and met with success on 16 May 1596. The excuse was made on 30 June: ibid., iv. 440, 581, 610.

were forthcoming from abroad. Worse still, the Swiss alliance signed by Henri III in 1582 was due to expire in 1597 and they were making it quite clear that they would break the alliance if their debts were not repaid.[1] Had the king already given up hope with the finance commission? Increasingly, he relied on Constable Montmorency-Damville, Sublet d'Heudicourt and Saldaigne d'Incarville for the day-to-day organization of war finance.[2] Though he sought and obtained loans from individual members of the finance commission,[3] the king had grave doubts about the honesty of some of them. He denounced their conduct to Sully, stating that the commission had made a worse mess of financial administration than François d'O. The number of *intendants des finances*, which had been increased to eight in 1594, was excessive.[4] They had bought up paper debts cheaply from the king's Swiss and German creditors and had obtained reimbursement both of principal and interest. The king alleged that 3.5 million *livres* had been misappropriated, enough to chase the Spanish out of his kingdom. Sully was appointed to the finance commission at the end of July 1596 to keep a check on its conduct.[5] At the same time, the king kept his options open. Acting on the advice of the finance commission, which in turn had been promp-

---

[1] Rott, *Henri IV, les Suisses et la Haute Italie . . .*, p. 168 n. 2. The Swiss ultimatum was dated 15 Nov. 1597, but their threats were clear earlier on. It appears that the last foreign loan was one of 900,000 *livres* from Ferdinand de Medici, grand duke of Tuscany, paid through the financier Hieronomo (Jérôme) Gondi at the time of the siege of La Fère: *Lettres . . . de Henri IV*, iv. 546.

[2] Ibid., iv. 512–15, 519–20, 527, 541–2. Sublet had been retained as an *intendant des finances* and Saldaigne as *contrôleur-général* on a special one-year commission on 11 Feb. 1596. Their letters patent argued that 'la multiplicité et le changement de personnes' caused 'confusion' in financial administration: P 2336, p. 315. Of Saldaigne, Henri said: 'Je ne puis passer de luy . . .'. For the seven volumes of registers of the *contrôle-général* in 1596: *Inventaire des arrêts du conseil d'état*, ed. Valois, no. 4275.

[3] Ibid., no. 2849. P 2337, p. 551, 14 Sept. 1596.

[4] The *Parlement* of Paris recalled in 1615 that one of Henri IV's great achievements had been to 'commettre à peu de personnes l'administration' of finance: Mayer, *Des États Généraux et autres assemblées nationales*, xvii. 165.

[5] *Lettres . . . de Henri IV*, iv. 564–8. Sully, *Oeconomies royales*, ed. Michaud and Poujoulat, i. 206–8. Both the authenticity and the date of this letter have been questioned. Sully gave the date as 15 Apr. 1596, written at Amiens, but the king was at Saint-Germain-en-Laye at that date. Valois gave the date as 15 Apr. 1597 (op. cit., i. p. lxxiv), but a more probable date for the letter was 15 Aug. 1596 when the king was at Amiens, before the meeting of the assembly of notables and about the time that Sully took up his appointment. Sully claimed that he burnt the original letter on the king's orders, which may account for part of the confusion. The idea that Sully was appointed to keep a check on the finance commission was questioned by Chamberland, who regarded Sully as just another servant of the king, but one who was younger and more vigorous than his colleagues: A. Chamberland, 'Le conseil des finances en 1596 et 1597 et les *Économies Royales*', *Revue Henri IV*, i (1905–6), 259. Of necessity, this view must regard the letter of the king as a forgery.

ted by Bellièvre,[1] Henri agreed on 25 July to summon an assembly of notables to discuss financial reform and other measures with comparable authority to that of an Estates-General. This assembly met at Rouen on 4 November and remained in session until 26 January 1597.

The 94 or so members who comprised the assembly of notables in 1596 were mostly nominated by the king. The government also held the initiative in the debates, drawing up specific proposals for the meeting to consider. It was thus a fairly tame assembly upon which Bellièvre and the other councillors hoped to foist unpalatable measures such as reductions in pensions, the interest rate on *rentes*, and the number and salaries of office-holders. In order to secure agreement to the reduction of royal expenditure on these and other matters, the government offered to divide royal revenues into two parts. The king was to make do with 15 million *livres* for his military and household expenses, while his contractual obligations to pay salaries to office-holders and interest to *rentiers* were to be paid from a slightly smaller fund administered separately from 'cet abisme de l'Épargne.'[2] This, and other proposals accepted by the assembly reveal a lack of realism on the part of both ministers and deputies. It is difficult to see how the king's expenditure on the war could be restricted to 15 million unless peace were signed immediately.[3] Yet the prospects for peace were not good. The crucial Spanish bankruptcy was not declared until 29 November 1596, and would take some time to work through to the Netherlands, with the inevitable consequence of a further round of mutinies. Meanwhile Mercoeur was still holding out in Brittany as the last supporter of the League. The

[1] Bellièvre's role is stressed by J. R. Major, 'Bellièvre, Sully and the assembly of notables of 1596', *Transactions of the American Philosophical Society*, new ser., lxiv (1974), p. 16 n. 90. However, the evidence is not clear-cut, and there is a danger of antedating the conflict on policy between Bellièvre and Sully. Bellièvre could argue the case for the king's financial necessity as well as any of the councillors. In a speech of 23 Jan. 1598 to the municipality of Paris, Bellièvre recognized that 'pendant la guerre durera il est impossible de mettre ordre ès affaires du royaume . . . toutes ses affaires (i.e. of the king) sont espuisées aux fraiz de la guerre': *Registres . . . de la ville de Paris*, ed. Tuetey, xi. 473.

[2] R. Charlier-Meniolle, *L'assemblée des notables tenue à Rouen en 1596* (1911), pp. 44, 69. The proposal (of Bellièvre?) was to administer the contractual obligations by a *conseil particulier* or *conseil de raison*, but this idea was not accepted: ibid., p. 73. N. Valois, 'Le "conseil de raison" de 1597', *Annuaire-Bulletin de la Société de l'Histoire de France*, xxii (1885), 248–56. Major, op. cit., p. 23.

[3] Henri IV pointed out that the figure of 15 million in expenses could not be guaranteed on secure revenues in view of the difficulty in levying the *taille* and the delay in establishing the *sol pour livre*: Chamberland, *Le conflit de 1597*, p. 30. *Chambre des Comptes*, ed. Boislisle, p. 230.

assembly of notables made no attempt, in this situation, to impose institutional checks on the king to prevent him diverting to the war effort revenues intended to meet his contractual obligations. Moreover, there were exaggerated hopes that better administration would improve the yield of the king's revenues in wartime. The likely yield of the proposed 5 per cent sales tax—the *sol pour livre* or *pancarte*—was overestimated: in the event, it aroused a storm of popular protest and had to be withdrawn in 1602.[1] The assembly proposed that office-holders should forego one year's salary, but did not accept the idea of reducing the interest rate on *rentes*. Royal commissioners were requested to investigate the validity of the *rentes*, the Swiss debt, and other royal obligations. The king's foreign creditors were to be repaid only after salaries to office-holders and interest to *rentiers* had been paid in a given year. The king was asked to hold a *chambre de justice* to eliminate corruption in financial administration.[2]

It is an open question whether the king intended to implement the proposals of the notables before all calculations were thrown into disarray by news of the Spanish capture of Amiens on 11 March 1597. The crisis was made much more serious by the discontent of the Protestants with a king who had not fulfilled their expectations. Bouillon and La Trémouille refused to cross the river Loire with their 6000 troops to assist the siege of Amiens, and began seizing the king's revenues in areas under their control.[3] It was not until 20 July that Schomberg negotiated an agreement with the Protestant leaders, who were granted 540,000 *livres* per annum for the upkeep of the garrisons in their *villes de sûreté*. The total sum payable to the Protestants was later increased in the settlement of Ñantes to 675,000 *livres*, though it is doubtful whether as much as this was ever paid in a single year.[4]

[1] Henri IV blamed the finance commission for the delay in establishing the sales tax, although this was chiefly caused by difficulty in obtaining registration of the edict, particularly at the *Cour des Aides*. It had not been established on 21 Aug. 1597: Chamberland, 'Le conseil des finances . . .', 279. The municipality of Paris wanted the removal of all direct taxes which had been increased since 1585 in return for the registration of the *pancarte*: *Registres . . . de la ville de Paris*, ed. Tuetey, xi. 355. For the general problem of the tax: R. É. Mousnier, *L'assassinat d'Henri IV. 14 mai 1610* (1964), p. 172.

[2] The letters patent revoking the *chambre de justice* specify that it was held on the advice of the notables: P 2337, p. 725, June 1597. There had, however, been talk of establishing one after the death of François d'O: *Mémoires-Journaux de Pierre L'Estoile*, ed. Brunet *et al.*, vi. 241.

[3] U 23, fo. 291, 9 May 1597.

[4] Mousnier, *L'assassinat d'Henri IV*, pp. 126–7, 330–1. Buisseret, *Sully*, p. 84. It is difficult to concur with the most recent verdict on Henri IV's dealings with the Huguenots in the 1590s, that the king 'declined to purchase the service of his subjects': N. M.

Once the crisis had broken, the king was prepared to agree to almost any expedient that secured money. The crucial difficulty was that he needed the compliance of the office-holders to register new fiscal edicts, and they refused. The *Chambre des Comptes* was sullenly unco-operative.[1] On 15 April, Constable Mont-morency-Damville and Bellièvre appealed to the assembled municipality of Paris and delegates of the sovereign courts to make a once and for all grant to the king. They recalled the grant made by the French towns to François Ier in 1536 to enable him to relieve the siege of Péronne. However, Martin Langlois, the mayor (*prévôt des marchands*) of Paris voiced the opinion of the assembly when he said that they had heard a great deal about the king's 'necessity' but not much about theirs. He protested at the king's failure to pay the *rentes* and at the alleged abuses in financial administration. Henri IV was requested to reduce his council of finance to the smallest number possible and to establish a *chambre de justice* to investigate corruption. In the meantime, all they were prepared to grant was 360,000 *livres* to pay 3000 Switzers for six months, a sum which could not be used for other purposes. The king had asked for more than this, and his total requirement was 3.6 million to raise an army and thereafter 450,000 *livres* a month to pay for its subsistence. The Parisian assembly reaffirmed the conditions of its grant on 28 April. In its view, further sums would simply be wasted: 27 million *livres* had been levied in taxes in 1596, yet this sum had been misused to pay for gifts to private individuals, to repay the king's creditors and to pay current interest on loans. The assembly considered the 'surprise' of Amiens to be symptomatic of 'la mauvaise ordonnance, dispensation et administration de voz finances . . .'[2] The *Parlement* of Paris also presented remonstrances on 26 April 1597 which were highly critical of financial administration and demanded the full implementation of the proposals of the assembly of notables. The abuse of the king's paper debts and the excessive gifts made since his accession were denounced. There was also the same emphasis on the reform

---

Sutherland, *The Huguenot struggle for recognition* (New Haven and London, 1980), p. 320. However, Dr Sutherland's discussion of the settlement of Nantes (pp. 328, 370–2) is valuable, because it places it within the context of earlier edicts of pacification.

[1] P 2337, p. 353, 23 May 1597: 'assistance en silence ne prestoit aucun consentement . . .'
[2] *Registres . . . de la ville de Paris*, ed. Tuetey, xi. 361–72. However, Henri IV blamed the loss of Amiens on the fact that the town had refused to accept a garrison of Switzers: *Lettres . . . de Henri IV*, iv. 695–7. P. Deyon, *Amiens. Capitale provinciale. Étude sur la société urbaine au xviie siècle* (Paris-The Hague, 1967), pp. 430–1. For the total cost of the army: U 23, fo. 291, 9 May 1597.

of the king's council and the holding of a *chambre de justice*.[1]

The king capitulated. He recognized there were abuses 'que la malice du temps a introduictz en l'administration de noz finances' and promised reform.[2] On 2 May, he set up a *chambre de justice*,[3] and a week later he agreed to an emergency war chest to be kept at the Louvre. This would have only one key, and the chest would not be opened except in the presence of a member of his council and two office-holders, one from the *Parlement* and the other from the *Chambre des Comptes*.[4] Finally on 19 May, he agreed to put into practice the principle established at the assembly of notables that there should be separate funds on the one hand to pay for the war and on the other to meet contractual obligations such as salaries to office-holders and interest to *rentiers*. Accordingly he established a *conseil particulier* to administer the contractual obligations under the presidency of the Cardinal de Gondi.[5] However, the new council did not achieve its purpose. War expenses drained off the funds allocated to meet the crown's contractual obligations: since it had no money to administer, the *conseil particulier* ceased to meet in July 1597.[6] Similarly the *chambre de justice* had to be abandoned with the financiers instead paying a composition of about 378,000 *livres*.[7] Instead of reforming his finances, the king made the situation worse by a further round of borrowing. Financiers such as Sébastien Zamet and Barthélémy Cénamy were only too willing to lend in the hope of obtaining reimbursement for outstanding debts from the years of the League.[8]

Henri IV felt badly let down by his office-holders. In a blister-

---

[1] Chamberland, *Le conflit de 1597*, pp. 10–15.

[2] *Lettres . . . de Henri IV*, iv. 753–5. *Registres . . . de la ville de Paris*, ed. Tuetey, xi. 374.

[3] Chamberland, *Le conflit de 1597*, pp. 22–4. *Chambre des Comptes*, ed. Boislisle, p. 230. E. Maugis, *Histoire du Parlement de Paris dès l'avènement des rois Valois à la mort d'Henri IV* (3 vols., 1913–16), ii. 264 n. 1.

[4] U 23, fo. 291, 9 May 1597.

[5] *Lettres . . . de Henri IV*, iv. 766–7. The decision was announced to the *Parlement* on 19 May: U 23 fo. 297ᵛ. Sully's account appears to be confused, but his hostility to the experiment is significant: Sully, *Oeconomies royales*, ed. Michaud and Poujoulat, i. 237–8, 240, 244–5.

[6] Though its fate is somewhat mysterious: Major, 'Bellièvre, Sully and the assembly of notables', 27.

[7] Clamageran gives the incredible figure of 3.6 million, exactly the amount required to pay for the levy of the army: Clamageran, *Histoire de l'impôt*, ii. 344. The lower total is derived from *Les papiers de Richelieu*, ed. Grillon, i. 115. On 4 June 1597, Henri IV told the *Parlement* that the 'longueur d'en faire les recherches particulières' could not be justified in 'la nécessité qui est si pressente'. He was talking about voluntary loans from office-holders, but presumably the same could be said of the financiers: *Lettres . . . de Henri IV*, iv. 772.

[8] Examples of loans: *Inventaire des arrêts du conseil d'état*, ed. Valois, nos. 3801, 3853. B.N. Clairambault 654, pp. 609, 621, 24 Dec. 1597 and 31 Jan. 1598.

ing speech to the *Parlement* of Paris on 21 May 1597, he accused them of a disloyalty during a national emergency.[1] The failure of the *robins* to assist the king left the initiative to the men of the sword: the king himself, the Constable Montmorency-Damville, who had gone to the *Parlement* wearing his sword,[2] and Sully, the confidant of the king and the man of the future. Sully's rise to power should not be antedated: there were senior and experienced councillors who contested his authority until at least 1599.[3] However, Sully had the reputation of a man of action from 1596, when he had gone on a *tournée* round the Orléanais and Touraine and returned with 72 cartloads of money.[4] Later, his 'rough courses' were to make him 'extremely odious to great and small' but Sully was more tractable in his first years in office, while his energy played a crucial part in organizing the two armies which recaptured Amiens (25 September 1597) and brought about the surrender of Mercoeur in Brittany (March 1598).[5] His rise to power was thus a return to the days of François d'O when a nobleman had 'commanded' the finances needed for the king's armies. The effort did not last for long: concessions were made to the Protestants at Nantes in April and May 1598 to convert the uneasy truce into a settlement, while peace with Spain was signed at Vervins on 2 May. The king recognized 'le besoing extresme que mon peuple avoit de repos',[6] but he never forgot the attitude of the officeholders during the Amiens crisis. Limitation on the king's independent control of finance would not be tolerated during the years of peace. Reform would be imposed by the king's council, and when it came it would not always be popular.

---

[1] Significantly, Henri IV's speech was much shorter than the earlier versions drafted by Bellièvre: Chamberland, *Le conflit de 1597*, pp. 43–8. *Lettres . . . de Henri IV*, iv. 764.

[2] U 23, fo. 297, 19 May 1597.

[3] The deaths of Chancellor Cheverny, Saldaigne d'Incarville and Sublet d'Heudicourt all occurred in 1599. Sully was appointed *grand maître de l'artillerie* on 15 Nov. 1599, and from this time he was given precedence in the king's council after other officers of the crown (the same precedence granted formally by a *brevet* to later *surintendants*): B.L. Egerton 1680, fo. 63. For a time, Sully acknowledged the seniority of the archbishop of Bourges. His predominance in the council was incomplete until the disgrace of Chancellor Bellièvre which occurred with the appointment of Brûlart de Sillery as Keeper of the Seals in Dec. 1604: B.N. p.o. 537 (Dr. 12,092), no. 666.

[4] A. Chamberland, 'La tournée de Sully et de Rybault dans les généralités en 1596', *Revue Henri IV*, iii (1909), supplement.

[5] Carew emphasized his 'rough courses': Carew, 'A relation of the state of France', p. 485. However, Barbiche produced evidence of early tractability: Barbiche, *Sully*, pp. 47–8. Sully emphasized his role in organizing the two armies in his resignation letter: A.A.E. France 768, fo. 172, 3 Mar. 1611.

[6] *Lettres . . . de Henri IV*, iv. 1008.

2. THE NEW ORDER: BANKRUPTCY AND REFORM

'When Sully came to the managing of the revenues, he found . . .
all things out of order, full of robbery of officers, full of confusion,
no treasure, no munition, no furniture for the king's houses and
the crown indebted three hundred million . . .' Sir George Carew
claimed to have heard this account of affairs from Sully himself.[1]
Gradually the king gave his confidant the fullest powers to remedy
the situation. He was given control not just of finance but of other
government activities which incurred expenses, such as roads,
artillery, fortifications, and buildings. He was made governor of
the Bastille in 1602, and the following year was rewarded with the
governorship of Poitou after his loyalty during the Biron conspiracy. Finally in 1606 he was raised to the status of duke and peer.
None of the later *surintendants des finances* enjoyed the king's
confidence in such an open way,[2] or for such a long period of
time—effectively from 1598 to 1610. This security of office must
be considered a crucial factor in Sully's success. Some of his more
interesting and far-sighted schemes date from quite late on in the
ministry. The *droit annuel* scheme was not established until 1604,
due to the resistance of Chancellor Bellièvre. The scheme for the
resumption of crown lands did not fully get under way until 1608.
A second reason for Sully's success was that the king gave him full
powers to resolve the issue of the royal debts. Some rulers would
have baulked at incurring the displeasure of legions of creditors, but
Henri IV had an 'oeconomical faculty (of) looking into matters of
profit'; 'the king supporting Sully in all his rough courses . . .',
wrote Sir George Carew, 'hath found great profit thereby . . .'[3] In
1614 there were many nobles who claimed to be owed money by
Henri IV but whom the king in his lifetime 'n'avoit voulu . . .
reconnaître ny faire payer.'[4] The same was true of virtually all the
king's creditors. Sully's later prestige as a financial reformer
should not hide the fact that he operated an undeclared bankruptcy after 1598.[5]

---

[1] Carew, 'A relation of the state of France', p. 486. Cf. R. Dallington, *The view of Fraunce*
(1604), pp. N and N2. Sully's total was 296.6 million if the alienated crown lands and
revenues are included in the calculations: Appendix Two, Table IX A ii.

[2] Though some, such as Schomberg, held the office of *grand maître de l'artillerie* as had
Sully. Sully regarded the control of the Bastille and of finance as 'les deux plus belles
marques . . . des bienfaitz et du ressentiment [*sic*] de mon bon m[aître]': A.A.E. France 768,
fo. 170, 3 Mar. 1611.

[3] Carew, op cit., pp. 480, 485.

[4] Mayer, *Des Etats Généraux et autres assemblées nationales*, xvii. 219.

[5] On 17 Mar. 1599, Sully told the *Chambre des Comptes* that 'il estoit impossible que S. M.
pust acquitter entièrement les charges, rentes et gages, et que s'il se faisoit quelque

Sully's figures for the debt need to be handled with caution since they include an element of irredeemable debt—the estimated 150 million *livres* of alienated royal demesnes and revenues. This debt was irredeemable without a special operation, which in turn would require finance, and Sully made no serious attempt to deal with it before 1608. With this element removed from the calculations, the redeemable debt stood at about 147 million in 1598: Sully did not try to repay this in full. The Swiss debt illustrates his methods. The king had used the great cost of the siege of Amiens as a further excuse for delaying repayment to the Swiss,[1] but by March 1599 it was clear that the issue could not be postponed much longer. Mortefontaine, the French ambassador to the Swiss cantons, counted himself lucky not to have been taken hostage. There were renewed Swiss threats not to renew the alliance unless the debt were repaid. They also insisted on a special French treasurer (the official who became known as the *trésorier des ligues suisses*) to handle the sums for their repayment. In 1602, the debt stood at 36 million *livres*—11 million in principal lent by the Swiss towns and cantons, and 5 million due to the Switzer colonels and captains. The rest of the debt was made up of the interest charge and arrears in the payment of pensions.[2] On 11 February 1596 the king had already ruled out the payment of compound interest as contrary to 'l'usage des lois . . . en ce royaulme.'[3] Sully's aim was to reduce the Swiss debt to more manageable proportions. By the agreement of Soleure, ratified by the king on 20 October 1602, France undertook to pay 1.2 million *livres* annually until the Swiss debt was repaid. It would thus take thirty years to repay the debt in full, without allowing for any new interest charge. Yet by 1607 the French government regarded the Swiss debt as having been reduced to 16.7 million, a reduction of nearly a half in five years. Clearly this had not been achieved by actual payments. The private creditors could not wait in the hope that the French crown would keep its word. 'Compositions' were made with the Swiss colonels who often accepted as little as one-seventh of their due: thus a payment of 1.7 million was taken

---

reculement, [c']estoit [par] la malice des comptables . . .': *Chambre des Comptes*, ed. Boislisle, p. 246.

[1] *Lettres . . . de Henri IV*, iv. 887–9.

[2] Barbiche, *Sully*, p. 79, gives different figures for the components of the debt. However, 120 a.p. 34, fo. 146 is quite explicit.

[3] *Lettres . . . de Henri IV*, iv. 499.

to write off a debt of nearly 9.2 million. In a sense the Treasury accounts show the savings made, not the payments actually handed over.[1]

The smaller foreign debts were treated in an equally cavalier fashion. Following the treaty of Hampton Court in July 1603, which was negotiated by Sully, one-third of the French subsidy to assist the Dutch rebellion against Spain was to count towards the reduction of the English debt. By 1613, France had written off the English debt because the French had paid more than 9,150,000 *livres* to the Dutch.[2] The debt to the English was discounted by one-third of this amount, that is to say 3,050,000 *livres*—but all James I received was 600,000 *livres*, paid not by Sully but by Jeannin in 1611–12. Had the French government any intention of repaying the debt in full, 2,743,550 *livres* would have remained to be paid.[3] Instead, it made the impertinent suggestion that there had been an overpayment of 306,450 *livres*!

When delaying repayment to England, Henri IV had told Elizabeth I that he was one of those who sought a good marriage to repay his debts from the proceeds of the dowry.[4] The attractions of Maria de Medici (later to be known as Marie de Médicis) were not very great in 1599: the king was turning his attentions from one mistress—Gabrielle d'Estrées—to another, Henriette d'Entragues. However, Maria was the niece of Ferdinand I de Medici, grand duke of Tuscany, and her dowry would help to offset the king's debts to the duke which stood at 3.5 million *livres*. Ferdinand would offer only 1.5 million at first, claiming that the Emperor Rudolf II would have accepted a smaller dowry. Henri IV asked for twice that sum. The negotiations dragged on until the grand duke was warned by Cardinal de Gondi that the king

---

[1] Rott, *Henri IV, les Suisses et la Haute Italie . . .*, pp. 169–70, 194–6. A. Chamberland, 'La comptabilité imaginaire des deniers des coffres du roi et les dettes suisses', *Revue Henri IV*, ii (1908), 50–60. Barbiche, *Sully*, pp. 79–80. *Traité* of Flory Simon (22 July 1601) to acquit 2,467,932 *livres* of Swiss debts for an actual payment of 687,201 *livres*: 120 a.p. 34, fo. 125ᵛ. Mallet's figures for payments by the *trésorier des ligues suisses* between 1600 and 1610 show a total of nearly 19.6 million: Buisseret, *Sully*, p. 81. For one such 'composition' with a Swiss colonel, cf. the instructions of the council of finance to Méric de Vic, Lefèvre Caumartin and Arnauld to draw up a contract for the benefit of Colonel Gaspard Gallaty of the canton of Claris including the payment of interest on arrears of the debt at 8 per cent: E 27c–28a, fo. 383, 18 Nov. 1610.

[2] B.N. MS fr. 23026, pp. 119–20. The payments were made in 1603–8, and agree with the figures given by Buisseret, *Sully*, p. 82.

[3] i.e. 3,343,550 *livres* minus 600,000 *livres*. The English calculation of the debt was somewhat higher: F. C. Dietz, *English public finance, 1558–1641* (London-New York, 1932), p. 459.

[4] *Lettres . . . de Henri IV*, viii. 763.

was on the verge of marrying Henriette d'Entragues.[1] If this happened, Ferdinand would obtain neither reimbursement of his debts—which the king could not afford—nor the marriage of his niece. The duke raised his offer, and on 7 March 1600 Constable Montmorency-Damville, Chancellor Bellièvre, and Sully signed the preliminary marriage contract, which was confirmed at Florence the following month. The dowry was fixed at 1.8 million *livres*, just over a million of which was in cash payable at Marseille. The rest of the dowry was to be partially offset against the debts to the duke. In spite of the arrangement, the Florentine debt had not been repaid by the time of Henri IV's death.[2] The same was true of the German towns and princes and the agreements made with the French nobles who had deserted the League. In December 1608, the crown refused to repay Henri III's debts on the grounds that many of the original loans had been fictitious.[3] When Sully's resignation was forced in the spring of 1611, there were a considerable number of foreign and domestic creditors awaiting a less inflexible approach.[4]

Sully succeeded in keeping Henri IV's creditors at bay, but did so by an act of bankruptcy: he renegued on all previous agreements. One of the first acts was to withdraw all revenues mortgaged to foreign creditors.[5] One group of royal creditors for whom the period of the League had been an acute crisis were of course the *rentiers*. The hopes when Henri IV arrived in Paris in 1594 had soon been dashed, and the failure of the *conseil particulier* in 1597 had brought the problem no nearer solution. By 1605 there were some *rentiers* who had received no interest payment for nineteen years, while the total arrears amounted to nearly 60.8 million

---

[1] The famous promise to marry Henriette within six months of her becoming pregnant was made on 1 Oct. 1599: ibid., v. 225 n. 2 (at p. 226). For the Florentine debt of 3,522,441 *livres*: Barbiche, *Sully*, p. 163.

[2] B. Zeller, *Henri IV et Marie de Médicis* (1877), pp. 16–18, 25, 27, 321–5. P 2341, p. 195, 25 Apr. 1600. The duke's agent was Hieronomo (Jérôme) Gondi, whose claims amounted to over 2.4 million, but he had bought up paper debts cheaply which inflated the total: 120 a.p. 33, fos. 125, 127. There were also debts to Orazio (Horatio) Rucellai, a member of the duke's household. Sully reduced the total by 496,845 *livres*: cf. Barbiche, *Sully*, pp. 80–1. 120 a.p. 34, fo. 42.

[3] *Inventaire des arrêts du conseil d'état*, ed. Valois, no. 12910.

[4] Examples of creditors of Henri IV: Appendix Two, Table IX A iii.

[5] Anquez, *Henri IV et l'Allemagne*, pp. 56–7. Of course, revenues were still assigned to creditors. Thus repayment to the Swiss tended to be assigned on the revenues of the Midi: Collins, 'Sur l'histoire fiscale du xviiᵉ siècle', 329. In 1600 Christian of Anhalt was assigned reimbursement of over 3.2 million *livres* on the *revente des aides anciennes: Chambre des Comptes*, ed. Boislisle, pp. 256–7. Presumably the *assignation* was subsequently changed since the Anhalt debt was not paid off.

livres.[1] In March 1599 Sully ordered an investigation of *rentes*
established since 1560. Since the great bulk of them dated from
this time, the investigation was wide-ranging and confirmed
Sully's impression that there had been considerable fraud at the
time the *rentes* had been originally established. In August 1604 it
was decided to put a stop on the payment of arrears, and henceforth to reduce the rate of interest on current payments. Some
rentes were to be abolished, others bought out cheaply by the
government. François Miron, the mayor (*prévôt des marchands*) of
Paris led a vigorous campaign against the proposals, which had to
be modified. The stop on arrears remained, but the repurchase
scheme was abandoned.[2] Later in his ministry, Sully returned to
this question as part of the process of repurchasing alienated
crown lands, but no permanent solution to the burden of the *rentes*
on the exchequer was found.[3] Nevertheless, the abandoning of
any attempt to pay arrears, the relative monetary stability after
1602, and above all the budgetary surplus enabled the payment of
rentes to be stabilized under Sully. Compared to the crisis of the
1590s, this was success.

The establishment of a budgetary surplus required both an
increase in revenues and a reduction in expenditure. In 1596 the
deficit on the current account stood at 18 million *livres*[4] and the
position probably worsened before peace was signed two years
later. The administration of the revenue farms was in disarray at
the end of the civil wars. Already in 1589 Henri III had had to
recognize debts to the farmers of the *gabelles de France* of over 3.9
million and to guarantee them payment of interest at 8.33 per cent
until the debt was honoured.[5] By the late 1590s the two principal
farmers of this tax were Sébastien Zamet and Barthélemy

---

[1] Barbiche, *Sully*, p. 83. Buisseret, *Sully*, p. 89. B.N. 500 Colbert 485, fo. 58ᵛ, 26 Apr. 1605.

[2] Ironically, Miron wanted repurchase of the *rentes* rather than a stop on interest
payments. He warned of the political dangers of alienating the *rentiers*: *Registres des
délibérations du bureau de la ville de Paris. XIII. 1602–1605*, ed. P. Guérin (1905), p. 427. B.N.
500 Colbert 485, fos. 63ᵛ–64ʳ, 27 Apr. 1605. For criticism of Sully's treatment of the *rentiers*:
B.N. MS. fr. 16626, fo. 151ᵛ. Lechassier argued that the king and not his subjects should
carry the loss if the establishment of the *rentes* had been mismanaged: B.N. 500 Colbert 485,
fos. 53ᵛ–54ʳ, 1605.

[3] In contrast, Schnapper talks of 'remèdes permanents': B. Schnapper, *Les rentes au xviᵉ
siècle. Histoire d'un instrument de crédit* (1957), pp. 276–80. However, as long as no new *rentes*
were established, and the arrears were written off, the burden on the exchequer was
probably acceptable.

[4] Appendix Two, Table IX A i.

[5] P 2330, p. 507, 12 Jan. 1589 (which gives the figure of 3,990,519 *livres*). Cf. 120 a.p. 33,
fo. 14 (which gives the figure of 2,874,432 *livres* from 1585–8).

Cénamy, who had bought out the interest of the other revenue farmers. They were certainly owed money by the crown, because on 19 April 1597 revenues assigned for their reimbursement had been diverted by the crown to help pay for the cost of the siege of Amiens.[1] On the other hand, Zamet and Cénamy had deliberately sought to make their position appear worse by speculating in the purchase of old debts from private creditors of the monarchy: they attempted to pass off these debts as outstanding from the administration of their revenue farm. Sully claimed to have repaid them more than 1.8 million between 1598 and 1605, but demanded restitution of an overpayment of 602,107 *livres*.[2] With the kingdom at peace, and the administration of the revenue farm cleared of debt, Sully was able to increase the rent payable annually from under 3.4 million in 1598 to over 4.6 million by 1605, although the actual yield of the taxes was usually less.[3] Sully greatly increased the burden of indirect taxes, although part of the increase was the result of improved collection.[4] He believed in the consolidation of leases into larger units, and after 1604 the *aides* were levied as a single revenue farm.[5] The contribution of the indirect taxes to the Treasury nevertheless remained disappointing. On Mallet's figures, they provided on average 16.5 per cent of total revenues between 1600 and 1604, and 19.1 per cent between 1605 and 1609. They provided a rather higher proportion of the 'ordinary' revenue[6] (respectively 20 and 29.3 per cent). However, the actual levy of the indirect taxes in the provinces was higher than the amounts paid to the Treasury, since some salaries to office-holders and privately-held tax rights were paid directly by the revenue farmers. It was not surprising that the income from the revenue farms grew in the years of peace after 1600. While prices remained at a high level, the abnormally high figures of the early 1590s were not repeated. French monetary problems could not be solved at a stroke, but the devaluation of September 1602 was beneficial and probably contributed towards the restoration

[1] 120 a.p. 33, fo. 48

[2] Barbiche, *Sully*, p. 82. 120 a.p. 33, fos. 76, 88–9.

[3] Barbiche, *Sully*, p. 95. Appendix Two, Table VI.

[4] Carew commented of Sully's increase that it was achieved 'without exacting any more upon the people than was paid before, but only by reducing that to the king's coffers which was embezled [*sic*] by under-officers': Carew, 'A relation of the state of France', p. 486.

[5] In 1607 there was a scheme for amalgamating several revenue farms into a general lease, the scheme which Colbert was to achieve with the *ferme générale*—but it came to nothing: Barbiche, *Sully*, p. 97.

[6] When referring to Mallet's figures, the term 'ordinary' revenue is taken to mean the total revenue after the deduction of the *deniers extraordinaires*.

of agricultural prosperity.[1] Agricultural rents undoubtedly rose in real terms; so too did urban rents. Manufacturing production, for example in textiles, reached its pre-war levels once again.[2] The payment of indirect taxes, which were levied either on consumption or the circulation of goods, was closely related to the strength of the economy. Greater prosperity made it easier to levy increased indirect taxes.

Nevertheless, the burden of direct taxes remained heavy. The alleged concern of the king and Sully that every Frenchman should have a chicken in his cookpot (*une poule au pot*) is a later myth.[3] On Mallet's figures, the direct taxes in the *pays d'élections* contributed on average 49.6 per cent of total revenues between 1600 and 1604, and 31.5 per cent between 1605 and 1609. The figures are much higher as a proportion of ordinary revenue, respectively 60 and 48.3 per cent. The amount of direct taxes payable by the *pays d'élections* to the Treasury was kept relatively stable, at less than 10 million *livres* per annum with the exception of 1601. However, the amount of tax levied in the provinces was higher, because of revenues assigned directly to royal creditors, local payments, and alienated taxes. In the case of Champagne, the total levy seems to have been almost double the amount paid to the Treasury.[4] In other provinces, the amount of additional tax levied was proportionately less, but the figures fluctuated from year to year. The total levy of direct taxes in any one year under Sully probably never exceeded 16.2 million (the figure for 1599) but nor did it fall below 13.5 million (the figure for 1602). However, as the figures for the *crue extraordinaire* indicate, when royal expenditure increased in 1601 with the cost of the war with Savoy and the renewal of the Swiss alliance, so too did the level of direct taxes.[5] The edict of March 1600, which sought to reduce fraudu-

[1] Spooner, *The international economy and monetary movements in France*, pp. 169–71, 337. B. Barbiche, 'Une tentative de réforme monétaire à la fin du règne d'Henri IV', *XVIIᵉ Siècle*, lxi (1963), 3–17. Jacquart, *La crise rurale*, pp. 256–9.

[2] E. Leroy-Ladurie, *Les paysans de Languedoc* (2 vols., 1966), i. 465–71. B. Veyrassat-Herren and Leroy-Ladurie, 'La rente foncière autour de Paris au xviiᵉ siècle', *Annales E.S.C.*, xxiii (1968), 546, 554–5. P. Couperie and Leroy-Ladurie, 'Le mouvement des loyers parisiens de la fin du moyen âge au xviiiᵉ siècle', *ibid.*, xxv (1970), 1018. J. Jacquart, 'La rente foncière, indice conjoncturel?', *Revue Historique*, ccliii (1975), 365–6. Deyon, *Amiens*, pp. 170–1 and graph 34 at pp. 536–7.

[3] Reinhard, *La légende de Henri IV*, pp. 54–9. Carew reported talk of Henri IV as the king of beggars ('roy . . . des gueux'): Carew, 'A relation of the state of France', p. 463.

[4] Collins, 'Sur l'histoire fiscale du xviiᵉ siècle', 342.

[5] Barbiche, *Sully*, p. 94. These royal expenses sent the *crue extraordinaire* up to 6.3 million, almost the level of the high figure for 1599 (nearly 6.5 million): 120 a.p. 16. Although the Swiss alliance was not renewed until 1602, they had to be calmed in 1601 by an immediate

lent exemptions and improve the efficiency of collection, probably facilitated payment of the *taille*. It appears fairly certain that there was no overall increase in the direct taxes under Sully.[1] What is less clear is whether improved collection offset the reduction in the overall levy after 1598.

One of Sully's basic aims was to obtain a firm, settled revenue—and this is well illustrated by the establishment of the *droit annuel* in 1604, which was unquestionably one of his most important achievements. This scheme allowed office-holders to resign their offices without significant restriction, even shortly before their death,[2] in return for paying in their lifetime an annual tax equivalent to one-sixtieth of the value of the office. The purpose of this scheme has aroused some controversy.[3] It may to some extent have had a political purpose, removing offices from the clientage network of powerful magnates such as the Guises and creating 'so many tenures which draw necessary dependence upon the king . . .'[4] On the other hand, in the long term the political advantages of systematizing the sale of offices seem slight, while the fiscal advantages are much more evident. In the 1580s and 1590s, the crown had enjoyed substantial revenue from offices,[5] but this had been of an irregular, accidental, and fortu-itous kind (hence the description of such revenue as *parties casuel-les*). What Sully did was to establish venality of office as a regular

---

payment of 3.6 million *livres* while negotiations continued: Rott, *Henri IV, les Suisses et la Haute Italie* . . ., pp. 181–2.

[1] On this point, Collins, art. cit., 343–6 appears to have the edge of the argument over Chartier (ibid., p. 343), although more evidence is needed. Barbiche, *Sully*, p. 94, suggests that Sully reduced the *taille* on average by 1.9 million a year. But because of the substantial arrears at the end of the civil wars, the high figure of 18 million was not in fact paid by the tax-payers.

[2] The so-called '40-day clause' was thus suspended for those paying the *droit annuel*. This had declared resignations of offices invalid unless the owner survived 40 days after making the act of resignation—a procedure which had been difficult to enforce and was obviously inconvenient to the office-holder.

[3] The classic discussion is Mousnier, 'Sully et le conseil d'état et des finances', 72–80, and Mousnier, *La vénalité*, pp. 594–605. A more recent discussion is Major, 'Henry IV and Guyenne', 365–7, reprinted in *State and society*, ed. Kierstead, pp. 4–5.

[4] This tended to be the view of the critics, notably Bellièvre, Richelieu and Fontenay-Mareuil. The quotation is from Carew, 'A relation of the state of France', p. 474. One critic considered that the scheme had caused 'tant de maux qu'il s'en pourroit escrire un gros volume': B.N. MS. fr. 16626, fo. 152.

[5] Seven million *livres* a year according to Dallington, *The view of Fraunce*, pp. O4ᵛ, and P2. This is no more than hearsay. In 1596 the figure was 450,000 *livres*: Charlier-Meniolle, *L'assemblée des notables*, p. 25.

revenue of the French monarchy, which could be farmed out to financiers.[1] The *parties casuelles* yielded on average 7.2 per cent of total revenues between 1600 and 1604, and 7.8 per cent between 1605 and 1609. The figures are higher as a proportion of ordinary revenue, respectively 8.7 and 12 per cent.[2] The *droit annuel* may not have been a great money-spinner under Henri IV but it was now a permanent revenue that could be more vigorously exploited in a later hour of need.

After 1607 Sully hoped to place the king's revenue on a firmer basis still by the resumption of crown lands and other revenues alienated during the civil wars. There were several possible approaches to this problem. The argument for repurchase was that the crown lands had originally been sold off too cheaply, and that the actual value of the lands was much higher on the private market.[3] The Estates-General of 1614–15 favoured two schemes. One was that rural parishes should directly reimburse existing occupants of crown lands—this approach was unlikely to prove successful because of the pressure of taxation on the countryside. A second scheme was that the crown should grant 'leases in reversion' on the English model: the new lessees would either reach a compromise with the occupants of crown lands, and take up half their holding, or else they would buy them out entirely. Occupants of crown lands were unlikely to be attracted by this offer, but could be obliged to agree. First, however, the crown would have to find lessees for what appeared a risky venture.[4] A third scheme, not discussed at the Estates-General, but proposed by Richelieu and d'Effiat to the assembly of notables in 1626–7, was to establish a sinking fund from which the resumption of

---

[1] Under Sully, the revenue farmers were Charles Paulet (hence the term *paulette*) and later Bénigne Saulnier: Mousnier, *La vénalité*, pp. 242–60.

[2] Mallet's annual figures for the *parties casuelles* were reproduced by Mousnier, op. cit., p. 421 for the years 1600–43. The figures given by Mousnier have been modified for the years 1607, 1610, 1615, 1617, and 1633 by reference to Mallet. On the whole, Hayden's strictures on the accuracy of Mousnier's table appear exaggerated: cf. J. M. Hayden, *France and the Estates-General of 1614* (Cambridge, 1974), p. 19 n. 8. Mousnier defines the *parties casuelles* as the proceeds from forfeiture of office, death in office, resignation, new creation, resale, heredity, *survivance, augmentation de gages*, and forced loans: Mousnier, *La vénalité*, p. 420 n. 7. The figures therefore include sums over and above the *droit annuel*.

[3] For the difference between the price at the original sale and the economic value: P 2332, p. 212, 30 Mar. 1593. For an English parallel, cf. D. L. Thomas, 'Leases in reversion on the crown's lands, 1558–1603', *Economic History Review*, 2nd ser., xxx (1977), 67–72.

[4] Mayer, *Des États Généraux et autres assemblées nationales*, xvii, pt. ii. 3–5. D'Effiat proposed three different schemes of this type c. 1626: J. Petit, *L'assemblée des notables de 1626–1627* (1936), pp. 99–100.

crown lands would be financed.[1] The drawback of this approach, and probably the reason why the suggestion was not accepted, was that the king would always be tempted to divert the fund to other purposes. There were thus several possibilities open to Sully who, characteristically, took a more pragmatic approach, treating proposals to repurchase crown lands much as he would have treated any other tax contract. About 140 proposals (*avis*) were received by the council of finance, of which nearly 70 were seriously considered. In 1610, 51 contracts with financiers such as Martin Lefèvre, Claude Barbin and Thomas Robin were under way for the resumption of alienated crown lands, *rentes* and offices. Sully hoped to recover royal assets with a capital value of more than 40 million *livres*, although the actual total of the contracts appears to have been somewhat lower. If Sully's estimates are reliable, this represented only about a quarter of the total value of alienated royal demesne and revenues.[2]

The difficulty with Sully's policy was that the process of redemption required stable political conditions for an unprecedented length of time: the leases negotiated in 1608 would not expire until 1624[3]—in the event, the beginning of Richelieu's ministry and thirteen years after the fall of Sully. Moreover, as the Estates-General of 1614–15 complained, the tax contractors had an interest in quick profits, not a long-term policy of increasing the king's revenue. Certain alienated crown lands and rights could be redeemed profitably only over a longer period than sixteen years: the Estates-General envisaged contracts lasting twenty or even thirty years.[4] Perhaps they were right, but time was not on their side. The king might decide on war, and revoke the contracts well before they expired. The weakening of the crown's political control after the death of Henri IV prevented even Sully's pragmatic scheme from reaching fruition. In 1615 Jeannin was forced to revoke the contracts which had not been completed,[5] doubtless in return for short-term financial gain. More royal taxes were alienated after this date, and though ideas

[1] A. D. Lublinskaya, *French absolutism: the crucial phase, 1620–1629* (Cambridge, 1968), pp. 315–16, 322. In effect the notables opted for the 'leases in reversion' proposal of the Estates-General.

[2] Barbiche, *Sully*, pp. 87–9. Buisseret, *Sully*, p. 90. 78 acts for *rachat de domaine* between 1599 and 1609, of which 66 were retained by the council: 120 a.p. 19.

[3] *Inventaire des arrêts du conseil d'état*, ed. Valois, no. 12149.

[4] Mayer, *Des États Généraux et autres assemblées nationales*, xvii, pt. ii. 1–2.

[5] A.A.E. France 787, fo. 204. Speech of d'Effiat to the assembly of notables in 1626–7. Barbiche notes that strict ministerial control of the contracts was a prerequisite, and that this was lacking under the Regency: Barbiche, *Sully*, p. 90.

chase were not dead the opportunity for putting them into effect
was past.

However, by no means all Sully's measures required political
stability in the long-term. There can be no more telling evidence
of Sully's preoccupation with short-term gain than his attitude to
the financiers. Extraordinary financial tribunals (*chambres de justice*) were held in 1597, 1601, 1605, and 1607.[1] Yet this was not an
attack on the financiers as such, for Sébastien Zamet, Barthélémy
Cénamy, Jean Moisset, Thomas Robin and Charles Paulet, and
newer men such as Philippe Collanges, Claude Barbin, Claude
Charlot and Antoine Feydeau although they were fined, were able
to reach agreements with Sully after the *chambre de justice* as before.
Indeed on 2 June 1608 a tax contract with drawn up by which
Jean Marteau, doubtless acting on behalf of a consortium of
financiers, undertook to levy the fines:[2] in this respect Sully set a
precedent for the future. Moreover some financiers were so important to the government that they were specially protected: Étienne
Puget, a *trésorier de l'Épargne*, was protected against the *chambre de
justice* of 1607, although later in the century his accounts were
reopened.[3] Prosecution was followed by amnesty, purchased by
payment of a fine: the king 'wringeth them like sponges and
ransometh every three or four years . . .', commented Sir George
Carew.[4] The successive fines on the financiers thus demonstrate
Sully's short-term objective of establishing a budgetary surplus,
rather than any concern for fundamental reform. Whereas in
1601, he had obtained only 600,000 *livres* from the financiers, in
1607 he sought nearly 1.2 million although it proved difficult to
levy this amount.[5] The best description of Sully's attitude was his

[1] Buisseret, *Sully*, p. 91. Barbiche, *Sully*, pp. 66–70. A. DesCilleuls, 'Henri IV et la
chambre de justice de 1607', *Comptes rendus de l'Académie des Sciences Morales et Politiques*, lxv
(1906), 276–91. P 2342, p. 1167, 23 Oct. 1604. P 2344, p. 331, Sept. 1607. B.L. Stowe MSS
169, fo. 9, 7 Apr. 1607.
[2] He was replaced by Germain Chalange on 12 Mar. 1613. The idea of a *chambre de justice*
had been suggested by two financial consortia in 1606. The first was on 2 Mar., by
Barthélémy Carteret; the second, which was accepted by the council of finance, on 9 Sept.
by Isaac Lacoste sieur de Barjau: *Inventaire des arrêts du conseil d'état*, ed. Valois, nos. 10102,
10570.
[3] Barbiche, *Sully*, p. 68. Supra, introduction.
[4] Carew, 'A relation of the state of France', p. 439.
[5] The original list of fines totalled 1,130,435 *livres* (B.N. MS. fr. 7583, pp. 368–84) but
this was slightly increased by a second list to 1,152,038 *livres*. On 30 Aug. 1611, 494,000
livres still remained to be paid, and on 12 Mar. 1613 part of this was remitted. On 7 Sept.
1613 it appears that the investigation was amnestied: A.A.E. France 768, fo. 179, 30 Aug.
1611. E 39b, fo. 84, 12 Mar. 1613. E 41c, fo. 26, 7 Sept. 1613. E 43b, fo. 87, 15 Mar. 1614.

own: 'his master had placed him in his office to increase his revenue and not to deliver justice'.[1]

The reforms of Henri IV and Sully had a limited purpose: the creation of an effective war machine. As Sir George Carew remarked, Sully 'prizeth himself for his military ableness, being offended when men ascribe the chiefest part of his sufficiency to the managing of the matters of the king's revenues and treasures'.[2] The siege of Amiens in 1597 had taught the king and Sully the need for a reserve fund for military contingencies. This in turn could not be established without careful economy during the years of peace. Sully closely supervised the accounting process and there is little doubt that he reduced the level of royal expenditure. In the years 1600–4, total expenses averaged just under 20 million *livres* per annum. The secret expenses, which had averaged 3.3 million per annum in 1595–9 were reduced to an average of 2.2 million in 1600–4. Such economy could not be maintained: even so, the average total expenditure in 1605–9 was only 30 million per annum, while the secret expenses had risen to 3.2 million per annum.[3] The most important achievement of Sully's administration was that for the first time in living memory he showed a significant budgetary surplus.[4] His projected budget for 1611, which was not implemented because of his resignation, envisaged expenses of 20.4 million and a surplus of 4.6 million.[5] The process of establishing a special emergency war fund had begun in July 1602, shortly after Sully was made captain of the Bastille: at the end of 1610, the surplus stood at perhaps ten million *livres* with a further five million in the Bastille.[6]

Why was this war fund needed? For much of the reign, the

---

[1] As reported by Carew, op. cit., p. 487. One contemporary considered that 'le grand abuz des partisans' continued under Sully; 'il faisoit party de tout et mettoit tout en party': B.N. MS. fr. 16626, fo. 151ᵛ.

[2] Carew, 'A relation of the state of France', p. 488.

[3] Appendix Two, Tables I and III.

[4] That is to say, the real budget in so far as it may be ascertained. Under single-entry book-keeping, the separate accounts of expenditure and income were almost always made to balance in theory. The method adopted by Guéry for unravelling the real budget from the theoretical balancing of the separate accounts is clearly unsatisfactory, because he arrives at a deficit for every year of Sully's administration: Guéry, 'Les finances de la monarchie française sous l'ancien régime', 236.

[5] 120 a.p. 28, fo. 40ᵛ.

[6] Barbiche, *Sully*, pp. 99–100. Buisseret, *Sully*, p. 80. L. Batiffol, 'Le trésor de la Bastille de 1605 à 1611', *Revue Henri IV*, iii (1909–12), 200–9. Contemporary estimates vary somewhat: Mayer, *Des États Généraux et autres assemblées nationales*, xvii. 222; xvii, pt. ii. 166, 168. A.A.E. France 768, fo. 172ᵛ, 3 Mar. 1611. A.A.E. France 772, fo. 288, n.d.

kingdom was at peace. In comparison with the troubled minority of Louis XIII, the years between 1598 and 1610 appear settled indeed. This impression is nevertheless misleading. Though Henri IV tried to keep his nobles in their place, he could not prevent them from conspiring against him; once his firm hand was removed, they would once more assume a predominant role in French domestic politics. Structural changes imposed by the king, such as the removal of appointments to the captaincy of towns and fortresses from the provincial governors[1] could be easily reversed. Perhaps, had the conspiracy of the duc de Biron succeeded in 1602, they would have been reversed much earlier, for it was said that the duke would have made the provincial governorships hereditary 'had not this king by his quick and advised proceeding in cutting off that dangerous head, and dispersing the rest . . . clean dissipated and overthrown their plot . . .'[2] Moreover, in the early 1600s the future of the Bourbon dynasty remained in doubt. The future Louis XIII was not born until September 1601, and the direct line was not completely secure until the birth of Gaston in April 1608. The issue of the succession played a crucial part in the d'Entragues conspiracy in 1604. Although the conspirators were arrested, and the most dangerous of them—the comte d'Auvergne—was imprisoned until 1616, the king legitimized Henriette d'Entragues's son:[3] in a sense the conspirators had gained part of their objective. The potential repercussions of the conspiracy become clear when it is remembered that François Balzac d'Entragues, father of the king's mistress, was a former supporter of the Catholic League.[4]

[1] Carew, 'A relation of the state of France', pp. 458–9. 'Pronostic que faisoient les mesdisans du temps du roy Henry quatriesme': *Les mémoires de Gaspard de Saulx-Tavannes*, ed. J. F. Michaud and J. J. F. Poujoulat, 1st. ser., viii (1838), p. 414. Bellièvre (and thus Henri IV) resisted the claims of d'Épernon and cited historical precedents: A.A.E. France 764, fo. 188, n.d. [*c.* 1596].

[2] Carew, op. cit., p. 459. Biron wanted the citadel of Bourg-en-Bresse, and to incorporate the citadel and the whole of Bresse in his governorship of Burgundy. He had dealings with Savoy and Spain to this purpose on 27 Jan. 1601. The report of the agreement by Fuentes, governor of Milan, to Philip III on this date reinforces Carew's comment. On the conspiracy: B. Zeller, 'La conspiration du maréchal de Biron', *Séances et Travaux de l'Académie des Sciences Morales et Politiques*, cxi (2nd ser., ii, 1879), 130–159 (esp. 137–8). A. Dufour, 'La paix de Lyon et la conjuration de Biron', *Journal des Savants* (1965), 428–55 (esp. 438–9). J. L. Cano de Cardoqui, *Tensiones hispanofrancesas en el siglo xvii. La conspiración de Biron, 1602* (Valladolid, 1970), pp. 49–56.

[3] For the legitimization of the d'Entragues children: Zeller, *Henri IV et Marie de Médicis*, pp. 213–14. The *duché-pairie* for Henri de Bourbon duc de Verneuil was only established in 1663, however: Labatut, *Les ducs et pairs*, p. 348.

[4] He held Orléans for the League after the rebellion of 1585: Girard, *Histoire de la vie du duc d'Espernon*, p. 39. However, he was removed from this post by Henri IV at the end of the

The third conspiracy, which lasted effectively from 1602 until 1606, was that of the duc de Bouillon. Although he proclaimed his innocence,[1] Bouillon was accused of participation in the Biron conspiracy. His prestige as Henri IV's lieutenant-general during the civil wars, his extensive landholdings in south-west France, and above all his principality of Sedan on the German frontier acquired in 1591 after his marriage to Charlotte de la Marck made him a powerful rallying point for discontent. Moreover, through his brother-in-law, Frederick IV of the Palatinate, he was allied to the Protestant princes of Germany. In 1603, he sought asylum there where he posed as a martyr to the cause of international Protestantism. A revolt of the French Protestants could not be ruled out: there had been talk of this two years earlier, and while Sully was a Protestant in high office, he was 'as harsh and rough to them as to any other . . .'[2] Bouillon hoped to capture a number of towns in south-west France with Spanish money and to bring in a German and Swiss army. With the possible exception of Spanish finance (which Henri of Navarre had been offered in his youth) it was in its structure almost a classic Protestant plot of the wars of religion.[3] All that was lacking was Protestant support for it within France, which in the end did not materialize. Faction rather than religion held together the uneasy coalition of Bouillon's clients, old friends of Biron and disgruntled former supporters of the League. Although Bouillon held out for a few months in Sedan in the hope of reinforcements, when the king marched against him with an artillery train in April 1606 he was forced to submit in return for a pardon and confirmation of all his offices.[4] Thereafter the kingdom was settled until Condé, suspecting Henri IV's attraction towards his wife, fled across the border to the Spanish

---

League without compensation: A.A.E. France 766, fo. 105. The link between the conspirators was that d'Entragues was the comte d'Auvergne's step-father, since he had married Marie Touchet. The count was Charles IX's bastard by Marie Touchet.

[1] As a Protestant, Bouillon asked to be tried before the *chambre de l'édit* of Castres, but this was no more than a ploy: A.A.E. France 764, fo. 243, 3 Nov. 1602.

[2] Carew, 'A relation of the state of France', p. 487. Cf. a letter from a Dutch agent dated 31 Dec. 1600: *Un envoyé hollandais à la cour de Henri IV. Lettres inédites de François d'Aerssen à Jacques Valcke, trésorier de Zélande, 1599–1603*, ed. J. Nouaillac (1908), p. 97.

[3] Tait, 'The king's lieutenants in Guyenne', p. 243. Dr Tait's account (op. cit., pp. 240–6), of which this is no more than a summary, demonstrates that the Bouillon conspiracy was much more serious than historians have sometimes argued. This may account for his immense prestige as 'un oracle en telles affaires' (i.e. conspiracies) in 1619: A.A.E. France 772, fos. 243–63, 'sur la sortie de la Reyne de Blois'.

[4] For Sully's part in the campaign: Buisseret, *Sully*, pp. 158–9. Barbiche, *Sully*, p. 156.

Netherlands in 1609. This became almost a re-run of the Bouillon conspiracy, except that Condé was a Catholic. The first prince of the blood would not return without serious guarantees, such as a fortress in his governorship in Guyenne,[1] which the king was not prepared to accept. The general mobilization in 1609 was the king's response to Condé's dealings with the Habsburgs: he replied in the same way that he had answered Bouillon's challenge three years earlier, although the international ramifications were much more serious.

What made the conspiracies against Henri IV so dangerous were the doubts concerning the validity of his divorce in 1599 and the legitimacy of Marie de Médicis's children. The Habsburgs naturally encouraged these doubts, since they had not lost their ambition to weaken France by challenging the principle of hereditary succession. Although ideas of electing the king had been dashed by Henri IV's victory over the League,[2] in one respect the opportunities for conspiracy had been increased by his victory. Henri IV's claim had seemed weak partly because he was so distantly related to the last of the Valois kings; if he could succeed to the throne, so might any other prince of the blood.[3] The agents of Philip III of Spain and the duke of Savoy, his diplomatic ally, fostered such ambitions in the French nobility. Biron was in informal alliance with Philip III of Spain and the duke of Savoy. The d'Entragues conspirators had been encouraged by Taxis, the former Spanish ambassador, to emulate Biron.[4] Bouillon took Spanish money, and support wherever he could find it. Condé was encouraged to press his claims to the French throne although the Pope would not allow the question of Henri IV's divorce to be reopened.[5] Quite apart from his personal preference for dealings with the Protestant powers, Henri IV could scarcely regard the attitude of Spain as conducive to international peace after 1598.

Although it was said of the king that 'he studiously avoideth all occasion of war, especially when he doubteth to find any strong

---

[1] P. Henrard, *Henri IV et la princesse de Condé, 1609–1610* . . . (Brussels, Ghent and Leipzig, 1870), p. 62. By August 1610, Condé's expectations had grown, and he wanted the position of Constable of France: ibid., p. 443.

[2] R. A. Jackson, 'Elective kingship and *consensus populi* in sixteenth-century France', *Journal of Modern History*, xliv (1972), 170–1.

[3] R. E. Giesey, 'The juristic basis of dynastic right to the French throne', *Transactions of the American Philosophical Society*, li (1961), 36, 40.

[4] The Spanish support was equivocal, because Taxis thought a successful conspiracy unlikely: A.A.E. France 766, fos. 20ᵛ, 27, 36.

[5] Condé recognized Louis XIII as king on 31 May 1610, which paved the way for his return to France in July: Henrard, op. cit., pp. 145, 148–9, 163.

opposition,[1] the fact remains that even in the decade of peace from 1600 to 1610 Henri mobilized three times. The first occasion was the war with Savoy. Henri IV went to war on 11 August 1600 because duke Charles-Emmanuel I had not returned the marquisate of Saluzzo which he had seized from France in 1588. Sully had to organize a substantial army which occupied Bresse.[2] The war was brought to a speedy conclusion by the treaty of Lyon (17 January 1601), which some contemporaries thought a bad bargain because instead of insisting on Saluzzo, Henri accepted instead Bresse, Bugey, Valromey, and Gex. With hindsight, the king appears to have made a better peace than it seemed to contemporaries: he had rounded off his territories in the east, made Lyon—an important financial and commercial centre— more defensible, and above all, he had cut one of the Spanish supply routes to the Low Countries.[3] The second war, against the duc de Bouillon in 1606, was a less serious proposition since the main bastion of resistance was Sedan, which capitulated at the approach of the king's army. The third war, the intervention in the Cleves-Jülich succession crisis in 1609–10, was the most serious of all. Henri IV ratified the treaty of Hälle with the Protestant Union in Germany on 23 February 1610. On 8 March, Boissize, his ambassador in Germany, promised the arrival of French troops. Shortly before his assassination, Henri was contemplating raising an army of 30,000 men,[4] and there is a serious possibility that had he survived Ravaillac's knife, the Thirty Years' War would have begun in 1610 and not 1618. Had this happened, what would have been left of Sully's financial reforms?[5]

In any judgement on the *grand dessein*, and more generally on

[1] Carew, 'A relation of the state of France', p. 477.

[2] Buisseret, *Sully*, pp. 156–8. Barbiche, *Sully*, pp. 155–6.

[3] P. F. Geisendorf, 'Le traité de Lyon et le pont de Grésin . . .', *Mélanges Paul-Edmond Martin. Mémoires et documents publiés par la Société d'Histoire et d'Archéologie de Genève*, xl (1961), 280.

[4] Anquez, *Henri IV et l'Allemagne*, pp. 171–89. Buisseret, *Sully*, pp. 159–60. Barbiche, *Sully*, pp. 156–7. Something of the scale of the preparations is indicated by the number of bread rations— 500,000 a day for three months—contracted for by Philippe de Coulanges and Claude Barbin on 22 Apr. 1610.

[5] Of course, the war might not have lasted for thirty years with France involved at the outset. But Sully's 'estat du fonds pour l'entretenement des armées du roy' is rather unconvincing: Sully, *Oeconomies royales*, ed. Michaud and Poujoulat, ii. 375–8. For a contrasting view of Henri's objectives as much more limited, cf. Hayden, *France and the Estates-General of 1614*, p. 44. However, even if the king's aims were for a limited strike against the Habsburgs on the Rhine, they could have gone seriously wrong, as did Louis XIV's in 1688.

Henri IV and Sully, it is not easy to disentangle fact from fiction. After the assassination, the king was soon given a mystique as *Henri le grand* which he had lacked in his lifetime.[1] It was even said by his funeral orators that he had paid his debts![2] In his enforced retirement after 1611, Sully wrote the *Sages et royales oeconomies d'estat . . . de Henri le grand* to immortalize, and exaggerate, their joint achievement. It was later said that Henri IV 'could always fall back on his Sully',[3] and it is certainly true that in comparison with Henri III's relationship with d'Épernon, Sully was good value to the king. Both d'Épernon and Sully were relative *parvenus*[4] raised to the status of duke and peer by their master; both were unpopular at the height of their power; both established considerable fortunes, and were accused of avarice by their opponents;[5] both indulged in rebellion against a later king when they no longer enjoyed royal favour.[6] In fact Sully's fortune appears to have been larger than d'Épernon's, for towards the end of his life it was estimated at nearly 5.2 million *livres*.[7] Foucquet later commented on the jealousy with which the finance minister guarded the independent status of his estate at Sully-sur-Loire; no later *surintendant* minted his own coins as Sully had done.[8]

Of course, Sully had political and financial abilities which were missing in d'Épernon. Yet if it is true that Henri IV 'could always fall back on his Sully', it was even more important that Sully could

---

[1] He was called *Henri le grand* in a decree of the council: E 40b–41a, fo. 215, 11 July 1613. The equestrian statue of *Henri le grand* set up at the Pont-Neuf in 1614 at the expense of the grand dukes of Tuscany added to the mystique: *Chambre des Comptes*, ed. Boislisle, p. 303.

[2] J. Hennequin, *Henri IV dans ses oraisons funèbres ou la naissance d'une légende* (1977), pp. 111, 113.

[3] Buisseret, *Sully*, p. 191. Buisseret correctly comments that d'Argenson, from whose writings this quotation is drawn, falsified the relationship between king and minister.

[4] Sully was the baron de Rosny before 1601, when his barony was raised to a marquisate: P 2341, p. 397, Aug. 1601. For the letters patent establishing the *duché-pairie* of Sully in Feb. 1606: P 2343, p. 651.

[5] The emissary of the comte d'Auvergne, one of the d'Entragues conspirators, to Spain in 1604 talked of 'l'avarice de celuy qui regist et de ses ministres': A.A.E. France 766, fo. 93ᵛ, n.d. [1604].

[6] For d'Épernon's rebellion in Provence in 1594–6: Mouton, *Le duc et le roi*, pp. 40–7. For his rebellion against Luynes in 1619 see below, Chapter II. Sully's alleged retirement from public life after 1611 is one of the myths attached to the servant of Henri IV, repeated even by recent biographers such as Buisseret, *Sully*, pp. 180–1 and Barbiche, *Sully*, pp. 169–70. For his participation in the Protestant revolts in 1615–16 and 1621–2: *Négociations, lettres et pièces relatives à la conférence de Loudun*, ed. L. F. H. Bouchitté (1862), p. 319. K 112, no. 5 [Musée AE II 798], 22 May 1622.

[7] Barbiche, *Sully*, pp. 170, 179.

[8] *Mémoires-Journaux de Pierre L'Estoile*, ed. Brunet et al., vii. 327. *Les oeuvres de Mʳ Foucquet, ministre d'état, contenant son accusation, son procez et ses défenses contre Louis XIV, roy de France* (16 vols., 1696), v. 342. The right to mint coins was regarded by Bodin and others as an important attribute of sovereignty.

always fall back on his Henri IV. Henri III had been forced to sacrifice d'Épernon in 1588 under pressure from the Catholic League. In contrast, Henri IV never sacrificed Sully, but supported him 'in all his rough courses'. It is most unlikely that the explanation for this was that Sully controlled the king 'by terror rather than obsequiousness'.[1] Rather, the king valued the objectives towards which Sully worked: he loved his buildings, but he kept such expenses in bounds; he paid 'more pensions than any of his predecessors . . . [but] distributeth them with great choice . . .';[2] his court was not as lavish as Henri III's had been. Not surprisingly, later financial reformers in the seventeenth century, such as d'Effiat, sought to model their budgets on those of Henri IV and Sully.[3] In all important matters, the king supported his finance minister. The *droit annuel* scheme was delayed for two years because of the opposition of Bellièvre, the Chancellor, but in the end Sully had his way. By 1605 a Keeper of the Seals was appointed which marked the king's disapproval of Bellièvre's conduct.

Henri IV also supported Sully in his arguments with the great nobility. Although Sully favoured the participation of nobles in the king's council,[4] he was prepared to criticize their conduct and resist their excessive demands for pensions and rewards. On 26 October 1598 Sully had a furious disagreement with d'Épernon. The duke protested that without his prior knowledge Sully had presented a complaint to the king's council about his conduct of financial administration while governor in the Saintonge and Angoumois. Sully replied rather tactlessly that the duke could have called on him to ascertain the nature of the complaint, which

---

[1] Both quotations are from Carew, 'A relation of the state of France', pp. 478, 485.

[2] Ibid., p. 480. Hennequin, op. cit., pp. 113–14. The average salary of a provincial governor rose from 33,950 *livres* in 1603 to 44,933 *livres* two years later. Salaries also increased during the reign of Louis XIII: Harding, *Anatomy of a power elite*, p. 139. M. Greengrass, 'War, politics and religion in Languedoc during the government of Henri de Montmorency-Damville, 1574–1610' (Oxford Univ. D. Phil., 1979), pp. 46, 49.

[3] D'Effiat took the year 1608 as his model: Petit, *L'assemblée des notables*, p. 105. Lublinskaya, *French absolutism*, p. 308. The budget for 1607 was published by A. Chamberland, 'Le budget de L'Épargne de 1607 d'après des documents inédits', *Revue Henri IV*, ii (1908), 312–26.

[4] Mousnier, 'Sully et le conseil d'état et des finances', pp. 82–3. According to the papal nuncio, Sully's quarrels with the great nobles caused him to lose favour temporarily with the king. The important point, however, is that he was never formally disavowed: Major, *Representative government in early modern France*, p. 279. N.B.: Major's account of Henri IV and Sully's motives differs substantially from the one presented here, particularly in his emphasis on their desire to 'secure a more absolutist regime' (p. 387). Major admits that much of his argument 'is mere conjecture. We have no contemporary evidence of why Henry and Sully acted as they did' (p. 390).

originated in a report from the *trésoriers de France* at Limoges. The
duke retorted that his status was not so abject that he had to go
calling on Sully, at which point the minister took offence: 'vous
avez parlé à moi comme si j'estois quelque petit financier . . .'
There was no difference in their families, he claimed, since he was
a 'gentilhomme et fort homme de bien'. If there was a present
difference in their status, that was merely because d'Épernon's
position had been raised by Henri III. The two men went for their
swords and were held back only by the presence of the Chancellor
and d'Épernon's doubt that the king would support him.[1] There
was a similar conflict with the comte de Soissons in 1603, after
which Henri 'caused it to be notified that whosoever should
attempt Sully should find the king's own person for his second'.
After the second incident, Sully was accompanied by an armed
retinue.[2] The finance minister held the purse strings tightly
because he had the full support of the king. Under a Regency with
the influence of powerful favourites such as Concino Concini and
his wife, this would not be possible. Perhaps Henri IV appreciated the danger, because in April 1610, he told the Queen in anger
that he would chase 'le Conchin et la Conchinne' back to Florence.[3] Before he had removed the threat he was assassinated by
François Ravaillac.

[1] *Mémoires-Journaux de Pierre L'Estoile*, ed. Brunet *et al.*, viii. 142–5.
[2] Carew, op. cit., pp. 484–5. A.A.E. France 764, fo. 158, n.d. [*c.* 1603]. Buisseret, *Sully*, p.
54, also mentions a conflict with the marquis de Vitry.
[3] Henrard, *Henri IV et la princesse de Condé*, p. 317. On the influence of Concini and his wife
during the reign of Henri IV: Zeller, *Henri IV et Marie de Médicis*, pp. 75–97.

Chapter II

Time of Troubles, 1610–1624

I. MARIE DE MÉDICIS AND CONCINI

The assassination of Henri IV on 14 May 1610 threw the political system of France into crisis. It is now fashionable to argue that public revulsion at the act of assassination was so great that in the long-term the French monarchy was strengthened: Ravaillac's knife, it is contended, assisted the growth of the absolute state.[1] Indirectly, this may have been the case, but such a consequence was by no means inevitable: few contemporaries would have dared hope for such an outcome. The immediate prospect was anarchy, comparable to the situation in France following the unexpected death of Henri II from a jousting accident in 1559. Both kings had been in their prime; both left male heirs who were too young to govern on their own. Louis XIII had not yet attained his ninth birthday and thus the Regency fell upon Marie de Médicis, the Queen Mother, who had already been appointed temporary Regent because of the imminent departure of Henri IV to the war-front. Recent studies have tended to re-establish Marie's reputation as a stateswoman,[2] yet in the circumstances of 1610 she was an untried force. She suffered from three disadvantages: she was a woman, she was inexperienced, and her Habsburg preferences were rather too obvious for comfort. Her assumption of the Regency would undoubtedly lead to ministerial changes.

The Chancellor, Brûlart de Sillery, and Villeroy had little to fear,[3] but this was not the case with Sully. Sully had been Henri IV's confidant: by paying Henri's gambling debts, placating his

---

[1] Mousnier, *L'assassinat de Henri IV*, p. 266.

[2] Hayden, *France and the Estates-General of 1614*, p. 173. Cf. his earlier paper, 'Continuity in the France of Henry IV and Louis XIII: French foreign policy, 1598–1615', *Journal of Modern History*, xlv (1973), 1–23. On the other hand, there is Marie's conduct after the fall of Concini to account for, and the case made out by Hayden for continuity in foreign and domestic policy between the reign of Henri IV and the Regency is unconvincing: cf. the comments by R. J. Knecht in *European Studies Review*, viii (1978), 158–9. However, in the most recent account of all (Major, *Representative government in early modern France*, p. 397) the Regent is depicted as 'jealous, quarrelsome and stupid . . . she had little concept of how to govern and had to follow the directions of her advisers'.

[3] Carew, 'A relation of the state of France', p. 492.

mistresses, and refusing the Queen objects she coveted[1] Sully had scarcely ingratiated himself with the new Regent. Above all, Sully and Marie disagreed on politics. Sully was a Protestant and supported the *grand dessein* against the Habsburgs; the Regent was a *dévot* Catholic, a friend of Spain, and naturally listened to the advice of former supporters of the Catholic League such as Villeroy and Jeannin. Even had Sully followed Henri IV's advice and abjured Protestantism[2] his position would not have been secure, for he was temperamental. His critics had an arsenal of weapons against him: they alleged that he wanted to become a *maréchal de France*, criticized his ferocious temper, his inability to co-operate with his ministerial colleagues, and his political intrigues both at home and abroad.[3] For his part, Sully over-dramatized his plight, claiming that he feared the fate of Enguerran de Marigny, the finance minister of Philip the Good who had been executed under Charles V in 1315.[4]

Sully was the ideal finance minister in wartime: the siege of Jülich was not completed until 2 September 1610, while it was not until 30 March 1613 that the Regent extricated herself from Henri IV's dangerous foreign policy by refusing to renew the treaty of Hälle.[5] At home, Sully's failure to adapt to the new régime was a tragedy for France, for his continuation in office was the best hope for financial stability and conciliation of the Protestants. In straight financial terms, Sully's stand against the Regent in 1610–11 was correct, but politically it made little sense. Marie must have been infuriated by Sully's contesting her right to announce that monies had been spent in Henri IV's lifetime when he claimed they had not.[6] He opposed the Regent's generosity towards the nobles, and was quite unwilling to compromise with the new power behind the throne, Concino Concini, the Italian favourite of the Regent, and Léonora Galigaï, his wife.[7] Indeed, Sully contested Concini's support for remissions on the revenue farms claimed by Jean Moisset and Antoine Feydeau. Above all, Sully tried to continue his policy of redeeming the crown lands in

[1] Buisseret, *Sully*, pp. 48–9.

[2] B. Barbiche and D. J. Buisseret, 'Les convictions religieuses de Sully', *Bibliothèque de l'École des Chartes*, cxxi (1963), 223–30.

[3] Sully rejected these accusations: A.A.E. France 768, fo. 171, 3 Mar. 1611.

[4] Carew, 'A relation of the state of France', p. 487–8. For Marigny: J. Favier, *Un conseiller de Philippe le Bel. Enguerran de Marigny* (1963).

[5] Anquez, *Henri IV et l'Allemagne*, pp. 193, 197.

[6] Buisseret, *Sully*, p. 54 and plate three facing p. 97. *Les Oeconomies royales de Sully*, ed. Michaud and Poujoulat, ii. 399–400.

[7] For the failure to create a *modus vivendi*: ibid., ii. 405–12.

the new and unfavourable circumstances of the Regency. Villeroy's son Halincourt wanted the revocation of the contract concerning the crown lands in the Lyonnais. It was this conflict which precipitated Sully's resignation, since the Villeroy family was supported by the Regent, Concini, and Chancellor Brûlart de Sillery. Already in October 1610 Sully had contemplated resignation, but had been dissuaded by his family; this time, on 26 January 1611, the break was complete and final. Sully left office at the age of fifty-one, with thirty years of active life still ahead of him. Far from being hanged, as he had feared, he received a royal gift of 300,000 *livres*.[1]

The fall of Sully left a power vacuum at the centre of the financial system, much as the death of François d'O had done in 1594. As on the earlier occasion, an attempt was made to abolish the position of *surintendant des finances* and instead, on 5 February 1611, a new finance commission was established—initially on an experimental, one-year basis.[2] Yet it is clear that there was more to this arrangement than simply a return to the collegiate form of administering finance which had proved unworkable in 1594–6. Overall responsibility for finance was taken in the first place by the Regent, the Chancellor, and Pierre Jeannin, who was appointed *contrôleur-général des finances* in the place of Gilles Maupeou. Jeannin, Sully's erstwhile rival, exercised day-to-day control jointly in 1611–12 with two other leading councillors of state, Châteauneuf and de Thou: they were called *intendants des finances*[3] although they did not buy their offices as did the other officials with this title. Thereafter, Jeannin's predominance was ensured by his friendship with Villeroy and the great prestige he enjoyed with the Regent. In Jeannin's words, Marie de Médicis gave him as controller-general the authority in financial administration normally enjoyed by a *surintendant*.[4] Thus in a real sense France was ruled by the 'greybeards' (*les barbons*)—Brûlart de Sillery, Villeroy, and Jeannin—whose main justification for the exercise of power was that they had outlived their rivals. All three were drawn from the *noblesse de robe*, and as such were likely to lack authority in dealing with the upper nobility. In particular, Jeannin was only the second finance minister in recent times not

---

[1] Barbiche and Buisseret, 'Sully et la surintendance des finances', 543. Barbiche, *Sully*, p. 171. B.N. Dupuy 90, fo. 204.

[2] Appendix One, Table I. Mousnier, 'Les règlements du conseil du roi sous Louis XIII', 128–31. Cf. also B.N. MS. fr. 16218, fo. 121. A.A.E. France 768, fo. 165.

[3] B.N. Dupuy 90, fo. 207, 5 Feb. 1611. A.A.E. France 768, fos. 235, 247, n.d. [1611–12].

[4] Quoted in the sources to Appendix One, Table I.

to have been a soldier by profession.[1] Perhaps inevitably, the three ministers believed that concessions to the upper nobility were unavoidable during a regency and preferable to civil war.[2]

The death of Henri IV and the fall of Sully led to a loosening of the purse strings, an outpouring of pensions and gifts that was unprecedented since 1594.[3] In the words of a foreign observer, 'chascun demande à la royne, l'espée au poing'. The magnates holding old debts of Henri IV's demanded repayment. For example, the Regent offered the duc de Guise repayment over six years in addition to a pension of 100,000 *livres* per annum: he held out in the hope of obtaining repayment within a two year period.[4] Between 1610 and 1614 the Regency government was forced to spend at least ten million on the magnates: 3.4 million to Condé, 1.7 million to Mayenne, 1.3 million to Conty, 1.2 million to Nevers, with smaller but very significant sums to Soissons, Longueville, Guise, Vendôme, d'Épernon, and Bouillon, to cite only the chief beneficiaries.[5] This pressure on the government might easily have led to a complete collapse of financial control, yet this did not happen. After the fall of Sully, the Regent, the Chancellor and Jeannin met at regular intervals—at first weekly, then fortnightly or even monthly—to review all unbudgeted expenses which the *trésorier de l'Épargne* was not allowed to acquit until they had been approved by this meeting. Between 1611 and 1613 these unbudgeted expenses averaged just under 5 million per annum, but they rose to well over 7 million in the crisis year of 1614.[6]

---

[1] The soldiers had been Artus de Cossé (1564), François d'O, and Sully. The other *noble de robe* had been Pomponne de Bellièvre in 1574–8. Jeannin was a *président* in the *Parlement* of Dijon.

[2] Jeannin's theory was expressed in his financial statement to the Estates-General of 1614–15 and in a letter of 26 June 1615 to Bouillon: Mayer, *Des États Généraux et autres assemblées nationales*, xvii. 225–6. *Négociations, lettres et pièces relatives à la conférence de Loudun*, ed. Bouchitté, p. 171. Hayden, *France and the Estates-General of 1614*, p. 18. In a meeting with the *Chambre des Comptes* on 14 Dec. 1613, the Regent had conceded that the gifts and pensions were large, but argued that they were conceded 'pour bonnes causes . . . pour entretenir la paix dans le royaume . . .': *Chambre des Comptes*, ed. Boislisle, p. 294 n.1.

[3] Sully had warned the *Chambre des Comptes* of the danger on 3 Dec. 1610 in a speech that paved the way for his resignation. In a remarkable *volte-face*—six years earlier Henri IV had told the *Comptes* that he was determined to limit their authority—Sully stressed the role of the court during a royal minority. Their authority should be used to oppose excessive secret expenses, pensions, and gifts: ibid., pp. 278, 291–2.

[4] Pecquius to archduke Albert, governor of the Spanish Netherlands, 24 July 1610. Quoted by Henrard, *Henri IV et la princesse de Condé*, p. 435.

[5] A.A.E. France 790, fos. 91, 104, n.d. [1615?].

[6] Thus 5,697,546 *livres* in 1611, 5,148,150 *livres* in 1612, 4,129,877 *livres* in 1613, 7,659,622 *livres* in 1614 and 918,591 *livres* from 1 Jan. to 6 June 1615: B.N. Dupuy 824–827, passim.

As early as 22 February 1611, the *Chambre des Comptes* protested at a breach of Henri IV's guidelines in a gift to Concini. On 31 January 1612 it presented remonstrances against the increase in gifts and pensions since the death of the king. If expenses continued to rise, the reserve fund at the Bastille would be used up and the crown would be forced to increase taxes.[1] Pensions and gifts averaged 3.4 million *livres* per annum in 1605–9 but had risen to an average of 6.5 million per annum between 1610 and 1614[2] despite the warnings of the *Comptes*. What the court would have found even more disturbing, had the information become public knowledge at the time, was that financial policy had become dominated by faction with royal patronage manipulated by the Regent's favourites. Léonora Galigaï, Concini's wife, was the dominant personality in the Queen's household. She it was who read and approved the list of pensions and gifts. No gifts were made without her consent.[3] Marie de Médicis and Jeannin could draw reasonable satisfaction from the fact that overall expenditure and the secret expenses remained approximately at the level of Henri IV's lifetime.[4] Moreover, the emergency war fund at the Bastille was not drawn upon until 1614.[5] On the other hand, the policy of the Regency government was related to short-term needs: the budget was reorganized so that the sums that might have been placed in reserve at the Bastille were distributed to the nobles as gifts and pensions. Critics of this policy argued that it was impossible to buy the loyalty of the king's subjects, and that royal expenditure should be lower during a minority than when the king was of age to rule.[6] The critics had a point, since the policies of the Regent and Jeannin failed to forestall the rebellion of 1614. On the other hand, the policies helped secure four years of civil peace. Without the increase in royal gifts and pensions, it is possible that the political disturbances would have occurred sooner.

The Regency government was blown off course not by its own policies but by a series of aristocratic rebellions which had

---

[1] *Chambre des Comptes*, ed. Boislisle, pp. 292–4.
[2] Appendix Two, Table II.
[3] F. Hayem, *Le maréchal d'Ancre et Léonora Galigaï* (1910), p. 310. B.N. 500 Colbert 221, fo. 410ᵛ. Interrogation of André de Lizza, 10 May 1617.
[4] Appendix Two, Tables I and III.
[5] Batiffol, 'Le trésor de la Bastille', p. 209. *Chambre des Comptes*, ed. Boislisle, pp. 298–300.
[6] This was the argument of the *Parlement* of Paris in 1615: Mayer, op. cit., xvii, pt. ii. 166–7.

threatened ever since 1610,[1] and which began four years later with the revolt of Henri II de Bourbon, prince de Condé. Condé's motives are difficult to disentangle, opportunism and self-interest figuring prominently along with aristocratic grievances and issues of state. Contemporaries talked of a 'league of public weal' as in 1465 during the reign of Louis XI.[2] By this they meant that the magnates, with foreign support if they could secure it, championed issues of public policy in the hope of extracting private concessions from the crown. In his manifesto, Condé claimed that confusion and disorder were so rife that only a meeting of the Estates-General could prevent the collapse of the state.[3] What were these confusions and disorders? In the negotiations between the government and the rebellious nobles, it emerged that Condé resented Concini's control of patronage resulting from his influence over the Regent, objected to the projected marriage of Louis XIII to Anne of Austria—the daughter of Philip III of Spain—and was prepared to play the 'Protestant card': he sought leadership of a rebellion of Catholic Malcontents and Protestants.[4] In his private conversations, Condé had already suggested that Henri IV's emergency war fund had been misused by the Regent.[5]

To counter the threat of the magnates, the government agreed to defer the conclusion of the Spanish marriage alliances until after the declaration of the king's majority, and to summon a meeting of the Estates-General. This arrangement, which was agreed at Sainte-Menehould on 15 May 1614, was bought at the price of a cash payment of 450,000 *livres* to cover Condé's expenses during his revolt.[6] Thus by the time that the Estates-General met—after the declaration of the king's majority, not before as the

---

[1] Henrard, *Henri IV et le princesse de Condé*, p. 439. The comte de Bucquoy reported to the archduke Albert on 27 July 1610, after Condé's return to France, that Condé intended civil war because he and his friends would no longer tolerate 'la forme de gouvernement de la royne . . .' Condé already intended to call for a meeting of the Estates-General according to Bucquoy.

[2] Ibid., p. 437. Rohan's comment on the treaty of Sainte-Menehould of 1614 echoed Commynes' on the treaties of 1465: Hayden, *France and the Estates-General of 1614*, p. 67.

[3] A.A.E. France 769, fo. 98, 19 Feb. 1614.

[4] The resentment of Concini was voiced as early as 1610 by Condé and other nobles. Pecquius also noted to the archduke Albert the possibility of an informal alliance between Catholic Malcontents and Huguenots: Henrard, op. cit., pp. 435, 437. For the instructions and negotiations of the royal commissioners (including Jeannin) with Condé: B.N. Dupuy 91, fos. 10, 31, 37, 7 Feb., 9 Apr. and 11 Apr. 1614.

[5] Henrard, op. cit., p. 440.

[6] Hayden, *France and the Estates-General of 1614*, p. 67. A.A.E. France 769, fo. 146, 15 May 1614. E 44, fo. 295, 22 May 1614.

rebellious nobles had wanted—the finances of the French crown were considerably less healthy than they had been, and part of Condé's prophecies had come to pass. The government had had to mobilize an army, and had paid for this by drawing 2.5 million from the war fund at the Bastille—despite the vigorous protests of the *Chambre des Comptes*.[1] It had also borrowed at least 910,000 *livres* at high rates of interest.[2] By his own actions, Condé had precipitated the crisis he claimed he wanted to prevent. The accounts were adjusted to balance at 29.4 million *livres*. However, in Jeannin's financial statement to the Estates-General a deficit of nearly 3.7 million was revealed on the current account. It has been estimated that the deficit was actually higher, amounting to nearly 8.8 million. Jeannin would naturally have sought to hide this unpalatable fact, if true, from the deputies, although it should be noted that the accounts had not been finalized, and thus the picture was unclear at the time he made his statement.[3]

Jeannin hoped that the Estates-General would propose positive measures to improve the financial situation and replace the war funds that had been withdrawn from the Bastille to meet the emergency in 1614. Yet when the 474 deputies (141 representing the first estate; 135 the second, 198 the third)[4] assembled on 27 October 1614, Jeannin soon found himself defending the Regency government from charges of maladministration and corruption.[5]

[1] Batiffol, 'Le trésor de la Bastille', p. 209. B.N. Dupuy 91, fos. 103–112ᵛ., 26 May–10 June 1614. P 2347, pp. 753, 877, 23 Feb. and 26 May 1614.

[2] *Les négociations du président Jeannin*, ed. J. F. Michaud and J. J. F. Poujoulat, 2nd ser., iv (1838), p. 677. Hayden, op. cit., p. 61. Appendix Two, Table VIII A. The interest rate was criticized by the *Parlement* of Paris in 1615: Mayer, *Des États Généraux et autres assemblées nationales*, xvii. pt. ii. 168.

[3] The fundamental account is R. Doucet, 'Les finances de la France en 1614 . . .', *Revue d'Histoire Économique et Sociale*, xviii (1930), 141–2. Doucet is particularly hostile to Jeannin. Hayden (op. cit., p. 19 n. 6) comments that 'Jeannin falsified less than Sully'. However, it is quite clear that Jeannin's figures given to the Estates-General were only estimates, even if they were over-optimistic. Whichever figure is accepted for the deficit on the current account, it is lower than that of 11.4 million suggested by Guéry. Guéry's calculations make the deficit *less* than in 1608–10 under Sully. The emergency war fund in the Bastille, which several contemporary sources confirm existed, could not have been established according to Guéry's estimates: Guéry, 'Les finances de la monarchie française', 236.

[4] Hayden, *France and the Estates-General of 1614*, pp. 234–83, lists the deputies. The actual number of votes within each estate was somewhat different: 156 for the clergy and 198 for the third estate. However since there are no voting records, these differences are unimportant. Moreover, since each estate deliberated separately, in a sense only three votes were cast.

[5] He rejected accusations made in 'écrits jettés au public . . . qu'il y a eu malversation au maniement des finances': Mayer, *Des États Généraux et autres assemblées nationales*, xvii, pt. i. 223.

To some extent, the government was saved from embarrassment by disagreements between the three orders: the proposals of the second estate, the nobility, for a new *chambre de justice* to investigate the conduct of finance found little support among the clergy.[1] For the first time since 1560 the crown managed to secure an Estates-General that was relatively favourable to the government in 1614: the final statements of all three estates show that there was no sympathy for Condé or for rebellion by the upper nobility. However, the deputies and especially the third estate went far beyond what the government wanted of them. They felt that the kingdom needed reform and were determined to provide the basis for it in their proposals.[2] In fact the *cahier* of the third estate, the widest-ranging financial statement of the three,[3] was heavily influenced, albeit unconsciously, by the Estates-General of 1588–9 and the propaganda of the Catholic League.

The third estate denounced the procedures of the finance commission since 1611. Although in 1614 Jeannin had been given the title of *surintendant*, the change had come too late to make any impact. The Regency government's aim of establishing a better 'ordre et règlement' than under Henri IV[4] had not been achieved in the view of the Estates-General which wanted to reduce membership of the council of finance to three or four senior councillors. Worse than incompetence, however, was the charge of corruption levelled against members of the king's council. The third estate wanted a new law prohibiting ministers and king's councillors from receiving pensions or gifts from tax farmers and contractors.[5] These pensions were common practice: Léonora Galigaï, the Queen's favourite, had taken a *pot de vin* of 60,000 *livres* and 30,000 *livres* a year as pension from the farmers of the *cinq grosses fermes* after 1613.[6] The third estate wanted all remissions granted to the

---

[1] P. Blet, *Le clergé de France et la monarchie. Étude sur les assemblées générales du clergé de 1615 à 1666* (2 vols., Rome, 1959), i. 36.

[2] Hayden, op. cit., p. 196.

[3] Picot, *Histoire des États Généraux*, v. 32. The *cahier* is in Mayer, op. cit., xvii, pt. ii. 1–88 ('Des finances et domaines') and pp. 88–108 ('Des suppressions et révocations'). Commentary by Picot, op. cit., v. 31–51, who compares the proposals with the two later assemblies of notables, and Hayden, op. cit., pp. 192–4.

[4] Ruling of 9 Feb. 1611: Mousnier, 'Les règlements du conseil du roi sous Louis XIII', 136.

[5] Though the penalty does not seem very severe, a fine of 2000 *livres parisis*, say 2500 *livres tournois*.

[6] Hayem, *Le Maréchal d'Ancre et Léonora Galigaï*, p. 263. G. Mongrédien, *Léonora Galigaï. Un procès de sorcellerie sous Louis XIII* (1968), pp. 187–9. B.N. 500 Colbert 221, fo. 176ᵛ. Galigaï was also accused of taking a *pot de vin* of 114,000 *livres* from the *gabelles de France*, of drawing off 'notables sommes' from the farm of the *parties casuelles*, and of taking her cut

revenue farmers since 1610 to be revoked.[1] They also wanted the leases of the farms to be registered in the sovereign courts—which was already current practice—but the verification by the court to precede the actual collection of taxes by the farmer, which was not usual. As suggested by the third estate in 1588, the participation of foreigners in the revenue farms and tax contracts was to be stopped: although Italian financiers were still involved, their influence was less than formerly, partly because of the economic decline of Italy and partly because both Henri IV and Sully favoured native Frenchmen.[2] As in 1588, the third estate wanted to reverse the trend towards the consolidation of leases on the revenue farms. Instead of a general lease for the *gabelles de France*, separate leases were to be negotiated within each locality. The revenue farm known as the *convoy de Bordeaux* was to be abolished, as was the levy of taxes to replace the *sol pour livre* which had been revoked in 1602. The current lease on the *aides* was to be withdrawn because the revenue farmer was allegedly paying only three-quarters of the *rentes*. Since the lease was not revoked, but continued to be held by Antoine Feydeau[3] until 1626, the reduction in the *rentes* had presumably been ordered by the government and not taken on the initiative of the farmer.

The third estate denounced the financiers as leeches (*sangsues*) both on the king and the people. They wanted the abolition of all tax contracts with the exception of those for the repurchase of alienated crown lands and rights, on which great emphasis—and false hopes—were placed. There was to be an investigation of all tax contracts since 1594 despite the fact that Sully's *chambres de justice* had amnestied the years between 1582 and 1607. In addi-

---

from the collection of fines from Henri IV's *chambre de justice*: Hayem, op. cit., pp. 261, 278. B.N. 500 Colbert 221, fos. 166, 170, 224. Concini, her husband, had been a councillor of state after 26 July 1610.

[1] Léonora Galigaï had ensured that the consortium of Pierre de la Sablière obtained the lease on the *cinq grosses fermes* from 1 Oct. 1613, even though the rent was lower than under the previous lease and a rival consortium offered a loan of 300,000 *livres* for six years without interest. In 1616, after the Estates-General, Galigaï allegedly had a remission of 600,000 *livres* accorded to the farmers, and took half for herself: Hayem, op. cit., p. 262. B.N. 500 Colbert 221, fo. 178. There were two remissions of 300,000 *livres* accorded to the consortium of Pierre de la Sablière in 1616: E 52c–53a, fo. 42, 25 June 1616. E 54a, fo. 7, 4 Oct. 1616.

[2] For Henri IV on the decline of Italian influence at Lyon: Carew, 'A relation of the state of France', p. 435. For Sully's preference for native Frenchmen in the farm of the *cinq grosses fermes*: Sully, *Oeconomies royales*, ed. Michaud and Poujoulat, i. 616–17.

[3] The third estate specified Denis Feydeau, his brother, as the farmer; but Antoine had held the lease since 1611: Hayden, op. cit., p. 193 n. 31. E 32a, fo. 294, 30 Aug. 1611.

tion to this investigation, a much broader *chambre de justice*[1] was envisaged, with no terminal date on the enquiry into the past, and no possibility of amnesty through purchase. The fines and restitutions ordered by this commission were to pay for the repurchase of unnecessary offices. To prevent the recurrence of financial abuses in the future, the *chambre de justice* was to be held every five years. Moreover, a much closer watch was to be kept on ministerial profiteering. As in 1588,[2] it was proposed that when entering office ministers, and presumably all royal officials, were to present to the *Chambre des Comptes* a full statement of their assets. Had this proposal been adopted, the later charges of corruption against La Vieuville and Foucquet could have been formally proven or the ministers cleared of the accusations. The procedures of the *Chambre des Comptes* were also to be made more effective, and to prevent collusion, the sons and relatives of *trésoriers de l'Épargne* and other accountants were not to be allowed to hold office in that court. (In fact, it became common in the course of the seventeenth century for financiers and financial officials to buy office in the *Chambre des Comptes*).[3] The system whereby accountants deposited a sum as surety against fraudulent bankruptcy was to be administered locally.

The third estate echoed previous meetings of the Estates-General in requesting a substantial reduction both in royal expenditure and taxation. Secret payments by the *comptants* were to be stopped altogether. The pensions and gifts of the Regency government were denounced as excessive. The third estate wanted awards to be made for services rendered and not in the hope of buying loyalty. Any budgetary surplus should be set aside as a special fund until the end of the accounting year. If no unforeseen emergency arose, up to half the surplus might be used to pay for gifts. However, in the future pensions should be granted sparingly since they entailed a permanent commitment. In the case of gifts, the true names of the beneficiaries and the awards made to them in the previous three years were to be stated in the letters patent. Gifts above 3000 *livres* were to require verification and registration by the *Chambre des Comptes*. This measure would

---

[1] The third estate envisaged the possibility of more than one, its phrase being 'une ou plusieurs chambres de justice'.

[2] For the proposal in 1588–9: Mayer, op. cit., xv. 192.

[3] It was also fairly common for *intendants des finances* to buy the office of *président des Comptes*. Charles Duret de Chevry, Claude Cornuel and Jacques Tubeuf all did so. Cf. Dent, *Crisis in finance*, p. 204.

have prevented Concini and later royal favourites from gaining a monopoly of royal patronage through secret royal payments and gifts to intermediaries. The salaries of officers of the crown and members of the king's council were to be reduced. Louis XIII was asked to revoke all payments and promises made to the rebellious nobles in 1614. A reduction in royal expenditure was considered necessary since it was currently higher than in 1576, when the kingdom was racked by civil war and had to pay for the upkeep of large armies. The logic of the deputies ignored the unpalatable truth that the cost of government had risen enormously in the intervening period with the continuing impact of inflation; moreover the kingdom could scarcely be regarded as settled in view of Condé's rebellion and the fear of further trouble. Nevertheless, the third estate pursued the theme still further, demanding a reduction of taxes to the level of 1576 and arguing that the increase in the intervening period had been intended as a temporary measure for causes which had since passed. The third estate also wanted to reduce the number of offices and thus the amount spent by the crown on salaries. The sale of offices was to be abolished and the *droit annuel* revoked. The right of an office-holder to resign his office as he saw fit was to be curtailed. The third estate included in their proposals a list of offices to be abolished. They were also prepared to contemplate a new capital offence for those who proposed the establishment of new offices or the restoration of offices which had been abolished.[1]

Payment of direct taxes in the provinces was to be facilitated by measures against undue fiscal exemption, including the full implementation of the edict of 1600 on the *taille*, and by other actions intended to reduce the costs of collection and frequency of lawsuits arising from disputed assessments. The deputies suggested that it would assist the payment of taxes if all arrears were remitted and further concessions made by the government on its collection until 1616. Rather than achieve its intended purpose, this idea was likely to encourage popular resistance to the levy of taxes.[2] Stricter accounting procedures were to be enforced in the provinces, and wherever possible payments were to be made locally to reduce the costs of transferring large amounts of coin

---

[1] They would be called 'ennemis et perturbateurs du repos général' and their wealth would be confiscated: in fact, such a definition of the offence would lead to a general witch-hunt against financiers.

[2] For the strength of the myth of *l'impôt remis au peuple* as a factor in revolt: Bercé, *Histoire des croquants*, ii. 611–15. The years of the Fronde were to illustrate the problem.

around the kingdom. There was also to be much stricter administration of the Treasury (*Épargne*) which in the view of the third
estate had become 'le réceptacle de toutes sortes de désordres et
divertissements'. Existing procedures for drawing up loan contracts and assigning revenues were regarded as open to abuse.
After the payment of local *charges*, taxes should be sent to the
Treasury 'sans qu'ils puissent être divertis ou menés ailleurs . . .'
The *cahier* of the third estate was the most far-reaching criticism of
financial administration since the manifestos of the Catholic
League, and greatly exceeded them in the penetration of its
analysis and the detailed proposals for change. It was presented
on 23 February 1615, which in effect marked the end of the
Estates-General. In the short term, the practical impact of the
proposals was small. As Richelieu later commented, it was not
enough to know all the abuses of the system if one lacked the will
to remedy them.[1] In the longer term, however, the *cahier* of the
third estate influenced all moves towards financial reform until
1630.

On 24 March 1615 the members of the Estates-General who had
remained at Paris to hear the royal reply to the *cahiers* were
informed that the crown had decided to abolish the sale of offices
and revoke the *droit annuel*. Pensions were to be cut and a new
chambre de justice established. The rest of the proposals of the
Estates-General would be considered as soon as possible.[2] The
sovereign courts were infuriated. It was one matter to talk about
the abolition of unimportant and unnecessary offices, quite
another to revoke the *droit annuel* and undermine the stability of
office-holding.[3] On 29 April, the *Parlement* of Paris decided to
present remonstrances, but before it could do so, the government
made concessions. On 13 May, it was announced that the *droit
annuel* would remain in force until the end of 1617. The government was nevertheless determined to reduce the number of offices
to the level of 1576.[4] However, by now the *Parlement* was committed to presenting remonstrances, and to have drawn back would
have led to the accusation that it had acted from motives of
self-interest.

---

[1] A. J. du Plessis, Cardinal de Richelieu, *Mémoires*, ed. R. Lavollée *et al.*, 10 vols.
(1907–31), i. 368. Hayden, op. cit., p. 165.

[2] Richelieu, *Mémoires*, i. 367. Mousnier, *La vénalité*, pp. 626–7. Hayden, op. cit., p. 161.

[3] The *Chambre des Comptes* presented remonstrances on 11 May 1615: *Chambre des Comptes*,
ed. Boislisle, pp. 304–5.

[4] Richelieu, *Mémoires*, loc. cit. Mousnier, *La vénalité*, p. 629. Hayden, op. cit., pp. 167–8.

The remonstrances were presented on 22 May 1615, and read like a summary of the *cahier* of the third estate with an equally vigorous attack on royal financial policy.[1] However, the remonstrances went further than the *cahier* by attacking the influence of Concini on the government. The king's council should be reformed, since in recent years it had been packed by 'ceux qui veulent y avoir des créatures' rather than filled with experienced councillors 'qui ont passé par les grandes charges'. Provincial governors were to be chosen from men of known loyalty and should not be foreigners, otherwise their appointment would be tantamount to handing the keys of the kingdom abroad. This remark can only have been directed at one man—Concini, who had been appointed lieutenant-general in Picardy on 9 February 1611, and who was also governor of the fortresses of Amiens, Roye, Montdidier, and Péronne. Lest there should remain any doubt about their hostility to his influence, the *Parlement* requested an investigation of new sects and *gens infâmes* such as anabaptists, Jews, magicians, and poisoners. The bad company kept by Léonora Galigaï, Concini's wife, was to provide considerable evidence at her trial two years later.[2] The *Parlement* denounced the 'avarice insatiable de ceux qui ont . . . la direction et maniement des affaires'. In particular, the excessive increase in royal pensions and gifts was criticized, as was the practice of accepting payments from the revenue farmers in return for influence to secure favourable leases or remissions of rent. There were too many financial administrators and their policy was misguided; in contrast, the achievement of Henri IV and Sully was praised. The speculation in the paper debts of the French monarchy was denounced. So too was abuse of royal gifts, many of which went to members of the court and government 'étant émployés sous noms supposés à personnes inconnues et de nul mérite . . .'[3] Finally the whole conduct of finance under the Regency was criticized in the strongest language: 'sire, la dissipation et profusion qui a été faite en vos finances depuis le décès du feu roi est incroyable'. Whatever the motives of the Parlement, in effect it was playing Condé's

---

[1] Hayden, op. cit., p. 168. Mayer, *Des États Généraux et autres assemblées nationales*, xvii, pt. ii. 138–73. *Recueil général des anciennes lois françaises depuis l'an 420 jusqu'à la Révolution de 1789*, ed. A. J. L. Jourdan, Decrusy and F. A. Isambert, 28 vols. (1821–33), xvi. 64–75. A.A.E. France 770, fo. 20.

[2] Cf. Hayem, *Le maréchal d'Ancre et Léonora Galigaï*, pp. 132–5, 195–6, 243. A Jew had entered her service in 1613.

[3] Of course this was not entirely true. On 11 Sept. 1613, Nicolas Harlay de Sancy had received a gift of 75,000 *livres* for services to Henri IV: B.N. p.o. 1484 (Dr. 33,585), no. 184.

game.[1] By calling for a meeting of the peers of the realm, and insisting on reforms, the *Parlement* was trying to force the hand of the government. On 24 May 1615, the council of state replied with a decree condemning the court's actions, and declaring that since the *Parlement*'s role was purely judicial it was not authorized to intervene in political affairs unless explicitly invited to do so by the sovereign.

No concessions were made on the central issue, the continuing influence of Concini on the government. Indeed, the reliance on him—and the exclusion of Condé—was made explicit in a letter from the king of 31 July 1615 in which Concini was given the task of suppressing the rebellion of the princes.[2] Condé replied with a manifesto issued at Coucy on 9 August which amounted to a far more serious indictment of royal policy than his attempt the previous year. The discussions of the Estates-General were now declared not to have been free and their proposals deliberately ignored. The *Parlement* had been 'gourmandé at indignement traité'. The foreign policy of the government—that is to say the Spanish marriages, which were being negotiated in Guyenne —was said to be shameful and a just cause for apprehension on the part of the Protestants. A thorough-going reform of the king's council was required to eliminate the influence of Concini and his select group of 'evil counsellors',[3] who it was said held the king in virtual captivity. Concini's objectives were condemned as avaricious and contrary to the true interests of France. It was claimed that the government had the intention of drastically increasing taxes,[4] while Concini had received more than six million *livres* in gifts, often through intermediaries to prevent discovery. Henri IV's war fund which had been built up to terrorize his foreign enemies had been used by Concini to oppress the true servants of the king—that is, the rebellious magnates. Detailed aspects of financial policy also received a mention: Jeannin had abandoned Sully's policy of redeeming crown lands, and this was

---

[1] Condé had supporters in the court, such as *président* Le Jay, who was placed under arrest. Luynes was ordered to release Le Jay on 25 Apr. 1616 towards the end of the Loudun negotiations: *Négociations, lettres et pièces relatives à la conférence de Loudun*, ed. Bouchitté, pp. 618–19.

[2] Bouchitté, op. cit., pp. 189–94. Condé's grievances with the government had become apparent in an exchange of letters with the king on 26–27 July 1615: A.A.E. France 770, fo. 46.

[3] Brûlart de Sillery, his son Puysieulx, Bullion, and Dollé were named specifically.

[4] Bouchitté, op. cit., p. 199: 'on a veu en mesme temps recevoir toutes sortes d'advis et inventions pour lever deniers sur le peuple, trente-cinq ou quarante édicts scellés pour cest effect . . .'

severely criticized. Condé's rhetoric against the Spanish marriages and in favour of the religious *status quo* also secured him the Protestant alliance on 27 November 1615. Bouillon, Sully, Rohan, La Trémouille, La Force and other Protestant leaders—though not Lesdiguières—joined the cause, but it is doubtful whether it was in the long term interests of the Protestant movement to do so. Du Plessis-Mornay warned that Condé's negotiations with the court would leave the Protestants with all the blame for the revolt.[1] The rebellion of some of the Protestant leaders was certainly motivated by self-interest. Bouillon wanted confirmation of the independent status of his principality of Sedan, Sully payment of the gift promised him on 26 January 1611 and full powers as governor of Poitou and *grand maître de l'artillerie*.[2]

The government was thus faced with a serious revolt and rapidly escalating costs. It resorted to borrowing to pay for the troops required immediately in the Île-de-France, Champagne, and Picardy.[3] There were reasonable hopes of separating Condé from his makeshift alliance with the Protestants when the negotiations, first for a truce and then for a more permanent settlement, began in January 1616.[4] Yet the longer the negotiations were drawn out, the greater the pressure on the government to agree to Condé's terms in view of the high cost of maintaining troops even during a truce. By April 1616 cash payments on the war effort and the anticipation of future revenues had assumed serious proportions[5] while revenues were falling because the magnates diverted funds in the areas under their control.[6] On 3 May 1616 the government made its peace with the rebels at Loudun, undertaking to increase the annual subsidy to the Protestants initially for three years and to grant 1.5 million *livres* to Condé and his supporters to cover their costs during the rebellion. The *demandes particulières* of the nobles were met, at least in part.[7] Yet the

---

[1] J. A. Clarke, *Huguenot warrior. The life and times of Henri de Rohan, 1579–1638* (The Hague, 1966), p. 56. Du Plessis-Mornay held his fortress of Saumur for the crown and was granted 58,696 *livres* to cover his costs: E 55b, fo. 229, 18 Apr. 1617.

[2] Both were promised what they wanted by the government, although in the event Rohan, not Sully's son, gained the governorship of Poitou: Bouchitté, op. cit., pp. 791, 794, 814. A.A.E. France 770, fo. 132, 5 May 1616.

[3] Appendix Two, Table VIII A.

[4] A.A.E. France 770, fo. 124, 20 Jan. 1616.

[5] Most of the volume E 52b—the decrees of the council of finance in Apr. 1616—is taken up by such business.

[6] E 51, fo. 228, 3 Nov. 1615.

[7] Bouchitté, op. cit., pp. 672–3, 752, 787–829. A.A.E. France 770, fo. 207, 'Estat des comptants à expédier suivant le traitté de paix de Loudun . . .'

concessions of the government did not end here. The most important change was Concini's removal from the post of lieutenant-general in Picardy and governor of Amiens. The Queen Mother and Léonora Galigaï had instructed Villeroy, the chief royal negotiator, to refuse this demand of the princes—but the secretary of state had recognized that such a course of action would wreck the conference. In the end, Concini's position was actually strengthened, since he was appointed lieutenant-general in Normandy, governor of Caen and Pont de l'Arche, and rewarded with 300,000 *livres*. The Queen Mother was governor of Normandy, and thus Concini had no rival to counter his power in the province as he had had with Longueville in Picardy.[1]

What the princes failed to achieve in the allocation of provincial governorships they sought to gain from a reorganization of the king's council and a reshuffle of ministerial posts. The seals were withdrawn from the Chancellor, who had been severely criticized by Condé, and transferred to Guillaume du Vair on 16 May. Three days later, Claude Barbin was made *contrôleur-général des finances*. Jeannin remained in the government, but although he was given the title of *surintendant* he was in fact Barbin's subordinate.[2] On 9 August, Villeroy and Puysieulx were forced out of office, and Puysieulx's secretaryship of state was taken by Claude Mangot.[3] In whose interest did the new regime operate? Guillaume du Vair was too independent to be Condé's man. Moreover, he had been invited to enter office by Léonora Galigaï. The exclusion of Villeroy and Puysieulx also seems to have been the work of this formidable lady, who had been kept informed of the Loudun negotiations by Louis Dollé, an *intendant des finances* and client of Concini. Léonora blamed Villeroy for her husband's loss of Amiens and the lieutenant-generalship of Picardy. The dismissal of the old servant of Henri III and Henri IV was an act of revenge for his concessions at Loudun. The new men, Barbin and Mangot, were clients of the Queen Mother and Léonora Galigaï, not Condé.[4] This was not immediately apparent in the aftermath of

---

[1] Hayem, *Le maréchal d'Ancre et Léonora Galigaï*, pp. 201–2. Bouchitté, op. cit., pp. 461, 480, 556–7, 655, 677.

[2] Appendix One, Table I.

[3] A.A.E. France 770, fo. 155.

[4] Hayem, op. cit., p. 309. B.N. 500 Colbert 221, fos. 408ᵛ–410ʳ. Interrogation of André de Lizza, 10 May 1617. According to Lizza, Galigaï read all the dispatches and took the decision to dismiss Villeroy 'de son propre mouvement'. Barbin had been *intendant-général de la maison de la Reine*, a position held previously by another great financier, Sébastien Zamet. He and his brother Dreux Barbin participated in the consortium holding the lease on the *droit annuel* under the name of Claude Marcel: E 33b, fo. 37, 10 Dec. 1611. According to

the ministerial reshuffle, because Condé attended council meetings assiduously and acted as a *de facto surintendant* while Guillaume du Vair turned from a supporter into a critic of Concini.[1]
This state of affairs could not long survive. Condé was arrested on
1 September, almost certainly on Barbin's advice, allegedly to
protect him from conspirators who wanted to use his name.[2] After
this time, Barbin was 'plus puissant que nul autre dans les affaires
. . .',[3] and his position was reinforced by the 'palace revolution' of
November 1616 in which the seals were transferred to Claude
Mangot and Richelieu was brought into the government to
occupy the secretaryship of state vacated by Villeroy.[4]

The arrest of Condé, who was not released until October 1619,
and the ministerial reshuffle which followed, marked the apogee
of Concini's power and influence. He saw the new team of Barbin,
Mangot, and Richelieu as a group capable of teaching the
'greybeards' a lesson and controlling the upper nobility.[5] In fact
the arrest of Condé had destroyed the last vestiges of Concini's
credibility. A Parisian mob sacked his residence in the rue de
Tournon following the news of the arrest of the first prince of the
blood,[6] and it was clear that Condé's supporters among the
magnates would not rest until the Italian favourite was removed
from power and influence. The duc de Bouillon was the first to
declare his rebellion on 6 January 1617; Nevers followed suit at
the end of the month, and they were joined by Vendôme and
Mayenne. The manifesto of the princes, which was issued at
Soissons on 4 February 1617, accused Concini of usurping the

---

the evidence of Germain Chalange on 28 June 1617, Galigaï had drawn off 'notables
sommes de deniers' during their lease: Hayem, op. cit., p. 261. B.N. 500 Colbert 221, fo.
170.

[1] Sully apparently warned Marie de Médicis of the threat posed by Condé: *Journal de ma
vie. Mémoires du maréchal de Bassompierre*, ed. Audoin de la Cropte, marquis de Chantérac, 4
vols. (1870–7), ii. 78–9. For du Vair as enemy of Concini: A.A.E. France 771, fo. 93ᵛ., n.d.
[1617?]. This was why the princes demanded his return to office in 1617. For Galigaï's
dealings with du Vair before he entered office: Hayem, op. cit., p. 270. B.N. 500 Colbert
221, fo. 202. Interrogation of Vincent Ludovici, 11 May 1617.

[2] *Chambre des Comptes*, ed. Boislisle, p. 313.

[3] Arnauld d'Andilly, *Mémoires*, ed. Michaud and Poujoulat, p. 426.

[4] B.L. Harleian 4472b, fo. 297, 25 Nov. 1616. P 2349, p. 133, 25 Nov. 1616. A.A.E.
France 771, fo. 168, 30 Nov. 1616. There was talk at the time of the 'palace revolution' of
making Barbin *surintendant*, and bringing in another great financier, Antoine Feydeau, as
controller-general, but the talk came to nothing: E. Griselle, *Louis XIII et Richelieu. Lettres et
pièces diplomatiques* (1911, repr. Geneva, 1974), p. 152.

[5] Richelieu, *Mémoires*, ii. 229. A.A.E. France 771, fo. 93ᵛ.

[6] Concini was accorded 450,000 *livres* in compensation by the crown: cf. E 55c–56a, fo.
348, 11 Aug. 1617.

administration of the kingdom and making himself master of the royal finances and patronage. The arrest of Condé was viewed as an abrogation of the peace of Loudun, while Concini's motives were seen as the desire to 'épuiser [les] finances par ses profusion[s et] suffoquer [le] peuple des charges excessives . . .'[1] Concini went to Normandy to organize resistance to the rebellion. Before leaving the capital he told Louis XIII that he would raise 6000 infantry and 800 cavalry and keep them in the field for four months at his expense. On 13 March 1617, he informed the king that he had levied the troops 'en vertu de vos commissions'. Over half the infantry and a quarter of the cavalry were foreign, recruited in Liège. The levy of foreign troops without royal permission later figured prominently among the charges against Concini, as did the accusation that they were raised 'pour la seureté de sa personne' and paid for at the expense of the crown and the French taxpayer.[2] Clearly either the king had not been consulted as Concini claimed, or else he later covered up his complicity in the resistance to the princes. In an attempt to hold the situation, the government began borrowing once more,[3] while Concini advanced considerable sums to protect his own regime, particularly through financiers such as Antoine Feydeau. He also borrowed from financiers to re-lend to the crown. Louis XIII later stated that Concini had 'vollé mes finances' and drawn off for his private use between 12 and 15 million *livres* since 1610. At the time of Concini's death promises from Antoine Feydeau, Nicolas Camus, and other financiers totalling 1,928,000 *livres* were found in the pockets of his breeches. All this was powerful evidence that Concini had controlled the process of royal borrowing in his own interest.[4]

---

[1] A.A.E. France 771, fos. 1, 4, 26–9, 6 Jan., 30 Jan., 4 Feb. 1617.

[2] Hayem, op. cit., pp. 206, 231. B.N. 500 Colbert 221, fo. 23ᵛ. Marillac's account of the years 1617–20: B.N. MS. fr. 17487, fos. 6ᵛ–7ʳ.

[3] Appendix Two, Table VIII A.

[4] Louis XIII cited the figure 1,973,000 *livres*: B.N. MS. fr. 17487, fo. 7. The lower figure comes from the inventory of Concini's papers by Gilles Maupeou and Isaac Arnauld on 26 Apr. 1617: Hayem, op. cit., pp. 235–6. P 2349, p. 441. The accusation at the trial was that Concini and his wife had 'usurpé un pouvoir si absolu et disposoient à leur volonté des finances du Roy, se faisant passer des obligations par les trésoriers et autres officiers de la guerre comme pour argent par eux presté, feignant mesme de faire prester au roi sommes excessives d'argent, sous noms supposés, dont ils tireroient déclarations et usures excessives à leur profit, et s'en faisoient paier à l'Espargne, prenant en plaine Espargne telles sommes d'argent qu'ils vouloient sans autre commandement du Roy, et ne baillant pour descharges que leurs promesses particulières': Hayem, op. cit., p. 234. B.N. 500 Colbert 221, fo. 26. Antoine Feydeau owed Concini 840,020 *livres*. Concini had borrowed from Feydeau and at least nine other individuals, including Beaumarchais, the *trésorier de*

If finance alone could have secured his survival, Concini might well have lasted out: but he had failed to take into account the attitude of the fifteen-year-old king, who was now firmly under the influence of a rising star, Charles d'Albert, seigneur de Luynes, first gentleman in the king's household, governor of Amboise and captain of the Tuileries.[1] Luynes was a protégé of Concini and a beneficiary of his patronage,[2] but he was ambitious and doubted the wisdom of confronting the nobles. Concini's difficulties offered Luynes a great tactical advantage which he was quick to exploit.

The conspiracy[3] was master-minded by Guichard Déageant, the secretary of the Queen Mother, who was rewarded for his part with the post of *intendant des finances*,[4] and put into effect by Nicholas de l'Hôpital, marquis de Vitry, the captain of the king's bodyguard, who was rewarded with the *baton* of *maréchal de France* and 200,000 *livres*. The king was a willing participant in the plot, hoping by this means to free himself from the influence of his mother. He may have been influenced by appeals to the good government of Henri IV and other propaganda against Concini;[5] he may genuinely have resented being forced to arrest Condé and declare his supporters guilty of rebellion. (One of the first acts of the new regime was to amnesty the rebels and place all the blame for the civil disturbance on Concini.)[6] Fear may well have

---

l'Épargne, and Duret de Chevry and Castille, two of the *intendants des finances*. The sums involved were respectively 223,717 *livres*, 18,000, 24,000 and 30,000 *livres*: E 55c/56a, fo. 203, 18 July 1617.

[1] For his commands: E 52b, fo. 131, 12 Apr. 1616. There had been talk at Loudun of making him lieutenant-general in Picardy and governor of Amiens: Bouchitté, op. cit., pp. 446–7.

[2] Concini brought him into the king's household in 1611: Hayem, op. cit., p. 148. On 10 June 1616, the *Chambre des Comptes* registered half the value of a royal gift of 100,000 *livres* to Luynes: *Chambre des Comptes*, ed. Boislisle, p. 312. The appointment as governor of Amboise on 1 Mar. 1615 was undoubtedly due to Concini's patronage. He bought the office of *grand fauconnier* for 135,000 *livres* in Oct. 1616, presumably largely from the proceeds of the royal gift: *Journal inédit d'Arnauld d'Andilly*, ed. Halphen, pp. 59, 222.

[3] M. de Marillac, *Relation exacte de tout ce qui s'est passé à la mort du mareschal d'Ancre*, ed. J. F. Michaud and J. J. F. Poujoulat, 2nd. ser., v (1837), pp. 447–84. L. Batiffol, 'Le coup d'état du 24 avril 1617', *Revue Historique*, xcv (1907), 292–308; xcvii (1908), 27–77, 264–86.

[4] Political influence in appointment to the office of intendant of finance seems to have been much greater before 1620 than after. Léonora Galigaï had obtained the office for Charles Duret de Chevry in 1615: Hayem, op. cit., p. 309. B.N. 500 Colbert 221, fo. 408ᵛ. Interrogation of André de Lizza, 10 May 1617.

[5] B.N. 500 Colbert 485, fo. 107. Anon. memorandum 'sur les misères de l'estat'. At the top of the document it states 'le Roy veut cette remontrance peu de jours auparavant la mort du Maral. d'Ancre'. There is some evidence of local propaganda against Concini shortly before his fall: Major, *Representative government in early modern France*, pp. 420–1.

[6] *Recueil . . . des lois*, ed. Jourdan et al., xvi. 103–5. P 2349, p. 587, May 1617.

strengthened the resolve of the conspirators. Louis XIII later claimed that Concini had planned a purge of the king's household, his councillors of state, and the *Parlement* of Paris: sixty or eighty names were on the list, and doubtless Luynes was one of them. Concini's arrest was required by 'la nécessité de mon estat et de ma personne'. Concini was to have been arrested and placed on trial by the *Parlement*, according to the official version of events. In this account, the *coup d'état* of 24 April 1617 misfired, because Concini resisted arrest and was killed by Vitry's guards. It is possible that the king and Luynes intended his murder from the outset, however. If so, they had nothing to fear. Concini was so detested by the *Parlement* that it praised the 'coup de [sa] mort',[1] and set about prosecuting Léonora Galigaï with vigour and perhaps even relish.

The trial of Léonora Galigaï, Claude Barbin, and their supporters on a charge of treason amounted also to the posthumous trial of Concini's regime. Apart from allegations of peculation and levying troops without royal permission, Concini was accused of establishing a clientage system at the expense of loyal servants of the crown and making himself master of Picardy and Normandy and the fortresses in those provinces. Concini and his wife were viewed as foreign adventurers who had held the king and his subjects to ransom since the death of Henri IV. They had come to France 'destituez de tous moiens'. They could not have acquired their great wealth—estimated by Bassompierre at 7.3 million *livres*, but perhaps as high as 8.4 million[2] except by 'des voyes extraordinaires et illicites' which had led to an increase in taxation. What must have particularly infuriated the judges was that some of this wealth—at least 675,000 *livres* and perhaps as much as 1.5 million[3]—had been transferred abroad and placed in state loans (*monte*) at Florence and Rome. Léonora Galigaï denied exercising a malevolent influence on Marie de Médicis through the arts of witchcraft. Nor had she interfered in the financial

---

[1] Louis XIII's grievances against Concini are in B.N. MS. fr. 17487 fos. 5ᵛ–8ʳ. (the praise for the *coup* is at fo. 5ʳ) and in the letters patent instructing the *Parlement* to prosecute Léonora Galigaï: Hayem, op. cit., pp. 220–1. B.N. 500 Colbert 221, fos. 383–4, 9 May 1617, registered in the *Parlement* on 12 May.

[2] Bassompierre had obtained his information from Concini himself: *Journal de ma vie . . .*, ed. Chantérac, ii. 109. The higher estimate is given by R. de Crèvecoeur, *Un document nouveau sur la succession des Concini* (1891), p. 20.

[3] Bassompierre gave the higher figure. The lower figure was given in testimony by Jean-André Lumagne, who had sent the sums abroad over a four year period: Hayem, op. cit., p. 237. B.N. 500 Colbert 221, fo. 36, 26 Apr. 1617.

process: 'elle ne se mesloit point de faire affaires'.[1] What she could not deny, however, was the enormous patronage she and her husband had enjoyed from the Queen Mother. This was proof enough. The result of the trial was a foregone conclusion.[2] On 8 August 1617, Concini and his wife were found guilty of *lèse-majesté*. Because of the experience of seven years of Concini's influence, it was declared that henceforth foreigners were to be prohibited from holding offices and governorships in France.[3] If the sentence on the husband was posthumous, that against the wife could be carried out the same day. Their wealth was confiscated to the crown: in fact Louis XIII granted it out to Luynes almost immediately, ostensibly as reimbursement for loans to the crown.[4] The trial of Claude Barbin was later transferred from the *Parlement* to the *grand conseil*, which Luynes tried to pressure into passing a severe verdict. However, Marie de Médicis intervened on Barbin's behalf and the Chancellor, Keeper of the Seals and Jeannin were opposed to the new favourite's vindictive approach. On 4 September 1618, Barbin was found guilty of treason and his wealth was confiscated to the crown. Instead of execution—the fate of Léonora Galigaï—Barbin's sentence was the lighter one of permanent exile abroad.[5]

2. LUYNES AND THE CATHOLIC CAUSE

Concini's precarious regime of 1616–17 had been destroyed by a royal *coup d'état*. Political trials followed and Richelieu was dismissed from office and exiled to his diocese at Luçon and later to Avignon. The Queen Mother was placed under house arrest at Blois. There was talk of shutting her up in Luynes's castle at

[1] Hayem, op. cit., p. 275. B.N. 500 Colbert 221, fo. 214, 24 May 1617.

[2] A good illustration of this point is that on 2 May 1617 Vitry was promised payment of 200,000 *livres* from the confiscation of Léonora Galigaï's wealth (in fact a payment extorted by her from Jean-André Lumagne). Yet the confiscation of her wealth did not take place until 8 Aug.: Crèvecoeur, op. cit., pp. 25, 61. The sum was mentioned in Lumagne's testimony on 26 Apr. 1617: B.N. 500 Colbert 221, fo. 35ᵛ.

[3] 'Dignités, charges et gouvernements' (Richelieu, *Mémoires*, ii. 218) was interpreted by some during the Fronde as meaning Mazarin's position as chief minister and governor of the Auvergne. The decree was read out by Viole in the *Parlement* of Paris on 22 Sept. 1648: Ormesson, *Journal*, ed. Chéruel, i. 578.

[4] Mongrédien regards this as the most important evidence demonstrating that the trial was a parody of justice: Mongrédien, *Léonora Galigaï) Un procès de sorcellerie sous Louis XIII*, p. 204. For the donation: Crèvecoeur, op. cit., p. 16. P 2349, p. 435, Aug. 1617.

[5] Richelieu, *Mémoires*, ii. 298, 301–4. Bassompierre, *Journal de ma vie* . . ., ed. Chantérac, ii. 127. V5 313 and U 785, fos. 176–7, 4 Sept. 1618. Barbin was obliged to sell his office of *intendant-général de la maison de la reine* for 75,000 *livres*: A.A.E. France 775, fo. 123, 8 June 1623. Despite the decree of the *grand conseil*, Barbin was still being held at the Bastille at the time of Condé's release in October 1619.

Amboise, and pressure was applied—which was ultimately successful in 1619—for her to exchange her governorship of Normandy for the less important province of Anjou.[1] The great beneficiary of the *coup d'état* was of course Luynes himself, who reaped the rewards of bold counsel to the young king. Four days after the *coup*, he took the oath as first gentleman of the king's chamber.[2] The provincial governorships were rearranged to the satisfaction of the new favourite. At first, Luynes became lieutenant-general of Normandy in Concini's place; later, in 1618, he obtained the appointment of Mayenne as governor of Guyenne to free the Île-de-France for himself; finally, on 6 August 1619 he became governor of Picardy.[3] Thus when the aggrieved Queen Mother listed the governorships and fortresses held by Luynes and his relatives and clients[4] the list was much more impressive than Concini's: in addition to Amboise, he had gained Amiens, Calais, La Fère, Soissons, Coucy, Chauny, Noyon and Concarneau; the last named fortress had cost 1.6 million *livres* and had been paid for with the king's money.[5] Yet more royal favours were to follow. In 1619 Luynes was raised to the status of duke and peer, and two years later appointed—apparently now by a rather reluctant king—both Constable of France and Keeper of the Seals.[6]

The ascendancy of Luynes was so all-encompassing that the

---

[1] Richelieu, *Mémoires*, ii. 309. The plan to move her to Amboise or Nantes was one of the justifications for her rebellion in 1619.

[2] Marillac, *Relation exacte*, ed. Michaud and Poujoulat, p. 469.

[3] Regrettably Harding's list of governors is inaccurate, failing to list either Mayenne or Luynes as governor of the Île-de-France, and giving different dates for the appointment of Longueville to Normandy, Luynes to Picardy, and Montbazon to the Île-de-France when one change was consequent upon another, and they all took the oath of allegiance on the same day: *Journal inédit d'Arnauld d'Andilly*, ed. Halphen, pp. 374, 440. Cf. Harding, *Anatomy of a power elite*, p. 224 no. 70, p. 226 nos. 111, 112, 124. The date of appointment given for Montbazon is clearly wrong: cf. B.N. MS. fr. 18147, fo. 182 and B.N. MS fr. 18148, fo. 186, 7 Aug. 1619 (instead of 9 Nov. 1620 as stated by Harding).

[4] B.N. MS. fr. 17487, fos. 21ʳ.–ᵛ., n.d. [1619]. At the time of writing, in February or March 1619, Luynes's control was less complete since Longueville was still governor of Picardy and the favourite had designs on, but had not acquired, Concarneau. Montbazon, who later gained Soissons, Noyon, Chauny, and Coucy, was Luynes's father-in-law.

[5] Richelieu, *Mémoires*, ii. 351–2. *Journal inédit d'Arnauld d'Andilly*, ed. Halphen, pp. 439, 441 (where the figure given is 1.6 million *écus*, which appears an error). For Calais: cf. E 66b, fo. 181, 24 Mar. 1621.

[6] Luynes's letters patent as duke and peer were registered on 30 Aug. 1619 and he took the oath on 14 Nov.: *Journal inédit d'Arnauld d'Andilly*, ed. Halphen, pp. 445, 454. He was appointed Constable on 31 Mar. 1621. Guillaume du Vair died on 3 Aug. 1621, and Luynes filled the post of Keeper of the Seals until his death on 15 Dec. 1621: B. Zeller, *Le connétable de Luynes. Montauban et la Valteline* (1879), pp. 43, 46, 94, 300–1. Lublinskaya, *French absolutism*, pp. 179–80, 190–1.

aristocratic rebellions of 1619–20 against his position are scarcely surprising. The remarkable fact is that rebellion was so long delayed, given the treatment of the Queen Mother and the imprisonment of Condé until October 1619.[1] Three factors worked to Luynes's advantage. Unlike Concini, he was a Frenchman: if the king had to have a favourite then, as that arch-conspirator the duc de Bouillon commented, perhaps Luynes was the most acceptable candidate for this position.[2] Secondly, the *coup d'état*, and the political trials which followed, had thrown his rivals into disarray. When the Queen Mother attempted her political comeback in 1619, it was with the assistance of the duc d'Épernon. She claimed that Luynes had deliberately alienated a favoured councillor of Henri IV with whom she had thrown in her lot. Louis XIII pointed out that Henri IV had not favoured d'Épernon at all; nor for that matter had Marie de Médicis when Regent; his disgrace in 1618 was due to his notorious temper and a blistering argument in council with the Keeper of the Seals.[3] The fact that the Queen Mother had to rely on Henri III's *mignon* in 1619 was a sign of weakness. Her second revolt the following year received more substantial support among the upper nobility, but by this time Luynes and Condé had been reconciled and the first prince of the blood led the royal army against the rebels.[4] The third factor working in Luynes's favour was the commitment to Henri IV's style and maxims of government. This was quite deliberate: the old guard of Brûlart de Sillery as Chancellor, Guillaume du Vair as Keeper of the Seals, Villeroy and Puysieulx as secretaries of state, Jeannin as finance minister and Maupeou as controller-general were reinstated after the *coup d'état*.[5] As Luynes manoeuvred to ensure complete political ascendancy, the government proclaimed reforming intentions which did much to forestall rebellion. In answer to the Queen

---

[1] V. Cousin, 'Le duc et connétable de Luynes', *Journal des Savants* (1861), pp. 355–6. Luynes visited Condé at the château de Vincennes on 4 Mar. 1619; Louis XIII returned Condé's sword on 8 Apr. 1619, both events during the Queen Mother's first rebellion: *Journal inédit d'Arnauld d'Andilly*, ed. Halphen, pp. 409, 416.

[2] Ibid., p. 406.

[3] Ibid., pp. 363–6, 372. B.N. MS. fr. 17487, fos. 38, 41, 23 Feb. and 12 Mar. 1619. D'Épernon's disgrace and the background to the revolt the following year emerge clearly from Girard, *Histoire de la vie du duc d'Espernon*, pp. 292–321. The small amount of support from the other nobles is emphasized ibid., pp. 334–5.

[4] Condé was reimbursed 200,000 *livres* by the crown to cover his costs: *Chambre des Comptes*, ed. Boislisle, p. 339. Condé's role in the war was stressed by d'Épernon's biographer: Girard, op. cit., p. 351.

[5] *Journal inédit d'Arnauld d'Andilly*, ed. Halphen, p. 295. A.A.E. France 771, fos. 101, 103, 26 and 31 Apr. 1617. Appendix One, Tables I, II.

Mother's criticisms in 1619, Louis XIII replied complacently that the country was well governed and that he himself was in charge of policy.[1]

At the end of April 1617, Jeannin's position was restored as the undisputed head of the financial system and he was able to operate in a more stable political situation. There is little doubt that the financial situation had deteriorated still further since the time of the Estates-General when a deficit of three million *livres* had been admitted publicly.[2] The rebellions of 1614–17 had cost approximately 31 million, and more than consumed the war fund build up by Henri IV and Sully, while expenditure had exceeded 34 million per annum in 1616 and 1617[3]—more than the figure in 1610 when Henri IV was mobilizing to intervene in the Cleves–Jülich succession crisis. Concini and Barbin had anticipated the revenues of 1617 by two million and those of 1618–20 by nearly as much. In Jeannin's view, the time had come to cut government expenditure by reducing pensions to the nobles and expenditure on the troops and garrisons. Taken together, these three items exceeded by six million the amount spent in the peace years of Henri IV's reign. Jeannin wanted an assembly of notables to meet and advise on how best to make these cuts in expenditure to avoid recourse to new levies (*affaires extraordinaires*). For their part, Louis XIII and Luynes saw the advantages of such a tame assembly, which would ratify the political arrangements since the assassination of Concini and demonstrate their reforming intentions and concern to implement the decisions of the previous Estates-General. Unlike Jeannin, they probably thought that new levies by means of the *affaires extraordinaires* were inevitable and would be suggested by the notables.[4]

The assembly, which met at Rouen from 4 to 28 December 1617, comprised 49 delegates appointed by the crown, with a

[1] B.N. MS. fr. 17487, fos. 41ʳ, 42ᵛ., 12 Mar. 1619.

[2] The financial difficulties of the crown had been admitted publicly on at least two occasions, 10 Jan. 1615 and 12 Dec. 1616: *Journal inédit d'Arnauld d'Andilly*, ed. Halphen, pp. 31, 246.

[3] *Les négociations du président Jeannin*, ed. Michaud and Poujoulat, pp. 685–6. A.A.E. France 772, fos. 73ᵛ, 288, 12 Mar. 1619 and n.d., *c.* 1617. Appendix Two, Table I.

[4] If this was not their attitude, the view of the nobles that the assembly was convoked 'principalement . . . pour tirer des impositions et levées de deniers . . .' is incomprehensible: *Journal inédit d'Arnauld d'Andilly*, ed. Halphen, p. 328. In the most recent account of the summoning of the notables, Luynes is considered 'hardly experienced enough to have planned so complex a meeting and must have acted upon the advice of Villeroy and his colleagues': Major, *Representative government in early modern France*, p. 411 n. 36. However, Fontenay-Mareuil attributed the initiative to Luynes, and Major himself admits (p. 410) that Villeroy 'left no memorandums advising Luynes what to do . . .'

specific mandate to advise on which proposals of the Estates-General should be enacted by royal legislation.[1] The deliberations were guided by proposals drawn up by the government which summarized the relevant articles of the three *cahiers* of 1615 on certain areas of policy. The assembly agreed to Jeannin's proposals to reduce expenditure by limiting the size of the king's household, and cutting the payments on troops and garrisons, for example by demolishing unnecessary fortresses within the kingdom. It agreed that a limit of 3 millipn *livres* per annum should be set for the royal pensions which would be distributed at the end of the year when it was clear whether the financial position of the crown permitted such largesse. The notables wanted the abolition of the two offices of *trésorier des pensions*, which had been established by edict of 24 November 1614 and had been a key factor in Concini's control of royal patronage.[2] They recommended that the crown revoke all previous gifts to private individuals and establish a new limit of 150,000 *livres* per annum for such payments, the details of which should be made public and not kept secret by using the *comptants*. Gifts made to the same individual in the last three years should be recorded in the letters patent, thus informing the *Chambre des Comptes* of disproportionately large payments to those enjoying royal favour. All this was as expected: in June 1617, the government itself had made some preliminary reforms in the area of the royal gifts.[3] The notables agreed to a proposal restricting the number of fiscal exemptions, particularly by revoking all letters of ennoblement 'falsely acquired' in the last thirty years.[4] The sale of offices in the king's household, in the army, and the sale of governorships of fortresses were to be abolished. The right of *survivance* to an office was also to be ended. It was recommended that the number of offices be reduced to the level of 1579.

[1] Mayer, *Des États Généraux et autres assemblées nationales*, xviii. 3–4. The figures for membership vary somewhat. Mousnier gives the figure of 27 office-holders, a clear majority; Mayer's figure was 25. Cf. Mousnier, *La vénalité*, p. 631. Arnauld d'Andilly records a vote of 34 to 17 in the debate of 23 Dec. 1617, which provides a total of 51 delegates: *Journal inédit d'Arnauld d'Andilly*, ed. Halphen, p. 339.

[2] Originally three offices had been established: B.N. MS. fr. 16627, fo. 98. Only two officials were reimbursed, however, Antoine Feydeau and Noel Hureau, who were paid 60,000 *livres*: E 59b, fo. 4, 5 Sept. 1618. Antoine Feydeau was already a great financier and a client of Concini when he acquired the office: P. Heumann, 'Un traitant sous Louis XIII: Antoine Feydeau', *Études sur l'histoire administrative et sociale de l'ancien régime*, ed. G. Pagès (1938), pp. 186–7.

[3] A.A.E. France 771, fo. 144, 21 June 1617.

[4] The phrase 'sous fausses causes' [Mayer, op. cit., xviii. 79] obviously posed great difficulty of interpretation.

It is by no means evident that the notables wanted to see the complete abolition of the sale of offices, however. Office-holders comprised just over half the assembly at Rouen, and what they wanted was to make their offices more, not less, important politically and to increase the value of their investment.[1] The crucial difficulty facing the government was the promise, made on 13 May 1615, that the *droit annuel* would cease at the end of 1617. The assembly was asked to propose an alternative source of revenue to the *droit annuel*, 'qui est un des principaux fonds . . . le plus prompt et le plus assuré . . .'[2] The notables refused to accept responsibility for this question: if this source of revenue was abolished, the king's council must decided on alternative measures without imposing additional taxes on the populace. By refusing to suggest a new source of revenue, the notables made it virtually impossible in the long term for the government to abolish the sale of offices or to reimburse the current holders of offices. The argument used by some of the notables in opposing the abolition of the *droit annuel* was that it had been established for thirteen years and had thus gained the status of a prescriptive law.[3] Apparently the king was infuriated by this argument: the suspension of the *droit annuel* from 15 January 1618 until 31 July 1620 probably owes more to the simple assertion of Louis XIII's authority over his office-holders than any coherent political or financial policy.[4]

Whatever the motives of the government, the aftermath of the assembly of notables at Rouen was little short of a disaster. The *droit annuel* provided a crucial proportion of the total yield of the *parties casuelles*: this in turn brought in to the crown an average of

---

[1] Mousnier, *La vénalité*, p. 634.

[2] Mayer, op. cit., xviii. 111. The decisions of the assembly are reprinted *in toto*, ibid. xviii. 53–113. The *Chambre des Comptes* argued that the *droit annuel* produced on average 1.2 or 1.5 million *livres* 'en la saison de l'année vous recevrez le moins et estés obligé à dépendre le plus . . .': *Chambre des Comptes*, ed. Boislisle, p. 321.

[3] *Journal inédit d'Arnauld d'Andilly*, ed. Halphen, p. 339: 'le Roy trouva fort mauvais . . . que la paulette estant establie il y a plus de dix ans, il y a prescription'. This comment was recorded on 23 Dec. 1617. On 2 Jan. 1618 the remonstrances of the *Chambre des Comptes* argued a strong case for the *droit annuel* in general and for its being a prescriptive law in particular: *Chambre des Comptes*, ed. Boislisle, pp. 320–1.

[4] Marie de Médicis, in her manifesto of rebellion in 1619, claimed that the assembly of notables had been called simply to 'rompre . . . la paulette' and that what Luynes wanted was to re-establish the noble clientage network among royal office-holders which had been broken by the establishment of the *droit annuel* in 1604: B.N. MS. fr. 17487, fos. 19ᵛ.–20ʳ., n.d. [1619]. This interpretation of both Henri IV's and Luynes's motives is questionable. Mousnier suggests that the suspension of the *droit annuel* led some office-holders to support the aristocratic rebellions of 1619–20: *La vénalité*, p. 636. According to this view, Luynes's action would have misfired. The evidence for the participation of office-holders appears slight, however.

over 5 million *livres* per annum between 1615 and 1619, equivalent
to 16 per cent of total revenues and 20.7 per cent of ordinary
income. However, the annual figure for the *parties casuelles* fluctuated greatly. In 1616, 10.7 million *livres* were raised from this
source, but the figure was lower the following year and with the
suspension of the *droit annuel* the yield became derisory (2.6 million
in 1618; 3.8 million in 1619).[1] By dispensing with this important
source of revenue, the government was gambling on continuing
peace at home and abroad. Jeannin was lucky in 1618, when he
was able to reduce royal expenditure from 34 to under 28 million
livres. However, to his consternation,[2] all hopes of strict economy
were dashed the following year with the revolt of the Queen
Mother. Immediately the government began borrowing once
more and anticipated some of the revenues of 1620.[3] Total royal
expenditure jumped from less than 28 million to 40 million; the
secret expenses nearly doubled from 3.8 million to 6.1 million.
The government was forced to seek additional funds from new
fiscal edicts registered at the *Parlement* of Paris, *Chambre des Comptes*
and other courts. This set the pattern for the following years.[4] It
was doubtless the collapse of his policy of retrenchment, combined with disenchantment at the conduct of the Queen Mother,
his patron, which led to the resignation of Jeannin in September
1619.[5] It is true that he was an octogenarian, and pleaded ill-
health: but his policy was in ruins.

It was ironic that the revolt which had these important financial consequences was an abortive affair. It began with a twenty–
day forced march by the duc d'Épernon from Metz to his governorship of the Limousin, Angoumois, Saintonge, and Aunis without royal permission, a heroic exploit given the small force at his
disposal. It was followed up by the escape of the Queen Mother
from house arrest at Blois on 22 February, an event later immor-
talized on canvas by Rubens, and her establishment at

---

[1] Mousnier, op. cit., pp. 635–6. Appendix Two, Table IV.

[2] *Les négociations du président Jeannin*, ed. Michaud and Poujoulat, pp. 686–7. A.A.E.
France 772, fo. 77, 17 Mar. 1619.

[3] Appendix Two, Table VIII A. Thomas Morant, *trésorier de l'Épargne* in 1619, advanced
415, 637 *livres* on the following year: A.A.E. France 773, fo. 191 and E 62c, fo. 104, 20 Dec.
1619.

[4] For the *Parlement*: A.A.E. France 772, fo. 73ᵛ., 12 Mar. 1619. For the registration of
fiscal edicts at the *Chambre des Comptes* on 30 Apr. 1619, 24 Feb. 1620, 5 April 1621, 4 May
1621 and 19 March 1622: *Chambre des Comptes*, ed. Boislisle, pp. 325, 332, 337–85, 341,
346–8.

[5] He was nevertheless rewarded with a pension of 26,000 *livres* per annum for life: O1 9,
fo. 127ᵛ.–128ʳ., n.d. [1619].

Angoulême, d'Épernon's *place de sureté*.[1] The rebels were desperately short of support among the upper nobility, lacked funds—d'Épernon tried to secure loans to finance the rebellion[2]—and battle-hardened troops. Due to the vigorous counter-measures taken by Mayenne, the governor of Guyenne, and Schomberg, the lieutenant-general in the Limousin, the rebels would almost certainly have met with military disaster but for the early negotiations and the patching up of a temporary peace on 12 May.[3] The propaganda was rather more important than the rebellion: by denouncing Luynes's control of the provincial governorships and important fortresses, and his dissipation of the king's finances, the Queen Mother effectively turned the tables on him, renewing past criticism of Concini against the new favourite. Marie de Médicis claimed that Luynes and his entourage participated in the tax contracts and took pensions and gifts from the revenue farmers. She denounced Jeannin's policy of reselling offices which Henri IV had repurchased, estimating that 6 million *livres* had been wasted in the process.[4] The 'tyrannies et vexations' committed by the guards whose task was to enforce the salt tax were also condemned.[5]

The specific criticisms levelled by the Queen Mother against royal financial policy are somewhat difficult to prove. It would seem that her comments on the guards of the salt tax (*gardes des gabelles*) reflect a general tightening up of the administration of the revenue farms in the second half of Jeannin's ministry. According to Mallet's figures, the revenue farms brought to the Treasury on average only 19.1 per cent of total revenues in the last years of Sully's ministry between 1605 and 1609; this proportion rose to an average of 22.1 per cent between 1610 and 1614, and in the second

[1] *Journal inédit d'Arnauld d'Andilly*, ed. Halphen, pp. 397, 402, 407.

[2] E 61b, fo. 143, 21 Mar. 1619. The rebels tried to seize the king's tax coffers in the *élections* of Niort, St-Jean d'Angély and Poitiers: E 61c, fo. 45, 2 May 1619. The dramatic financial consequences of the rebellion are explained not so much by the seriousness of the revolt itself as the government's determination to secure overwhelming military superiority.

[3] Preliminary treaty of Angoulême, 30 Apr. 1619 in J. Dumont, baron de Cakels-Croon, *Corps universel diplomatique du droit des gens* ..., 8 vols. (Amsterdam, 1726–31), v. 332. Peace of St-Germain-en-Laye, 12 May 1619: A.A.E. France 772, fo. 89. The respective roles of the participants were reversed from the revolt of 1617, when Mayenne had rebelled against Concini while d'Épernon had opposed the movement in the Limousin, Angoumois, Saintonge, and Aunis and been accorded 220,173 *livres* to cover his costs: E 55c/56a, fo. 168, 15 July 1617. Mayenne was not governor of Guyenne at the time of the earlier revolt, however.

[4] The *revente des greffes* had occurred before 27 Nov. 1617: *Chambre des Comptes*, ed. Boislisle, p. 317.

[5] B.N. MS. fr. 17487, fos. 18ᵛ., 20ʳ.–ᵛ., n.d. [1619].

half of Jeannin's ministry between 1615 and 1619 it reached an average of 26 per cent. The revenue farms represented a considerably higher proportion of ordinary income—on average 29.3 per cent per annum in the years 1605–9, 32.1 per cent in the years 1610–14 and 33.7 per cent in the years 1615–19—and second only to the yield of the *taille* from the *pays d'élections*.[1] These high proportions whether of ordinary or total royal income were never reached again before 1661, due to the economic dislocation caused by the civil war of the 1620s and the impact of increased direct taxes in the following decades. On the other hand, the Queen Mother's argument that after the assembly of notables in 1617 so many new taxes had been established that the populace was 'du tout accablé' seems to have been false—at least at the time the charge was levelled in February 1619. According to Mallet's figures, Jeannin was more sparing in his recourse to *affaires extraordinaires* in the second half of his ministry than in the first, and in both periods his reliance on such measures was less than in the last years of Sully's ministry. The *deniers extraordinaires* comprised an average of 34.8 per cent of total revenues between 1605 and 1609, 31.2 per cent in the years 1610–14, but only 22.9 per cent in the years 1615–19. However, in 1619, 11.9 million *livres* were raised from this source, which was the highest figure since 1610, the year of mobilization for the Cleves–Jülich crisis.[2]

If Jeannin's financial record was better than some contemporaries allowed, his ministry was nevertheless characterized by weakness: weakness towards the nobles which had led to an unparalleled increase in royal gifts and pensions; weakness towards the financiers, with no check on their profiteering by a *chambre de justice* and many of the new tax contracts carrying high rates of interest; finally, it was marked by weakness towards the *intendants des finances*, whose number had been increased to four, who were often clients of the royal favourite and who had appropriated an excessive amount of power over financial administration.[3] Jeannin was an honest man, an experienced and perhaps

---

[1] The preponderance of the *taille* from the *pays d'élections* was reduced as the yield from the revenue farms increased. From an average of 48.3 per cent of ordinary income in 1605–9, the *taille* fell to 45.7 per cent in 1610–14 and 38.2 per cent in 1615–19: Appendix Two, Table V.

[2] Appendix Two, Table IV.

[3] General criticisms of his policy in B.N. MS. fr. 16626, fos. 152ᵛ–153ᵛ. The growing power of the *intendants des finances* was implicitly recognized by the ruling of 5 Aug. 1619 which distributed the tasks between them and envisaged a change of responsibility every three years to give them experience on all financial questions: Mousnier, 'Les règlements du conseil du roi sous Louis XIII', 156–8.

even a great statesman: but he was an incompetent finance minister.[1] In the search for his successor, Luynes wanted a loyal client
who would provide firm government. In the first week of September 1619, his choice fell on Henri de Schomberg, comte de
Nanteuil.[2] The son of a great mercenary captain under Henri III
and Henri IV, who had sat in the finance commission of 1594–6,[3]
Schomberg was lieutenant-general in d'Épernon's governorship
of the Limousin,[4] where he had earned Luynes's gratitude for his
vigorous opposition to the rebellion earlier in 1619. He had also
served as ambassador to England and Germany and commander
of the army in Piedmont in 1617–18. There was thus a return to
the time of Sully, when a military man had 'commanded' financial
administration: indeed, the ruling of 5 February 1611 abolishing
the *surintendance* was formally withdrawn, while in 1621–2
Schomberg also held Sully's other great office, that of *grand maître
de l'artillerie* during the rebellion of the Protestant duke and his
son.[5]

Schomberg's promotion came at a particularly difficult moment.
Royal expenditure was increasing at a time when the wealth of
France was probably less than it had been in the peace years of

[1] Favourable verdicts on his stature in Arnauld d'Andilly, *Mémoires*, ed. Michaud and
Poujoulat, p. 427. André Lefèvre d'Ormesson called him a 'grand personnage': B.M.
Rouen, MS. Léber 5767 t.1, fo. 230ᵛ. In the autumn of 1622 he was Puysieulx's candidate
for the post of Keeper of the Seals: A.A.E. France 775, fos. 111ᵛ., 207ᵛ., 5 Oct. 1622. Sully
criticized both his competence and his alleged dishonesty, but his reasons for a jaundiced
view scarcely need emphasizing: cf. Sully, *Oeconomies royales*, ed. Michaud and Poujoulat, ii.
386.
[2] There had been talk of the appointment of Déageant as *surintendant* in Apr. 1618, but he
had fallen out of favour the following year: L. Batiffol, 'Louis XIII et le duc de Luynes',
Revue Historique, cii (1909), 256. The negotiations for Jeannin's resignation were carried out
by the marquis d'Effiat, who was to obtain this position in 1626: *Arnauld d'Andilly, Mémoires*,
ed. Michaud and Poujoulat, p. 433. Cf. Appendix I, Table I. Schomberg had been chosen
as Jeannin's replacement by 3 Sept. 1619, but he did no formal work in the council of
finance until 16 Oct.: *Journal inédit d'Arnauld d'Andilly*, ed. Halphen, p. 446. E 62c, fo. 9. His
brevet gave him precedence over all councillors of state after the officers of the crown: O1 9,
fos. 126ʳ-ᵛ, 6 Sept. 1619. Cf. B.L. Egerton 1680, fo. 63.
[3] B.I. Godefroy 145, fos. 56, 58, 16 and 19 Jan. 1595. Godefroy 144, fos. 9, 11, 13, 4 Feb., 7
Mar. and 14 Mar. 1595.
[4] He was lieutenant-general in the Limousin and Marche in 1615: B.N. p.o. 2664, no. 75,
31 Jan. 1615. By 1626 he was both governor and lieutenant-general in the Limousin,
Saintonge and Angoumois: B.N. p.o. 2664, no. 97, 2 Aug. 1626.
[5] Arnauld d'Andilly, *Mémoires*, ed. Michaud and Poujoulat, p. 435. Le Père Anselme de
Sainte-Marie (Pierre de Guibours), *Histoire généalogique et chronologique de la maison royale de
France, des pairs, grands officiers de la couronne . . .*, 3rd ed., 9 vols. (1726–33), viii. 186. Article
14 of Sully's treaty of capitulation envisaged that his son, the marquis de Rosny, would
resume the functions of his office of *grand maître* which he had held since 30 Apr. 1610: K 112
no. 5 [Musée AE 798], 22 May 1622.

Henri IV's reign. There was a short-term economic depression throughout Europe in 1619–22, to which France was no exception.[1] Although agriculture seems to have been less affected —indeed, cereal prices reached their highest level since the peace of Vervins in the harvest year 1617–18, just before the onset of the depression—the ability of the French peasants to pay their taxes must have been affected. In foreign policy there were difficult decisions to be made which had important financial implications. Henri II had supported the Lutheran rebellion in the Holy Roman Empire in 1551. Should Louis XIII support the Calvinist rebellion in 1619? The Queen Mother, in her manifesto that year, had already criticized Luynes's neglect of the traditional English and Dutch alliances. Matters were made worse by the tacit support given to the Emperor Ferdinand II in his struggle against the rebels of Bohemia.[2] Acting on a memorandum written by Jeannin, the French diplomatic effort centred on neutralizing Germany from the conflict—an impossible task, since the Calvinist candidate for the throne of Bohemia was the elector of the Rhine Palatinate. The French policy culminated with the signing of the treaty of Ulm between the Catholic League and the Protestant Union on 3 July 1620. This was a disaster for French foreign policy. Not merely did it facilitate a Habsburg victory in Bohemia, it led directly to the collapse of the Calvinist party in Germany and thus to a reversal of traditional French support to the Protestant princes under Henri II and Henri IV.

Apart from the personal preferences of Louis XIII and Luynes,

---

[1] J. D. Gould, 'The trade depression of the early 1620s', *Economic History Review*, 2nd ser., vii (1954), 81–90. R. Romano, 'Encore la crise de 1619–22', *Annales, E.S.C.*, xix (1964), 31–7. R. Romano, 'Between the sixteenth and seventeenth centuries: the economic crisis of 1619–22', *The general crisis of the seventeenth century*, ed. N. G. Parker and L. M. Smith (1978), pp. 165–225. At p. 206 Romano notes the very low issue of coin in France in 1622. At 163,236 *livres*, this was the lowest figure recorded since 1493; only the figure for 1625 would lower. Cf. Spooner, *The international economy and monetary movements in France*, pp. 337–8. On the European dimension to the crisis: P. Jeannin, 'Les comptes du Sund comme source pour la construction des indices généraux de l'activité economique en Europe, xvie–xviiie siècle', *Revue Historique*, ccxxxi (1964), 324. B. E. Supple, *Commercial crisis and change in England, 1600–1642. A study in the instability of a mercantile economy* (Cambridge, 1959), pp. 52–81. Difficulties in the Amiens textile industry: Deyon, *Amiens*, p. 170 and graph 34 at p. 536.

[2] V. L. Tapié, *La politique étrangère de la France et le début de la guerre de Trente Ans, 1616–1621* (1934), pp. 461–5, 509–10, 627. For Jeannin's memorandum: *Les négociations du président Jeannin*, ed. Michaud and Poujoulat, pp. 688–95. For Luynes's preferences: Fontenay-Mareuil, *Mémoires*, ed. J. F. Michaud and J. J. F. Poujoulat, 2nd ser., v (1838), p. 143. Support for Louis XIII's campaign against the Protestants and the Emperor's against the Bohemian rebels in the *Chambre des Comptes* on 24 Feb. 1620: *Chambre des Comptes*, ed. Boislisle, p. 333.

there were two pressing reasons for this timid foreign policy: a further revolt of the Queen Mother in 1620, and the burning question of the restoration of Catholicism in Béarn. On 11 April 1620, the Queen Mother mounted a rebellion from her new governorship in Anjou, allegedly because of 'disorders in the state' and threats to the person of the king,[1] in fact because of her continuing opposition to the ascendancy of Luynes. The revolt received much more support than the previous year, and involved Longueville, the new governor of Normandy, Mayenne in Guyenne and the Protestant Henri de Rohan in Poitou. The comte de Soissons and the ducs de Vendôme,[2] Retz, Nemours, Roannez and Châtillon were also implicated. Although a formidable movement on paper, the rebellion was hopelessly divided in practice: it lacked a clear military leader. This explains why, after some initial gains, the revolt collapsed after the destruction of the main rebel force at the battle of Les Ponts de Cé (8 August 1620). Almost the only concession made to the rebels was that repayment of the Queen Mother's debts would be assisted by a grant of 600,000 *livres* from the crown, payable over two years.[3]

Nevertheless, the rebellion had two important consequences. The first was financial: once more the crown had had to mobilize troops, to anticipate revenues and secure loans to pay for the army.[4] The second consequence was to settle the fate of Béarn. Luynes distrusted the Huguenots and in an unguarded moment commended the Spanish policy of expelling the Moriscos.[5]

[1] A.A.E. France 773, fo. 38, 11 Apr. 1620.

[2] Three members of the royal family participated in the revolt apart from the Queen Mother: Louis de Bourbon, comte de Soissons ('Monsieur le Comte'); César, duc de Vendôme, and Alexandre de Vendôme ('Monsieur le grand prieur de France'). The last two were bastards of Henri IV by Gabrielle d'Estrées. Vendôme was governor of Brittany, Soissons of the Dauphiné—but his real power there was slight because of the enormous prestige of Lesdiguières, the lieutenant-general.

[3] Dumont, *Corps universel diplomatique du droit des gens . . .*, v. 370. Participation in the rebellion established from Girard, *Histoire de la vie du duc d'Espernon*, p. 346, and A.A.E. France 773, fos. 38, 43, 44, 49, 66, 11 and 26 Apr., 30 May, and 20 July 1620. For the reconciliation of the Queen Mother and Rohan: G. Serr, 'Henri de Rohan. Son rôle dans le parti protestant. II. 1617–22', *Divers aspects de la réforme aux xvi* et xvii* siècles. Études et documents.* [*Supplément de la société de l'histoire du protestantisme français*] (1975), p. 374.

[4] Appendix Two, Table VIII A.

[5] Quoted by Patry, *Philippe du Plessis-Mornay*, p. 578 n. 172. Major (*Representative government in early modern France*, p. 455) argues that 'Luynes usually counseled caution, for he feared the hazards of war, and there were others who thought it wiser to proceed slowly with Béarn for fear of provoking a general Protestant revolt. Under such circumstances we can only conclude that Louis himself was taking more direct control over his government.' The fact is that Luynes had himself elevated to the position of Constable—the head of the army—on 31 Mar. 1621. There is no reason to suppose a conflict between king and favourite on the issue of Béarn.

Rohan's participation in the second rebellion of the Queen
Mother, and her opposition to the 'innovation des affaires de
Béarn'[1] served to convince the king and his favourite that the
Protestants had rallied to the cause of the magnates in
1620—which was untrue. Instead of demobilizing after signing
peace with Marie de Médicis, Louis XIII marched south to
restore Catholicism in Béarn and incorporate this independent
state into the kingdom of France.

The invasion of Béarn, the restoration of Catholicism and the
incorporation of Béarn and Basse Navarre into the kingdom of
France were achieved without great difficulty in October 1620.[2]
However, this was the lull before the storm, for these measures
precipitated nine years of intermittent warfare between Louis
XIII and the Protestants. If the expedition to Béarn was a great
success for the government,[3] a further Protestant rebellion in May
1621 marked the beginning of a long and desperate struggle which
the royal finances could ill afford. The revolt was precipitated by
the deliberations of the Protestant assembly which met at La
Rochelle after 25 December 1620—above all, the decision taken
on 10 May 1621 to appoint a member of the Protestant upper
nobility as military head of each of eight territorial units (*cercles*)
into which France and Béarn were divided. This may well have
been less a grandiose and reactionary scheme for the dismember-
ment of France than a desperate attempt to hold on to the *status
quo*: but Luynes regarded it as an act of rebellion, a latter-day
Dutch revolt, and even one of the Protestant *chefs généraux*—
Lesdiguières—agreed.[4] The government had already taken the
precaution on 6 March of transferring the bureaux for tax collection from Protestant *villes de sûreté* to Catholic-held towns. The
Protestant governor of Saumur, Du Plessis-Mornay, who had
held his town loyally for thirty-two years, was removed from his

---

[1] Expressed in her manifesto in 1619: B.N. MS. fr. 17487, fo. 22. Marie de Médicis was
referring to the decision to incorporate Béarn into the kingdom of France, taken in the
king's council on 31 Dec. 1616, and the *édit de mainlevée* to restore Catholicism, signed by
Louis XIII on 25 June 1617: Tucoo-Chala, *La vicomté de Béarn et le problème de sa souveraineté*,
pp. 130–1.
[2] Ibid., p. 132. A. D'Estrée, *La Basse Navarre et ses institutions de 1620 à la Révolution*
(Paris-Zaragoza, 1955), p. 35.
[3] Lublinskaya, *French absolutism*, p. 172.
[4] Ibid., p. 173. Clarke, *Huguenot warrior*, pp. 77–8. D. Parker, 'The social foundation of
French absolutism, 1610–1630', *Past and Present*, liii (1971), 71, 76–7. Luynes's reaction is
quoted by Patry, op. cit., p. 588. Cf. D. Parker, *La Rochelle and the French monarchy: conflict and
order in seventeenth-century France* (1980), p. 155. Dr. Parker's chronology, which varies from
some earlier accounts, has been followed.

post by a shabby manoeuvre.[1] The king then marched against Saint-Jean d'Angély, which was taken on 23 June after a month's siege. Further gains were made in July and early August. However, the siege of Montauban which began on 18 August had to be lifted on 18 November. Its outcome was less a victory for the Protestants than a result of the decimation of the royal army by epidemic.[2]

The failure of the siege of Montauban left the government vulnerable to domestic criticism. It had already been said of Luynes that he was a good Constable only in peacetime and a good Keeper of the Seals only in wartime—thus insinuating that he was fit for neither post.[3] With Luynes's death on 15 December 1621, Schomberg was left as *de facto* head of the government, acting in an informal alliance with Cardinal de Retz, the nominal president of the king's council, and Condé. Schomberg's control was incomplete because there was an important rivalry for influence with Chancellor Brûlart de Sillery and his son, Puysieulx, who was foreign minister.[4] The death of Retz on 2 August 1622 and Condé's decision to withdraw from government and go abroad to Italy—a result of the king's policy of seeking a compromise peace with the Protestants—removed Schomberg's most important allies. At the same time, the promotion of Lefèvre de Caumartin, Schomberg's long-standing enemy, to the post of Keeper of the Seals in September 1622[5] marked the beginning of a campaign for the dismissal of the finance minister which eventually met with success the following January.

Schomberg's position proved vulnerable because he was too closely associated with the war party which had failed to capture

---

[1] Patry, op. cit., pp. 589, 594–5. For the decision of 6 Mar. 1621: ibid., p. 584.

[2] Serr, op. cit., p. 484, calls it 'une grande victoire pour le parti réformé'. On 19 Mar. 1622, Condé commented that the experience the previous year had shown that the Protestant garrisons were less vulnerable than the king's besieging army to the ravages caused by 'la saison des chaleurs et maladies': *Chambres des Comptes*, ed. Boislisle, p. 346.

[3] Lublinskaya, *French absolutism*, pp. 190–1.

[4] Cf. Lublinskaya, p. 200, who comments 'there remained only the Brûlarts'. Bassompierre emphasized the triple alliance, which was reduced to a double alliance on Retz's death: Bassompierre, *Journal de ma vie* . . ., ed. Chantérac, iii. 56–60, 100, 131–40. However, as late as Oct. 1622 it was said that Louis XIII took no action without first consulting Schomberg: A.A.E. France 775, fos. 111ᵛ., 207ᵛ., 5 Oct. 1622.

[5] Méric de Vic had held the Seals from 24 Dec. 1621 until his death on 2 Sept. 1622. Schomberg wanted Aligre to succeed him; Puysieulx originally wanted Jeannin, but agreed with Bassompierre on Lefèvre de Caumartin. Cf. B.L. Harleian 4472b, fos. 293, 295, 24 Dec. 1621 and 23/25 Sept. 1622. Bassompierre, *Journal de ma vie* . . ., ed. Chantérac, iii. 165.

Montauban during the great siege of 1621. He had given a hostage to fortune by promising the king on his life that the town would fall to the besieging army.[1] As *grand maître de l'artillerie*, it was suggested that he had concentrated too much on military affairs to the exclusion of finance; later Richelieu was to recall that instead of costing two million *livres* as envisaged, the siege of Montauban had cost fifteen, largely as a result of peculation.[2] Moreover, in 1622 the council of finance had been divided into two sections, one operating at Paris and the other at Lunel in Languedoc. It must have been impossible for Schomberg, based as he was for part of the time in the Midi, to keep a close eye on all the transactions of the section of the council of finance which remained at Paris.[3] Pierre Castille, the controller-general appointed at the same time as Schomberg, was one of those accused of corruption.[4] Louis XIII tended to believe the worst in others. He was an avaricious king and thus predisposed to consider high expenditure a sign of extravagance. In this area, Schomberg appeared to have lost control since total expenditure rose from 37 million *livres* in 1620 to 43 million the following year, and the record figure of 49 million in 1622. The secret expenses, at 11.6 million, were not far below Henri IV's record of 1594.[5] Robert Arnauld d'Andilly had to defend Schomberg's conduct to the king against the charge of peculation, an accusation which was ill-founded because all objective commentators agreed that the *surintendant* was scrupulously honest,[6] but which nevertheless demonstrates the extent of the king's doubts about his servant.

Rather than his integrity, Schomberg's financial acumen and dealings with the financiers were open to question.[7] He committed a cardinal error in 1622 in allowing the two most important revenue farms—the *gabelles de France* and the *aides*—to fall into the

---

[1] The promise was made on 13 Oct. 1621: ibid., ii. 347.
[2] Richelieu, *Mémoires*, iii. 165.
[3] E 72b, Aug. 1622, *passim*.
[4] *Les négociations du président Jeannin*, ed. Michaud and Poujoulat, pp. 715–16. A.A.E. France 779, fo. 87. 'Mémoire contre le sieur de Castille', n.d., *c.* 1623.
[5] Appendix Two, Tables I and III.
[6] Arnauld d'Andilly, *Mémoires*, ed. Michaud and Poujoulat, p. 442. Fontenay-Mareuil, *Mémoires*, ed. Michaud and Poujoulat, p. 173. *Mémoires du Cardinal de Richelieu*, ed. J. F. Michaud and J. J. F. Poujoulat, 2nd ser., viii (1838), p. 428.
[7] As Richelieu commented. On 19 Mar. 1622 the *Chambre des Comptes* asked Condé to prevent funds for the army being 'divertis comme au passé'. Earlier, on 4 May 1621, the excessive profits of the financiers had been denounced by that court: *Chambre des Comptes*, ed. Boislisle, pp. 341, 348.

hands of one financier, Antoine Feydeau.[1] Schomberg had been able to borrow successfully in 1621–2,[2] but there were suggestions that his ability to obtain loans from the financiers was at a low ebb because he had anticipated too much of the revenue of 1623. Nevertheless, Schomberg boasted that he had 8 million *livres* ready when needed in *affaires extraordinaires* and a change of financial leadership might 'fermer toutes les bourses des partisans'.[3] Overall, it seems much more probable that Schomberg's dismissal resulted less from clear-cut financial reasons than from a political *coup*. Beaumarchais, the *trésorier de l'Épargne* for 1623, refused to make any loans while Schomberg continued in office:[4] but his alleged financial reasons for this decision are no more eloquent than the fact that he was the father-in-law of La Vieuville, the frontrunner for Schomberg's position.[5] There is little doubt that Schomberg was in part the victim of the peace of Montpellier concluded by Constable Lesdiguières with the Protestants on 19 October 1622. The early hopes of a rapid and complete royalist victory had been dashed. Although the crown had made significant gains—Béarn did not recover its former autonomy; Rohan was removed from his governorship of Poitou; the Huguenots lost nearly half their *villes de sûreté*—the peace of Montpellier was really only a truce, not the end of the war. It provided Chancellor Brûlart de Sillery, Lefèvre de Caumartin and Puysieulx with the opportunity to make Schomberg the scapegoat for the failures of the war effort. The appointment of La Vieuville as *surintendant* in January 1623 nevertheless resulted less from his qualities and claims to office than from the failure of Schomberg's opponents to unite in support of an alternative candidate.[6] While La Vieuville had been appointed commander

---

[1] Feydeau had held the *aides* since 1611 and gained the *gabelles de France* on 16 Mar. 1622 with effect from 1 Oct. 1622: E 70b, fo. 202, 16 Mar. 1622. The risk was that if Feydeau went bankrupt, two farms instead of one would be affected.

[2] Appendix Two, Table VIII A.

[3] Bassompierre, *Journal de ma vie . . .*, ed. Chantérac, iii. 171.

[4] Louis XIII may have panicked, believing that 'sans ce secours il n'auroit pas de quoy vivre': Fontenay-Mareuil, *Mémoires*, ed. Michaud and Poujoulat, p. 172. Lublinskaya, *French absolutism*, p. 246.

[5] For the La Vieuville–Beaumarchais marriage in 1610: Labatut, *Les ducs et pairs*, pp. 146–7.

[6] It seems probable that Louis XIII would have chosen Henri Bauffremont, marquis de Senecy, but for his premature death in 1622. The recall of Sully was favoured by Bassompierre; Puysieulx favoured Halincourt, Villeroy's son, or Nicolas Clausse, seigneur de Fleury, the *grand maître des eaux et forêts*. A scheme for the appointment of six *directeurs des finances* was rejected by the king: Bassompierre, *Journal de ma vie . . .*, ed. Chantérac, iii. 166–7.

of an army of some 3000 men in Champagne in 1622, his prestige had not been dented by failure: the army under his command had not fired a shot in anger, since the threatened invasion by the great mercenary captain, Ernst von Mansfeld, had never materialized.[1]

La Vieuville was appointed finance minister on 23 January 1623,[2] with Bochart de Champigny as controller-general in place of Pierre Castille (Castille's integrity was open to question and he was demoted to the post of *intendant des finances*). La Vieuville was a lieutenant-general in Champagne and captain in the king's body-guard—a man, moreover, with a personal grievance against Schomberg, who had cut his pension.[3] He was the great-nephew of François d'O, the finance minister of Henri III and Henri IV. He had been trusted in financial matters by Beaumarchais, his father-in-law, and had access to his wealth and credit: Beaumarchais not only had great experience, he was considered the richest man in France.[4] Moreover, La Vieuville was a financier in his own right, having presented two proposals to the council of finance in 1620 for the establishment of new taxes.[5] He thus had a better claim than many for the post of finance minister. His weakness was the absence of a firm power base within the central government. Chancellor Brûlart de Sillery and his son Puysieulx, the foreign minister, had agreed on La Vieuville's promotion simply as a device to get rid of Schomberg. The new *surintendant* was frequently in conflict with the other ministers until he succeeded in ousting the Brûlarts on 4 February 1624. In order to achieve this aim, however, La Vieuville had to find allies. One of these seems to have been Aligre, the Keeper of the Seals appointed on 6

---

[1] Mansfeld's invasion of France was negotiated by the arch-conspirator of the Protestants, the duc de Bouillon: KK 1358, p. 311 [Musée AE II 797], 10 Apr. 1622. A.A.E. France 777, fos. 8, 46, 7 Aug. and 5 Sept. 1622. Cf. Lublinskaya, op. cit., p. 245.

[2] Appendix One, Table I. Many of the copies of his *brevet* give the date of appointment erroneously as 6 Jan. 1623, while Schomberg was still in office. The date of appointment might be 26 Jan., but Bochart was appointed on 23 Jan. [cf. O1 9, fo. 133] and Beauclerc was appointed as intendant of finance on 24 Jan. [cf. O1 9, fo. 133ᵛ.]. It is most unlikely that the king decided on La Vieuville's name after these important decisions.

[3] The pension was a continuation of compensation paid to his father, Robert de la Vieuville, for the loss of the fortress of Mézières which was seized in 1614 by the rebellious duc de Nevers: Bassompierre, *Journal de ma vie . . .*, ed. Chantérac, iii. 169–70. For the seizure: B.N. Dupuy 91, fo. 31ᵛ., 9 Apr. 1614. For La Vieuville as captain of the king's bodyguard: B.N. p.o. 2989 (Dr. 66,403), no. 72, 12 Aug. 1616.

[4] Fontenay-Mareuil, loc. cit., is a good witness to his wealth and experience. He had been *trésorier de l'Épargne* since 1599: Appendix One, Table IV.

[5] If these proposals raised a million *livres* in revenue, as envisaged, then La Vieuville would have received 100,000 *livres* for his *droit d'avis*: E 63a, fo. 99, 5 Feb. 1620.

January 1624 after a vacancy of almost a year:[1] Aligre was the
king's nominee, not La Vieuville's, but the Seals had been
removed from the Chancellor's custody to make way for his
appointment. A more important ally was the Queen Mother. Her
influence over the king had increased somewhat since the death of
Luynes, as the appointments of d'Épernon as governor of
Guyenne and of Richelieu as Cardinal (respectively on 28 August
and 5 September 1622) testify.[2] However, the price La Vieuville
had to pay for the support of Marie de Médicis and her religious
advisers such as Bérulle was a heavy one: the entry of Richelieu
into the king's council on 29 April 1624.[3] From this moment on, it
seems that La Vieuville's position as *de facto* chief minister, foreign
minister, and *surintendant* was vulnerable to an alliance between
Richelieu and Aligre, although as late as 3 August the king denied
rumours of impending ministerial changes.[4]

Did La Vieuville have a credible financial alternative to
Schomberg's policy of high expenditure? The new finance minister claimed that Louis XIII was the 'principal directeur de ses
finances' and that the king personally supervised the expenditure
accounts. La Vieuville saw his task as one of retrenchment
although '[il] n'était que le ministre'.[5] He succeeded in reducing
royal expenditure from 49 million *livres* in 1622 to 33 million in
1624. There was a similar dramatic fall in the secret expenses.[6] It

[1] Lefèvre de Caumartin had died on 21 Jan. 1623, and Louis XIII refused to replace him
until he found a candidate who would be dependent on the king, and not one of the other
ministers: B. Zeller, *Richelieu et les ministres de Louis XIII de 1621 à 1624* (1880), pp. 226, 238–9.
B.L. Harleian 4472b, fo. 288, 6 Jan. 1624. Though Aligre was not supposed to be
committed to any of the factions, the fact remains that the interregnum had worked in
favour of the Brûlarts since the Chancellor had held the Seals. For Aligre's period in office:
D. J. Sturdy, 'The formation of a "robe" dynasty. Étienne d'Aligre II (1560–1635),
chancellor of France', *English Historical Review*, xcv (1980), 59–60.

[2] The promotion of Richelieu had been promised by Louis XIII at the time of the two
treaties with the Queen Mother in 1619–20. The appointment of d'Épernon was suggested
to the king by Condé, but the memory of his service to the Queen Mother in 1619 was still
very much alive: Girard, *Histoire de la vie du duc d'Espernon*, pp. 381–2 (who gives the date as
27 Aug.).

[3] Zeller, *Richelieu et les ministres de Louis XIII*, p. 241. Lublinskaya, op. cit., pp. 263–4.
Bérulle at this time was head of the congregation of the Oratory. In 1627 he was promoted
as Cardinal.

[4] *Chambre des Comptes*, ed. Boislisle, p. 350. As early as 3 Jan. 1624 Ottavio Corsini, the
papal nuncio, had considered La Vieuville's position vulnerable: Zeller, op. cit., p. 237.
For a suggestion of an alliance between Richelieu and Aligre: A.A.E. France 778, fo. 196, 12
Aug. 1624. The point was made after the event by Marillac's apologist: B.N. MS. fr. 17486,
fo. 183'.

[5] *Chambre des Comptes*, ed. Boislisle, p. 358. On 15 Dec. 1623, Giovanni de Pesaro, the
Venetian ambassador, concluded that La Vieuville's policy was one of retrenchment:
Zeller, op. cit., p. 233.

[6] Appendix Two, Tables I and III.

is true that these savings were made possible by reduced military expenditure, an option that had not been open to Schomberg in 1621–2 because of the war with the Protestants. La Vieuville seems to have hoped that civil peace would lead to French commercial recovery from the European trade depression,[1] and that if agriculture and trade prospered, payment of direct and indirect taxes would be facilitated. There was much to be said for this policy after the trauma of the war against the Huguenots. The yield of both direct and indirect taxes had diminished in absolute terms in the years 1620–4, and relatively in comparison with the last years of Jeannin's ministry, while reliance on the *parties casuelles* and the *affaires extraordinaires* had increased. For example, the *taille* from the *pays d'élections* had contributed on average 38.2 per cent of ordinary royal income between 1615 and 1619, but the proportion fell to 27.7 per cent between 1620 and 1624. In the same period, the average yield of the revenue farms fell from 33.7 per cent to 20.1 per cent per annum. Not inappropriately, in view of the continuing reliance on the *affaires extraordinaires*, La Vieuville was regarded as a specialist in establishing new taxes: he hoped to establish four or five million *livres* immediately on his appointment, and financial proposals came pouring into the council in the succeeding months.[2] Perhaps he even intended reviving Sully's policy of redeeming the *rentes* and crown lands, although it is more likely that he regarded the investigation of fraudulent leases simply as a means of obtaining additional revenue from fines.[3]

There is little doubt that La Vieuville's policy of retrenchment made him extremely unpopular. Those who had suffered cuts in their salaries and pensions would certainly not mourn his passing,

---

[1] On 20 Dec. 1623, he undertook to examine measures to halt piracy and re-establish trade which had been depressed 'for three years'. He was to be assisted by Bochart de Champigny, de Bisseaulx and Châteauneuf: E 77b, fo. 219.

[2] Bassompierre, *Journal de ma vie . . .*, ed. Chantérac, iii. 171. The success of La Vieuville is revealed by the number of financial proposals (*avis*) received by the council in comparison with the period of Schomberg. From Mar. to Dec. 1621, the council received 34 proposals; in 1622 it received 53; once La Vieuville took over in 1623, the council received 104 proposals, of which 51 came in between Jan. and Mar. However, the number of proposals fell in 1624 (only 41 between Jan. and 13 Aug. 1624).

[3] E 75b, fo. 10, 5 July 1623. All contracts signed between 1 Jan. 1600 and 31 Dec. 1622 were to be investigated by Maupeou and Duret de Chevry. Major (*Representative government in early modern France*, p. 475) considers La Vieuville's policies 'similar to (those) of Bellièvre and other reformers. He believed that it was necessary to reduce expenses and to abandon the use of expedients that proved costly in the long run.' The new minister's reliance on the *affaires extraordinaires* belies this assessment.

though they could not force the finance minister from office. Only a realignment of the factions at court and in the government could do this, and La Vieuville appears to have achieved the remarkable feat of alienating the three most important members of the royal family (Louis XIII, Marie de Médicis, and Gaston d'Orléans) at the same time.[1] In Richelieu's celebrated phrase, La Vieuville was like a drunkard who could not walk a step without stumbling.[2] A vigorous pamphlet campaign was conducted against La Vieuville by Fancan, acting as Richelieu's publicist,[3] and the finance minister proved vulnerable to the criticism because he had tried to arrogate too much power to himself and because of serious mistakes in foreign policy.[4] On 12 August 1624, La Vieuville offered his resignation. Instead of accepting this, Louis XIII had him arrested and appointed Richelieu as chief minister the following day. The reasons for La Vieuville's disgrace need to be distinguished from the charges that were later brought against him. False accounting figured prominently among these charges—Beaumarchais, his father-in-law, was accused of buying up old treasury bills and debts of Henri III and Henri IV, reassigning them on good revenues and adjusting the accounts for 1620 and 1622 to cover up his transactions. Beaumarchais's reputed wealth of 12 million (such a significant factor in Schomberg's removal from office in 1623) was now turned against him: it was argued that since he was of humble social origins, this wealth must have been acquired illegally.[5] The suggestion that the accounts had been adjusted retrospectively to the convenience of Beaumarchais would have been sufficient to convict La Vieuville on grounds of complicity, but the charges against the former *surintendant* were much more serious. He was accused of having profited by 600,000 *livres* in Beaumarchais's dealings in treasury bills and old debts. He was charged with participating in a consortium headed by the financier Nicolas Camus which administered an important tax contract[6]—or, at the very least, of

---

[1] A.A.E. France 778, fo. 195, 12 Aug. 1624.

[2] Richelieu, *Mémoires*, iv. 107.

[3] Zeller, *Richelieu et les ministres de Louis XIII*, p. 292. Lublinskaya, *French absolutism*, pp. 265–6. W. F. Church, *Richelieu and reason of state* (Princeton, N. J., 1972), p. 100.

[4] Zeller, op. cit., pp. 293–5. Lublinskaya, op. cit., p. 268.

[5] Beaumarchais's arrest was ordered on 8 Nov. 1624, and his execution (in effigy, since he had fled to the island of Noirmoutier) followed on 25 Jan. 1625: A.A.E. France 779, fo. 106. B.N. Dupuy 93, fo. 5. B.N. MS. fr. 7583, pp. 543–50. The trial papers indicate clearly that the accounts of 1622 were adjusted retrospectively, although Morant, and not Beaumarchais, had held the fund in that year: Appendix One, Table IV.

[6] Presumably the *traité* establishing the *greffes des élections*: E 74a, fo. 37, 2 Mar. 1623.

accepting an illegal bribe from this consortium. It was also claimed that his dealings with the revenue farmers had been illegal, that he had accepted bribes in return for renewing Antoine Feydeau's lease on the *aides*,[1] and that he had prevented an investigation into some of the more dubious activities of Claude Charlot as farmer-general of the *cinq grosses fermes*.[2]

Even assuming that the French judicial system tended to make life easy for the prosecution and that some of the testimony was falsified, the charges amounted to a massive indictment of nineteen months' of financial administration by La Vieuville. He remained in prison for thirteen months until he managed to escape and flee abroad. After an appeal by his wife, Louis XIII allowed him to return: but La Vieuville joined the revolt of Gaston d'Orléans in 1631 and his lands and wealth were expropriated.[3] He remained in exile in Lorraine, the Spanish Netherlands, and eventually England for the rest of Richelieu's ministry and was not amnestied until 11 June 1643.[4] The years in exile turned La Vieuville in popular estimation from a corrupt finance minister into a martyr for his opposition to Richelieu: it was said that he had exercised his office with integrity,[5] and that the charges against him were trumped up. Nevertheless, in the short term La Vieuville brought about his own downfall, and in so doing he imperilled the future of his office. Richelieu was determined that the post of finance minister should no longer be held by an ambitious magnate seeking offices and provincial governorships but instead by someone appointed from among the *noblesse de robe*. The finance minister should be neither too great nor too humble in his social origins. Above all, his political ambitions should be limited by his exclusion from the council of state.[6] Although the post of *surintendant* was not abolished as in 1594 and 1611, the reaction against the development of its power in 1624 was almost

---

[1] For the renewal of the lease: E 74b, fo. 43, 11 Apr. 1623.

[2] Richelieu, *Mémoires*, iv. 287–90. For the general political reasons for his arrest: *Les papiers de Richelieu*, ed. Grillon, i. 96–9, 101–5, 108–10.

[3] D. Gallet-Guerne, 'Une conséquence des troubles féodaux sous Louis XIII: les confiscations royales de 1629 à 1641', *Bibliothèque de l'École des Chartes*, cxxvii (1969), 340, 345–7. Saint-Simon, the current royal favourite, received a gift of part of the confiscations: E 107b, fo. 283, 10 Nov. 1631. The *chambre de justice* at the Arsenal found La Vieuville guilty of treason and ordered his execution in effigy: A.A.E. France 802, fo. 11, 10 Jan. 1632.

[4] B.N. MS. fr. 17331, fo. 118. In these letters of amnesty he was called a former 'principal ministre' of the king.

[5] Omer Talon, *Mémoires*, ed. J. F. Michaud and J. J. F. Poujoulat, 3rd ser., vi (1839), p. 248.

[6] Richelieu, *Mémoires*, iv. 113–14. Bochart and Marillac were excluded from the council of state unless specially summoned: B.N. MS. fr. 18152, fo. 81, 27 Aug. 1624.

as great as on those two previous occasions. It remained to be seen whether a return to a collegiate form of control would prove sufficiently dynamic to resolve the fundamental problems of French financial administration in the later 1620s.

Chapter III

Richelieu and Marillac: War or reform?

Richelieu's ministry was quite different in character from its predecessors since 1610. There was a new Chancellor, Aligre, who was promoted from the post of Keeper of the Seals in October 1624.[1] There was also a secretary of state for war, Beauclerc, who had been promoted from the office of *intendant des finances* in February 1624 to what amounted to a new ministry. On the other hand, the older office of secretary of state for foreign affairs remained vacant after the dismissal of Puysieulx in February 1624, with responsibility for this function being divided between the other secretaries of state until 11 March 1626. Richelieu was thus effectively chief minister and foreign minister. His grip on the council of state was reinforced by the recall of Schomberg.[2] The Cardinal and the former *surintendant* were friends, and indeed in 1624 Richelieu was prepared to make an exception to his preference for a member of the *noblesse de robe* as finance minister had Louis XIII been prepared to take Schomberg back. However, the king was willing to allow Schomberg to enter the council of state, but vetoed his appointment as finance minister because of his alleged lack of expertise.[3] Other names, including Sully provided that he changed religion,[4] were canvassed and rejected. In the end, Richelieu was forced to propose a collegiate system of financial control with himself at the head, the others being Jean Bochart de Champigny, Michel de Marillac, and Mathieu Molé. Molé refused to serve on the grounds that his office of *procureur-général* in the *Parlement* of Paris was incompatible with that of *surintendant*.[5] (Nearly thirty years later Nicolas Foucquet would

---

[1] B.L. Harleian 4472b, fos. 286, 290, 3 Oct. 1624. Brûlart de Sillery died on 1 or 2 Oct. 1624.

[2] The impression of the ministry of 1624–6 as a triumvirate comprising Richelieu, Aligre, and Schomberg was given by the *premier président* of the *Parlement* of Paris on 27 Sept. 1626: cf. *Chambre des Comptes*, ed. Boislisle, p. 367.

[3] Richelieu, *Mémoires*, iv. 113. Richelieu had sympathized with Schomberg on his disgrace in Jan. 1623; Schomberg had congratulated Richelieu on his entry into the king's council in 1624. A.A.E. France 778, fo. 12, 12 Jan. 1624. *Les papiers de Richelieu*, ed. Grillon, i. 76.

[4] The other name canvassed was Fleury, *grand maître des eaux et forêts*, as in 1623.

[5] Bassompierre, *Journal de ma vie . . .*, ed. Chantérac, iii. 193. Interestingly, Molé is silent on this incident in his own memoirs.

not be so reticent.) The other two agreed and took up their appointment on 27 August.[1] Bochart retained his office of controller-general, and this fact, together with his seniority in the king's council,[2] should have given him the predominant voice. In the event, owing to Bochart's ill health and perhaps a superior financial mind (Marillac's father had been controller-general under Charles IX),[3] Marillac quite quickly took charge. When Bochart resigned on 20 February 1626, leaving Marillac in sole command, this merely confirmed the existing state of affairs.

The predominance in the king's council of a Cardinal who was not the royal favourite provides a strong contrast between Richelieu's ministry and the successive governments after the death of Henri IV. The powers of the *surintendants* were reduced to those of directors of finance as in 1611-12. Marillac's position was somewhat stronger than Jeannin's had been:[4] but the ruling of 2 September 1624 circumscribed the powers of the finance ministers, particularly in their ordering of day to day expenses where they were restricted to sums not exceeding 1000 *livres*: above that figure, they had to receive authorization from the king or his council. In other crucial areas of policy, the ruling sought to reverse the trend towards a strong, independent finance ministry between 1611 and 1624. The *surintendants* in September 1624 had no automatic right of entry into the council of state (*conseil d'en haut* or *conseil des affaires*); similar restrictions had applied to the directors of finance in February 1611.[5] As in 1611, the finance ministers' right to make secret payments (*comptants*) was restricted by the need to obtain the approval of the king and his council and the signature of the Keeper of the Seals. Tax contracts, remissions accorded to the revenue farmers, and repayments of outstanding

---

[1] Appendix One, Table I.

[2] B.L. Egerton 1680, fo. 63ᵛ. An idea of Bochart's seniority is obtained from the fact that he became a *maître des requêtes* on 10 July 1585. Marillac took up the same position nearly ten years later, on 25 Jan. 1595.

[3] Bochart's age and ill health were stated as the reasons for his resignation: cf. B.N. MS. fr. 16626 fo. 235, 20 Feb. 1626. Guillaume II de Marillac was *intendant* and *contrôleur-général des finances* in 1569: cf. *Dictionnaire de la noblesse*, ed. Aubert de la Chenaye des Bois and Badier, 3rd. ed., 19 vols. (1863–76), ix. 544. B.N. p.o. 1854 (Dr. 42,783), no. 65, 13 Feb. 1598.

[4] Marillac had the support of a king who had come of age; Jeannin depended on the Regent. There are other similarities (both had supported the Catholic League) and contrasts (Marillac was a dedicated reformer; Jeannin was not). Major (*Representative government in early modern France*, p. 498) comments that 'little is known of (Marillac's) work beyond that he continued La Vieuville's economy efforts'. The expenditure statistics do not bear out this verdict.

[5] A.A.E. France 768, fo. 247, n.d. [Feb. 1611].

royal debts were all to receive final approval in the council of state. The overall impression is that Louis XIII, Richelieu, and Aligre intended to keep the activities of the *surintendants* under careful scrutiny.[1] Bochart and Marillac were not appointed on a one-year commission as has sometimes been said.[2] Nevertheless, their powers were certainly more restricted than those enjoyed by Schomberg and La Vieuville.

Richelieu exercised a determining influence on financial policy through his conduct of foreign affairs and his attitude to La Vieuville and the financiers. The distinctive feature of the years between 1607 and 1624 was that while everyone was in agreement that there had been abuses in financial administration, there had been no prosecution of the financiers, despite the promise made to the Estates-General in 1615. After lengthy debates in the king's council, a *chambre de justice* was set up which lasted from October 1624 until May 1625.[3] Richelieu seems to have participated fully in the debates and to have influenced the terms of reference of the tribunal and the amount levied in fines: Condé later praised the chief minister's efforts in obtaining 10.8 million *livres* in fines on the financiers, double the sum originally envisaged.[4] The debate within the king's council reveals a great deal about prevailing social attitudes and ministerial expectations of the financiers and financial officials, especially their integrity and standard of service. Was it possible or desirable to push the judicial prosecution of cases of corruption to the ultimate limit, resulting in the execution of offenders and the confiscation of their wealth? Was the

[1] Mousnier, 'Les règlements du conseil du roi sous Louis XIII', 163–5 and B.N. MS. fr. 18152, fo. 81.

[2] Their powers were confirmed on 26 Dec. 1625: cf. B.N. MS. fr. 16626, fo. 235, 20 Feb. 1626. Boislisle argued from this evidence that they were originally appointed on a one-year commission: Boislisle, 'Semblançay et la surintendance des finances', 267 n.3. However, the commission of 27 Aug. 1624 made no mention of a time-limit and since all commissions were revocable by the crown at will it would have been unnecessary to do so. It was quite common for financial officials to be confirmed in office (for example, Bochart was confirmed as controller-general on 31 Jan. 1624 and subsequently: cf. 01 9, fo. 136'). Nevertheless, the confirmation of their powers in 1625 reinforces the impression of the relative loss of authority of the finance ministers over the previous year.

[3] For the edicts creating and abolishing the *chambre de justice: Recueil . . . des lois*, ed. Jourdan *et al.*, xvi. 147. B.N. MS. fr. 7583, pp. 439–50. P 2353, p. 439. For the debates: Richelieu, *Mémoires*, iv. 134–58 and 273–85 (who recalls at iv. 134 the promise made to the Estates-General). *Les papiers de Richelieu*, ed. Grillon, i. 116–22.

[4] Petit, *L'assemblée des notables de 1626–1627*, p. 81. B.N. MS. fr. 7583, p. 581. For Condé's view: Richelieu, *Mémoires*, vi. 54. For an earlier list of fines totalling 7.5 million: A.A.E. France 780, fo. 199. Richelieu later claimed that 'j'ai refusé cent mil pistoles des financiers qui me les offroient, sans diminution d'un sol du traicté qu'ils faisoient avec Sa Majesté . . .': *Lettres, instructions diplomatiques et papiers d'état du Cardinal de Richelieu*, ed. D. L. M. Avenel, 8 vols., (1853–77), iii. 204.

chambre de justice to take place once and for all, or was it necessary to set up a permanent body to review allegations of corruption? Was there a case for devising new laws against peculation and new procedures for gathering evidence against offenders? Could realistic distinctions be made between certain posts where pecula-tion was more common and others where it was not? Each course of action presented difficulties and possible dangers. Only a thoroughgoing prosecution of offenders would restore public confidence in the integrity of financial administration. Yet, as the clergy had pointed out in 1615,[1] the social connections of many financial administrators were very respectable. Were noble families, whether of the robe or the sword, to be hounded because they had contracted marriages with financiers' children?[2] The issues were extremely wide-ranging. On the other hand, all the various schemes had the common problem of the practical difficulty of putting them into effect. Sully's method was tried and tested. This was to assume that all financial officials were corrupt and tax them according to their length of service. This might be considered rough justice, but it was easy to administer and was likely to yield more revenue than alternative schemes which tried to ascertain the extent of individual corruption. At first Richelieu seems to have condemned out of hand the idea of an amnesty with financiers paying fines or 'compositions'; later, perhaps under the influence of Fancan his publicist,[3] he seems to have come round to this view as the only practicable alternative.

Despite all the fears which had been reflected in the debate in the king's council, the long-term social consequences of the *chambre de justice* of 1624–5 were slight. No permanent body was established to review allegations of corruption;[4] instead, a *chambre de justice* was to be held every ten years.[5] The financiers were not

---

[1] Blet, *Le clergé*, i. 36.

[2] For Richelieu's hostility to *mésalliances*: Richelieu, *Testament politique*, ed. André, p. 251. Devyver, *Le sang épuré*, p. 157.

[3] *Les papiers de Richelieu*, ed. Grillon, i. 263–4. Richelieu, *Testament politique*, ed. André, p. 252. Fancan was probably the author of the 'mémoyre touchant la composition des finances' published by G. Fagniez, 'Fancan et Richelieu', *Revue Historique*, cvii (1911), 311–12.

[4] This idea was later incorporated into article 411 of the *Code Michaud* of Jan. 1629. The difference in attitude between Aligre and Marillac as Keepers of the Seals is significant. Marillac was prepared to establish a new institution comparable to a *chambre de l'édit*, but dealing with cases concerning financiers. Aligre told the members of the *Chambre des Comptes* on 23 Apr. 1624 that they should fulfil their functions properly and thus avoid royal commissions such as the *chambre de justice: Chambre des Comptes*, ed. Boislisle, p. 358.

[5] This decision was recalled in the amnesty to the financiers of 31 Mar. 1635: E 122d, fo. 215. P 2370, pp. 975–80.

hounded to destruction. Though certain financiers and financial officials were closely investigated,[1] the penalties seem to have been moderate. Beaumarchais's death sentence was withdrawn and he was ordered to pay a fine of one million *livres*. Two other *trésoriers de l'Épargne*, Raymond and Baltazar Phélypeaux, were to pay 300,000 *livres*. The other financial officials were to pay according to the number of years of their service since 1 October 1607.[2] The collection of fines was carried out by Guillaume Mesnager, a financier in his own right:[3] the *chambre de justice* thus in a sense became an exercise of revenge, whereby one financier could profit at the expense of others. Nevertheless, the financiers obtained important concessions from the crown. The *chambre de justice* was excluded from jurisdiction over the revenue farms, loans, and tax contracts,[4] the area of financial policy which required closest investigation. Business had to continue as usual and the king's 'credit' had to be maintained. Two of the leading financiers, Claude Charlot and Antoine Feydeau, were granted a dispensation from investigation by the *chambre de justice* in view of the great loans they had made to the crown and the size of the tax contracts which they had entered.[5] For others, exemption could be purchased: Raymond and Baltazar Phélypeaux lent 200,000 *livres* to the crown and thus were discharged from their fine.[6]

As a result of the investigation by the *chambre de justice*, two offices of *trésorier de l'Épargne* (those belonging to Beaumarchais and Morant) were sold. The government seems to have regarded these sales as a means of ridding itself of corrupt officials whose fines at the *chambre de justice* could be paid from the proceeds of the sales.[7] In seeking to avoid corrupt officials at the head of the Treasury, Richelieu, Bochart, and Marillac seem to have paid too little attention to the continuing business interests of the new appointees, Antoine Feydeau and Pierre Payen. Feydeau was the most important revenue-farmer in France, and by becoming *trésorier de l'Épargne* was given direct access to royal funds to assist his private business operations.[8] In January 1626, Feydeau went into

[1] 'Liste des financiers compromis en 1624': Richelieu *Mémoires*, iv. 285–7. *Les papiers de Richelieu*, ed. Grillon, i. 140–1.
[2] Cf. E 83c, fo. 360, 27 Sept. 1625.
[3] E 84a, fo. 103, 25 Oct. 1625.
[4] B.N. MS. fr. 7583, pp. 518–22, 13 Nov. 1624. E 84a, fo. 103, 25 Oct. 1625.
[5] B.N. MS. fr. 7583, pp. 505–6, 28 Oct. 1624.
[6] B.N. MS. fr. 7583, pp. 610–12, 24 Feb. 1627.
[7] Richelieu, *Mémoires*, iv. 147. *Les papiers de Richelieu*, ed. Grillon, i. 120. La Vieuville was still trying to pay Beaumarchais's fine on 30 Sept. 1628: A.A.E. France 791, fo. 133.
[8] '. . . ayant diverty et employé en ses affaires particulières, emporté ou aultrement

hiding from his creditors. When his affairs were investigated, he was found to owe over a million *livres* to the crown.[1] Payen was one of the most important financiers of his time. When he died unexpectedly in April 1626, he left debts of three million, of which 1.8 million was owed to the crown.[2] The seriousness of these collapses threatened to bring about a more general bankruptcy. As it was, the subsidiary financiers with whom Feydeau and Payen had dealt had to be kept solvent by the council of finance, which suspended actions at law by their creditors.[3] At such times, the crown was the priority creditor,[4] and although the private creditors organized themselves into an association and elected an agent to act on their behalf, their requests for compensation dragged on into the 1630s.[5]

In comparison with Schomberg's errors of judgement in 1622, for which he was severely criticized and ultimately dismissed, these were more serious miscalculations by Bochart and Marillac. At best the *chambre de justice* had been largely irrelevant to the financial problems of the French monarchy;[6] the hopeless delays in the accounting procedure, the imbalance between revenues and expenditure, the excessive rates of interest paid on covering loans, all remained in 1626 at the end of Marillac's ministry.[7] At worst, the *chambre de justice* may be seen as a grotesque failure, leading indirectly to the bankruptcy of two financiers, the subdivision of the farm of the *gabelles de France* and a severe threat to the farm of the *aides*.[8] In other crucial areas of financial policy

---

disposé contre le deub de sa charge . . .': E 85a, fo. 263, 28 Jan. 1626. Heumann ('Antoine Feydeau', p. 217) considered that Feydeau gave up his business interests on becoming chief treasurer. However, he retained them through agents: cf. Minutier Central LI 145, 29 July 1625. Minutier Central LI 147, 20 Jan. 1626. E 83b, fo. 26, 2 Aug. 1625.

[1] E 93b, fo. 114, 14 Aug. 1627.

[2] E 87a, fo. 189, 2 May 1626. E 106a, fo. 295, 20 June 1631. E 114a, fo. 313, 31 Mar. 1633. B.N. Morel de Thoisy 157, fo. 10.

[3] Numerous examples in the decrees of the council of finance for 1626–7, affecting Philippe and Pierre Guerin, Jean le Conte, the brothers Nicolas Mallebranche, Guillaume Menant, and Bernard d'Alsol.

[4] Cf. the phrase 'le premier créancier' in E 93b, fo. 114, 14 Aug. 1627.

[5] Meetings of the creditors of Payen: Minutier Central LXXXVI 233–7, 1626–30.

[6] It was not until 7 Apr. 1626 that the tax-farmers and tax-contractors (as opposed to the financial officials) were fined, and then only by the trifling sum of 80,000 *livres*: cf. E 87a, fos. 139–40, 25 Apr. 1626.

[7] *Lettres . . . de Richelieu*, ed. Avenel, ii. 207–11. *Les papiers de Richelieu*, ed. Grillon, i. 346–9. Lublinskaya (*French absolutism*, p. 303 n.4 at p. 304) correctly ascribes this document to d'Effiat, but it was probably written later than she suggests.

[8] For the division of the revenue farms: Bonney, 'The failure of the French revenue farms', 13–14, 22. Matters were made worse by Pierre Payen's assuming the lease on the *aides* after Feydeau's bankruptcy: ibid., 27.

there was a similar contrast between the high hopes of 1624 and the actual achievement two years later. Overall expenditure had risen from about 34 million *livres* in 1624 to over 44 million two years later. The secret expenses had nearly doubled to over 12 million, despite the specific instructions to the *surintendants* to use this method of payment as sparingly as possible. The overall impression is one of failure. Marillac struggled on until 1 June 1626, when he was appointed Keeper of the Seals.[1] The immediate reason for his elevation was the disgrace of Chancellor Aligre for apparent weakness in dealing with Gaston d'Orléans, and the need for a strong prosecutor in the trial of Chalais, who was accused of high treason.[2] Yet Richelieu could not have been displeased at this ministerial reshuffle, which provided the opportunity for the appointment of an abler finance minister who was also his client: Antoine Coiffier de Ruzé, marquis d'Effiat.[3]

In stressing the failures of Bochart and Marillac's ministry in 1624–6, due allowance must be made to the overwhelming foreign and domestic difficulties faced by the French government in these years. French foreign policy was exceedingly tortuous, partly because of the complexity of the issues at stake in the Thirty Years' War, partly because of the desire to keep French military commitments to a minimum, and partly because of the difficulty in giving due weight to foreign rather than domestic policy when some members of the council (notably Marillac) argued for the opposite set of priorities. Richelieu's foreign policy centred in these years on the question of the Valtelline passes and the fate of the Grisons, whose control of the passes had been destroyed by the efforts of the Spanish government.[4] For a Cardinal of the Church who had become chief minister in a predominantly Catholic country, the Valtelline conflict posed an acute dilemma since the natural allies of France (the Grisons) were Protestant while the

[1] B.L. Harleian 4472b, fo. 285.

[2] Richelieu, *Mémoires*, vi. 46, 65, 73. Significantly, Richelieu praised Marillac's 'probité' but not his 'force et résolution de son esprit' (vi. 65 n.4) – although undoubtedly this was a later amendment to the memoirs after Marillac's arrest.

[3] Appendix One, Table I. Marillac's apologist naturally gives a more favourable verdict on his *surintendance* while emphasizing chiefly his probity: B.N. MS. fr. 17,486, fos. 74ᵛ–78ʳ.

[4] R. Pithon, 'Les débuts difficiles du ministère de Richelieu et la crise de la Valteline, 1621–1627', *Revue d'Histoire Diplomatique*, lxxiv (1960), 298–322. Idem, 'La Suisse, théâtre de la guerre froide entre la France et l'Espagne pendant la crise de Valteline, 1621–1626', *Schweizerische Zeitschrift für Geschichte*, xiii (1963), 33–53. Lublinskaya (op. cit., pp. 278–81) modifies Pithon's interpretation of the peace of Monzón of 1626 in important respects. However, it should be noted that her verdict is at variance with Richelieu's own, particularly with regard to the role of the French ambassador in Spain, du Fargis.

opponents of French policy included not only Catholic Spain but the Papacy itself. (From May 1623 the forts controlling the Valtelline passes had been garrisoned by Papal troops.) This explains the care with which Richelieu sought to publicize the issues to a rather bemused French public.[1]

The decision of the French government to resort to force was taken at the council meeting of 11 July 1624 before the arrest of La Vieuville. An ultimatum was issued to the Papacy to hand over the fortresses. The ambassadors of Savoy and Venice were notified of the French intention to put the (dormant) triple alliance of February 1623 into effect by taking active military measures. The marquis de Coeuvres was dispatched to the Swiss Cantons with secret instructions to provoke a rising of the Grisons and prepare for open French military involvement. The arrest of La Vieuville made no difference to the policy, since the ultimatum to the Papacy was renewed on 5 September while the military preparations continued.[2] The strategic objective was to cut communications between Genoa and Milan, thus hampering Spanish attempts to defend the Valtelline passes from French invasion. However, this operation required naval support for success and in 1624–5 France had no navy worth speaking of, being totally dependent on a loan of twenty ships from the Dutch which would not become available until March 1625. (As a result of the treaty of Compiègne of 10 June 1624, signed before Richelieu became chief minister, France had lent the Dutch 1.2 million *livres* with a commitment to further loans of one million in both 1625 and 1626. The loans became subsidies if the Dutch offered France reciprocal military assistance, but were repayable if they did not. The agreement to supply the ships was reached on 24 December 1624.)[3] However, by the time the ships were ready, the domestic situation had taken a dramatic turn for the worse and they had to be diverted to meet the challenge from Soubise and the Protestant navy based on La Rochelle. Without the expected naval support, the French strategy in Italy collapsed. The army under Constable

---

[1] E. Thuau, *Raison d'état et pensée politique à l'époque de Richelieu* (1966), pp. 178–97. Church, *Richelieu and reason of state*, pp. 103–72.

[2] *Lettres . . . de Richelieu*, ed. Avenel, vii. 545–8 and 938–9 (Avenel dates Coeuvres's instructions as 10 June, the day before the council meeting). Richelieu, *Mémoires*, iv. 218–21.

[3] Richelieu, *Mémoires*, iv. 88–9, 230; v. 31. The threats in 1627 to make the Dutch repay the loans should be noted: ibid., vii. 88. On the weakness of the French navy at this time: R. Pithon, 'La marine de guerre française au début du ministère de Richelieu. Contribution à l'étude des origines de sa réforme', *Schweizerische Zeitschrift für Geschichte*, x (1960), 18–42.

Lesdiguières captured Gavi on 26 April 1625, but the Spanish retook this fortress on 24 July. In June 1625 Coeuvres was forced to lift the siege of Riva di Chiavenna. The only good news for the French was the successful defence of Verrue after a siege of three months and ten days. By the autumn of 1625 Richelieu was under considerable domestic pressure to negotiate a settlement with the Pope and Philip IV of Spain.

The new element which had upset all Richelieu's calculations was the revolt of Soubise in January 1625, acting in the interests and perhaps the pay of the Spanish government.[1] Later Richelieu recalled that in 1597, when Henri IV had been preoccupied with the siege of Amiens, the Huguenots had seized the opportunity to mount the rebellion which had secured the edict of Nantes.[2] Nevertheless, when he embarked on the Valtelline war Richelieu does not seem to have harboured any fears of a comparable Protestant rising, and the revolt of Soubise followed by that of the duc de Rohan, his elder brother, in February, and the great fortress of La Rochelle in May, seems to have taken him completely by surprise. The chief minister immediately grasped the financial danger posed by fighting a war on two fronts: 'les dépenses sont si excessives en France', he told Louis XIII in May 1625, 'qu'il n'y a personne qui puisse respondre qu'on puisse tousjours fournir à si grands frais . . .'[3] Cardinal Barberini, the papal legate, arrived in France in that month to negotiate a settlement of the Valtelline conflict, while the following July serious negotiations began with the Protestant leaders. The king thus had to choose which conflict to settle first, and the price of both was high. The Protestants wanted the demolition of the royal fortress near La Rochelle known as Fort-Louis, which Richelieu refused point blank. Rohan wanted a military command in Italy and payment of 450,000 *livres* which had been promised as part of the terms of the peace of Montpellier (19 October 1622) but which the finance ministers had not honoured.[4] Should the government

[1] C. S. R. Russell, *Parliaments and English politics, 1621–1629* (Oxford, 1979), pp. 71, 211. Richelieu had his suspicions about Spanish involvement almost from the outset: Richelieu, *Mémoires*, v. 27. *Les papiers de Richelieu*, ed. Grillon, i. 184. Schomberg told the notables on 29 Sept. 1625 that Spain had 'suscité la rébellion' of the Protestants: *Chambre des Comptes*, ed. Boislisle, p. 367.

[2] Richelieu, *Mémoires*, v. 26. *Les papiers de Richelieu*, ed. Grillon, i. 184.

[3] *Les papiers de Richelieu*, ed. Grillon, i. 185.

[4] Richelieu, *Mémoires*, v. 46–7. Richelieu was critical of other misjudgements or omissions by the finance ministers which had contributed to the revolt of the Huguenots, notably the failure to pay for the defence of Blavet and 12 ships seized by Soubise: ibid. v. 5–6.

reach a compromise settlement with the Huguenots in order to pursue its military objectives in Italy? The debate was fiercely contested in the king's council which in July and early August was probably fairly evenly divided.

Marillac, the finance minister, was the chief proponent of peace with Spain and the Papacy.[1] He argued that it was against the interests of the Catholic faith to support the cause of the Grisons, and that this course of action risked divine retribution. The Valtelline war, in his view, was a costly enterprise of little benefit to France (he called it a war 'pour sauver un morceau de terre à des Suisses'). In order to avoid war on two fronts, the king was obliged to seek a compromise peace with the Huguenots, but in Marillac's view such a peace would prove to be 'la ruine de l'état'. The war against the Protestants presented the most favourable opportunity to date of destroying the political and military power of the Huguenots and making the king 'seul et absolu maître de son état'. The king should concentrate on this task and abandon foreign alliances with Protestant states which were likely to assist the rebellion of the Huguenots. Underlying Marillac's argument was a compelling financial logic: war against the Huguenots was a cheaper option than the Valtelline war; two concurrent wars risked a royal bankruptcy. If the war continued for long, the king would be unable to pay the *rentes* and salaries to office-holders. He would be forced to resort to extraordinary fiscal measures, that is to say the establishment of new taxes. These measures would provoke public discontent, which would be made worse by the knowledge that the opportunity for peace had existed but had been rejected by the king and his counsellors.

Richelieu was forced to take these arguments seriously. In a

---

[1] The divisions within the king's council are revealed in a letter of Richelieu to the Queen Mother on 16 Aug. 1625: *Les papiers de Richelieu*, ed. Grillon, i. 205–6. The memoirs make no allusion to a debate in the council until early 1626, at which point Marillac is depicted as the chief proponent of peace: Richelieu, *Mémoires*, v. 206–8. A complication arises in that Marillac is referred to as Keeper of the Seals (ibid., v. 207, 320). However, the speech must have been made while he was *surintendant*: peace was signed with the Protestants on 5 Feb. 1626, yet Marillac only became Keeper of the Seals on 1 June 1626. (It is true that under the terms of the ruling of 2 Sept. 1624 Marillac did not have an *automatic* right of entry to the council of state; but he could be summoned to attend, and presumably was whenever there were important financial principles at stake, as there were in any discussion of foreign policy.) The crucial evidence with regard to the dating of Marillac's speech is his reference to continuing negotiations with the papal legate: these broke down on 24 Sept. 1625, and the speech must have been made before this event. It seems clear from the speech that the debate within the king's council had not been concluded. When Richelieu wrote to the king on 3 Sept. 1625 he wrote 'au nom de tous ceux de son conseil' and argued for rejection of the papal legate's terms: Marillac's speech must have been delivered before this memorandum.

memorandum to the king on 3 September, he pointed out that there was considerable propaganda, inspired by Spain and the Papacy, to the effect that peace was attainable and was only prevented by the attitude of Louis XIII's council. Richelieu rejected this argument: peace was not possible except on terms dictated by the enemies; 'faire mal une paix', he argued, 'c'est préparer une nouvelle guerre . . .' The chief minister also pointed out that Spain and the Papacy were spreading rumours that the king of France lacked financial resources to continue the war, that the Huguenots were nearly victorious, and that Louis XIII's Catholic subjects were ill-disposed (*mal affectionnez*) to the Valtelline war. An assembly of notables was needed to disprove these rumours and to demonstrate that there was public support in France for the policy adopted by the king's council. In Richelieu's view, a compromise peace with the Huguenots was desirable so that an undivided French military effort could be mounted in the Valtelline conflict.[1] The assembly of notables would also be useful as a means of preparing the way for the acceptance of additional fiscal measures and inducing the French clergy to make an appropriate grant to the king.[2]

Further arguments along these lines were presented by Richelieu to the assembly of prelates, nobility, and office-holders which met at Fontainebleau on 29 September 1625.[3] The chief minister emphasized the great issues at stake in the Valtelline conflict and the danger of giving way to Spanish intransigence over the right of free passage for its troops through the passes. The Cardinal stressed the importance of maintaining French diplomatic alliances which a premature unilateral peace would jeopardize. He expressed his confidence in the ability of France to sustain the foreign war: he had been assured by the *surintendants* that there were sufficient funds for the army for four months without recourse to extraordinary fiscal measures or anticipating

---

[1] Richelieu may well have been influenced in reaching this decision by a memorandum from Fancan, his publicist: *Les papiers de Richelieu*, ed. Grillon, i. 218–20.

[2] *Lettres . . . de Richelieu*, ed. Avenel, ii. 119–24. At the time of writing this memorandum, Richelieu considered that the papal legate would prove more flexible in his negotiating position once he understood the French commitment to the Valtelline war. Here he miscalculated. Once Barberini learnt of the projected assembly of notables, he assumed that it was summoned to reject this peace terms and broke off further relations.

[3] Richelieu, *Mémoires*, v. 120–2, 309–10. *Chambre des Comptes*, éd. Boislisle, pp. 366–7. Richelieu's seems to have been by far the most important speech. The presence of the Queen Mother and Marillac, the two most prominent *dévots*, is worth noting. Cf. Major, *Representative government in early modern France*, p. 495.

the revenues for 1626.[1] Richelieu claimed (quite erroneously)[2] that the clergy had pledged its fullest support for a campaign against the Huguenots thus leaving the king's revenues free to pay for the Valtelline war. He dismissed the dangers of pursuing war on two fronts. It is very unlikely that the assembly would have shared his confidence but for one recent event: the defeat of Soubise by an Anglo-Dutch fleet in the French service under the command of Admiral Montmorency (15 September).[3] The remnants of Soubise's fleet had been forced to seek refuge abroad. After this 'signalée victoire' there was little to be feared from the Huguenots, and Richelieu's advice to reject the terms offered by Cardinal Barberini, the papal legate, was accepted by the assembly of notables. As a result, the peace settlements were negotiated in the order determined by Richelieu. The compromise Peace of Paris with the Huguenots came first, on 5 February 1626, and was no more than a truce. The treaty of Monzón, negotiated by Le Fargis the French ambassador in Spain on 5 March, was subsequently modified in detail and not ratified by Louis XIII until 2 May at the earliest.[4] The Valtelline conflict proved exceedingly difficult to resolve. The French allies (the Grisons, Savoy, and Venice) were infuriated by the unilateral peace which took no account of their interests. French diplomacy later tried to retrieve the situation by making secret undertakings to the allies which contradicted the public treaty with Spain. Meanwhile, the Papacy refused to order the demolition of the fortresses until November 1626, and it was not until a year later that this was carried out. The outcome of the Valtelline conflict was not the definitive victory for which Richelieu had hoped.

Louis XIII's financial problems were an important factor leading to the compromise settlements at home and abroad in the spring of 1626.[5] By June 1626, most of the revenues of 1627 had

---

[1] Richelieu used the expression 'quatre montres', which is not quite the same. The text in the memoirs, 'sans toucher au courant', is clearly unsatisfactory, and the other two versions of the speech make it clear that Richelieu meant 1626.

[2] The assembly of the clergy had heard rumours of a settlement with the Huguenots, and on 16 Sept. (before news of the victory over Soubise had arrived) voted to refuse a grant of taxes. On 20 Sept., Schomberg asked for a vote of 3 million *livres* but was rebuffed. It was not until 10 Nov. that the assembly agreed to vote 1.5 million over ten months beginning on 1 Jan. 1626 for the specific purpose of besieging La Rochelle 'et non pour autre sujet': Blet, *Le clergé*, i. 287–92.

[3] Russell, op. cit., pp. 264–5, misdates the victory. Cf. Richelieu, *Mémoires*, v. 58–9.

[4] Cf. Lublinskaya, *French absolutism*, p. 281 n. 2, who argues that the date of ratification was later than is usually accepted.

[5] Cf. Pithon, 'Les débuts difficiles du ministère de Richelieu', 315, who comments 'mais cela n'explique pas tout'.

been anticipated and the deficit on the current account stood at about 52 million *livres*.[1] Richelieu's public statements the previous September thus seem to have been too optimistic. The pressing financial problems of the crown were undoubtedly one reason for the summoning of another assembly of notables—but the notables did not meet until 2 December 1626, and there is little evidence to support the view that France was actually forced out of the Valtelline War because it lacked the resources to continue fighting. If any outside event influenced the decision to ratify the treaty of Monzón, it was not bankruptcy but domestic political conspiracy: two days after the treaty was ratified, Louis XIII ordered the arrest of the maréchal d'Ornano, the nobleman charged with Gaston's education (4 May 1626).[2] This was only the first step in the disclosure of a wide-ranging conspiracy. On 12 June, the duc de Vendôme and his brother, the *grand prieur*, were arrested. After a summary trial, and damaging confessions, Henri de Talleyrand, comte de Chalais, was executed on 19 August. Just as the last embers of the fire were being put out, Ornano died while imprisoned at the Château de Vincennes (2 September). The disgrace of François de Baradat, the royal favourite (2 December) and the conspiracy of the comte de Soissons the following year were both indirect consequences or extensions of the crisis in the summer of 1626.

The motives of the conspirators are exceedingly difficult to unravel and varied according to participant, the aims of some contradicting those of others. In part it was a conspiracy against Richelieu's control of patronage. The Cardinal accused Baradat of overweening ambition: he had received royal gifts and pensions to the value of over 900,000 *livres* in less than two years yet still remained dissatisfied.[3] The Chalais conspiracy was an attempted *coup* in the manner of April 1617: the participation of Guichard Déageant, the former intendant of finance and one of the conspirators against Concini, is significant. Déageant was arrested on 5 May. Louis Tronson, an *intendant des finances* actually in office, was disgraced in August.[4] However, these individuals were exceptions. Richelieu's grip on the king's council seems to have

[1] Estimates in Petit, *L'assemblée des notables de 1626–1627*, pp. 82, 86.

[2] Pithon, art. cit., p. 318. Of course, if Lublinskaya's argument is correct that the treaty was ratified later than 2 May 1626, Ornano was actually arrested before the final settlement of the Valtelline conflict.

[3] The link with the conspiracy is that Baradat had opposed Gaston's marriage: Richelieu, *Mémoires*, vi. 304–19, especially vi. 308 for the pensions.

[4] Ibid., vi. 44, 100. Déageant was a confidant of Ornano.

remained reasonably firm throughout the crisis. It was a court conspiracy, not an intrigue within the central government: at court, even the king's household was affected.[1] On the other hand, if the conspirators were not members of the central government, they certainly wanted a reorganization of the king's council. One of their most important demands was the participation of Gaston d'Orléans in the council of state, which was conceded on 3 May 1626. The highly equivocal role played by Gaston in the affair (characteristically participating in the intrigues and then making damaging confessions which implicated others whose position was more vulnerable than his own)[2] highlights another important feature of this and all other conspiracies before 1638. Louis XIII at this time had no direct male heir. Since Gaston was heir presumptive he was a powerful rallying point for discontent in the way that Alençon had been during the reign of Henri III.

The question of Gaston's marriage and the establishment of an appropriate apanage for the heir presumptive were two of the central issues of the Chalais conspiracy. Should Gaston be allowed to marry into the House of Lorraine, which risked raising the fortunes of the Guises to a summit even higher than that reached in the 1580s? Was it safe to create a vast apanage for Gaston which would serve as power base in any Malcontent movement, such as Alençon had led in 1574–6? One of the great obstacles to this establishment was Gaston's admission that he had resolved at an early stage in the conspiracy to withdraw from court and seek allies for his cause in the provinces.[3] The strength of support for his 'reversionary interest' at this date is indicated by the concessions the government was forced to make. On 31 July 1626, Gaston was accorded the Orléanais, the duchy of Chartres and the county of Blois (but not the Touraine as well, as he had requested), as apanage, at an estimated annual value of 100,000 *livres*.[4] The grant had fiscal implications, since Gaston strove throughout his lifetime to moderate the levy of royal taxes within his apanage.[5] In addition, the crown had to pay heavily to keep

---

[1] Chalais was *maître de la garde robe*, and according to Richelieu other members of the household were implicated: ibid. vi. 26.

[2] *Les papiers de Richelieu*, ed. Grillon, i. 414–23.

[3] Ibid., i. 382–91, 417, 421. Gaston recalled Alençon's apanage as a precedent, but not his rebellion. Richelieu argued that it had been Henri IV's intention to grant Gaston 'de grosses pensions' but not an apanage: Richelieu, *Mémoires*, vi. 80–2.

[4] Ibid., vi. 123–4. *Chambre des Comptes*, ed. Boislisle, p. 375.

[5] In 1652, Gaston asked for a reduction of the taxes of the Orléanais as part of his settlement at the end of the Fronde: B.N. Dupuy 775, fo. 202, 28 Oct. 1652. He asked for

Gaston quiet: 560,000 *livres* became payable annually from the Treasury and a further 100,000 *livres* direct from the *recette-générale* of Orléans.[1] Finally, on 5 August Gaston married Marie de Bourbon (Mademoiselle de Montpensier) despite the earlier fears of the government.[2]

In defusing the political crisis, Richelieu displayed considerable political skills. He recognized the need to attempt a reconciliation with Gaston and to avoid the appearance of attacking the upper nobility as a group. The government had to appear to be acting from a position of strength. Chalais's fate was sealed: he served as sacrificial victim in place of Gaston, who could not be punished.[3] Vendôme, who had talked to Ornano of placing the crown on Gaston's head, was lucky to escape with his life, and was probably saved only because the blood of Henri IV flowed in his veins.[4] Vendôme was also accused of reasserting Breton autonomy: he never regained his governorship, which ironically devolved upon Richelieu in 1631. What the government had feared above all was a rebellion of the three leading princes of the blood, Gaston, Condé, and the comte de Soissons, 'qui renverseroit tout le royaume.'[5] Richelieu's prompt action in seeking a reconciliation with Condé, who had been in disgrace since his disavowal of the Peace of Montpellier, was one of the crucial

---

another reduction in 1659–60: L. Jarry, *La guerre des Sabotiers de Sologne et les assemblées de la noblesse, 1653–1660* (Orléans, 1880), pp. 67–8. E 331a, fo. 295, 14 Jan. 1660.

[1] *Brevets* of 31 July and 5 Aug. 1626 cited in Richelieu, *Mémoires*, vi. 124. The crown appropriated the pension on 3 Aug. 1652 because of Gaston's participation in the Fronde, and presumably did so during his earlier rebellions: cf. *Arrêts du conseil du roi*, ed. Le Pesant, no. 1748.

[2] *Les papiers de Richelieu*, ed. Grillon, i. 424–6. As a result of the marriage, Charles de Lorraine, duc de Guise, became Gaston's father-in-law, but the fears were short-lived because Marie died in June 1627. One of the reasons why some of the conspirators opposed the marriage of Gaston (apart, in the case of the comte de Soissons, from the desire to marry Marie himself) was that if Louis XIII died, Gaston would be free to marry Anne of Austria: ibid., i. 423.

[3] Richelieu used the phrase 'battre le chien devant le lion' to describe Chalais's fate: Richelieu, *Mémoires*, vi. 39.

[4] The fate of Biron was recalled in Vendôme's interrogation: *Les papiers de Richelieu*, ed. Grillon, ii. 29. It is true that Vendôme had not specified who would put the crown on Gaston's head, but this was dangerous talk: A.A.E. France 781, fo. 195. Vendôme had also remarked that 'il n'y a plus de seureté pour les gouverneurs que dans leurs gouvernemen[t]s' (fo. 194ᵛ.) and had opposed the appointment of a provincial intendant: A.A.E. France 782, fos. 131, 132ᵛ., 8 Aug. 1624 and 28 Mar. 1626. Chalais had been executed because of the (probably false) testimony of Roger de Louvigny that he intended to assassinate Louis XIII 'avec ung cousteau large': A.A.E. France 783, fo. 34.

[5] Richelieu, *Mémoires*, vi. 42.

reasons for the defeat of the conspiracy. On 30 May 1626, the chief minister neutralized the threat posed by potentially the most audacious of the conspirators on terms which, in comparison with the concessions later made to Gaston, can only be described as cheap.[1] This event, together with the failure of conspirators' foreign paymasters to provide the promised troops[2] and money, led to the collapse of the Chalais conspiracy.

Despite continuing domestic and foreign problems, the years between 1626 and 1630 saw serious attempts at the reform of government and particularly financial administration. Marillac's apologist later claimed that whereas the Keeper of the Seals was committed to reform, Richelieu 'vouloit la guerre et craignoit la paix . . .'[3] Nothing could be further from the truth in the years 1626–7: before the crisis of the English invasion and the third revolt of the Huguenots, Richelieu seems to have been intent on far-reaching structural reforms and to have shared common objectives with Marillac and d'Effiat, the new finance minister. The Cardinal seems to have had a general reform plan 'pour toutes les affaires du royaume' by late 1625 or early 1626,[4] which included provision for the reduction of expenses on the king's household to the level of Henri III's reign, the abolition of the sale of offices (and thus royal income from the *parties casuelles*) and the reduction in the number of offices to the level of 1574. The *comptants* were condemned by Richelieu as 'une des principales causes de la dissipation de(s) . . . finances' and were not to be used in the future at all. Salaries of office-holders were to be reduced to the level of 1576; royal gifts were also to be restricted. The *Chambre des Comptes* was to carry out a permanent investigation of financial corruption without 'compositions, grâces ou remises' to the financiers. A special commision of twelve financial experts (*conseil de*

---

[1] *Les papiers de Richelieu*, ed. Grillon, i. 339–43. All Condé had asked for was to be recalled to court and to have his pensions paid: Richelieu, *Mémoires*, vi. 340–2. Vendôme had certainly attempted to attract him into the conspiracy, talking of the state being governed by 'des gens qui ne devront se mesler que de leur bréviaire': A.A.E. France 781, fo. 194ᵛ.

[2] Particularly the duke of Savoy, acting out of pique at the French attempt to negotiate a unilateral settlement of the Valtelline conflict. Cf. A.A.E. France 783, fo. 34: 'que Mr. de Savoye en estoit [duparti] aussy et debvoir fournir 10,000 hommes . . .' The duke promised assistance to the comte de Soissons in 1627: cf. *Les papiers de Richelieu*, ed. Grillon, iii. 46–7.

[3] B.N. MS. fr. 17486, fos. 116ᵛ.–117ʳ. Cf. Major, *Representative government in early modern France*, p. 581. Earlier (p. 496) Major discusses Richelieu's reforming intentions in 1625.

[4] *Les papiers de Richelieu*, ed. Grillon, i. 248–69. The dating of the plan is uncertain, but it refers to the position of Constable (i. 249) and must precede the death of Lesdiguières on 28 Sept. 1626 and the subsequent abolition of the office.

réduction) was to be set up with the purpose of investigating procedures for the resumption of alienated crown lands.

In addition to this general plan of reform, Richelieu seems to have devised a more detailed set of proposals for restoring stability to the king's finances by creating a budgetary surplus for the first time since the ministry of Sully.[1] Royal expenditure was to be reduced drastically from 44 million *livres* in 1626 to 25 million 'after the peace'. All areas of royal expenditure were to be pruned, but the reduction in the military establishment was to be so drastic that the king's ability to fight another foreign war would have been seriously affected. On the other hand, Richelieu envisaged total royal income of over 58 million and thus presumably a very useful war reserve of 33 million a year. This royal income would be provided from a redistribution of taxes. The chief direct tax, the *taille*, would be abolished. It would be replaced by the salt tax, which would be extended uniformly throughout the kingdom (and would raise 30 million) and a new 5 per cent sales tax (which would raise 12 million).[2] Whether a redistribution of taxes on this scale was possible in *ancien régime* France seems unlikely. Traditionally, the areas exempted from the salt tax, or which carried a relatively light burden, had displayed stern resistance to the loss of their privileges, as in the great revolts of 1542 and 1548 in south-west France. The introduction of new taxes always carried risks and the experiment with the sales tax or *pancarte* under Henri IV and Sully had been a failure: the new tax had had to be withdrawn in 1602. However, Richelieu was essentially a pragmatist. He may well have thought that far-reaching reform was desirable, but the application of reform was to be tempered by his

[1] Several examples exist of the 'projet pour augmenter le revenu de Sa Majesté et décharger son peuple' and the 'projet de dépense après la paix': *Recueil . . . des lois*, ed. Jourdan *et al.*, xvii. 101–2, 106–9. K 891, no. 2. B.N. MS. fr. 4520, fo. 202ᵛ. MS. fr. 11138. MS. fr. 18491, fo. 232. Other examples are cited by R.É. Mousnier, 'Le testament politique de Richelieu . . .', *Revue Historique*, cci (1949), 64 n.6. The peace referred to may be the treaty of Monzón. On the other hand, several copies of the document link it to the year 1639, and a two-month truce began in Italy on 14 Aug. 1639. The evidence for Richelieu's 'grand dessein du sel' at an earlier date in his ministry (Feb. 1627) is in Richelieu, *Mémoires*, vii. 32. [This summarizes a memorandum from Condé which refers to Richelieu's appointment as governor of Brouage (4 Feb.) but the notables still in session (they were dismissed on 23 Feb.).] The usual judgement on this plan is that it showed Richelieu's ignorance of financial questions: cf. H. Hauser, *La pensée et l'action économiques du Cardinal de Richelieu* (1944), p. 178. However, this verdict in turn rests on the inaccurate (and thus incomprehensible) figures in Richelieu, *Testament politique*, ed. André, pp. 437–8, 441–3. (André's edition in 1947 did not correct the mistakes in the figures in the earlier editions.)

[2] The reading in the *Testament politique*, ed. André, pp. 437–8, gives respectively 25,000 *livres* and 12,000 *livres*! The figure of 12 million was also the estimated yield of the sales tax in 1641–2: cf. A.A.E. France 872, fo. 460, *c.* 1650.

other political objectives and the opportunities presented by the foreign and domestic situation.[1]

Nevertheless, significant changes were introduced. One of the most important of these was the abolition of the offices of Constable and Admiral of France in January 1627. The abolition of Constable was made possible by the death of Lesdiguières, the last holder of the office; but Admiral Montmorency had to be bought out for 1.2 million *livres*.[2] There were certainly political reasons for this decision. Earlier Constables had either been powerful magnates in their own right (such as Montmorency-Damville) or else royal favourites (such as Luynes) who had obtained the office through influence. They had not necessarily been safe choices as the head of the army. With regard to the position of Admiral, Richelieu wanted to build up a French navy and in October 1626 had himself appointed *grand maître, chef et surintendant général de la navigation et commerce de France*.[3] Yet though there were political reasons for abolishing two of the great semi-independent offices of the crown, the financial arguments seem to have been paramount. The existence of these offices prevented the finance minister from supervising all the detailed aspects of military and naval expenditure: 'de l'abus de ces puissances sont arrivés les désordres qui ont mis en arrière les finances du roi', Richelieu concluded. For his part, d'Effiat estimated the savings as at least 400,000 *livres* a year.[4] In the short term, it was essential to wrest control of the 'deniers du roi' from semi-independent officials of the crown.[5] In the longer term, the abolition of these

---

[1] Thus in 1639, during the war against Spain and after the revolt of the *Va-Nu-Pieds* had broken out, Richelieu condemned Bullion and Bouthillier's attempted extension of the *gabelles* into the *pays de quart bouillon* in Normandy: M. Foisil, *La révolte des Nu-Pieds et les révoltes normandes de 1639* (1970), p. 157. *Lettres . . . de Richelieu*, ed. Avenel, vi. 494–5. B.N. MS. fr. 18510, fo. 266, 27 Aug. 1639. It is significant that although the 'grand dessein du sel' appears to have existed in embryonic form at the time of the assembly of notables it was not presented to them for formal approval. Perhaps Richelieu feared the idea would be rejected. When Chevalier, a *président* of the *Cour des Aides* of Paris, proposed the extension of the land tax throughout the kingdom, the notables rejected the idea. The *Parlement* of Bordeaux had been suspended in the years 1548–50 following the great revolt against the *gabelle*. The majority of the notables in 1626–7 were office-holders who would be inclined to side with provincial privileges.

[2] Lublinskaya, *French absolutism*, pp. 287–8. B.N. n.a.f. 7228, fo. 69/2, Jan. 1627. Cf. *Les papiers de Richelieu*, ed Grillon, iii. 503.

[3] *Les papiers de Richelieu*, ed. Grillon, i. 511–15. Richelieu was already head of French commerce, a position to which he was appointed in Jan. 1626, with d'Effiat as his *intendant de commerce*: A.A.E. France 782, fo. 33, 19 Jan. 1626.

[4] Richelieu, *Mémoires*, vi. 297. Petit, *L'assemblée des notables de 1626–1627*, p. 84.

[5] Cf. the later judgement of Servien and Foucquet on the abolition of the Constableship: A.A.E. France 892, fo. 379, 25 Sept. 1653. After the death of Lesdiguières, the activities of

offices helped make possible the improvement in the performance of the French army and the establishment of a French navy.

Other measures of reform were proposed to an assembly of notables comprising 13 members of the clergy, 13 nobles (including Gaston d'Orléans, the president) and 29 office-holders which met at Paris between 2 December 1626 and 24 February 1627.[1] Richelieu, Marillac, Schomberg, and d'Effiat all made speeches to the assembly, demonstrating the commitment of the ministers to reform. Several important ideas were discussed, including the establishment of trading companies and the improvement of internal communications by a canal-building scheme even more ambitious than Sully's.[2] However, the problem of the king's finances dominated the meeting, partly because the financial outlook was so gloomy, partly because the ministers were extraordinarily frank in their assessment of the situation after the Valtelline war. Richelieu stated categorically that it was impossible to introduce new taxes because the people would not be able to pay them ('les peuples ne sçauroient plus porter'). In his view, the way to solve the problem of the king's finances was by a resumption of alienated crown lands.[3] D'Effiat proposed various alternative methods of funding such a scheme, but what is striking is the relatively modest objective of repurchasing lands to the value of 25 million *livres*.[4] (Sully had estimated alienated royal lands and revenues at 150 million, and had signed leases for repurchase to a value approaching 40 million.) It is doubtful whether the income produced from this relatively modest scheme would be sufficient to solve the crown's financial problems. D'Effiat pointed out that royal expenditure had increased substantially since 1608–9, yet net income had actually fallen. He

his munitions contractors in the army of Italy (Jacques Artault, Charles Perinet and Jean-Baptiste Palleologo) were investigated by Nesmond, a *maître des requêtes*, acting on the orders of the council of finance: E 91b, fo. 113, 27 Mar. 1627.

[1] The list in Petit, op. cit., pp. 233–45 is more complete than that used by Lublinskaya, *French absolutism*, p. 296. Cf. also the recent discussion in Major, *Representative government in early modern France*, pp. 501–8.

[2] Hauser, op. cit., p. 50. Lublinskaya, op. cit., p. 300. G7 722, 'extrait de la harangue de Monsieur le Chancelier Séguier [*sic*: in reality of Marillac as Keeper of the Seals] . . .', included in a memorandum of Cazier to Desmaretz, 9 June 1710.

[3] Lublinskaya, op. cit., p. 299.

[4] Lublinskaya, loc. cit., gives Richelieu's figure of 20 million. D'Effiat's estimate was higher, 25.6 million: Petit, op. cit., pp. 98, 278–80. It should be noted that this was the capital value of the scheme, not the annual revenue. Lublinskaya's verdict (based on Richelieu's speech) that it would be 'possible to balance the budget permanently' appears questionable.

estimated the revenues for 1627 at 39 million yet a sum of 22 million was to be levied as *charges* in the provinces. (The increase in local payments and alienated taxes is one of the distinctive features of financial administration in the 1620s.)[1]

When faced with this sombre financial picture, the notables reacted predictably. The reflex response was voiced by Antoine Nicolay, the *premier président* of the *Chambre des Comptes*, who denounced the abuses in financial administration and the excessive profits made by the financiers. He and his colleagues had heard d'Effiat's report with astonishment: there should be an immediate reduction in the secret expenses and the sums paid out in royal gifts and pensions.[2] The notables refused to establish a working fund for the resumption of alienated crown lands, opting instead for a repurchase scheme spread over sixteen years. For success, this scheme would require conditions of civil and foreign peace until 1643. (In the case of both France and Spain, 1627 presented one of the last opportunities for domestic reform in peacetime, since war began in Italy between the two powers the following year.)[3] Instead of establishing a fund for the repurchase of crown lands, the notables suggested that the French budget should be balanced by drastic reductions in royal expenditure. They agreed that the army should be based in the provinces, but two-thirds of the cost was to be borne by the central treasury. They agreed to establish a navy comprising 45 ships at an estimated cost of 1.2 million *livres*, but declined to comment on the source from which the finance for building the fleet was to be raised. Despite energetic speeches and clear proposals from the ministers, the notables decided little of any lasting value or importance.[4]

As with the previous assemblies of notables in 1596–7 and 1617, the crown was left with no choice but executive action. Attempts at financial reform did not end with the meeting of the notables in 1626–7. The efforts of Marillac and d'Effiat ensured that they continued and were brought to fruition in the form of royal legislation: the most important measures were the rulings on finance of 26 June 1627 and 18 January 1630, the decision to keep

[1] Petit, op. cit., pp. 109, 274–8. Collins, 'Sur l'histoire fiscale du xviie siècle', 332.

[2] *Chambre des Comptes*, ed. Boislisle, pp. 371–4.

[3] Cf. J. H. Elliott, 'The statecraft of Olivares', *The diversity of history. Essays in honour of Sir Herbert Butterfield*, ed. Elliott and H. G. Koenigsberger (1970), pp. 138–40.

[4] The judgement of Petit, op. cit., p. 229 is more charitable than Lublinskaya, op. cit., pp. 324–5.

proper records at the *contrôle-général des finances* (13 September 1628),[1] and above all, clauses 344 to 411 of the royal ordinance of January 1629 known as the *Code Michaud* after the most decisive influence on its drafting, Michel de Marillac.[2] Taken together, the royal ordinance and the various supplementary rulings provided clear guidelines and procedures for financial administration in peace-time. Leases on the revenue farms were to be granted by the king's council in the customary manner, but the procedures for taking sureties were tightened up, and the revenue farmers were to present their annual accounts within three months of the end of each year of the lease. A special committee of the king's council, comprising the controller-general, an intendant of finance, and seven councillors of state, was established to supervise their activities. (The same committee also discussed proposals for fiscal expedients such as the creation of new offices.)

Comparable procedures were established for the administration of direct taxes. The *brevet* ordering the levy of the *taille* was to be sent out each year by the end of July. In each parish, the *commissaire des tailles* was to keep an accurate record of all levies of taxation. The royal edict on the *taille* of 1600 was to be implemented by the *élus*, together with a subsequent edict of 1614 which had limited fiscal exemptions. There was a general tightening up of the rules of ennoblement and an attempt to prevent tax evasion by false claims to nobility. These concerns foreshadow the sending out of *commissaires pour le régalement des tailles* in 1634–5.[3] The investigation of noble titles had a fiscal purpose: in 1627 it was suggested that 9.5 million *livres* could be raised in fines from a *réformation de noblesse*, although this estimate was probably exaggerated.[4] (In one respect the *Code Michaud* liberalized the laws of *dérogeance*: a noble was henceforth free to participate in maritime

---

[1] Mousnier, 'Les règlements du conseil du roi sous Louis XIII', 169–73, 177–81, 191–6.

[2] *Recueil . . . des lois*, ed. Jourdan *et al.*, xvi. 223–342, esp. 305–26. For Marillac's influence on the *Code Michaud*: L. Desjonquères, *Le garde des sceaux Michel de Marillac et son oeuvre législative* (1908), pp. 95–222. Richelieu later implied that there had been conflict between Marillac and d'Effiat over the wording of the *Code Michaud*, but the reference is obscure: *Lettres . . . de Richelieu*, ed. Avenel, vi. 69. Ranum, *Richelieu and the councillors of Louis XIII*, pp. 151–2. Louis XIII told Antoine Nicolay, the *premier président* of the *Comptes* to 'garder et faire garder (the *Code Michaud*), observer et entretenir inviolablement . . .': *Chambre des Comptes*, ed. Boislisle, p. 380. A recent discussion of the *Code Michaud* and the difficulty in obtaining registration is provided by Major, *Representative government in early modern France*, pp. 512–17.

[3] Cf. Bonney, *Political change in France under Richelieu and Mazarin*, pp. 181–3.

[4] A.A.E. France 787, fo. 157. However, the example of the *généralité* of Caen suggests the hopes were optimistic: cf. D. J. Sturdy, 'Tax evasion, the *faux nobles* and state fiscalism: the example of the *généralité* of Caen, 1634–35', *French Historical Studies*, ix (1976), 549–72.

commerce provided that he did not engage in any retail business.)[1] A fundamental principle of French law was reasserted, namely that there could be no unauthorized additions to the *état des finances*. Governors, lieutenants-general, and other officials of the crown were prohibited from levying taxes unless specifically empowered to do so by letters patent. Between 1627 and 1631, the amount of direct taxes was reduced by three million *livres* and the arrears of the *taille* up to the end of 1624 were remitted. A second committee of the king's council, comprising the intendant of finance with responsibility for the particular province under discussion,[2] and six councillors of state, dealt with the detailed aspects of the administration of direct taxes.

The same committee of the king's council was also empowered to investigate the validity of claims for repayment of debts owed by the crown. Article 378 of the *Code Michaud* specifically prohibited the making of royal gifts as repayment of debts, which had been common practice during the minority of Louis XIII. Instead, the Chancellor or the Keeper of the Seals and the finance minister were to order repayment of debts at the end of each year on the basis of a list authorized and signed by the king. Similarly, royal gifts were not to be paid out until the end of the year, when all other burdens on the king's finances had been met. All previous royal gifts were revoked by article 381 of the *Code Michaud*.[3] Henceforth royal gifts of less than 3000 *livres* could not be made out in the form of a secret payment (*comptant*), while gifts above this amount were subject to registration by the *Chambre des Comptes*.[4] All beneficiaries of royal gifts were to declare the total amount of income they had received from this source over the previous three years. Royal gifts issued under false pretexts or in the name of agents rather than the real beneficiaries were revocable and a fine could be levied for the offence. Royal pensions were also to be reduced. A separate list was to be drawn up at the end of the year and signed by the king himself, with payments made only

[1] Article 452. Cf. D. Bitton, *The French nobility in crisis, 1560–1640* (Stanford, Ca., 1969), pp. 70, 73.

[2] Each intendant of finance was allocated special responsibility for a number of provinces according to a *département* drawn up by the Chancellor, Keeper of the Seals or finance minister from time to time. Cf. Mosser, *Les intendants des finances au xviii⁰ siècle*, pp. 276–7, who publishes the *département* of 31 Dec. 1641.

[3] They could subsequently be confirmed by letters patent counter-signed by a secretary of state and sealed with the great seal: doubtless some were. According to Mallet's figures the total spent by the crown on pensions and gifts fell from 5.1 million in 1626 to under 3.3 million in 1630: Appendix Two, Table II.

[4] D'Épernon's pension of 11,000 *livres* per annum was registered by the *Comptes* on 29 Dec. 1629: P 2357, p. 729.

when the true state of his finances were known. (In this respect, d'Effiat's ministry was fairly successful: the amount spent on pensions fell from nearly 3.6 million *livres* in 1626 to less than 2.7 million in 1631.[1]) The salaries of the king's councillors were set within clear limits. According to the ruling of 18 January 1630, Richelieu as chief minister was to receive 18,000 *livres* a year; d'Effiat, Marillac and Schomberg 14,400 each; the four secretaries of state, three intendants of finance, controller-general and *trésorier de l'Épargne* were each to receive 7,200 *livres* a year. Article 61 of the *Code Michaud* revoked the *brevets* of all councillors of state. Many were reinstated,[2] but there was a serious attempt to reduce the size of the council and thus the amount spent in salaries on the king's councillors. Similarly, other administrative costs were closely scrutinized. The legal fees (*épices*) of the *Chambre des Comptes* were not to be increased. The salaries, fees, and transportation costs of the accountants (*comptables*) were regulated; receipts had to be produced before their incidental costs were reimbursed. Accountants had to specify the sums they had received in cash or else they were liable to prosecution on the charge of peculation.

Throughout the *Code Michaud* considerable emphasis was placed on establishing procedures to ensure better accounting, from the *trésorier de l'Épargne* down to the bottom of the hierarchy of treasurers and accountants. In this respect, Marillac seems to have been reacting to his own difficulties as *surintendant*. When d'Effiat entered office in June 1626, he was confronted by 'une montagne de papiers'. More than 250 million *livres* had not been satisfactorily audited, including the accounts of ten *trésoriers de l'Épargne*[3] and more than 400 treasurers, revenue farmers, and tax-contractors. The accounts which had not been satisfactorily audited went back some five or six years. D'Effiat claimed that by a 'merveille[ux] travail et labeur continuel' he had reviewed more accounts than all his predecessors put together.[4] The *Code Michaud* reasserted

<hr />

[1] A.A.E. France 783, fo. 200. A.A.E. France 797, fo. 217.

[2] Reinstatement of Antoine Nicolay, 15 Jan. 1630: *Chambre des Comptes*, ed. Boislisle, p. 382. The reinstatement of other councillors may be traced from B.N. MS. fr. 16218, fo. 330 and MS. fr. 18152, fo. 119.

[3] Because of the rapid change-over of chief treasurers in 1625–6, this would take accounting back only to 1621: Appendix One, Table IV.

[4] Petit, op. cit., p. 271. *Les papiers de Richelieu*, ed. Grillon, i. 347. Attempts by the council of finance to enforce better accounting procedures: E 85b, fo. 280, 28 Feb. 1626. E 88b, fo. 240, 24 Sept. 1626. E 93b, fo. 167, 30 Aug. 1627. E 99b, fos. 170, 343, 21 and 26 Feb. 1629. D'Effiat attributed his illness in 1628 to this excessive burden: A.A.E. France 795, fo. 184. Cf. the supervision of the accounts of Claude du Floz, *receveur général* at Poitiers in 1628 by d'Effiat and Sublet des Noyers: E 102, fo. 224, 6 Mar. 1630.

the time limit on the submission of accounts and the rules laid down in previous royal ordinances on the subject of peculation. Considerable stress was placed on the investigation of fraudulent bankruptcy, and three witnesses were sufficient to provide proof of peculation.[1] The government recognized that there had been frequent abuses in royal financial administration in the past, and under article 411 of the *Code Michaud* envisaged the establishment of a permanent *chambre de justice* drawn from the officeholders but appointed under a royal commission.[2] A distinction was made between corrupt officials and financiers and 'nos bons et fidèles officiers', particularly the *trésoriers de l'Épargne*, who might later hope to be promoted to senior positions within the *Chambre des Comptes* or the king's council. Article 151 of the *Code Michaud* described interest rates on the private market above *denier* 16 (6.25 per cent) as usurious, but made the exception of interest rates paid by the crown to financiers 'que les nécessitez de nos affaires nous obligent de faire . . .'

Underlying the various aspects of Marillac's financial legislation were two fundamental purposes. The first was to keep much closer scrutiny over all aspects of financial administration than ever before. Indeed, his attempt at record-keeping and the supervision of accounting was more ambitious than that of any other minister before 1661. The ruling of the council of 13 September 1628, which established the guide-lines for keeping records at the *contrôle-général des finances*, pointed out the multitude of abuses which had occurred because of the ineffectiveness of government: tax contracts had been continued by financiers even after the government had ordered the abolition of the taxes being collected; royal debts had been repaid yet were still claimed by creditors; royal gifts were enjoyed by private individuals after the expiry of the time-limit on the act of donation; acts of surety could not be found when a particular revenue farmer or tax contractor went bankrupt; leases and contracts for the alienation or resumption of crown lands could not be found, which prevented the government from ascertaining the true extent of alienated crown lands.[3] Marillac's

---

[1] D'Effiat had wanted proof from two witnesses to be sufficient and the 'exhibition des partages et des titres des successions': Petit, op. cit., p. 285. Marillac appears not to have accepted the necessity, or desirability, of granting these wider powers to the government.

[2] Article 411 specified that it was not necessary for the government to make 'autre publication ni enregistrement que cesdites présentes' to establish the *chambre de justice*. However, the royal commissions appointing individuals to serve appear never to have been issued.

[3] That this was not known is indicated by d'Effiat's decision to carry out an investigation: E88b, fo. 120, 12 Aug. 1626. E96b, fos. 145, 184, 30 June and 6 July 1628. Article 24 of

innovation as Keeper of the Seals was less the concern for record-keeping as the determination to enforce new procedures: all royal acts and copies of deeds (*expéditions*) were declared null and void unless they had been registered and certified by the controller-general. However, the application of these measures was possible only with the good intent of reforming ministers: Marillac himself, d'Effiat as *surintendant* and Simon Marion as controller-general. Marion died in December 1628, Marillac was arrested on 12 November 1630, and d'Effiat died on 27 July 1632. Their successors were unable or unwilling to implement the reforms.

The second fundamental purpose of the legislation was to ensure the balancing of the budget at peace-time levels of expenditure. The ruling of 18 January 1630 envisaged Henri IV's expenses in 1610[1] as the model on which the finance minister would base his estimates at the beginning of the year. A fund of three million *livres* was to be set aside for unforseen contingencies. Further amounts could be anticipated by a loan from the *trésorier de l'Épargne* who would hold the fund in the following year, but interest would be paid on the loan and the implication was that the amount of revenue to be anticipated would not be large. Strict control over increases in royal expenditure would be ensured by the fact that the council of state (*conseil des affaires et dépêches*) had to discuss any increase and the king had to write a personal authorization before it could take place. Overall, Marillac's legislation seems to have reflected the aspirations and preoccupations of the Estates-General of 1614–15 and the two assemblies of notables of 1617 and 1626–7. Indeed, the *Code Michaud* was declared to have been drawn up 'sur le(urs) plaintes'.[2] The problem with the legislation was that it came over a decade too late.

As has been seen, legislation in itself was not enough. The new

---

the ruling of 13 Sept. 1628 envisaged the completion of the investigation within three months.

[1] Strictly speaking, the year 1608 was the last year of Henri IV's peacetime expenditure, since in 1609–10 he was preparing for intervention in the Cleves-Jülich succession crisis. In 1630 France was fighting the war of the Mantuan succession. The parallel reflects Marillac's concern to ensure that the Italian intervention proved to be a war of limited purpose and duration.

[2] *Recueil . . . des lois*, ed. Jourdan *et al.*, xvi. 223. Thus Picot, *Histoire des États-Généraux*, v. 31–51, discusses the financial proposals of the three meetings and their influence on the *Code Michaud* in one section. Hayden, *France and the Estates-General of 1614*, pp. 211–13 presents the proposals and their enactment in legislation as a comparative table. At p. 215 he comments that the *Code Michaud* was only a partial enactment, more closely related to the proposals of the notables in 1626–7 than the Estates-General of 1614–15.

rules had to be applied in practice by the finance minister. Antoine Coiffier de Ruzé, marquis d'Effiat was an ideal choice. The son of a lesser noble in the Auvergne who had been a loyal supporter (and creditor) of Henri IV, d'Effiat had been a leading figure in Louis XIII's household and was sent on important diplomatic assignments in 1619 and 1624.[1] He had linked himself firmly to Richelieu's cause in May 1624 when he had denounced the budgetary deficit and the excessive pensions paid to the nobles.[2] In January 1626, he had been appointed *intendant de commerce*, a position directly subordinate to Richelieu himself. Thus by the time of his elevation to the *surintendance des finances* later in the year, d'Effiat had obtained useful experience in government. In his own words, he was able to set to work immediately with experience behind him, when a period of apprenticeship would have been 'très dangereux à l'estat' and likely to cost the king several million in lost revenue.[3] On several occasions, d'Effiat reflected on the qualities required in a finance minister: in his view, foresight, vigilance, intelligence, and diligence were the most important. The *surintendant* must have imagination to think up ideas for new taxes, persuasiveness in order to enlist the services of the financiers, integrity so that the king's 'credit' be maintained and the financiers allowed honest profits, resoluteness in the handling of council business, and the ability to bring to heel those who owed the king money. Above all, he must be a good administrator with book-keeping expertise to avoid confusion in the registers of expenses and revenues. He must be able to delegate. In peace-time, the task of the finance minister was simple enough. It was true that the public revenues were insufficient,[4] but in peace-time they could be increased gradually and there was no need for extraordinary taxes such as the creation of *rentes*. In wartime, the tasks of the finance minister were much more difficult and even the most able tended to lose their reputation

[1] Gilbert II Coiffier d'Effiat was a 'capitaine de 50 hommes d'armes des ordonnances de Sa Majesté' and had served as governor of Clermont-Ferrand: cf. E 92b, fo. 173, 16 June 1627. For Henri IV's debts to him: Appendix Two, Table IX A iii. Antoine Coiffier was 'premier escuyer de la grande escurie . . . intendant et ordonnateur des bâtiments en ses (i.e. the king's) maisons et châteaux de Moulins et Riom': E 74b, fo. 188, 5 May 1623. In 1624 he carried out the negotiations for the Anglo-French marriage alliance.

[2] *Les papiers de Richelieu*, ed. Grillon, i. 88–90.

[3] A.A.E. France 795, fo. 184, undated memorandum entitled 'voicy l'estat auquel Monsieur le marquis d'Effiat laisse les affaires des finances', presumably written when he was seriously ill in 1628.

[4] In d'Effiat's words, an increase in revenues was necessary because of 'la foiblesse présente de l'estat': A.A.E. France 797, fo. 215, *c.* 1631–2.

because they were forced to rely on expedients. D'Effiat thus had few illusions about the difficulties he faced, but modelled himself firmly on the maxims and methods of Henri IV and Sully.[1] Although d'Effiat was unable to reduce royal expenditure to 33 million *livres*, the level of the last years of Henri IV's reign, one of his more remarkable achievements was to check the rise in royal expenditure in the 1620s. For reasons of foreign and domestic war, 1629 was a record year with total expenditure exceeding 54 million. However, the trend was firmly reversed the following year, when expenses were cut to less than 42 million.[2] D'Effiat's own calculations demonstrated that there was scarcely any increase at all in royal expenditure in the quinquennium 1626–30 as against the previous five years.[3] The average annual expenditure of the crown in the 1620s was about 42 million *livres*. By comparison with the later 1630s, these were peace-time levels of expenditure.

How had d'Effiat maintained such economy? The campaign to eliminate waste at all levels of financial administration had undoubtedly produced some positive results, although it is doubtful whether it alone could have halted the trend towards increased royal expenditure. D'Effiat sought to halt the process of alienating royal revenues which had been under way since the time of Jeannin. Of course, he had to create some new *rentes* in time of crisis,[4] but he redeemed more than he alienated. Claude Charlot's lease on the *gabelles de France*, signed under the name of Thomas Guyot, specified that the revenue farmer was to redeem 8.5 million *livres* in *rentes* established previously on this revenue.[5] D'Effiat claimed to have redeemed 12 million *livres* in *gages*, offices, and other alienated rights of the crown in 1629.[6] He also sought to borrow less frequently and to reduce the interest rate payable to financiers on loans to the crown: he claimed that his predecessors had often had to borrow at rates of interest of up to 30 per cent, but

[1] He recalled a maxim of Henri IV (though hardly a reforming one) with regard to the alienation of crown lands: A.A.E. France 779, fo. 35. His concern to model the accounts on the year 1608 attests to his admiration of Sully's methods. He cited a maxim of Sully: A.A.E. France 797, fo. 215.

[2] Appendix Two, Table I.

[3] D'Effiat calculated total expenditure in the quinquennium 1621–5 as 209,448,168 *livres* as against 210,207,130 in the quinquennium 1626–30: A.A.E. France 797, fo. 206.

[4] Véron de Forbonnais, *Recherches*, i. 212, stated that there was no alienation of revenues in 1628. In fact, 120,000 *livres* in *rentes* were created which ought, in theory, to have yielded 1.44 million to the Treasury: V6, 69, no. 2, 6 Nov. 1628.

[5] Clause 38 of his lease specified that this was the capital value of the redemption: P 2356, p. 681 and AD IX 413, no. 33, 30 Mar. 1628. Other evidence of redemptions in E 99b, fo. 454, 26 Feb. 1629. E 103a, fo. 97, 18 Apr. 1630. V6 79, no. 11, 31 Dec. 1630.

[6] A.A.E. France 797 fo. 208ᵛ.

that he had paid only 10 per cent. In part, the smaller borrowing requirement would have accounted for the fall in the rate of interest.[1] All finance ministers had to sign tax contracts (*traités*); even Marillac left some in readiness for his successor.[2] Nevertheless, since tax contracts tended to carry high rates of interest, the key to efficient financial adminstration was to use them as sparingly as possible. D'Effiat's preference was to have recourse to extraordinary taxes only in absolute necessity.[3] However, according to Mallet's figures, the proportion of total royal income derived from the *affaires extraordinaires* rose from 20 per cent in the years 1620–4 to 31.6 per cent in the years 1625–9. The situation worsened in the last two years of d'Effiat's ministry.[4]

Mallet's figures also indicate that the *parties casuelles* represented a somewhat larger proportion of ordinary royal income under d'Effiat than under his predecessors (49 per cent of ordinary income in the years 1625–9 as against 46.4 per cent in the years 1620–4). The proportion was to rise still further in the 1630s, partly as a result of d'Effiat's efforts in 1630–1 to extract higher payments from the office-holders in return for the renewal of the *droit annuel*. When the lease on the *droit annuel* expired on 31 December 1629, d'Effiat appears to have hoped to obtain a forced loan from all office-holders equivalent to a quarter of the value of their offices. The conditions proposed in the royal declaration of 27 January 1630 provoked howls of protest from the office-holders and had to be modified on 21 December: the members of the sovereign courts were to pay a forced loan equivalent to 12.5 per cent of the value of their offices; the *trésoriers de France* and members of the *présidiaux* were to pay 16.6 per cent; the other office-holders were to pay a forced loan of 20 per cent. This policy of divide and rule was reasonably successful in damping down the opposition, although by August 1631 most of the sovereign courts had been allowed the renewal of the *droit annuel* without paying any forced loan at all.[5] Despite the crisis in relations between the crown and the office-holders in 1630–1, d'Effiat's policy towards the tribun-

---

[1] Petit, *L'assemblée des notables de 1626–7*, pp. 83–4. He gave conflicting reports on the previous rate of interest: Lublinskaya, *French absolutism*, pp. 305, 307. Appendix Two, Table VIII A.

[2] B.N. MS. fr. 17,486, fo. 78.

[3] A.A.E. France 853, fo. 164ᵛ.

[4] Appendix Two, Tables IV, V and VII A.

[5] Mousnier, *La vénalité*, pp. 292–5, 656–61. A. L. Moote, *The revolt of the judges. The Parlement of Paris and the Fronde, 1643–1652* (Princeton, N. J., 1971), pp. 59–62. A.A.E. France 796, fo. 328, 6 Dec. 1630.

als seems to have been reasonably moderate. The salaries of the office-holders were paid and so were the *rentes*. D'Effiat did not act on Condé's advice in 1627, which was to appropriate the *rentes*, a policy which might have raised 15 or 20 million *livres* in revenue to the crown.[1]

Instead, d'Effiat concentrated his efforts on attempting to increase the rents payable by the revenue farmers of the indirect taxes. He claimed to have increased rents by over six million *livres* during his ministry,[2] a boast that cannot be accepted uncritically. Nevertheless, there was undoubtedly a significant increase in rents during the earlier years of his administration. Antoine Feydeau had paid less than 6 million *livres* a year for the *gabelles de France*, yet Claude Charlot was paying 8.5 million a year after 1628. Étienne Brioys paid nearly 2.5 million as against 2.2 million under the previous farmer of the *aides*.[3] Mallet's figures suggest that the revenue farms represented a slightly larger proportion of total royal income under d'Effiat, and a significantly larger proportion of ordinary income (24 per cent of ordinary income came from the revenue farms in the years 1625–9 as against 20.1 per cent in the years 1620–4).

The increase would have been greater but for the fact that the revenue farmers used the subsistence crisis of 1629–31 as an excuse to demand remissions on their rents. Claude Charlot led the way, complaining to the council of finance of reduced consumption of salt because of 'la pauvreté du peuple et la maladie contagieuse'. Substantial remissions had to be accorded on his rents and on 29 January 1631 the government had to resort to direct administration of the *gabelles de France* because Charlot was bankrupt: when his business was investigated, Charlot was found to owe 1.4 million *livres*, including a million to the crown.[4] (D'Effiat had repeated the mistake of Bochart and Marillac in allowing a revenue farmer to hold too many leases at the same time: apart from a number of smaller farms,[5] Charlot held the lease of the *cinq grosses fermes*, which was worth 1.65 million a year in rent and was also affected by his bankruptcy.)[6] Other revenue

---

[1] Richelieu, *Mémoires*, vii. 33. Condé proposed that the *rentiers* be reimbursed at 5 per cent interest.

[2] A.A.E. France 795, fo. 184ᵛ., n.d., *c.* 1628.

[3] Appendix Two, Table VI, and ultimately Bonney, 'The failure of the French revenue farms', 26–7.

[4] Ibid., 14 n. 1 and 18 n. 1.

[5] For example, the farms of the *écu pour tonneau de mer* and *tonneau de vin* of Normandy and the *traites domaniales* of Poitou: E 101a, fos. 410–14, 30 Jan. 1630.

[6] Minutier Central XVI 51, 23 Dec. 1624. E 114a, fo. 164, 23 Nov. 1633.

farms, such as the *gabelles de Languedoc*,[1] experienced comparable difficulties and remissions had to be allowed to the revenue farmers. D'Effiat did not lightly accord these remissions. On 27 July 1628, he had ordered a thorough investigation of current claims.[2] In the long term the policy of granting remissions was disastrous, since it destroyed the basic purpose of the revenue farm, which was to secure a stable and regular income for the crown and thus cushion it from the effects of short-term economic depression. D'Effiat reserved his wrath for revenue farmers such as Étienne Brioys, whom he accused of inefficiency and excessive demands for remissions.[3] On the other hand, he probably had no choice but to accord reasonable remissions, because the alternative was to bankrupt the revenue farmers. As it was, the shock waves from the collapses of Feydeau, Payen, and Charlot were felt throughout the financial system, and at the end of d'Effiat's ministry the need to 'restablyr le crédict' was taken for granted.[4]

The difficulties with regard to the indirect taxes were paralleled by difficulties in the collection of direct taxes, above all the *taille*. Mallet's figures indicate that the amount paid in *taille* by the *pays d'élections* fell as a proportion both of total and ordinary revenue of the French monarchy (in the case of ordinary revenue, from 27.7 per cent in the years 1620–4 to 19.9 per cent in the years 1625–9). However, these figures reflect the amount of money paid to the Treasury. Some of the local evidence suggests that the amount of taxes paid in the provinces was actually on the increase, despite the subsistence crisis, much of the increase paying for alienated royal taxes and local *charges* such as *rentes*.[5] There was also an increase in payments in the *pays d'états*.[6] D'Effiat was no friend of the fiscal privileges enjoyed by the provincial estates and it was with good reason that the rioters at Aix in 1630 burnt

---

[1] In the earlier 1620s, this farm had been held by Charlot under the *prête-nom* of Brussel de Vailleconte: P 2355, p. 773, 30 Mar. 1623. Cf. E 114b, fo. 395, 31 Dec. 1633. However, the consortium had changed by the time the remissions were requested: cf. E 106a, fo. 320, 20 June 1631. E 113b, fo. 30, 4 Aug. 1633.
[2] E 96b, fo. 413.
[3] Cf. A.A.E. France 853, fo. 164ᵛ., and A.A.E. France 842, fos. 50ᵛ.–51ʳ, 21 Feb. 1642. Guillaume Menant, another financier, claimed that Brioys had obtained nearly 3 million *livres* in remissions on rents on the *aides* and nearly 20 million in remissions on all the farms he had held between 1619 and 1631: A.A.E. France 801, fo. 224, *factum c.* 1631. Nevertheless, when Brioys died in 1636, he left debts.
[4] A.A.E. France 801, fo. 304. Ironically, the author of the memorandum contrasted d'Effiat's ministry with the alleged halcyon days of Schomberg who had been able to borrow without money becoming scarce on the open market.
[5] Collins, 'Sur l'histoire fiscale du xviiᵉ siècle', 342.
[6] Leroy-Ladurie, *Les paysans de Languedoc*, i. 425–6; ii. 1026 (graph 41).

his effigy.[1] It seems that the *surintendant* was the driving force behind the attempt to establish *élections* in the Dauphiné, Burgundy, Languedoc and Provence between 1628 and 1630. The creation of *élections* was a fiscal device, one of the numerous *traités* prepared by the finance minister and the intendants of finance. It could be prevented by a province if satisfactory compensation were offered to the financiers who had contracted with the government. Thus the Estates of Languedoc agreed to pay Jacques Le Feroz and Claude Vanel nearly 2.9 million *livres* as compensation for their revoked tax contract to establish 22 *élections*, although the Estates agreed to do so only after the failure of the Montmorency revolt in 1632. The Estates of Provence offered 1.5 million, those of Burgundy 1.6 million, but again only after the failure of revolts at Aix and Dijon in 1630 and the arrival of Condé with an army the following year.[2] The history of these negotiations demonstrates that however desirable the objective of increasing the levy of taxation in the *pays d'états*, d'Effiat's methods carried risks. The attempts were not repeated until the years 1658–60, shortly before Louis XIV's personal rule. D'Effiat's other efforts to facilitate the payment of direct taxes, for example by the redemption of municipal debts particularly in Languedoc, met with only partial success.[3] Nevertheless, d'Effiat was one of Richelieu's greatest servants: like Sully, the *surintendant* on whom he modelled himself, d'Effiat was both competent and honest,[4] an unusual combination in seventeenth-century France.

That any comparison is possible between Sully and d'Effiat is

---

[1] R. Pillorget, *Les mouvements insurrectionnels de Provence entre 1596 et 1715* (1975), pp. 327, 352. A.A.E. France 796, fo. 276, 23 Oct. 1630.

[2] Bonney, *Political change in France under Richelieu and Mazarin*, pp. 349–50. This interpretation is in contrast to that of Major, *Representative government in early modern France*, pp. 519–67. Major contends (p. 492) that Marillac was 'much more authoritarian and inflexible than Richelieu'; Marillac, it is argued (p. 619), wanted 'a centralized, absolute state administered by a loyal, nonhereditary, and probably non-venal bureaucracy' and sought to weaken the power of provincial estates by the introduction of *élections*. There is, however, no contemporary evidence apart from a claim made by Marillac's opponents after his arrest (cited at p. 580) that the Keeper of the Seals had such an intention. Sir Thomas Edmondes attributed the introduction of *élections* to Richelieu, and the Cardinal took credit in his memoirs for their establishment in Languedoc (ibid., pp. 554–5, 569–70). Major also concedes 'that (d')Effiat was a partisan of the *élus*' (p. 590).

[3] Bonney, op. cit., pp. 338–9.

[4] In 1629, d'Effiat listed all his assets, which he valued at under a million *livres*: A.A.E. France 795, fo. 189. However, he was accused of dishonesty by certain members of the *Parlement* of Paris on 5 July 1630: Mousnier, *La vénalité*, p. 657. It should also be noted that his widow, Dame Marie de Fourcy, was well off and participated in financial ventures: cf. E 382b, fo. 28, 15 Oct. 1665.

remarkable, for the situation after 1626 was much more difficult than at the turn of the century. It was a considerable achievement of d'Effiat not to have made the financial position of the crown any worse:[1] he succeeded in maintaining a peacetime financial structure in time of war. The period of foreign and civil peace following the treaty of Monzón and the failure of the Chalais conspiracy was short-lived. Relations between England and France deteriorated sharply in 1626, partly as a result of Charles I's inability (under pressure from Parliament) to honour the terms of his marriage treaty with Henrietta Maria, partly because of the failure to develop the marriage agreement into a general offensive–defensive alliance. In the years 1624–6 Buckingham had high, and in the event quite unreasonable, expectations of the French.[2] Matters came to a head with the mission of Bassompierre to England in the autumn of 1626: his instructions contained a formal French refusal to join the alliance of the Hague.[3] Nevertheless, war was started by Charles I and Buckingham, not France. Refuge was given to Soubise, the exiled Huguenot leader, and the English decided to apply pressure on the French government by provoking a further rising of the Huguenots. There is much to be said for Richelieu's view that the anti-French turn in Buckingham's foreign policy was motivated largely by pique.[4] In July 1627, an English fleet was sent to the Île-de-Ré in preparation for large-scale assistance to La Rochelle. Yet at this time the great Protestant stronghold was not even in rebellion: Buckingham's manifesto of 21 July preceded the negotiations for an alliance with the town (which at first proved difficult to achieve), while a general rising of the Huguenots was not declared until 10 September.[5]

[1] Cf. Véron de Forbonnais, *Recherches*, i. 215.

[2] S. L. Adams, 'Foreign policy and the Parliaments of 1621 and 1624', *Faction and Parliament. Essays on early Stuart history*, ed. K. M. Sharpe (Oxford, 1978), pp. 153, 157. Russell, *Parliaments and English politics*, pp. 210, 265–7, 300, 328–9, provides valuable information on the breakdown in Anglo-French relations but does not focus on the mission of Bassompierre as the turning-point. He was forced to justify the French rejection of the alliance on 6 Nov. 1626: Richelieu, *Mémoires*, vi. 287–93, 334–5. Bassompierre, *Journal de ma vie . . .*, ed. Chantérac, iii. 269.

[3] The alliance of the Hague was signed on 9 Dec. 1625 between England, the United Provinces, and Denmark.

[4] Richelieu, *Mémoires*, vii. 45. On the other hand, it could be argued that Buckingham was simply reacting to the Franco-Spanish treaty of 20 Mar. 1627 by a pre-emptive strike. Under the terms of this treaty, France was to join Spain in the war against England. However, the French entry into the war was not to take place until June 1628. The prospects of a Franco-Spanish invasion of England were remote, since the size of the respective fleets was not agreed until 8 July 1628: ibid., vii. 58; viii. 39–41.

[5] Russell, op. cit., pp. 329–30. Lublinskaya, *French absolutism*, p. 217. Parker, 'The social foundaton of French absolutism', 87. Manifesto of Buckingham summarized in

Louis XIII decided to conduct the siege of La Rochelle personally, with Richelieu as his lieutenant-general.[1] They determined strategy in consultation with Schomberg, who led the force which successfully re-occupied the Île-de-Ré.[2] D'Effiat's task was to ensure that sufficient money was sent from Paris to support the cost of the siege of La Rochelle and the other military operations.[3] Because the English landing on the Île-de-Ré was a fiasco (they were forced to evacuate with heavy losses in November 1627) there is a tendency to regard the siege of La Rochelle as a foregone conclusion. Yet it was not regarded as such by contemporaries: it was a costly business for both sides in manpower, while the besieging army faced severe logistical and strategic problems. Initially, there had been almost no money in the Treasury to meet the threat of invasion. Richelieu had to borrow on the private market and his loans to the crown during the siege of La Rochelle exceeded a million *livres*.[4] Matters were still so serious on 6 October that Condé proposed to Richelieu the dramatic measure of bankrupting the private owners of alienated royal taxes, which he estimated would bring in ten or eleven million to the Treasury.[5] (This proposal was later adopted in 1634, although the private owners of the alienated royal taxes were offered new *rentes* as partial compensation.) Condé's plan was not adopted, because Richelieu hoped that Pope Urban VIII would agree to his financing the war effort from the wealth of the clergy. What he wanted was agreement to a French version of the *cruzada* accorded to the kings of Spain. He obtained much less: Urban VIII suggested that the French clergy vote 3 million *livres* for the siege of La Rochelle. Even so, the negotiations with the assembly of the French clergy were protracted. In May 1628, Louis XIII rejected outright a vote of 2 million, since the army was costing this amount each month. It was not until 17 June 1628 that the

---

Richelieu, *Mémoires*, vii. 96–7. Declaration of La Rochelle: A.A.E. France 784, fo. 194, Aug. 1627. Declaration of Rohan: A.A.E. France 787, fo. 47. The reluctance of La Rochelle to renounce its allegiance to Louis XIII is very evident: Parker, *La Rochelle and the French monarchy*, pp. 15–16, 52, 167.

[1] Richelieu was appointed lieutenant-general on 4 Feb. 1628 (*Les papiers de Richelieu*, ed. Grillon, iii. 48–50) but seems to have exercised the reality of power earlier.
[2] The strategy for the relief of the Île-de-Ré was determined on 14 Sept. 1627: Richelieu, *Mémoires*, vii. 156. A.A.E. France 784, fo. 246.
[3] Véron de Forbonnais, *Recherches*, i. 212. Cf. A.A.E. France 790, fo. 189, 3 June 1628.
[4] Richelieu, *Mémoires*, vii. 107, 127; ix. 48.
[5] *Les papiers de Richelieu*, ed. Grillon, ii. 564.

assembly agreed to accord three million.[1] Since La Rochelle capitulated on 28 October,[2] the French clergy contributed too little too late to rescue the crown from in its financial emergency. The surrender of La Rochelle did not end the war against the Huguenots, but it freed one French army for action elsewhere – in what had become the war of the Mantuan succession.

Vincent II Gonzaga, duke of Mantua and marquis of Montferrat, had died on 26 December 1627 without leaving a direct male heir. There were various claimants to the succession, but in his last will and testament Vincent II handed over all his lands to Charles III Gonzaga, duke of Nevers, who was a subject of the king of France (indeed, he was governor of Champagne from 1589 until his resignation in May 1628).[3] There was little the French could do to bolster up Nevers' position in Mantua, which depended on his own efforts and assistance from Venice. However, French military intervention in Montferrat was a distinct possibility, and it became essential once Gonzalo Fernández de Córdoba, the governor of Milan, moved on his own initiative to partition Montferrat between Spain and Savoy:[4] Nevers' position rapidly deteriorated until only the fortress of Casale held out for him. An additional complication was that both Mantua and Montferrat were nominally fiefs of the Empire. The Emperor Ferdinand II, acting in the interests of his Spanish Habsburg relatives, refused to 'invest' Nevers with the fiefs and ordered their sequestration (20 March 1628). After the peace of Lübeck, and despite the misgivings of Wallenstein, the Imperial generalissimo,[5] Ferdinand II sent an army of invasion into Mantua under the command of Collalto (5 June 1629). Louis XIII and Richelieu consistently championed the justice of Nevers' cause. Later, considerations of revenge for Spanish assistance to the Huguenots (on 3 May 1629 Philip IV agreed to subsidize Rohan's rebellion by 900,000 *livres* paid in three instalments)[6] and the desire to achieve 'collective security' for the smaller Italian princes against Habsburg aggression would reinforce these sentiments. However, the Mantuan war was far more dangerous than the previous incon-

---

[1] Blet, *Le clergé*, i. 370–98. *Les papiers de Richelieu*, ed. Grillon, iii. 275.

[2] A.A.E. France 788, fo. 93.

[3] Harding, *Anatomy of a power elite*, p. 222 (no. 27). *Les papiers de Richelieu*, ed. Grillon, iii. 263.

[4] On Spanish policy during the war: Elliott, 'The statecraft of Olivares', pp. 139–42.

[5] Cf. G. Mann, *Wallenstein. His life narrated*, trans. G. Kessler (1976), pp. 473–5. The peace of Lübeck was signed on 7 June 1629.

[6] B.L. Add. MS. 30599, fos. 254–62.

clusive Valtelline conflict, which it threatened to reopen. It is true that Nevers was a Catholic ally, whereas in the Valtelline conflict the Grisons were Protestants. Moreover, on this occasion the Pope sided with French rather than Spanish policy. Nevertheless, four foreign enemies at once (England, the Emperor, Philip IV, and his ally Charles-Emmanuel of Savoy) threatened to be too many. When peace was signed with England at Susa on 24 April 1629, after the French intervention in Italy had begun, it was criticized within the council by Cardinal de Bérulle.[1]

The debate within the king's council[2] on the question of French intervention in the Mantuan war is one of the turning-points in Richelieu's ministry. Most of the arguments against intervention championed by the Queen Mother, Bérulle, and Marillac proceeded either from fear of the risks or from other priorities (desire for peaceful co-existence with the Habsburgs abroad and suppression of heresy at home). In essence, it was the same argument as in 1625–6: the war against the Huguenots should be concluded first as the main priority of the crown. The danger of intervention in the Mantuan conflict was that it would lead to a 'guerre immortelle' involving Milan and reopening the Valtelline question. As late as 21 February 1629 both Bérulle and Marillac argued against Louis XIII's conducting the Italian campaign in person because of the danger to the dynasty should he die abroad and the risk of leaving France undefended against a possible invasion from Germany or the Spanish Netherlands. They pointed to the threats posed by popular unrest in France, the general resistance to taxation, and indifference if not outright hostility to the French war aims. Marillac contrasted the financial and administrative consequences of war in Italy with his own (and to some extent, Richelieu's) reforming intentions: 'il est . . . de la gloire du bon gouvernement de penser au soulagement des sujetz et aux bons règlement(s) de l'estat qui ne se peuvent faire que par la paix'.[3]

A further consideration added weight to the objections of Bérulle and Marillac. Louis XIII could scarcely leave France for

[1] M. Houssaye, *Le Cardinal de Bérulle et le Cardinal de Richelieu, 1625–1629* (1875), pp. 479–80. Bérulle had been elevated to the Cardinalate on 30 Aug. 1627.

[2] At various points in the memoirs, Richelieu suggests that the debate was accompanied by a pamphlet war. However, the two authorities on the pamphlet debates produce evidence that is exclusively after the Day of Dupes: Thuau, *Raison d'état et pensée politique . . .*, pp. 120–9. Church, *Richelieu and reason of state*, pp. 212–24.

[3] G. Pagès, 'Autour du "grand orage". Richelieu et Marillac. Deux politiques', *Revue Historique*, clxxix (1937), 66, 77–8. A.A.E. France 788, fo. 173, 21 Feb. 1629. A.A.E. France 793, fos. 74ᵛ, 79, 15 Feb. and 21 Feb. 1629.

the Italian campaign without establishing a regency council. In view of the recent unreliability of Gaston d'Orléans and the comte de Soissons, and Condé's preoccupation with the war against the Huguenots in the Midi,[1] the king would have to establish a regency for Marie de Médicis. During his absence from the capital to conduct the siege of La Rochelle, Louis XIII had appointed the Queen Mother as his regent in northern France (27 September 1627). These powers were renewed at the time of Louis XIII's departure for Savoy.[2] Not surprisingly, the increased authority enjoyed by the Queen Mother made her advisers more important too. Marie de Médicis's preferences were for a period of peace abroad after the fall of La Rochelle.[3] Her reluctance to see Louis XIII become deeply embroiled in the Italian conflict was reinforced by a personal dislike of Nevers, who had been one of the leaders of the aristocratic revolts against Concini and had boasted that the Gonzaga were princes in Italy before the Medici were gentlemen.[4] A further complication was Gaston's wish to marry Nevers' daughter: for a time Maria-Louisa Gonzaga had to be arrested to prevent a clandestine marriage.[5] While this was not the only cause of a new round of difficulties with Gaston (he wanted an increased apanage, a *place de sûreté* such as Amboise and either Burgundy or Champagne as a provincial governorship), it led to a period of self-imposed exile in Lorraine from September 1629 to January 1630. With Gaston abroad, the risks posed by the Italian campaign appeared even greater, and a full reconciliation between the king and his brother was not achieved until May 1630.

Richelieu accepted the argument that only limited assistance could be offered to Nevers until the fall of La Rochelle provided the government with greater freedom for manoeuvre.[6] In December 1628, however, the chief minister was convinced that the king could march into Italy and relieve Casale by May 1629. The king could then march back to Languedoc, finish off the war against the Huguenots and return to the capital in triumph by

---

[1] On 10 Oct. 1627 Condé had been appointed lieutenant-general in the army of Languedoc, Guyenne, the Dauphiné, and the Lyonnais.

[2] Pagès, art. cit., 75. B.N. MS. fr. 18147, fo. 219, 27 Sept. 1627. Cf. Marillac's comments: A.A.E. France 793, fo. 85, 26 Feb. 1629.

[3] *Les papiers de Richelieu*, ed. Grillon, iii. 303. In a letter of 23 May 1628, Marie expressed the hope that 'le Roy puisse donner la paix à son peuple'.

[4] *Mémoires de . . . Montglat*, ed. J. F. Michaud and J. J. F. Poujoulat, 3rd ser. v (1838), p. 18.

[5] A.A.E. France 793, fos. 100ᵛ., 106, 11 and 12 Mar. 1629.

[6] *Les papiers de Richelieu*, ed. Grillon, iii. 202–10.

August 1629.[1] It was a very tight schedule and Bérulle and Marillac must have viewed with considerable misgivings Richelieu's avowed aim of making Louis XIII 'le plus puissant monarque du monde et le prince le plus estimé.'[2] In the first week of March 1629 the French army with Louis XIII personally in command and Richelieu as his lieutenant-general captured the Mount Cenis pass and the fortress of Susa. On 11 March Charles-Emmanuel of Savoy accorded the French army free passage to Casale and agreed to assist in the provisioning of the troops. He also reluctantly joined a French league for the defence of Italy, to which Venice and Mantua later acceded. The Spanish army withdrew from the siege of Casale and supplies reached the garrison on 18 March. The difficulty was to turn the French victory over Savoy into a firm peace that would guarantee French interests and Nevers' position. Louis XIII left for Languedoc on 28 April and Richelieu followed on 11 May without this having been achieved. Nevertheless, the return of the king speeded the collapse of Protestant resistance in France. The peace of Alais (28 June 1629) ended eight years of intermittent civil war. The edict of Nantes was guaranteed, but the political and military organization of the Huguenots was destroyed. Moreover, the Protestant leader Rohan was sent into exile, although his title of duke was restored and he received 300,000 *livres* in reparations. His troops were to serve the cause of the king of France in Italy.

Louis XIII returned to Paris in August 1629, as Richelieu had predicted, but while the Huguenot problem had been settled once and for all, the Mantuan conflict remained unresolved. Mantua was invaded by imperial forces and the Spanish renewed their offensive in Montferrat, culminating in a second siege of Casale. Nevers' position was no stronger in the winter of 1629–30 even if the French hold on Susa facilitated a second campaign. Richelieu argued the necessity for renewed French intervention and rejected the claim that the king lacked sufficient resources for the war: d'Effiat's diligence as finance minister would ensure that all would be well.[3] On 24 December 1629, Richelieu was appointed lieutenant-general in a new army to be sent to Italy which provided him with the authority to make preparations.[4] A second invasion followed in March 1630 and the French troops captured

---

[1] Ibid., iii. 587–8.

[2] *Lettres . . . de Richelieu*, ed. Avenel, iii. 179–81. They must have viewed Richelieu's aim of establishing gateways (*portes*) into Italy and Germany with similar apprehension.

[3] Richelieu, *Mémoires*, x. 335, 343, 406–7.

[4] A.A.E. France 794, fo. 311. A.G. A1 12, no. 127.

the strategic fortress of Pinerolo, which secured their supply lines to the Dauphiné. The capture of Pinerolo on 29 March was a decisive event in the breakdown of relations between Richelieu and his critics in the king's council. In the view of the chief minister, it offered Louis XIII the chance to become the 'arbitre et maître de l'Italie'. If Pinerolo were given up, the prospects for French power in Italy would be dashed. On the other hand, the retention of Pinerolo would in all probability lead to the continuation of the war. In Richelieu's view, d'Effiat would be able to ensure that the army would receive sufficient funds, which he estimated at 1.8 million *livres* every three months.[1] Richelieu was well informed about military expenses. Before he left Pinerolo, he made a personal loan of half a million and further assistance for the army was negotiated on his return to Grenoble.[2] Nevertheless, on this crucial point the Cardinal seems to have been over-optimistic. One of Marillac's arguments for halting the war effort was 'la nécessité des finances',[3] and even with d'Effiat personally supervising military expenditure as lieutenant-general the cost reached 1.2 million in July and 1.5 million in August 1630.[4] Richelieu's underestimate may have been sleight of hand, but he recognized the extent of the financial commitment. As he told the king in his memorandum of 13 April, '. . . il faut quit(t)er toute pensée de repos, d'espargne et de règlement du dedans du royaume'. He was also aware that the French war effort was proportionately greater than the figures might seem to indicate because of the need to pay the army in cash rather than assigning payment on future revenues.[5]

At crucial moments in the summer and early autumn of 1630 Richelieu was forced to justify his policy to Marie de Médicis and Marillac. It is possible that as early as June the Queen Mother had decided that the Cardinal had to be dismissed on the grounds that he sought to prolong the war in Italy 'pour estre plus néces-

---

[1] Pagès, art. cit., 84 omits the figures from Richelieu's memorandum of 13 Apr. 1630. They are taken from *Mémoires du Cardinal de Richelieu* . . ., ed. Michaud and Poujoulat, 2nd ser. viii, p. 190.

[2] *Lettres . . . de Richelieu*, ed. Avenel, iii. 694–5.

[3] Ibid., iii. 775 n. at p. 776.

[4] At its peak the army reached 20,000 infantry and 2700 cavalry: J. Jacquart, 'Le marquis d'Effiat, lieutenant-général à l'armée d'Italie (été 1630)', *XVIIᵉ Siècle*, xlv (1959), 308–9.

[5] Pagès, art. cit., 85. Pagès does not quote the important comment 'en telles occasions on ne subsistoit pas par assignations, mais par argent comptant . . .': *Mémoires du Cardinal de Richelieu* . . ., ed. Michaud and Poujoulat, loc. cit.

saire et plus absolu dans les affaires et les finances'.[1] The chief minister pointed out, not unreasonably, that rumours of a split within the king's council encouraged Spanish intransigence.[2] He suspected that the Emperor might be more flexible than Philip IV, which explains the decision to pursue negotiations concurrently with Ferdinand II at Regensburg and through papal mediation in Italy. Perhaps even Richelieu was unable to keep abreast of the two sets of simultaneous negotiations; certainly Marillac was not properly informed and came to the conclusion that the Cardinal sought to increase the complexity of the negotiations in order to prevent peace.[3] On 4 September 1630, d'Effiat signed the truce of Rivalto which led to a cessation of hostilities in Italy until 15 October. He returned to France shortly afterwards, to explain the truce to Richelieu and obtain more funds.[4] Richelieu accepted the truce because it left a beleaguered garrison loyal to Nevers defending the citadel of Casale. He was much more alarmed when he learnt the terms of the peace of Regensburg which had been signed by the French and imperial representatives on 13 October. For although the treaty envisaged that after compensation to the other claimants, Nevers would be invested with the duchy of Mantua and marquisate of Montferrat and take possession of Casale, he would not be allowed to fortify the citadel, which would thus become defenceless to any later Spanish attack from Milan. Under the terms of the peace, the Spanish would withdraw from Montferrat and the imperial forces from Mantua; but the French had to withdraw completely from Italy, with the exception of the fortresses of Susa and Pinerolo which they would be allowed to retain. A further difficulty was provided by article one of the treaty, which talked in terms of a general peace and the renunciation of French assistance to the enemies of the Emperor. French negotiations were already under way with Gustavus Adolphus, who had invaded the empire on 6 July when he landed on the Pomeranian island of Usedom. Moreover, on 17 June 1630 Louis XIII had undertaken to pay the Dutch one million *livres* per annum for seven years provided that they continued to fight

---

[1] B.N. MS. fr. 17486, fos. 127, 164.

[2] *Lettres . . . de Richelieu*, ed. Avenel, iii. 740.

[3] B.N. MS. fr. 17486, fo. 168. It is an open question whether Richelieu was properly informed of the Regensburg negotiations. Richelieu had limited the powers of the French negotiators to 'a general peace in Italy' and Brûlart de Léon was told categorically on 22 Oct. that he had exceeded his authority: D. P. O'Connell, 'A *cause célèbre* in the history of treaty making. The refusal to ratify the peace treaty of Regensburg in 1630', *British yearbook of international law*, xliii (1967), 81, 84. *Lettres . . . de Richelieu*, ed. Avenel, iii. 960–4.

[4] Jacquart, art. cit., 313.

Spain. An important clause bound the allies not to undertake separate peace negotiations. (Significantly, Marillac had criticized the treaty.)[1] The treaty of Regensburg would thus appear to Gustavus Adolphus and the Dutch as a piece of double-dealing, which was a powerful motive in Richelieu's repudiation of the peace terms on 22 October.[2]

Whatever view the Queen Mother and Marillac formed of the Regensburg peace terms,[3] they must have regarded the repudiation of a treaty with the Emperor as a deliberate affront to their policy of peaceful co-existence with the Habsburgs. It would be much more difficult to secure a peace treaty in the future, while the war in Italy appeared no nearer solution with the French generals instructed to pursue the war with vigour, relieve Casale (which was achieved on 26 October), and make further conquests in Piedmont.[4] Louis XIII's recurrent illness steeled the Queen Mother's resolution. On the Day of Dupes (11 November 1630), 'la plus étrange révolution qui fût jamais',[5] Marie de Médicis and her cabal thought that they had persuaded the king to dismiss Richelieu. They were 'duped' because the king had made no decision, misled them, or changed his mind. Since the decision was a personal one by Louis XIII, the outcome of the crisis of Richelieu's ministry was unpredictable. Saint-Simon, the king's current favourite, may have exercised a degree of influence in the Cardinal's favour to offset the hostility of Père Suffren, the king's confessor. Richelieu seems to have retained majority support among the ministers (even though this support was not a critical factor on the Day of Dupes), with d'Effiat, Schomberg, Bullion, and Bouthillier all defending his views.[6] The great exception, of course, was Marillac who was the first victim of the Day of Dupes:

---

[1] B.N. MS. fr. 17486, fo. 132. He also considered that 'le Cardinal seul a conclu . . . le traitté' (fo. 177ᵛ).

[2] O'Connell, art. cit., 84. *Lettres . . . de Richelieu*, ed. Avenel, iii. 951.

[3] The terms were criticized by Marillac's apologist, who blamed Richelieu's confidence in Père Joseph: B.N. MS. fr. 17486, fo. 168ᵛ, 169ʳ.

[4] *Lettres . . . de Richelieu*, ed. Avenel, iii. 958–60, 964–8. Richelieu instructed Brûlart de Léon to obtain modifications of the treaty of Regensburg, but these were not forthcoming from the Emperor.

[5] *Mémoires du Cardinal de Richelieu*, ed. Michaud and Poujoulat, p. 307. The various contemporary or near-contemporary accounts are conveniently reprinted in G. Mongrédien, *La journée des Dupes. 10 novembre 1630* (1961), pp. 187–203. Additional evidence on the question, and an important modification of the dating, is provided by P. Chevallier, 'La véritable journée des dupes (11 nov. 1630). Étude critique des journées des 10 et 11 nov. 1630, d'après les dépêches diplomatiques', *Mémoires de la Société Académique de l'Aube*, cviii (1978), 1–63. Cf. Major, *Representative government in early modern France*, p. 576 n. 21.

[6] B.N. MS. fr. 17486, fos. 113, 123ᵛ.

on 12 November the Seals were removed from his custody and he was arrested. The same day orders were sent for the arrest of his brother, who was serving in the army in Italy.[1] (The maréchal de Marillac was later placed on trial and executed on 7 August 1632). Opinion at court may have been more evenly divided. Members of the house of Lorraine seem to have been prominent in their support for the Queen Mother. Gaston d'Orléans vacillated, as usual, and declared open hostility to Richelieu only at the end of January 1631. Following this event, the Queen Mother was placed under house arrest at Compiègne (23 February).[2] By March Gaston and his supporters were in rebellion.

Because of the attempted reconciliation with the Queen Mother and Gaston in the immediate aftermath of the Day of Dupes, the full extent of aristocratic support for the *dévots* was not revealed until Gaston's rebellion in March 1631. The ducs de Bellegarde and d'Elbeuf, the governors of Burgundy and Picardy, facilitated Gaston's escape to Lorraine and joined him in exile after the collapse of resistance in the Orléanais. The duc de Guise, the governor of Provence, went into exile abroad to avoid arrest. Other nobles joined the conspirators in Lorraine, while the loyalty of some of those remaining in France was suspect: when Gaston invaded in the summer of 1632, the duc de Montmorency, the governor of Languedoc, declared his support for the king's brother. Precautions had to be taken by the government to prevent Sedan falling into the hands of the rebels due to suspicions about the loyalty of the duc de Bouillon. Finally, Marie de Médicis escaped from house arrest on 18 July, and went into exile first in the Spanish Netherlands, later in England and Germany. She remained abroad until her death five months before that of Richelieu, her former protégé and now arch-enemy. All the later attempts at reconciliation with her son, for example by Charles I in 1637, were brusquely rebuffed.[3] The size of her court in exile was a continuing threat since it was estimated to number some 600 Frenchmen when she went to England.[4] So too was the Queen Mother's wealth, which left open the possibility of a further invasion by the exiles after the failure of Gaston's intervention in

---

[1] *Lettres . . . de Richelieu*, ed. Avenel, iv. 7–11.

[2] *Chambre des Comptes*, ed. Boislisle, p. 385. Bassompierre, *Journal de ma vie . . .*, ed. Chantérac, iv. 131. Bassompierre's own arrest followed two days later: iv. 137.

[3] *Mémoires de . . . Montglat*, ed. Michaud and Poujoulat, pp. 88–9. A.A.E. France 828, fo. 128, 19 Nov. 1637. B.N. MS. fr. 18431, fo. 231.

[4] R. M. Smuts, 'The Puritan followers of Henrietta Maria in the 1630s', *English Historical Review*, xciii (1978), 41.

1632. Even after the long years in exile she left a fortune of nearly 8.5 million *livres* on her death in 1642, of which Louis XIII received over 2.4 million.[1]

The postscript to the struggle between Richelieu and his critics in the king's council is provided by Gaston's manifesto, issued from exile at Nancy on 30 May 1631. The king's younger brother depicted Richelieu's hold on power in terms comparable to those used by aristocratic critics of Concini and Luynes. Richelieu held all the important fortresses in France, according to Gaston. He was effectively in charge of French artillery having disgraced the marquis de Rosny and given d'Effiat a commission as *grand maître de l'artillerie*.[2] Gaston criticized Richelieu's control of the French navy and the administration of the king's finances by d'Effiat ('une de ses créatures'). As with earlier manifestos against Concini or Luynes, Gaston singled out the uneven distribution of royal patronage and abuses in financial administration for particular criticism. In his view, the burden of taxation was excessive in France. He estimated the cost of the Mantuan war at more than 50 million *livres*. Richelieu, he claimed, had championed French intervention in Italy 'pour sa vanité, son ambition et son intérêt, au détriment de la France . . .'[3] Richelieu was infuriated by Gaston's accusations, perhaps because there was more substance to them than he cared to admit.[4] While he may not have held as many fortresses as Luynes, Richelieu held Le Havre,[5] the most important fortress in the kingdom, and refused the Queen Mother and Gaston comparable *places de sûreté*. The chief minister was quick to fill the provincial governorships vacated by Gaston's supporters in Burgundy, Picardy and Provence. He made himself governor of Brittany (before the Day of Dupes, the provincial estates had asked for the Queen Mother as governor).[6] Marie de

---

[1] A.A.E. France 845, fo. 320. Of course, Marie de Médicis also had debts, which were still being paid off in 1646: *Arrêts du conseil du roi*, ed. Le Pesant, nos. 117, 133, 195, 270, 284, 441, 499.

[2] Anselme, *Histoire généalogique* . . ., viii. 186. Lublinskaya, *French absolutism*, pp. 304–5. Dissatisfaction with Rosny was evident in 1627–8: *Les papiers de Richelieu*, ed. Grillon, ii. 665; iii. 176.

[3] Mongrédien, op. cit., pp. 215–18. A.A.E. France 798, fo. 293.

[4] *Lettres . . . de Richelieu*, ed. Avenel, iv. 153–61, 177–81. *Mémoires du Cardinal de Richelieu*, ed. Michaud and Poujoulat, pp. 325–6.

[5] Le Havre had cost Richelieu 345,000 *livres* on 18 Oct. 1626, but he was probably reimbursed by the king: Richelieu, *Mémoires*, ix. 48. *Lettres . . . de Richelieu*, ed. Avenel, ii. 275; iii. 205.

[6] B. Pocquet, *Histoire de Bretagne. La Bretagne province, 1515–1715* (Rennes, 1913), pp. 393–4, 402. Harding, *Anatomy of a power elite*, p. 221 (no. 10). Richelieu profited from the largesse of the Breton estates: Major, *Representative government in early modern France*, pp.

Médicis' former province of Anjou was conferred on d'Effiat, who on 1 January 1631 was made a *maréchal de France*, and appointed governor of the Auvergne the following year.[1] The extent to which Richelieu relied on d'Effiat in 1630–1 demonstrates the reversal of his earlier policy of excluding military men and provincial governors from the position of finance minister.

Gaston denounced 'la dissipation de(s) ... finances' and Richelieu's control of 'l'argent comptant du royaume'. The criticism sounded extreme, yet the *Chambre des Comptes* had condemned the conduct of financial administration only a few months earlier. On 10 February 1631, Nicolay, the *premier président*, had severely criticized excessive profiteering by the financiers and declared that the king should take greater care for the 'soulagement du peuple'. Nicolay had argued that fiscal edicts recently presented to the tribunal for registration were not the true wish of the king but a consequence of pressure from the financiers.[2] If some contemporaries shared Gaston's doubts about d'Effiat's financial policy, there is no clear evidence to justify the charge that Richelieu directly profited from the French intervention in the Italian war. As has been seen, at crucial moments such as the siege of La Rochelle and the capture of Pinerolo, the chief minister had lent money to the crown: but the true extent of his wealth in 1630–1 is shrouded in mystery, although there is little doubt that bankruptcy and perhaps confiscation of his assets would have followed a *dévot* victory on the Day of Dupes. By the time of his death in 1642, it was said that Richelieu had built up an immense private fortune of 22.4 million *livres*, although debts of 6.5 million reduced the total to under 16 million.[3] He had received massive gifts from the king and was also a great ecclesiastical pluralist. But was all the wealth of the Cardinal derived from legitimate sources? Bullion, whose own hands were not clean and who had to defend his conduct as finance minister in the 1630s to the king, claimed that there were three yawning abysses (*gouffres*) in French financial administration: the navy, the artillery, and the 'maison du Cardinal'. Effec-

---

565–6. B.N. MS. fr. 21542, fo. 145. Bellegarde resigned his governorship of Burgundy on 10 Oct. 1632, while at Nancy: A.A.E. France 805, fo. 112. The post had been filled the previous year with the appointment of Condé.

[1] Bassompierre, *Journal de ma vie* ..., ed. Chantérac, iv. 128. B.N. n.a.f. 7228, fo. 76/2. B.N. MS. fr. 21542, fo. 46.

[2] *Chambre des Comptes*, ed. Boislisle, pp. 383–5.

[3] L. Batiffol, 'La fortune du Cardinal de Richelieu', *Revue des Deux-Mondes*, 8th ser., xxvii (1935), 896. The subject merits a more satisfactory examination, but this was the claim of Hilaire, *avocat* of the duchesse d'Aiguillon.

tively all three areas of royal expenditure were controlled by Richelieu, not the finance minister.[1] (Significantly, after d'Effiat's death Richelieu had his cousin La Meilleraye appointed as *grand maître de l'artillerie*).[2] Critics such as the pamphleteer Mathieu de Morgues claimed that Richelieu increased his personal fortune by misusing the secret expenses (*comptants*),[3] but there is no positive proof of this accusation. More than simply securing Richelieu's personal fortune, the outcome of the Day of Dupes had immense consequences for the conduct of the king's finances generally, the rise in the secret expenses in the 1630s being just one aspect. It was with good reason that the *Chambre des Comptes* later came to regard the year 1630 as the turning-point, after which the abuses in financial administration reached disastrous proportions.[4]

[1] *Mémoires de . . . Montglat*, ed. Michaud and Poujoulat, pp. 101–2. In 1638, the crisis year in the relations between Richelieu and Bullion, expenditure on the artillery and the marine reached nearly 9.2 million *livres* (5.8 million on the artillery, 3.3 million on the marine): A.A.E. France 832, fo. 250.

[2] Anselme, loc. cit., gives La Meilleraye's first date of appointment as 11 Aug. 1632, within a month of d'Effiat's death. The marquis de Rosny never recovered favour and died on 1 Sept. 1634, at which point the office reverted to Sully, his father. Sully resigned his interest on 18 Sept. in return for appointment as a *maréchal de France: Lettres . . . de Richelieu*, ed. Avenel, iv. 611, 614. P 2365, pp. 233–42, 26 Sept. 1634.

[3] Batiffol, art. cit., 894. Morgues was later to make the same allegation against Mazarin.

[4] Cf. A.A.E. France 860, fos. 204ᵛ., 208ᵛ., 14 Oct. 1648.

Chapter IV

From the Day of Dupes to Rocroi, 1630–1643

The aftermath of the Day of Dupes left Richelieu in undisputed control of the king's council, filling the vacant posts of Keeper of the Seals and war minister with his own appointees, Châteauneuf and Servien.[1] D'Effiat remained a loyal supporter until his death on 27 July 1632 near Lutzelstein while commanding a French army to defend the elector of Trier against the Spanish. It was at this time that Le Bret described the office of finance minister as 'maintenant une des plus importantes du royaume'[2] and perhaps the appointment of Claude Bullion and Claude le Bouthillier as joint *surintendants* on 4 August 1632 was a reaction against this development. Richelieu may well have decided to return to his earlier principle that it was unwise to appoint to the post of finance minister ambitious magnates who would seek other important offices and governorships. Schomberg may have been consulted by Richelieu on the choice of successor to d'Effiat; he certainly approved the decision.[3] Bullion was a member of the Parisian *noblesse de robe*. His career was the classic one, from councillor in the *Parlement* of Paris (1595), to *maître des requêtes* (1605) and king's councillor (including membership of the finance commission of 1611), with intendancies in the army and diplomatic missions on the way. Bouthillier's career was less typical: a member of the lesser nobility who had risen to prominence in the service of Marie de Médicis, he had transferred his allegiance to Richelieu on becoming secretary of state in 1628.[4] Both men were older than the chief minister and experienced in office. Richelieu had no difficulty in exerting his authority over Bouthillier, but seems to have been more cautious in his attitude to Bullion, whose maxims and methods prevailed in financial policy until his death in 1640.[5]

[1] The post of war minister was vacated by the death of Beauclerc. Châteauneuf had intrigued to become Keeper of the Seals as early as 1628: *Les papiers de Richelieu*, ed. Grillon, iii. 258

[2] Le Bret, *De la souveraineté du roy*, p. 172. Le Bret was given royal permission to publish this work on 10 Dec. 1630.

[3] A.A.E. France 802, fo. 328, 5 Aug. 1632.

[4] *Les papiers de Richelieu*, ed. Grillon, iii. 527, 531–5.

[5] Bullion was born in 1569, Bouthillier in 1581, and Richelieu in 1585. Cf. Montglat's

The Day of Dupes did not bring an end to all debate and division within the king's council. Châteauneuf was arrested in February 1633 after intrigues pursued with Madame de Chevreuse in England aimed at toppling the governments both there and in France.[1] Pierre Séguier, the new Keeper of the Seals, came into conflict with Bullion before the end of the year, although the disagreement does not seem to have amounted to very much and was resolved by Bouthillier.[2] Much more serious was the dispute between Bullion and Servien over the war estimates, which led to the war minister's resignation in February 1636.[3] Servien was replaced by Sublet des Noyers, one of the intendants of finance. Sublet in turn was forced to resign in April 1643, some months after Richelieu's death. While it is probably true that Sublet was in part the victim of an intrigue led by his rivals Mazarin and Chavigny (Bouthillier's son who was foreign minister), another factor in his forced resignation was a dispute with king over the war estimates.[4] Le Tellier's promotion to war minister in 1643 was thus very similar in circumstances to Sublet's appointment seven years earlier. Disputes and disagreements in the king's council did not come to an end in November 1630. What changed, however, was the whole atmosphere in which the choices in foreign and domestic policy were debated. No one seriously challenged the view, presented to Louis XIII by Richelieu in the spring of 1632, that Spain, the Emperor and the duke of Lorraine were allied against France and that a general war was inevitable.[5] Richelieu and the other ministers could present proposals to the king in the confident expectation that he would accept their advice. Even after the Mantuan war was settled by the two treaties of Cherasco (6 April and 19 June 1631), Louis XIII

comment that Bullion was 'un des plus grands hommes d'état de son temps': *Mémoires . . . de Montglat*, ed. Michaud and Poujoulat, p. 101. Véron de Forbonnais (*Recherches*, i. 215) commented that Bullion 's'empara des principales fonctions . . .'

[1] *Lettres . . . de Richelieu*, ed. Avenel, iv. 431–41. Smuts, art. cit., p. 34.

[2] *Lettres . . . de Richelieu*, ed. Avenel, iv. 507.

[3] Ranum, *Richelieu and the councillors of Louis XIII*, p. 161. A.G. A1 41, fo. 117, 27 Feb. 1636. A.A.E. France 820, fo. 119, 15 Feb. 1636. Mazarin noted the dispute and rather surprisingly talked in terms of a 'peace party' led by Bullion: G. Dethan, *The young Mazarin*, translated S. Baron (1977), pp. 106–7.

[4] There is a considerable difference in emphasis in the accounts of Montglat and d'Ormesson: *Mémoires . . . de Montglat*, ed. Michaud and Poujoulat, pp. 135–6. Ormesson, *Journal*, ed. Chéruel, i. 23, 25.

[5] *Lettres . . . de Richelieu*, ed. Avenel, iv. 270, 293–4. A clear account of Louis XIII's grievances against the duke of Lorraine by 19 Sept. 1633 is in *Chambre des Comptes*, ed. Boislisle, pp. 387–8.

moved ineluctably towards further conflict with the Habsburgs. That the declaration of war against Spain came as late as May 1635 was not due to the absence of a *casus belli*. Rather it was the result of a positive decision to postpone the conflict for as long as possible while the French resources for the war effort were built up.

One reason why full French participation in the Thirty Years' War was delayed for as long as possible was that conspiracies and rebellions aimed at removing Richelieu from office and reversing his foreign policy continued after 1630–1. In the summer of 1632, Gaston d'Orléans invaded France with 2500 cavalry from the Spanish Netherlands, crossing Burgundy and the Auvergne and entering Languedoc where he met up with the duc de Montmorency, who had timed his rebellion to coincide with the invasion. Fortunately for Richelieu, the rebel army was defeated by the forces under the command of Schomberg at the battle of Castelnaudary, although the chief minister's loyal supporter died of his wounds shortly after the victory. Montmorency was placed on trial before the *Parlement* of Toulouse and executed. Negotiations with Gaston proved abortive, and he went into exile again in the Spanish Netherlands, where he remained until October 1634. Conspiracies did not cease with Gaston's return to France and appointment to the governorship of the Auvergne.[1] Gaston was implicated in the conspiracy of the comte de Soissons. The comte fled to Sedan in November 1636, where the duc de Bouillon gave him refuge before he entered the service of the king of Spain.[2] In July 1641, the comte de Soissons, the duc de Guise, and the duc de Bouillon issued a manifesto at Sedan which was directed against Richelieu's foreign policy and couched in language to appeal to the widest possible spectrum of French public opinion. They claimed that their objective was to restore order 'dans les conseils, dans la guerre [*sic*] et dans les finances qui ont esté divertis . . .' Their true purpose, however, was to stop the war. They were in military alliance with the Habsburgs, who provided Soissons with an army which routed the king's troops at the battle of La Marfée

---

[1] While in Lorraine in Jan. 1632, Gaston had secretly married Marguerite of Lorraine. Fear of Louis XIII's reaction to this discovery was a powerful reason for Gaston going into exile, as Bullion told the king: A.A.E. France 803, fo. 292, 13 Nov. 1632. For the conditions of the reconciliation, and Gaston's treaty of 12 May 1634 with Spain: *Lettres . . . de Richelieu*, ed. Avenel, iv. 372–8, 587–8. A.A.E. France 811, fos. 59, 63ᵛ., 115, 2 and 30 Oct. 1634.

[2] A.A.E. France 822, fos. 237, 240, 247, 262, 320, 20 Nov.–3 Dec. 1636. Richelieu rejected the need to conciliate the comte de Soissons: A.A.E. France 827, fo. 271, July 1637.

(9 July 1641). However, Soissons was killed in the battle and the rebellion collapsed within a month.[1]

The duc de Bouillon was also heavily implicated in the conspiracy the following year led by Cinq-Mars, d'Effiat's son who had become the king's favourite partly through Richelieu's influence. Gaston d'Orléans was also involved in the plot: on 13 March 1642, he accepted the provisions of a treaty negotiated on his orders at Madrid. Philip IV was to supply Gaston with a down payment of 1.2 million and an annual pension of 432,000 *livres* a year. The king of Spain would also supply the rebels with 5000 cavalry and 12,000 infantry and pay 100,000 *livres* a month towards their upkeep. Cinq-Mars and Bouillon were each to receive pensions and the rebels were to fight on the orders of Philip IV and the Emperor Ferdinand III against enemies of the Habsburgs, such as the Swedish allies of France. Gaston was empowered to grant terms to any French provinces and towns which sought peace with the Habsburgs.[2] Part of the significance of the Cinq-Mars conspiracy arises from the suggestion that the king's support for his chief minister wavered in the early months of 1642.[3] However, Louis XIII's commitment to Richelieu and his policies were reinforced with a vengeance on 3–4 August, when the king denounced his brother and instructed the Cardinal and Chancellor Séguier to obtain proof of the complicity of Cinq-Mars and Bouillon.[4] On 12 September Cinq-Mars and another of the conspirators, de Thou, were declared guilty of treason and executed. Five days later, Bouillon's life was spared in return for handing Sedan over to the crown.[5] Gaston's complicity in this conspiracy could not be overlooked, and on 1 December he was deprived of his governorship of the Auvergne and debarred from holding public office in France.[6]

[1] *Chambre des Comptes*, ed. Boislisle, p. 408. B.N. MS. fr. 17331, fo. 46. A.A.E. France 839, fos. 9, 14, 32, 123, 9 July–5 Aug. 1641. In his submission to Louis XIII, the duc de Bouillon asked pardon for his treaties with the Habsburgs. The Soissons treaty was taken as the precedent for the Cinq-Mars treaty in 1642.

[2] B.N. MS. fr. 17331, fo. 97. A.A.E. France 842, fos. 82, 89.

[3] J. Orcibal, 'Richelieu, homme d'église, homme d'état . . .', *Revue d'Histoire de l'Église de France*, xxxiv (1948), 96–7. V. L. Tapié, *La France de Louis XIII et de Richelieu* (1967), p. 394.

[4] B.N. MS. fr. 3843, fo. 62, 3 Aug. 1642. B.N. MS. fr. 18431, fo. 400, 4 Aug. 1642. K 114b, no. 50/6 [Musée AE II 833], 1 Aug. 1642.

[5] On the trial of Cinq-Mars: M. Faucheux, 'Le procès de Cinq-Mars', *Quelques procès criminels des xviie et xviiie siècles*, ed. J. Imbert (1964), pp. 77–100. B.N. MS. fr. 17331, fos. 101, 105–6, 12 and 17 Sept. 1642. Cardinal Mazarin negotiated the transfer of Sedan.

[6] G. Dethan, *Gaston d'Orléans. Conspirateur et prince charmant* (1959), p. 284. B.L. Harleian 4472b, fos. 159–61, 1 Dec. 1642. The king later withdrew the decision: Gaston was made president of the regency council envisaged in Louis XIII's last will and testament dated 20

The threat posed by domestic conspiracy and faction with Habsburg support was a powerful factor delaying direct French intervention in the Thirty Years' War. So too was the military unpreparedness of France and the parlous state of the king's finances. Richelieu had underestimated the true cost of the Mantuan war. Yet this was a war on only one front once the Huguenot rebellion was quelled in the summer of 1629. Participation in the Thirty Years' War would result in warfare on at least three fronts at the same time. France tasted this experience in 1632, when one army was needed to invade Lorraine, another to defeat Montmorency in Languedoc and a third to bolster up the position of the pro-French elector of Trier. The condition of the third army at the time of d'Effiat's death is a telling comment upon the financial plight of the French monarchy. The troops were unpaid, and it was only their loyalty to the finance minister, and their grief at the news of his death, which prevented a mutiny.[1] The decision to delay French participation in a general war and instead to fight the Habsburgs by proxy thus made clear financial sense. On 17 June 1630, the French had agreed to pay the Dutch a million *livres* per annum. This was less than Henri IV had paid them between 1603 and 1607 at a time when the *livre tournois* was a stronger currency.[2] Not surprisingly, Charnacé was empowered to offer the Dutch three million if necessary to maintain the alliance, but on 15 April 1634 a new treaty was signed which increased the annual French subsidy to 2.3 million.[3] On 13 January 1631, by the treaty of Bärwalde, the French undertook to subsidize Gustavus Adolphus's war in Germany until 1 March 1636 to the tune of 400,000 *riksdaler* a year which was estimated at a million *livres tournois*. 120,000 *riksdaler* were to be paid retrospectively to help defray Gustavus's costs in 1630. The French fell behind in their payments in 1632. When Gustavus Adolphus was killed at Lützen on 16 November, further payments were suspended (much to the relief of Bullion) on the grounds that the treaty of Bärwalde was

---

Apr. 1643. He did not regain a provincial governorship (Languedoc) until after the king's death. Charles de Schomberg was demoted to lieutenant-general on 25 Apr. 1644, to make room for Gaston as governor. The change had been talked about since Feb.: A.A.E. France 849, fos. 53, 183, 1 Feb. and 25 Apr. 1644.

[1] The witness was an impeccable one, Sublet des Noyers: A.A.E. France 804, fo. 299, 27 July 1632.

[2] Henri IV had paid 1,350,000 *livres* in 1603–4 and 1,950,000 *livres* in 1605–7: Buisseret, *Sully*, p. 82. B.N. MS. fr. 23026, pp. 119–20.

[3] J. de Pange, *Charnacé et l'alliance franco-hollandaise, 1633–1637* (1905), p. 102. *Lettres . . . de Richelieu*, ed. Avenel, iv. 526.

an agreement between two kings, and was abrogated by the death of one of them.[1] By the treaty of Heilbronn signed in April 1633, France was due to pay a further million *livres*, although whether this sum was actually paid is an open question.[2] In December 1634, by the terms of the treaty of Paris, the French undertook to make a once and for all payment of 500,000 *livres* instead of the million envisaged the previous year. Chancellor Oxenstierna refused to ratify the treaty, but the French seem to have paid the money over all the same.[3] These sums were small indeed when one recalls that d'Effiat's army in Italy was costing 1.5 million a month in August 1630.

The cautious attitude of the French government in delaying involvement in the Thirty Years' War is explained by the seriousness of the financial position revealed by Guénégaud's accounts as *trésorier de l'Épargne* for 1632.[4] It is true that there had been a significant increase in revenues since 1630, from 43 million to nearly 57.5 million. However, there was a serious imbalance in the revenues paid to the Treasury. Nearly half the total (28.2 million) came from the *parties casuelles*. Almost a fifth (11 million) came from *deniers extraordinaires* such as the creation of *rentes* on the *aides*, the alienation of certain royal taxes and incidental items such as the expropriation of Montmorency's wealth.[5] The total net payment to the crown from the *recettes générales* was a derisory

---

[1] L. Weibull, 'Gustave Adolphe et Richelieu', *Revue Historique*, clxxiv (1934) p. 224. M. Roberts, *Gustavus Adolphus. A history of Sweden, 1611–1632* (2 vols., 1953, 1958), ii. 466. (I am indebted to Professor Roberts for his elucidations of the tortuous history of the French subsidy to Sweden.) For Bullion's relief: A.A.E. France 803, fo. 329, 4 Dec. 1632. On the other hand, Bullion claimed on 1 Dec. (fo. 324) that he had paid Sweden, apart from 80,000 *livres* which had been assigned on future revenues.

[2] The arrears of 1632 do not seem to have been paid, and Sweden protested. There were no protests about non-payment in 1633. The sum is bracketed in S. E. Åström, 'The Swedish economy and Sweden's role as a great power, 1632–1697', *Sweden's age of greatness, 1632–1718*, ed. M. Roberts (1973), p. 95.

[3] The League of Heilbronn ratified the treaty, and may have received the money. On 2 Nov. 1634 [*sic*] Richelieu told Louis XIII that 'l'argent des Suédois est party'; a letter from Bullion on 25 Oct. had referred to 'les 500,000 livres des Suédois': *Lettres . . . de Richelieu*, ed. Avenel, iv. 636 and n. 1. Åström, loc. cit., records no payments to Sweden in 1634–6.

[4] B.I. Godefroy 144, fo. 259. The accounts were authenticated by Séguier, Bullion and Bouthillier, Duret de Chevry, Mallier and d'Hémery on 13 June 1633. They confirm the impression given by Mallet's figures for this year.

[5] The enumeration of the *deniers extraordinaires* in the 1632 accounts (B.I. Godefroy 144 fos. 294–300ᵛ) demonstrates that Guéry's assumption that this revenue was simply the borrowing requirement is misplaced. Guéry calculated the theoretical deficit for 1632 as 38.2 million, but his estimate is wildly inaccurate. Quite apart from the false premise, he failed to include the *parties casuelles* in the total of revenues. Mallet's total should read 57,504,923 *livres* (not 29,273,895 *livres* as given by Guéry). The authenticated accounts give the figure as 57,450,336 *livres*. Cf. Guéry, 'Les finances de la monarchie française', 236, 238.

8.4 million, much less than the total levy in the provinces to meet assigned payments, local *charges*, and alienated royal taxes.[1] The income from the revenue farms was also low, being largely consumed by payments of *rentes* and salaries to office-holders. The very low yields from the various farms of the *gabelles* reflected the remissions accorded to the revenue farmers as a result of the recent subsistence crisis. Thus the total payment to the Treasury from all the farmers of the *gabelles* was a mere 1.5 million. The single most important farm, the *gabelles de France*, paid the ridiculously small sum of 138,111 *livres*. Yet the reduced annual rent payable by a new consortium holding the lease under the name of Philippe Hamel and effective from 1 October 1632 was 6,650,000 *livres*.[2] It is difficult to separate the various component elements in a general crisis of the revenue raising system. The single most important factor, however, appears to have been the very rapid alienation of royal taxes in 1632–3 which is partly reflected in the large sums raised from tax contracts (*traités*) in these years.[3]

In their first eighteen months in office, Bullion and Bouthillier made the problem of alienated royal taxes much worse. Thus the *brevet* for 1634, determined by the king at Monceau on 30 July 1633, envisaged a total levy in direct taxes from the *pays d'élections* of 22.6 million. Only 14.1 million would be paid directly to the Treasury from the *taille*, the *taillon* and *crues*. The rest (8.5 million) would not go to the Treasury at all, but would pay the private owners of alienated royal taxes.[4] In the event, these sums were never levied. In February 1634, in a remarkable *volte-face*, Bullion and Bouthillier adopted part of Condé's strategy to meet the crisis of the English invasion of the Île-de-Ré seven years earlier. Rather than 'surcharger nos sujets' with heavier direct taxes, the government abolished the alienated taxes: instead, it issued 8 million *livres* in *rentes* on the *taille* and 3 million in *rentes* on the *gabelles*. Not surprisingly, the proprietors protested vehemently, but they were overruled.[5] The virtual bankruptcy of the private proprietors was

---

[1] Excluding the *taillon*, which would raise the total to nearly 9.5 million. Cf. the general argument of Collins, 'Sur l'histoire fiscale du xviiᵉ siècle', 325. His criticism of the incompleteness of Mallet's figures applies equally to the authenticated accounts. French accounting procedure before 1661 reflected payments to the Treasury rather than the total levy of taxes in the provinces.

[2] The lease was signed on 31 Mar. 1632: E 108a, fo. 474.

[3] Collins, art. cit., 332, 342. Appendix Two, Table VIIA.

[4] B.N. n.a.f. 200, fo. 2.

[5] AD + 226, Feb. 1634. The *rentes* were to be issued to the proprietors in the form of a supplementary tax organized on behalf of the government by the financier Denis Marin: P 2363, p. 645, 29 May 1634. E 117a, fo. 500, 27 May 1634. E 117b, fo. 318, 17 June 1634. E

in one sense unquestionably a reform. The levy of alienated royal taxes was extremely unpopular and was an additional burden on the peasants that was of no great value to the government.[1] The original sales of these revenues had taken place at only five or six times the annual interest, whereas it was intended that the sales of *rentes* in 1634 take place at 14 times the annual interest. Thus the creation of *rentes* should have produced the gross yield of 154 million *livres*.[2] The sums mentioned in the accounts for the years 1634–6 were dramatically increased by the 'convertissement des droits en rentes' in terms both of royal income and expenditure.[3] Yet these were essentially paper transactions. In practice, the expected yield from the sales of *rentes* failed to materialize.

What went wrong? The unprecedented scale of the operation stretched the resources of the money market to its limits. Although initially a great deal of revenue was raised from the sale of *rentes*, the market soon became flooded and the capital value fell, a situation made worse after 1638 with the decision to reduce the payment of interest to *rentiers*.[4] Thus by 1641, an annual *rente* of 1000 *livres* which in 1634 ought to have been worth 14,000 *livres* was selling at a mere 4000 *livres*.[5] As late as January 1639, 600,000 *livres* in *rentes* remained unsold from the creation nearly five years

---

119a, fos. 223, 227, 14 Aug. 1634. *Procuration* of Marin for the *recette* in the area of the *gabelles de Lyonnais*: Minutier Central XIV, 44, 26 May 1635. Two of Marin's subcontracts in Minutier Central XIV 52, 5 July 1638.

[1] Collins, 'Sur l'histoire fiscale du xviiᵉ siècle', 332–3. Bercé, *Histoire des croquants*, i. 70; ii. 737.

[2] That is to say 11 million *livres* in annual interest (8 million on the *taille*, 3 million on the *gabelles*) multiplied by 14. There seem to have been some creations of *rentes* in 1634 at *denier* 18 rather than *denier* 14, however: Minutier Central XIV 40, 41, 43 and especially 49, *passim*. Cf. the important comment of Véron de Forbonnais, *Recherches*, i. 222.

[3] Mallet's comment (p. 228) was that 'cette augmentation n'est qu'une fausse finance, dont une partie procède . . . du grand nombre des rentes qui furent crées en ce temps-là, que pour le remboursement des droits aliénés, lequel remboursement suivant l'usage ordinaire de l'Épargne a été emploié dans les comptes de ces années comme s'il avoit été fait en deniers comptants; bien que ce n'est qu'une simple commutation de la jouissance de ces droits en rentes sur les tailles et sur les gabelles.' On the expenditure account, this conversion of *droits* into *rentes* was passed through the item of *deniers payés par ordonnance*. On the revenue account, the conversion was passed through the item of the *deniers extraordinaires*, which reached the massive figure of 156 million in 1635.

[4] Cf. E 183b, fo. 586, 19 Sept. 1643. B.N. MS. fr. 18494.

[5] 'Mémoire sur l'état des finances depuis 1616 jusqu'à 1644', *Archives curieuses de l'histoire de France*, 2nd ser., vi (1838), p. 64. A.A.E. France 845, fo. 175ᵛ., n.d., *c*. 1641–2. Cf. E 377b, fo. 282ᵛ., 31 Mar. 1665: '. . . le pied du prix courant qui estoit le denier 4'. Already by 1635, the value had been reduced to 8000 *livres*: E 124b, fo. 203, 30 June 1635. Forbonnais believed that it sank eventually to 2000 or 3000 *livres*: Véron de Forbonnais, *Recherches*, i. 222. The title of *petites rentes* given to those issued in 1634 was therefore particularly appropriate: E 196a, fo. 311, 12 Nov. 1644.

earlier. An attempt was made to force the sale by a tax on the well-to-do (*taxe des aisés*), a policy which was desperately unpopular and ultimately failed.[1] From the outset in 1634, the credibility of the operation was undermined by government reliance on a consortium of financiers comprising Thomas Bonneau, Germain Courtin, and Jean Galland. The gross amount (*forfait*) of the tax contract was 19.5 million and the interest payment 4.7 million for the total operation of issuing the *rentes* and taxing the holders of the *droits aliénés*. The net payment envisaged to the government was only 14.8 million.[2]

Even more serious was the opportunity for speculation provided to the financiers,[3] which was an important contributory cause in the rapid decline of the capital value of the *rentes*. The financiers were more favourably placed to secure redemption of the new *rentes* at a later date than private purchasers. After 1636, the government allowed financiers to redeem *rentes* as part of their fixed-term payments under both loan and tax contracts.[4] The redemption failed to increase the market value of *rentes* and did nothing to alleviate the discontent caused by the reduction in interest payments. On the other hand, the financiers were allowed enormous speculative profits, since the *rentes* were redeemed at the official and not the market value. Thus a financier could buy an annual *rente* of 1000 *livres* for a capital payment of as little as 4000 *livres* and then resell to the government for as much as 18,000 *livres*.[5] On paper it might appear that the conditions of a loan contract had been fulfilled: but in fact the government was getting much the worse of the bargain and could ill afford to discount payments owed by financiers, or for that matter redeem *rentes*, in wartime. The policy came under severe criticism in 1648, but was

[1] Bonney, *Political change in France under Richelieu and Mazarin*, pp. 327–8.

[2] *Traité* signed by Robert Souart: B.N. MS. fr. 18205, fo. 234ᵛ., 14 Mar. 1634. Acts of association summarized in E 392, fo. 27, 7 Oct. 1666.

[3] This opportunity was facilitated by many of the original sales being contracted with the name of the purchaser in blank: E 116a, fo. 359, 14 Mar. 1634. E 120a, fo. 25, 7 Sept. 1634.

[4] For example, *traité* of 15 Dec. 1636 by a consortium comprising Antoine Boyer, Jean Galland, Jean de Vouldy, and Pierre Puget de Montauron under the name of Charles Pinert. The crown redeemed 124,815 *livres* in *rentes* to the consortium (i.e. discounted 2,246,667 *livres* from the *traité*): cf. E 392, fo. 146, 7 Oct. 1666. Similarly the loan of 5 million by a consortium under the name of Jean Levesque (2 July 1639). The crown reimbursed 103,704 *livres* in *rentes* (i.e. discounted 1,451,852 *livres* from the loan): cf. E 392, fo. 11, 7 Oct. 1666. There are examples of redemptions of *rentes* to the financier Jean Galland in 1641–2 in Minutier Central XIV 56.

[5] As was recognized by Jacques Tubeuf in 1648: Z1a 163, fos. 78ᵛ.–79ʳ., 11 July 1648. Mallet noted (p. 228) that *comptants* were issued 'pour la différence du fond du denier 14 au denier 18'.

not effectively reversed until 1664. Bullion had created the worst of all worlds: an illogical and unpopular system that worked to the advantage of few at the expense of many without any real gain to the crown, a system moreover that became much worse as time went on.[1] Much of the financial confusion and disorder which lasted until 1661 was a direct consequence of the excessive issue of *rentes* in 1634 and the subsequent redemptions.[2] Well might Omer Talon conclude that as a result of the excessive sales of offices and *rentes* in the 1630s 'les richesses de la France pour la plupart ont été imaginaires . . .'[3]

The French retention of the fortress of Pinerolo as a result of a secret agreement with duke Victor-Amadeus of Savoy on 31 March 1631—despite the official terms of the peace of Cherasco—was regarded by Philip IV as a legitimae *casus belli*. There is little doubt that a Spanish declaration of war on France would have resulted had there been a clear alliance between Spain, the Emperor, and the dukes of Lorraine and Savoy. Under the influence of his confessor, Lamormain, the Emperor was however unwilling to declare war on Louis XIII who had quelled his own Protestant subjects—and with the Swedish invasion of 1630 he had more than enough difficulties on his hands in the empire. Moreover the French king had strengthened his borders by neutralizing one unreliable neighbour (Savoy) and evicting another (Lorraine). Thus when the Spanish council of state debated the possibility of declaring war on France on 13 April 1634 it found that the necessary European coalition to sustain such a war did not exist, and the declaration was postponed.[4] Louis XIII, however, remained profoundly distrustful of Spanish intentions and in a secret memorandum to Richelieu, dated 4 August 1634, argued at length the case for a 'vigorous open war against Spain in order to secure a beneficial general peace'. The king's concerns were primarily defensive: his country could not afford to be left isolated if the Dutch signed a truce with Spain or if the Heilbronn League made their peace with the Emperor. On the other hand a French declaration of war against Spain would

---

[1] As is suggested by the figures of 'remboursement des rentes accordés pour les prestz' which rose from 5.8 million in 1639 to 10.7 million in 1640 and exceeded 11 million in 1641: A.A.E. France 832, fo. 317. A.A.E. France 837, fo. 58. A.A.E. France 844, fo. 128.

[2] Véron de Forbonnais, *Recherches*, i. 223. Cf. Dent, *Crisis in finance*, p. 50.

[3] Omer Talon, *Mémoires*, ed. Michaud and Poujoulat, p. 270.

[4] A. Leman, *Urbain VIII et la rivalité de la France et de la maison d'Autriche de 1631 à 1635* (Lille-Paris, 1920), p. 382.

forestall a Dutch truce and give new heart ('grand courage') to the evangelical league in Germany. The king argued that open war with Spain would be a relatively cheap solution compared to the burden of annual subsidies to the Dutch and Sweden. In 1634, these subsidies stood at about 3.3 million *livres* per annum (one million to Sweden, perhaps less; 2.3 million to the Dutch). Louis XIII thought that the war would cost only an extra million *livres* a year! The underlying assumption was that the German war would not be a central French concern,[1] an assumption which to some extent had to be revised by the scale of the Swedish disaster at Nördlingen the following month.

From December 1631, Louis XIII had offered to protect all Catholic princes in Germany who needed his help, either against Spanish or Swedish troops. Of the three ecclesiastical electorates in the Rhineland, only Trier took up this offer, but the territory was of the greatest strategic importance. The key points were the great fortresses of Coblenz and Ehrenbreitstein, together with Philippsburg which belonged to the elector in his capacity as bishop of Speyer. In April 1632 Gustavus Adolphus recognized the neutrality of the electorate and agreed that the key fortresses should be occupied by the French (the first two were taken over in May and June 1632; Philippsburg was not obtained until August 1634 and its capture by Imperial forces in January 1635 was one of the factors precipitating French intervention in the war). Trier was a testing ground for the principle of French protection: once the war was over, it would revert to its former status within the empire. The French declared war against Spain in May 1635 following the arrest on 26 March of the elector of Trier by a column of Spanish soldiers. The council of state of Louis XIII, discussing the event, concluded that 'the king cannot avoid taking up arms to avenge the affront which he has received by the imprisonment of a prince who has been placed under his protection'.[2] In fact the defeat and dispersal of the Swedish army and the collapse of the Heilbronn League necessitated decisive intervention by France in order to prevent Swedish capitulation. Most of the German princes had followed the lead of John George of Saxony and made their peace with the Emperor at Prague.[3] Nevertheless, French intervention was intended to be both

[1] *Acta pacis Westphalicae. Serie I. Instruktionen. Frankreich. Schweden. Kaiser*, ed. F. Dickmann *et al.* (Münster, 1962), i. 18–20.

[2] Leman, *Urbain VIII et la rivalité*, p. 492.

[3] The recent interpretation of French foreign policy in the 1630s by Major (*Representative government in early modern France*, p. 621) is untenable.

limited and indirect. France would make a powerful 'war by diversion' but keep its commitment in Germany to a minimum. The assumption behind this strategy was that it was the king of Spain, not the Emperor, who provided the most serious threat to European security. If Philip IV's power was decisively weakened, the French believed that the Emperor would no longer make war or unacceptable political demands on his Protestant subjects. Thus the declaration of war on the Emperor was delayed until the Franco-Swedish alliance was renewed at Wismar on 30 March 1636.

From the early months of 1636 Bullion was haunted, perhaps even obsessed, by fears of a sudden cash crisis which might precipitate bankruptcy and force France out of the war on disadvantageous terms.[1] The development of royal monetary policy, and especially the devaluation of the *livre tournois* in March 1636, must be viewed as a key element in the strategy to win the war. Despite the traditional prohibition on the export of specie, much gold and silver had been exported from the kingdom between 1633 and 1635. The devaluation was aimed at reversing this trend, and the associated phenomenon which was the rapid appreciation of the Spanish gold *pistole* against the *livre tournois*. It was reinforced by further measures in 1640–1 which cumulatively had the effect of strengthening the monetary position of France against Spain and were a vital factor in winning the war.[2] Spanish coin flooded into the kingdom and was reissued as French coin. Under Richelieu and Mazarin, twice as much coin was issued as in the previous 130 years, although the figures are somewhat distorted by the fall in the value of the *livre tournois* in the intervening period.[3] The great issues of coin occurred in the years 1640–4 and 1649–53, and much of the process was simply French recoinage of foreign

[1] Ranum, *Richelieu and the councillors of Louis XIII*, p. 157. While lacking penetrative analysis of financial policy, Ranum's chapter is a good characterization of the embattled tone of Bullion's correspondence with Richelieu. Cf. A.A.E. France 820, fos. 93ᵛ., 119ᵛ., 131ᵛ., [?] Jan, 15 Feb. and 22 Feb. 1636. A.A.E. France 833, fo. 98, 11 Apr. [1639]. A.A.E. France 834, fo. 92, 11 Oct. [1639].

[2] Deyon, *Amiens*, p. 120. J. G. da Silva, *Banque et crédit en Italie au xviiᵉ siècle* (2 vols., 1969), i. 703.

[3] Less than 139 million *livres* in coin were issued between 1493 and 1624, but 280 million *livres* were issued between 1625 and 1659. Calculations based on Spooner, *The international economy and monetary movements in France*, pp. 334–9. The silver content of the *livre tournois* declined from 18 grams in 1513 to 8.3 grams in 1641, with a low point of 7.16 grams in 1653. Morineau's recent comment on Spooner's figures is self-contradictory and misleading: cf. M. Morineau, 'France', *An introduction to the sources of European economic history, 1500–1800. I. Western Europe*, ed. C. H. Wilson and N. G. Parker (1977), p. 178.

specie. However, as early as December 1632 Bullion decided on a policy of monetary expansion as a means of helping provide funds to pay for the war.[1] The devaluation of 1636 was thus part of a wider process of monetary expansion. It also had three important consequences. The first was to make French trade more competitive by stimulating exports. The impact was less great than might have been hoped, because in practice perhaps only one-fifth of all commercial transactions concerned foreign trade, and most of this was with Spain. Once the embargo on trade with Spain was declared in 1635, the traditional pattern of trading relationships was disturbed and French commerce suffered.[2] (The devaluation thus brought few profits except for munitions contractors and financiers servicing letters of change, who could play the exchange rates at the expense of the crown.)[3] A second, and more important, effect was to encourage private investment in royal financial transactions such as tax and loan contracts. By 1636 Bullion was extremely concerned at the lack of investment: 'l'argent . . . ne fust jamais si rare qu'il est', he told the king.[4] The devaluation was aimed at discouraging the hoarding of coin, since inactive cash deposits lost their value. Omer Talon considered that 'les marchands avoient la plupart abandonné leur trafic actuel' in order to invest in tax and loan contracts.[5] If his observation was correct the reasons may well have been the greater return on financial investment and the embargo on trade with Spain rather than the devaluation of 1636. From the point of view of the government perhaps the most important consequence of the devaluation was to reduce the real cost of subsidies paid to the French allies, which for the most part had to be paid in cash.

The two most important annual subsidies paid by France before 1635 were to the Dutch Republic and Sweden. By 1636,

[1] A.A.E. France 803, fo. 329ᵛ., 4 Dec. 1632.

[2] Véron de Forbonnais, *Recherches*, i. 229, considered that the edict of 1636 'dérangea extraordinairement le commerce'. Bullion's intentions were the opposite: Ranum, op. cit., p. 133. For the effect of the war on the textile industry: Deyon, *Amiens*, pp. 170–1 and graph 34. Noel de Paris, the farmer-general of the *cinq grosses fermes*, demanded remissions on his rents because of the prohibition of grain exports and of trade with Spain: E 134a, fo. 405, 27 Oct. 1636.

[3] *Lettres, instructions et mémoires de Colbert . . .*, ed. P. Clément, 10 vols., (1861–82), vii. 249. J. Sanabre, *La acción de Francia en Cataluña en la pugna por la hegemonía de Europa, 1640–1659* (Barcelona, 1956), p. 656. Both examples are rather later, respectively 1643 and 1645.

[4] A.A.E. France 820, fos. 93ᵛ., 259ᵛ [?] Jan. and 9 May 1636.

[5] Talon, *Mémoires*, ed. Michaud and Poujoulat, p. 300.

Bullion was castigating the demands of the Dutch as 'tyrannical',[1] and the value of the subsidy was cut as direct French involvement in the war increased. Thus the amount paid by the French fell from 2.3 million *livres* per annum, agreed in 1634, to 1.5 million (6 September 1636) and 1.2 million (17 September 1637). At the same time, the depreciation of the *livre tournois* was much faster than that of the guilder at Amsterdam.[2] After the Swedish army in Germany met disaster at Nördlingen (6 September 1634) it was clear that France would once more have to assist its northern ally with subsidies. In March 1636, the French and Swedish negotiators at Wismar agreed on the resumption of an annual subsidy of one million *livres*, and this arrangement was confirmed at Hamburg in March 1638. Payment of the subsidy seems to have been resumed in 1637 before the Wismar treaty was fully ratified, and continued until the end of the fighting in Germany in 1648. By the second treaty of Hamburg in July 1641, the rate of annual subsidy was increased to 480,000 *riksdaler*, which was taken to be equivalent to 1.2 million *livres*. This calculation was based on the same rate of exchange as in the original treaty ten years earlier, yet in the meantime the French had devalued the *livre tournois*. The real rate of subsidy had therefore not increased, but had actually fallen; at current rates of exchange 1.4 million *livres* would have been a more accurate conversion.[3] Apart from smaller payments, the French were also committed to substantial subsidies to the Grisons to finance their rebellion in 1635, although the collapse of the French position in the Valtelline two years later was closely related to Bullion's inability to keep the funds flowing smoothly.[4] The other great French commitment between October 1635 and July 1639 was to pay 4 million a year towards the upkeep of the army of duke Bernard of Saxe-Weimar. In return, Bernard was to maintain an army of 18,000 men in the

[1] A.A.E. France 820, fo. 266ᵛ., 14 May 1636.

[2] Comparative rates of exchange of the *livre tournois* with the Amsterdam *Gulden* or *Florijns Banco* and the Hamburg *Reichsthaler Banco* (the latter mentioned in the 2nd treaty of Hamburg between France and Sweden) are given by J.J. McCusker, *Money and exchange in Europe and America, 1600–1775* . . . (Chapel Hill, 1978), p. 306.

[3] Annual payments in riksdaler given by Åström, 'The Swedish economy . . .', *Sweden's age of greatness*, ed. Roberts, loc. cit. Converted into *livres tournois* on the basis of McCusker's figures. Richelieu sought a resumption of payments in 1636: *Lettres . . . de Richelieu*, ed. Avenel, vii. 1017.

[4] Ranum, *Richelieu and the councillors of Louis XIII*, pp. 149–50. Bullion's protests to Louis XIII: A.A.E. France 820, fo. 258, 9 May 1636. It is significant that Martin Lyonne, the *trésorier des ligues suisses*, went bankrupt in 1637: E 139b, fo. 241, 12 Sept. 1637. Mallet records a noticeable fall in payments to the *ligues suisses*. 1634: 1,675,826 *livres*; 1635: 1,708,658 *livres*; 1636: 60,000 *livres*; 1637: 416,300 *livres*; 1638: 62,075 *livres*.

field in Germany. The *surintendants* frequently complained about the excessive expenses of this great mercenary captain, and an investigation was ordered after Bernard's death in 1639.[1]

These subsidies to the allies of France were paid for the most part in cash. Yet even at the highest estimate, they can have accounted for only a relatively small proportion of royal expenditure at the time of Bullion. The difficulty was less their cost than the fact that they were rigid commitments, which had to be met at certain fixed dates each year, regardless of the state of the French treasury.[2] This was also true of the main item of expenditure in the 1630s, which was the army, or more precisely, the five or six armies envisaged for different war fronts. Different estimates were produced of the size of these armies between 1634 and 1636. The lowest figure was 9,500 cavalry and 115,000 infantry, which on Bullion's calculations would have cost over 27 million *livres* a year.[3] Precise calculations of the size of the French army are impossible since no series of muster rolls survives. The real cost would tend to fluctuate, though Mallet's figures indicate a rapid increase in military expenditure coinciding with the French entry into the Thirty Years' War. Military expenditure had averaged less than 16 million a year in the 1620s. After 1630, it was still averaging less than 20 million, but after 1635 it rose to over 33 million and after 1640 to over 38 million a year.[4]

Nevertheless, it ought to have been possible for the crown to meet these expenses because in 1636, the first full year of war, the accounts were adjusted to balance at 108 million.[5] The actual

---

[1] A.A.E. France 822, fo. 52, 13 Oct. 1636. A.A.E. France 834, fo. 11ᵛ., [1639]. A.A.E. France 839, fo. 392, 15 Dec. 1641.

[2] Cf. the difficulty in paying Bernard of Saxe-Weimar at the correct moment in 1637: A.A.E. France 826, fo. 261ᵛ., 6 Apr. 1637.

[3] A.A.E. France 811, fo. 120, [7] Nov. 1634. A.A.E. France 819, fo. 29, [1635]. A higher estimate of 12,000 or 12,500 cavalry and 132,000 infantry is given in A.A.E. France 813, fo. 301ᵛ., 23 Apr. 1635. E 122d, fo. 216, 31 Mar. 1635. A higher estimate still of 27,400 cavalry and 172,000 infantry is given in A.A.E. France 820, fo. 200 [1636] and A.A.E. France 823, fo. 255 [1636]. Bullion's calculations in 1632 were that an army of 1,500 cavalry would cost 666,848 *livres* per annum and 16,000 infantry would cost 3,252,848 *livres* per annum. This provides unit costs of 444.6 *livres* per cavalryman and 203.3 *livres* per infantryman. The unit costs tended to rise during the war, so that the calculations err on the cautious side. Cf. A.A.E. France 806, fo. 173.

[4] The quinquennial averages, based on figures in Appendix Two Table II, are: 1620–4: 15.5 million; 1625–9: 16.2 million (average for the decade 15.9 million); 1630–4: 19.7 million; 1635–9: 32.2 million (average for the decade 26.4 million); 1640–4: 38.6 million; 1645–9: 35.9 million (average for the decade 37.3 million).

[5] Apart from Mallet's figures, the sources are A.A.E. France 823 fo. 116 (which gives revenues as 108.9 million) and B.N. MS. fr. 10410 (which gives revenues and expenses as 108.9 million). The *rôles de l'Épargne* give total expenses of 96.8 million but are incomplete: B.N. n.a.f. 164.

revenue enjoyed by the French monarchy in 1636 was less than the official total of 108 million. Ordinary revenue accounted for less than half (52.3 million) and there was continuing reliance on the *parties casuelles*, which alone provided 28.8 million.[1] Only part of the 56.4 million from the *deniers extraordinaires* would have provided genuine income. How many royal payments were genuinely made in cash rather than as paper transactions?[2] Part of the expenses for 1636 were deferred to the next year by the procedure known as the *ordonnance de remise en d'autre épargne*: this sum amounted to 11.7 million. The *deniers payés par ordonnances* resulting from the conversion of alienated taxes into *rentes* (which has been seen were paper transactions, the actual amount raised from the conversion being much lower) amounted to a fictitious 20.8 million. Part of the secret expenses (*comptants*) of over 31 million were also paper transactions.[3] With these three items removed from the calculations, royal expenditure would be reduced to about 45 million, the annual total which Colbert later considered to have been 'useful' and 'necessary'.[4] The figure of 40 million in cash expenses was the one most frequently cited by Bullion. According to the finance minister, the crown had never spent more than 35 million in cash in peacetime, and the more useful figure had been 30 million.[5] The financing of French inter-

[1] Guéry, loc. cit., seriously underestimates total revenues by his failure to include the *parties casuelles*. Thus the *parties casuelles* have been added to Mallet's figure of ordinary income (23.5 million) to reach the total of 52.3 million.

[2] Guéry's method of calculation assumes that all expenses were 'genuine' but some royal income was 'fictitious'. In fact, there were paper transactions underlying the figures for both income and expenditure, as Foucquet made clear at his trial when discussing the procedure known as the *ordonnance de remise en d'autre épargne*: Foucquet, *Défenses*, v. 103–8.

[3] Mallet's comment (p. 250) is important: 'on a employé . . . toutes les ordonnances expédiées pour les différences de fonds, pour les remises des traités, intérêts de prêts, réformation de billets et autres de cette nature. C'est pourquoi toutes ces dépenses ne sont pas plus fortes ni plus effectives que les recettes des deniers extraordinaires, puisqu'elles ne sont toutes qu'entrées et sorties dans les comptes.' It should be noted that Mallet's figures for extraordinary expenses, with the exception of the year 1635, are consistently higher than the contemporary figures for the *comptants*. It is not known how Mallet arrived at his figures, and whether he tried to incorporate all paper transactions under the heading of extraordinary expenses. Contemporary expenditure accounts were drawn up according to procedures dating from before the reform of the *Épargne* in 1523, and which are particularly unhelpful to the historian. Paper transactions were included under the four most important items of expenditure in these accounts (*comptables; pensions; deniers payés par ordonnances; comptants par certification*).

[4] Mallet's figure for 'ordinary' expenditure was nearly 42.5 million in 1636. For Colbert's comment: *Lettres . . . de Colbert*, ed. Clément, vii. 237.

[5] Bullion informed Louis XIII of his view: A.A.E. France 820, fo. 259, 9 May 1636. There are various references to the 40 million limit in 1634, 1636 and 1640: A.A.E. France 811, fo. 120, [7] Nov. 1634. A.A.E. France 822, fos. 72, 74, 185ᵛ., 18 Oct. and 9 Nov. 1636. A.A.E. France 835, fo. 257, 6 July [1640].

vention in the Thirty Years' War was an elaborate structure built up very largely on paper transactions, rather less than half the total royal expenditure of 108 million in 1636 being actually paid in cash. A massive operation on paper was required to produce proportionately quite a small increase in specie available to the government. The transfer of paper debts from one accounting year to the next, and the payment of interest on the debt, contributed to a staggering increase in the secret expenses, the item of royal expenditure which included most of the interest payments to finance the debt. The secret expenses had averaged just under 20 million in the years from 1630 to 1634, but more than doubled in the years between 1635 and 1644. After 1635, the secret expenses alone equalled the total of *all* expenses in 1630.[1]

The increased importance of paper transactions under Bullion is demonstrated by the growth of the extraordinary revenues, the *deniers extraordinaires*. According to Mallet's figures, these had amounted to only 5.6 million in 1630, but the annual average between 1633 and 1640 was 51.8 million. From less than 30 per cent of the total income of the French monarchy in the years 1630–4, the *deniers extraordinaires* rose to over 52 per cent in the years 1635–9.[2] As has been seen, part of this increase is explained by fictitious accounting of such operations as the conversion of alienated taxes into *rentes*. It is misleading, however, to attribute the whole increase to sleight of hand in the accounts. Part of the increase arose from royal borrowing. The statistics on the French borrowing requirement in the 1630s are incomplete. Nevertheless, it appears that over 5 million a year was borrowed after 1634, and over 10 million a year after 1638; by 1640 the total amount of borrowing had reached nearly 38 million.[3] Yet the French borrowing requirement would be higher in the 1640s. Above all, Bullion's ministry was an age of 'extraordinary taxes' (*affaires extraordinaires*) in a way in which d'Effiat's was not. Looking back on his conduct of financial administration in 1640, Bullion claimed that each year he had had to find more than 40 million *livres* from new tax contracts (*traités*), a claim which does not seem

---

[1] Mallet's figure for total expenditure in 1630 was 41.9 million, in which case the average of 41.6 million in secret expenses between 1635 and 1639 was slightly less. However, B.N. MS. fr. 10410 gives the figure for 1630 as 41.2 million, in which case the average was slightly higher. Cf. Appendix Two, Table III.
[2] Appendix Two, Tables IV and V.
[3] Appendix Two, Table VIII A.

far from the truth.[1] By almost any calculation this was an enormous effort. Bullion's emphasis on tax-contracts was probably more significant in financial terms than the later (and more notorious) policies of Pontchartrain, Chamillart and Desmaretz during the wars of the League of Augsburg and the Spanish Succession.[2]

What type of taxes were raised by the method of *traités*? Clearly one test of the abilities of a finance minister was his acumen in selecting from the numerous financial proposals (*avis*) which came before the council of finance those which were likely to be least damaging and most remunerative in terms of revenue. Much of the preliminary work was done by the *intendant des finances* appointed to examine the merits of the different proposals. Bullion obtained the appointment of Claude Cornuel as an intendant of finance precisely because he had had a direct interest and was thus experienced in such matters.[3] A rather untypical example of a tax contract was the tax levied on the clergy in 1641 by a decision taken by their assembly at Mante after much wrangling and great pressure from the government. The tax of 4.5 million in the form of a *droit d'amortissement* was levied by a contract with Jean Doublet, who subcontracted with the clerical collectors (*receveurs des décimes*) in order to ease his task of revenue collection.[4] This is an unusual case, however, and in general the French clergy was not heavily taxed. The vast bulk of the *traités* concerned two types of revenue, the sales of *rentes* and taxes on office-holding, especially creations of offices and the forced sale of salary increases (*augmentations de gages*). Bullion's ministry was the high point of the fiscal exploitation of office-holders by the crown, surpassed only during the later wars of Louis XIV's reign.[5] This is reflected in the yield

---

[1] A.A.E. France 835, fo. 306, 26 July 1640. This does not seem to have been the case in 1636: Appendix Two, Table VII A.

[2] Appendix Two, Table VII B and C.

[3] Ranum, *Richelieu and the councillors of Louis XIII*, p. 162 n. 4. Cornuel participated in the *traités* of Robert Souart (5 Feb. 1633) and Nicolas Husson (5 Mar. 1633). Cf. E 381b/382a, fo. 473, 1 Oct. 1665, *liquidation* concerning the heirs of Cornuel. He had formerly been a clerk of Antoine Feydeau and a secretary of the council.

[4] Blet, *Le clergé*, i. 494–530. Doublet's original *traité*, under the name of Toussainctz de la Ruelle, was with a *forfait* of 6 million. This was over-optimistic, in view of the opposition of the clergy, and had to be reduced progressively to 5.5 million and ultimately 4.5 million with a *remise* of 1.07 million *livres*: B.N. MS. fr. 18212, fo. 23ᵛ., 12 Dec. 1640. B.N. MS. fr. 18215, fo. 89ᵛ, 31 Aug. 1641. Cf. E 164b, fo. 354, 28 Sept. 1641. For Doublet's subcontracts: Minutier Central, XXI, 139–141, *passim*. Doublet himself was a former *receveur des décimes* at Troyes.

[5] Cf. J. J. Hurt, 'Forced loans and the sale of offices under Louis XIV: the ordeal of the *parlementaires*' (unpublished paper delivered to the American Historical Association, 28 Dec. 1979). My thanks to Professor Hurt for allowing me to consult this paper. Technically

of the revenues raised from the *parties casuelles*, which reached a peak in 1633 but produced substantial amounts of revenue throughout the 1630s. In this decade, the *parties casuelles* produced over a quarter of the total revenues (nearly 39 per cent in the years 1630–4, 24.5 per cent in the years 1635–9) and over half the ordinary revenue.[1] D'Hémery's regime was even more unpopular in the 1640s, but it actually raised less revenue from this source. Mazarin and his finance minister suffered much odium from the excesses of the previous administration.

Bullion presided over a massive increase in both direct and indirect taxes. The *brevet* of 30 July 1633 ordering the levy of direct taxes for 1634 had envisaged a total levy of 22.6 million, including all items.[2] By 1635, the total levy of the *taille* in the *pays d'élections* was 36.2 million.[3] After 1637 a new military tax, the *subsistances*, was levied annually for the maintenance of the army during the winter quarter. The new tax rose from 8.5 million a year at the outset to 13.6 million by 1640–1 and was levied at the same time as the *taille* after 1642.[4] Bullion and Bouthillier issued a new ruling on the administration of the *taille* in January 1634, before the massive increase in direct taxes. However, legislation in itself could not deal with abuses in collection and popular resistance to increased taxes. By 1640, the arrears of the *taille* were accumulating in the provinces at an alarming rate. In part, this explains the low net payments to the Treasury. A more general explanation, however, is the practice of assigning royal expenses directly on local revenues. The total levy was thus bound to be higher than the net receipts. Nevertheless, the proceeds from the *taille* in the *pays d'élections*, as reflected in payments to the Treasury, were very low in the 1630s: they amounted to about 10 per cent of total revenue and about 18 per cent of ordinary revenue.[5]

Similar problems arose with regard to the levy of the indirect taxes. Bullion progressively increased the rents payable by certain

---

the *augmentation de gages* was a *rente* or bond which an office-holder had to buy if he wished to be re-admitted to the *droit annuel*. Professor Hurt demonstrates that office-holders had to borrow money, and indeed contract mortgages on their offices, to pay the *augmentations de gages* during the later wars of Louis XIV. This does not seem to have happened under Richelieu and Mazarin.

[1] Appendix Two, Tables IV and V.
[2] B.N. n.a.f. 200, fo. 2. The items included were the *taille*, the *taillon*, the *crues* and the *droits aliénés*.
[3] The total levy including the *droits aliénés* was 40,049,708 *livres*: B.N. MS. fr. 4520, fo. 1ᵛ. B.N. MS. fr. 7736, fos. 2ᵛ–3ʳ.
[4] Bonney, *Political change in France under Richelieu and Mazarin*, pp. 184, 274–6.
[5] Detailed figures in Appendix Two, Tables IV and V.

revenue farmers and new rights (that is to say, heavier indirect taxes) were accorded. Thus the rents on the *gabelles de France* were increased from 6.6 million *livres* in 1632 to 10.5 million in 1634, 11.9 million in 1637 and 12.4 million in 1638. Rents from the other revenue farmers showed a less dramatic but nevertheless perceptible rise.[1] However, the indirect taxes were extremely difficult to levy, because of rural poverty, the insufficiency of coin in circulation before the great issues in 1640–4,[2] and the devastating effects of plague, famine, and the passage of troops. In 1621, 11,351 *muids* of salt had been sold in the twelve provinces chiefly in northern France which constituted the farm of the *gabelles de France*.[3] Yet only 10,500 *muids* were sold in 1635–6, 8,221 in 1638, 8,142 in 1639 and 9,318 in 1640.[4] Since the crown had undertaken in 1632 to guarantee the consortium of Philippe Hamel sales of 10,225 *muids*, it was obliged to grant the tax farmers remissions on their rents virtually every year.[5] Sometimes, the government was able to avoid remissions only by according new leases with reduced rents.[6] Generally, it was able to retain the services of the most important financial consortia only by further committing them in the hope that they would recover previous losses. It was important not to break faith with a group of financiers who behaved well in Bouthillier's view, because the failure to honour a lease might lead to the collapse of the administration of the revenue farm.[7]

The situation was undoubtedly difficult, but Bullion's policy with regard to the revenue farms was little short of a disaster. Over-renting was followed by remissions to the farmers. This virtually destroyed the purpose of the revenue farms, which was to guarantee a stable revenue regardless of economic fluctuations. Between 1637 and 1641, the revenue farm of the *aides*, the second most important in the kingdom, was on the verge of collapse, and its administration was subdivided after François Chandonnay was discharged from the lease in 1637.[8] These difficulties explain

[1] Bonney, 'The failure of the French revenue farms', 26–7. Appendix Two, Table VI.
[2] This was noted by Bullion in Dec. 1635: Ranum, op. cit., p. 155. Cf. E 135a, fo. 105, 17 Jan. 1637. The general point was made by J. Meuvret, *Études d'histoire économique . . .* (1971), pp. 127–37.
[3] J. Récurat and E. Leroy-Ladurie, 'Sur les fluctuations de la consommation taxée du sel dans la France du nord au xviie et xviiie siècles', *Revue du Nord*, liv (1972), 385, 398.
[4] E 135a, fos. 105, 109, 17 Jan. 1637. E 159c, fo. 27, 6 Feb. 1641. E 171b, fo. 410, 28 June 1642.
[5] Bonney, 'The failure of the French revenue farms', p. 19 especially notes 2 and 3.
[6] For example, the renewal of the *cinq grosses fermes* in 1635: Ranum, op. cit., p. 130.
[7] A.A.E. France 842, fos. 50^v.–51^r., 21 Feb. 1642. This part of Bouthillier's letter is not quoted by Ranum, op. cit., pp. 175–6.
[8] E 136a, fo. 183, 28 Mar. 1637. E 137b, fos. 196, 373, 21 and 23 May 1637.

in part the low net payments by the revenue farmers to the Treasury, although as with the direct revenues, certain types of royal expenses were assigned locally on the indirect taxes. The proceeds from the revenue farms, as reflected in payments to the Treasury, were very low in the 1630s: they amounted to about 11 per cent of total revenue and about 19 per cent of ordinary revenue.[1]

There were several fundamental objections to Bullion's fiscal policies, however useful his methods proved after 1635. One objection was political: his readiness to pressurize the office-holders left a legacy of resentment which would assume serious proportions once Louis XIII and Richelieu were removed from the helm. The violent methods used to increase the amount of forced loan payable by the office-holders in return for the confirmation of the *droit annuel* in October 1638 could not easily be repeated when the nine-year term of the confirmation expired at the end of December 1647.[2] Bouthillier was much more circumspect after Bullion's death, recognizing that the office-holders were willing to co-operate with the government provided that they were not pushed too hard[3] — but by 1641 the damage had been done. A second objection to Bullion's policy was financial. He sacrificed the long-term interest of the crown for short-term advantage. The creation of offices and *rentes* was in reality an extension of the consolidated debt of the French monarchy. It brought a sudden windfall to the Treasury, but at the cost of a long-term increase in expenditure, because office-holders had to be paid their *gages* and *rentiers* the interest on their *rentes*. By 1640, according to Mallet's estimate, these payments absorbed perhaps 45.8 million *livres* (19.7 million on *rentes*, 26.1 million on *gages*) and Bullion had no choice but to cut back on payments. He commended the attitude of Henri IV in 1609–10, claiming that the king had cut these payments by half to pay for his armies.[4] The risk of provoking a political crisis was very real, however, if the constant criticism by the sovereign courts of Henri IV's policies in the 1590s is borne in mind.

---

[1] Appendix Two, Tables IV and V, provide more detailed figures.

[2] Mousnier, *La vénalité*, pp. 300–8. Mousnier's calculations (p. 421) of the *parties casuelles* as a proportion of total revenues give a misleading impression. The yield was higher in the 1630s than the 1620s as expressed as a proportion of ordinary revenue.

[3] A.A.E. France 839, fo. 246ᵛ., 13 Sept. 1641.

[4] Mallet, p. 94. A.A.E. France 833, fo. 93ᵛ., 8 Apr. [1639]. E 151a, fo. 35, 4 June 1639. Reductions by one quarter in the *gages* in 1639 and thereafter are mentioned in A.A.E. France 839, fo. 386, 12 Dec. 1641.

Bullion's preferred method of revenue raising by the *traités* accentuated the political difficulties of the government and was both inefficient and expensive. The average rate of interest paid on tax contracts in the 1630s was about 24 per cent,[1] and while any investment in royal financial transactions carried risks there is no doubt at all that the proliferation of new tax contracts brought a bonanza to the financiers. Bullion appears to have abandoned any attempt to keep a check on profiteering. Although it had been decided in 1625 to investigate the activities of the financiers every ten years, no *chambre de justice* was held in 1635. Instead, only 3.5 million *livres* were levied in fines.[2] This was a meaningless gesture, which had at its most obvious motive the desire to gain a small additional revenue while attempting to retain the confidence of the financiers in the forthcoming struggle against the Habsburgs. The fines were levied by the financiers themselves as a tax contract. Neither the scale of the operation, nor the method by which it was organized, would have impressed the sovereign courts who enjoyed the power of disrupting Bullion's policy by delaying registration of the fiscal edicts which formed the juridical authority for new tax contracts. Registration was not obligatory on the government, but it helped allay public disquiet and ensure public acquiescence to the taxes. Without registration, the tax contractors had great difficulty in levying the taxes and they required the approval of the sovereign courts for their own security. The disadvantage of submitting new fiscal legislation to the courts was that registration was not always forthcoming. The courts tended to oppose increases in taxation generally, and the fiscal exploitation of office-holders in particular. 'Extraordinary taxes' thus became the focus of political controversy, part of the struggle between the crown and the office-holders. Bullion was responsible for much of the conflict between the government and the *Parlement* of Paris, for example in 1636 and 1639.[3] These political difficulties explain in

---

[1] Appendix Two, Table VII A.

[2] E 122d, fo. 215, 31 Mar. 1635, P 2363, p. 707, 21 June 1635. *Traité* of Jean des Montz (or de Mons) with a *forfait* of 4.9 million (including taxes of 3.5 million on the financiers) and a *remise* of 1.5 million: B.N. MS. fr. 18206, fo. 128ᵛ., 4 Sept. 1635. E 126a, fos. 23, 76, 4 Sept. 1636. The consortium levying the taxes comprised the financiers Jean Galland, François le Gros and Nicolas Colbert (the father of the minister of Louis XIV). That Colbert's father was a tax-contractor is well known, though his participation in this venture is not: J. L. Bourgeon, *Les Colbert avant Colbert. Destin d'une famille marchande* (1973), pp. 203–13.

[3] Mousnier, *La vénalité*, pp. 205–10. Moote, *The revolt of the judges*, pp. 59–60. Ranum, op. cit., p. 138. A.A.E. France 820, fos. 14, 39ᵛ., 6 and 28 Jan. 1636. A.A.E. France 826, fo. 4, 1 Jan. 1637. A.A.E. France 836, fo. 61, 21 Aug. [1640]. Ironically, Bullion himself bought an office of new creation in the *Parlement* of Paris: an office of *président à mortier* acquired in Mar. 1636.

part the inefficiency of the tax-contract system. Many of the new taxes were never registered by the sovereign tribunals, and the tax contractors were unable to levy them. Others were registered, but with modifications which made them an unprofitable investment to the contractors. Still more eventually produced revenues, but intermittently and much less than had been expected.

Each tax contract had its own history, and it must have been very difficult for the government to keep an adequate check on the profits made by the financial consortium holding the contract. The only practicable method of keeping a check on profiteering was the scrutiny of the records of the interest payments made to financiers through the secret expenses (*comptants*). The document sent to the *Chambre des Comptes* called the *acquit de comptant* was simply the annual total of the secret expenses, but up to 1634 the council of finance had kept the minutes of all payments (*menus de comptant*). When Cornuel became intendant of finance in that year, however, he commenced the practice of burning this detailed record, a decision taken almost certainly with the knowledge and approval of Bullion.[1] For four years it became almost impossible to keep a track on interest payments to financiers and ministerial profiteering. It seems probable that it was in this period that Cornuel and Bullion made the bulk of their fortunes, respectively of 1.8 and 7.8 million *livres*.[2] It is impossible to determine precisely how these sums were acquired. The finance minister, for example, prudently dispersed the fruits of his corruption[3] by purchasing lands and offices which represented about three-quarters of his fortune. Bullion had used his position to acquire a much more secure fortune than Cornuel: the debts of the *surintendant* were scarcely a quarter of those of the intendant yet his fortune at his death was four times as great.[4] Both fortunes are striking to the extent that the amount of money involved in royal financial transactions, with the exception of offices, was very small (18 per cent in the case of Bullion, although the total

[1] Ranum, op. cit., p. 153. *Lettres . . . de Colbert*, ed. Clément, vii. 174.

[2] J. P. Labatut, 'Aspects de la fortune de Bullion', *XVII*ᵉ *Siècle*, lx (1963), 11–39, especially 24–5, 39. For Cornuel's fortune: Dent, *Crisis in finance*, p. 167. Minutier Central LI 191, 15 Dec. 1638. Cornuel's fortune of 1,866,000 *livres* was drastically reduced by liabilities of 842,045 *livres* to a total of 1,023,955 *livres*.

[3] For Bullion's reputation of corruption, apart from the evidence of conflict with Richelieu, there is the story told by Tallemant des Réaux (Labatut, art. cit., 17)), Schomberg's comment on his death (A.A.E. France 1632, fo. 19, 7 Jan. 1641) and above all Servien's denunciation: 'une des principales parties luy manquast, qui est la probité . . .'; A.A.E. France 891, fo. 54 and A.A.E. France 892, fo. 148, 25 Jan. 1653.

[4] Bullion's debts were only 245,000 *livres*. Cornuel's debts were 842,045 *livres*.

amounted to 1.4 million; less than 6 per cent in the case of Cornuel, a mere 107,800 *livres*). Yet almost certainly the origins of both fortunes are to be found in royal financial transactions, such as rewards (*pots de vin*) from financiers, the illegal participation in loan or tax contracts, and the misappropriation of the secret expenses.[1]

On the last point, the clearest evidence is provided by the crisis in relations between Richelieu and the *surintendant* in 1638–9. Bullion wanted to marry his son, who held the *survivance* of his office in the *Parlement* of Paris, to Charlotte de Prie, daughter of the marquis de Toussy. However, the marriage required the agreement both of Richelieu and the king. The chief minister refused to speak to the king about the matter for over six months until Bullion met certain of his specific requirements, and at one point he may even have considered dismissing the *surintendant*.[2] Nevertheless, the marriage contract was eventually drawn up towards the end of February 1639 in the presence of the entire ministerial team.[3] In return, Bullion had to agree to act with more moderation than he had sometimes shown in the past (for example, in his conflict with Servien). He was to limit his fortune to its extent in January 1639: although this agreement precluded further illicit gains, it implicitly protected Bullion from subsequent confiscation of his wealth. The finance minister also undertook to implement the ruling of 19 July 1638 which had limited the financial rewards of members of the king's council and specifically outlawed 'récompense(s) par extraordinaire et par co(mptant)'. The ruling had also specifically ordered the Chancellor and the finance ministers to keep a copy of the minutes of the secret expenses ordering interest payments 'pour les remises des traitants'. Among the other provisions was a commitment to implement the *Code Michaud* of January 1629, although it is an open

---

[1] For a claim that Bullion had received a *pot de vin* of 200,000 *livres* from a tax contract: cf. E 384b, fo. 206, 1 Feb. 1666. For Cornuel's continued involvement in financial consortia and perjury before the *Chambre des Comptes*, cf. introduction.

[2] The crisis lasted from the ruling of 19 July 1638 until the settlement of the marriage contract on 24 Feb. 1639. Richelieu's comment quoted by Montglat ('voilà le procès de Bullion tout fait quand il me plaira') may be related to the ruling: *Mémoires . . . de Montglat*, ed. Michaud and Poujoulat, p. 101. In the context of Bullion's marriage plans for his son, the later policy of Foucquet in marrying his daughters into the upper nobility is worth recalling and the contemporary criticism, for example from Colbert.

[3] Labatut, art. cit., pp. 34–5. Y 180, fo. 88, 24 Feb. 1639. Among those present was a future finance minister, La Meilleraye, who at the time held the office of *grand maître de l'artillerie*. He was present as Richelieu's cousin.

question whether this was possible in wartime.[1] Bullion also undertook to keep three copies of the minutes of the secret expenses, one for himself, one for the Chancellor, and one for the *trésorier de l'Épargne*. The practice of burning the records of the secret expenses during Cornuel's lifetime was abandoned after 1639. According to Foucquet, Cardinal Mazarin and Chancellor Séguier had been prepared to resume the practice in the 1650s, but he opposed the idea which was not accepted.[2] The crisis in relations between Richelieu and Bullion thus produced one lasting reform, albeit one of a fairly elementary kind which removed an abuse of recent origin. Richelieu clearly intended that Bullion should implement more fundamental reforms for the public benefit. Richelieu's own reform plans of 1626–7 seem to have been taken out of the files and dusted off in 1639, and Bullion made suggestions of his own.[3] What was lacking was a context of peace in which these plans for financial reform could be seriously applied.

Two important consequences of this financial review became apparent in November 1640, just a month before Bullion's death. One was the revocation of letters of ennoblement granted over the previous thirty years. This was a reform aimed at facilitating the levy of the *taille* which had been rendered difficult by the grant of an excessive number of fiscal exemptions.[4] The second important measure was the introduction of the *sol pour livre* or *subvention générale*, a 5 per cent sales tax, which was none other than Henri IV's *pancarte* under a different name.[5] It is a common element in both Richelieu and Bullion's reform plans, and it seems that the chief minister had discussed the details of the scheme on 2 January 1636 with the great financier Pierre Puget de Montauron. Montauron appears to have believed that the sales tax could raise

[1] Ranum, *Richelieu and the councillors of Louis XIII*, pp. 197–8. For the agreement on 10 Jan. 1639: ibid., pp. 152–3 and *Lettres . . . de Richelieu*, ed. Avenel, vi. 271–2.
[2] Cornuel died in Nov. 1638. B.N. Morel de Thoisy 156, fo. 15: '. . . depuis l'année 1639 les menus de comptant . . . ont esté soigneusement conservez par ordre du Roy . . .' Foucquet's comment is cited below in Chapter VI. The Chancellor's copy provides the only record of the secret expenses between 1644 and 1661. Cf. Appendix Two, Table III, sources.
[3] As observed in Chapter III, several copies of Richelieu's plan of reforms link it with the year 1639. For Bullion's reform plan: B.N. 500 Colbert 194, fo. 273, 'ordre à préparer lors qu'il plairra à Dieu donner la paix au Royaume'. Above the title, in another hand, is the statement that 'l'original de ce mémoire est escrit de la main de M. Bullion . . .' Bullion wanted to see the abolition of the *comptants*, a reduction in direct taxes by 8 or 10 million and an increase in the sales tax ('outre ce qu'il est affermé presentement') by 2 million.
[4] AD + 263, Nov. 1640.
[5] AD IX 8, Nov. 1640.

80 million *livres* in addition to the *taille*, a figure which was wildly exaggerated but in some measure accounts for the stormy reception of the tax.[1] When the edict was presented to the *Cour des Aides* of Paris for registration, Chancellor Séguier gave assurances that if the sales tax produced very large amounts of revenue the *taille* would be remitted. He also commented that the sales tax was levied in all the best administered states, and had been in existence in the Netherlands for a hundred years.[2] His words were hardly reassuring. Séguier was distrusted and considered a corrupt Chancellor.[3] The great underlying fear of the sales tax, which led to widespread resistance and eventually forced the government to abandon the measure, was that it would become a permanent additional revenue, not an alternative to the *taille*—in other words that Montauron would be proved right and the government would not keep its word. The members of the government seem to have believed that as a tax on consumption the sales tax spread the load more widely over the nation than existing direct taxes such as the *taille*. The rich, so the theory ran, consumed more than the poor, and therefore paid more in tax.[4] Yet quite apart from the political dangers presented by the opposition of vested interest groups such as butchers and wine growers, who stirred up riots against the tax, it is questionable whether the reasoning behind the *sol pour livre* was correct. To the poor, or even

[1] Montauron mentioned a total levy of 120 million. The *taille* was levied at 40 million in 1636. Cf. A.A.E. France 819, fos. 178–9ᵛ., 217–18, 1635 and 2 Jan. 1636. Figures of 100 million and 50 million were mentioned by members of the *Cour des Aides* of Paris. For the stormy reception of the tax: Bonney, *Political change in France under Richelieu and Mazarin*, pp. 328–30.

[2] Z1a 161, fos. 29ᵛ.–30ʳ., 4 Dec. 1640. The original 5 per cent sales tax in the Netherlands dated from 1569, but had applied only to the sales of landed property. A ten per cent sales tax was to apply to all other sales: Parker, *The Dutch revolt*, p. 115. The opposition to the 'tenth penny' in the Netherlands is worth recalling.

[3] When Séguier died in 1672, he left a fortune of 4 million *livres*: *Lettres et mémoires adressés au Chancelier Séguier*, ed. R. É. Mousnier, (2 vols., 1964), i. 34. As Chancellor, Séguier was able to defend his activities in the council of finance and in 1665 he was discharged from taxes on his redemptions of *rentes* because of his 'grandes et notables services' to the king: E 383a, fo. 55, 5 Nov. 1665.

[4] A.A.E. France 839, fo. 303ᵛ., 17 Oct. 1641. Bouthillier wrote to Richelieu: 'ce sont les riches du royaume qui la paient comme consommantz incomparablement plus que les pauvres des denrées et marchandises qui y sont subjettes.' He called the sales tax 'la plus innocente imposition qui puisse se faire . . .': A.A.E. France 842, fo. 43, 17 Feb. 1642. Séguier had stated in 1640 that 'cette nouvelle imposition se payeroit plus par les riches que par les pauvres . . .' These arguments are borne out to the extent that the edict establishing the tax carefully excluded two articles from the *sol pour livre*, grain for consumption within the kingdom (i.e. not intended for export) and 'les menus denrées que les gens de village et menu peuple vendent en détail et non en gros'. There was either misunderstanding about the nature of the tax, or the exclusion clauses proved unworkable in practice.

the relatively poor, any amount of sales tax represented an additional burden. Had the tax been established without provoking riots, it might have proved administratively convenient to levy as one large revenue farm. But the early difficulties, and the recourse to enforcement by the provincial intendants and the troops created havoc with the marketing of leases. Financiers were willing to enter only small commitments, at the level of the province or the large town. It would thus have proved difficult to increase rents from the farms of the sales tax above the figure of 12 million *livres*, which was the estimated yield in 1641–2.[1] For both administrative and political reasons it was inevitable that the tax would be abandoned, although it was not withdrawn until 25 February 1643.

Bullion did not live to see the revocation of the sales tax, which had been one of the key elements in his and Richelieu's reform plans. He died on 23 December 1640 and had to be buried secretly for fear of a popular demonstration of joy at his death.[2] Bouthillier was left as sole finance minister, but was generally regarded as less capable than Bullion. Jacques Tubeuf, an intendant of finance, was given special authority as his assistant.[3] Tubeuf was later criticized personally for the escalation of borrowing,[4] but he defended his conduct on the grounds that the revolt of the Catalans in 1640 had expanded French military commitments and the

---

[1] Cf. Bouthillier's comment on the difficulty in increasing yields from the sales tax: A.A.E. France 842, fo. 72, 10 Mar. 1642. Examples of leases: E 161a, fo. 292, 8 May 1641. E 162a, fo. 350, 8 June 1641.

[2] *Lettres . . . de Richelieu*, ed. Avenel, vi. 735 n. 2.

[3] For Bouthillier: Ranum, *Richelieu and the councillors of Louis XIII*, pp. 166–80. Montglat commented that Bouthillier 'n'étoit pas si habile que l'autre [i.e. Bullion]. Tubeuf, qui travailloit sous le défunt fut mis auprès de celui-ci pour le soulager, et avoir l'oeil sur ce qui se passeroit': *Mémoires . . . de Montglat*, ed. Michaud and Poujoulat, p. 102. Bullion had obtained the appointment of Tubeuf as Cornuel's replacement in Nov. 1638, and he had had charge of the loan contracts under Bullion. Cf. Ranum, op. cit., p. 162.

[4] The *Catalogue des partisans*, a *Mazarinade* from the time of the Fronde, claimed that 'Tuboeuf dans ses commencemens scribe à la suite du Conseil, estant parvenu à l'intendance, a introduit les prests sur les deniers du roy . . .': *Choix de Mazarinades*, ed. C. Moreau (2 vols., 1853), i. 123. M. N. Grand-Mesnil, *Mazarin, la Fronde et la presse, 1647–1649* (1967), pp. 87–8. The first part of the statement is true, since Tubeuf had been a protégé of d'Effiat, a *trésorier de France* at Riom and *contrôleur des restes du conseil*: Y 172, fo. 345ʳ., 28 Jan. 1632. The second part of the statement is more doubtful. Cornuel seems to have presided over an initial escalation of borrowing in 1637–8. The decision on 12 Feb. 1637 to remove the restrictions imposed in 1626 on the anticipation of revenues was a symbolic act by the council of finance, made on Cornuel's recommendation: E 135b, fo. 216, 12 Feb. 1637. For the apparent participation of Tubeuf in the loan contracts on the *généralité* of Limoges as the assignee of Charles de Pradines (*c.* 1642–6): cf. E 300a, fo. 423, 12 Apr. 1657.

need for cash payments.[1] In fact, the escalation of borrowing seems to have preceded the revolt of the Catalans: Bullion and Tubeuf negotiated loan contracts totalling 15.9 million in 1639 and 37.6 million in 1640. Bouthillier and Tubeuf borrowed 41.6 million in 1641, a relatively small increase over the previous year.[2] Yet whatever the precise reasons for the increase in royal borrowing, it is clear that the receipts of all forms of taxation, including the *taille*, were being anticipated systematically during Louis XIII's lifetime. Thus the responsibility for this decision cannot be placed (as it frequently has been by historians)[3] on the Regency government and Mazarin and d'Hémery in particular. By 1642 the revenues of the *taille* had been anticipated at least one year in advance by the method of loan contracts negotiated with the financiers. The growing arrears of the *taille* were thus extremely serious. Not only did they threaten the credibility of the revenues upon which future loans were to be contracted. They led the financiers to panic about the security of their investment. Throughout 1642, Bouthillier warned Richelieu of the need to reduce government expenditure, to improve the collection of the *taille*, and to bolster up financial confidence. A threatened strike by the financiers in the summer of 1642 led to dramatic changes. On 5 June, the council of finance pledged full repayment to the financiers for loans, if necessary by replacement of the revenues upon which repayment was assigned. On 22 August 1642, the assessments of the *taille* were conferred upon the provincial intendants.[4] It seems clear that by the time of Louis XIII's death on 14 May 1643 at least 12 million *livres* had been anticipated on the revenues of the next two years with interest paid on the debt at a minimum of 15 per cent.[5]

Borrowing on this scale brought with it an inherent risk of bankruptcy. The first year of Bouthillier's administration was rocked by the bankruptcy of François Sabathier, one of the leading financiers of the crown, whose private disaster threatened to bring about a more general collapse.[6] The trouble began with the difficulties experienced by a secondary financier, Louis le Barbier,

---

[1] Z1a 163, fo. 79ᵛ., 11 July 1648. Séguier had made a similar point in 1640: Z1a 161, fo. 29ᵛ.,–30ʳ., 4 Dec. 1640.

[2] Appendix Two, Table VIII.

[3] For example, Moote, *The revolt of the judges*, p. 80. The mistake was originally made, it seems, by the usually reliable Véron de Forbonnais, *Recherches*, i. 250.

[4] Bonney, *Political change in France under Richelieu and Mazarin*, p. 184.

[5] This statement of Gaston d'Orléans on 31 Aug. 1647 was almost certainly an underestimate: Talon, *Mémoires*, ed. Michaud and Poujoulat, p. 206.

[6] Ranum, op. cit., pp. 178–9.

who had participated in several tax contracts and revenue farms in the 1630s, but who was owing the government money by late 1638:[1] at his request the council of finance blocked legal actions by his private creditors in the spring of 1641.[2] Barbier's difficulties caused a crisis of confidence among the secondary tier of private investors in the financial system, who took panic measures to secure their assets held by a much more considerable financier, François Sabathier.[3] Sabathier had risen to prominence through the provision of saltpetre and gunpowder to the crown,[4] a splendid monopoly to hold at the beginning of France's entry into the Thirty Years' War. He bought the office of *trésorier des parties casuelles* in 1638[5] and most of his important financial dealings dated from this time: he claimed to have entered into tax contracts and loans to the crown worth 22 million *livres* in the two years 1639–41.[6] Sabathier's biggest contract was a loan of 9 million contracted on 20 February 1640 under the name of François Brunet,[7] which anticipated a certain number of revenues of 1641 and 1642. This was certainly the largest single loan contract negotiated by Bullion and Tubeuf, and was one of the largest for the entire period of Richelieu's and Mazarin's administration. Sabathier undertook to pay the crown 6 million *livres* in 18 equal monthly instalments and to present 3 million in *rentes* for redemption (bought up on the open market at the cheap rate of *denier* 4 but redeemed at the high rate of *denier* 18).[8]

[1] The fear was expressed that he might 'divertisse les deniers desd[ites]fermes [of the *entrées*] pour en payer ses autres créanciers . . .': E 147a, fo. 218, 20 Nov. 1638. In the event, Barbier was accused of utilizing 1.45 million *livres* from his *traité d'amortissements* (cf. B.N. MS. fr. 18210, fo. 8ᵛ., 6 Apr. 1639) to satisfy his private creditors: E 170a, fo. 117, 7 May 1642. François le Massonet was appointed to take over the administration of the *traité* and three important financiers (Guillaume Cornuel, Germain Courtin, and François Tardif) acted as surety and liquidated Barbier's assets: E 173a, fo. 235, 22 Aug. 1642. However, although Barbier had died in Dec. 1641, this work was still continuing in 1648: E 228c, fo. 187, 5 Feb. 1648. In Sept. 1641 a preliminary estimate was drawn up of total debts to the crown of 2.7 million in the form of arrears of payments on the farms and tax-contracts held by Barbier: E 164a, fo. 377, 11 Sept. 1641.

[2] Cf. E 160c, fo. 742, 30 Apr. 1641, which refers to earlier decrees of 30 Jan. and 6 Mar.

[3] E 160c, fo. 10, 6 Apr. 1641. At this moment, Sabathier claimed that his assets stood at 10.7 million while his debts amounted to about 8 million.

[4] He held a nine-year lease from 1 July 1634: cf. E 118a, fo. 186, 15 July 1634. For a sidelight on his activities: J. U. Nef, *Industry and government in France and England, 1540–1640* (repr. Ithaca and London, 1969), p. 64.

[5] Cf. E 147b, fo. 320, 18 Dec. 1638. Once he went bankrupt, he had the office exercised by an agent: E 160c, fo. 631, 24 Apr. 1641.

[6] E 160c, fo. 10, 6 Apr. 1641.

[7] E 154b, fo. 365, 20 Feb. 1640.

[8] Cf. E 377b, fo. 282, 31 Mar. 1665. *Liquidation* concerning the heirs of François Sabathier.

Despite the high interest payments, it is easy to imagine how Sabathier's creditors came to regard him as over-committed and thus a dangerous investment: once confidence was lost, his bankruptcy was only a matter of time. On 6 April 1641, at his request, the council of finance blocked legal actions by his creditors, which was the beginning of the rot.[1] The suspension was renewed successively[2] while a commission of enquiry was set up by the council of finance to receive the complaints of the association of Sabathier's creditors.[3] Hardly surprisingly, the royal commissioners, Aligre and Tubeuf, found it difficult to reconcile the contradictory statements of the financier and his creditors. Sabathier claimed that the figure for his private debts alleged by his creditors—11 or 12 million *livres*—was too high and ought to be halved: but neither side could demonstrate their case.[4] Thus when Sabathier died in 1646, his accounts had not been finalized, and it was claimed that his assets had been diverted fraudulently to avoid paying off his creditors.[5] The liquidation of his debts continued into the 1650s, when it was claimed that he owed the crown 4.3 million *livres*.[6] The scale of the collapse of François Sabathier was thus much greater than the previous bankruptcies of Feydeau, Payen and Charlot. He was undoubtedly one of the most important financiers of his time, and the government was able to weather the storm in 1641 only because Sabathier's position was not unrivalled: Bouthillier could turn to other, very considerable, financiers such as Jean Galland, Antoine Boyer, Thomas Bonneau, and Denis Marin.

Looking back on the reign of Louis XIII, and reflecting on the origins of the Fronde, Omer Talon, the *avocat-général* in the *Parlement* of Paris, concluded that scandalously large sums of money had been levied, so much so that it was scarcely an exaggeration to say that more taxes had been raised by Louis than all his predecessors put together. Cardinal de Richelieu, in Omer Talon's view, had secured his political ascendancy by control of patronage

---

[1] E 160c, fo. 10.

[2] E 168a, fo. 584, 15 Mar. 1642. E 179a, fo. 37, 15 Apr. 1643. In Feb. 1644, Sabathier went into hiding [E 187a, fo. 388, 17 Feb. 1644] until a new suspension was granted: E 189a, fo. 72, 6 Apr. 1644.

[3] For a reference to the *syndics* of the creditors: E 168a, fo. 65, 8 Mar. 1642.

[4] A.A.E. France 845, fo. 175. Memorandum of Aligre to Richelieu, n.d., *c.* 1641–2.

[5] E 208a, fo. 231, 7 Feb. 1646.

[6] On the process of *liquidation*: E 212a, fo. 358, 13 June 1646. E 230b, fo. 48, 20 May 1648. E 249b, fo. 264, 18 Nov. 1651. E 256b, fo. 326, 29 May 1653.

and the financial system (*la profusion des finances*). Moreover, the creation of offices and *rentes* in this period had reached epic proportions, so that any and everyone bought these titles and considered themselves rich as a result. Yet Talon considered that this new wealth of France was illusory and rested on an insecure foundation: if the crown renegued on its obligations, the new *rentes* and offices would be worthless.[1] An anonymous memorandum on the state of the royal finances in the second year of the Regency concluded that more than 700 million *livres* in taxes had been brought to the Treasury since 1620, while the gains of the financiers had been enormous—172 million from the *traités* alone on a conservative estimate.[2] Underlying both these verdicts on financial administration during the reign was the assumption that in real terms the crown was bankrupt by the time of Louis XIII's death. Technically, of course, this was not the case: François Sabathier's collapse did not bring about the general bankruptcy that had been feared, and his loan contract of 9 million *livres* was reallocated among other financiers apparently without great difficulty.[3] But the consequences of the great issue of *rentes* in 1634 were already clear, and by 1647 the government was prepared to admit publicly that there had been a 'manquement de bonne foi . . . capable de ruiner les affaires publiques . . .'[4]

Neither Richelieu nor Louis XIII lived to see the younger Condé's great victory over the Spanish at Rocroi on 19 May 1643, the sort of military triumph which they had been seeking throughout the war. In fact, Rocroi settled nothing. The arbitration of a single battle could not be final or definitive in a war which was essentially a struggle for resources.[5] The question faced by the French government in 1642–3 was whether royal expenditure could be maintained at the high levels of the first eight years of the war and whether new revenues could be found, or existing

---

[1] Talon, *Mémoires*, ed. Michaud and Poujoulat, pp. 270–1, 299.

[2] 'Mémoire sur l'état des finances depuis 1616 jusqu'à 1644', *Archives curieuses de l'histoire de France*, 2nd ser., vi (1838), 60–1. Between 1631 and 1641, 133.6 million was paid out in *remises* on the *traités*: Appendix Two, Table VII C.

[3] Parts of the loan were taken over by the following *prête-noms*—Michel Collin (1.8 million *livres*): E 156b, fo. 654, 29 Aug. 1640. François le Bert (2.7 million): E 159c, fos. 437, 440, 27 Feb. 1641. Thomas le Clerc (2 million): E 160b, fo. 385, 30 Mar. 1641. Noel Petu (600,000): E 160c, fo. 612, 20 Apr. 1641. Guillaume Bossuet (700,000): E 160c, fo. 615, 20 Apr. 1641.

[4] 'Car depuis de ce temps', Gaston d'Orléans declared on 31 Aug. 1647, 'personne n'a voulu contracter avec le roi . . .' He also pointed out the fall in the value of the *rentes* on the open market: Talon, *Mémoires*, ed. Michaud and Poujoulat, p. 206.

[5] Cf. R. Stradling, 'Catastrophe and recovery: the defeat of Spain, 1639–43', *History*, lxiv (1979), 219.

revenues exploited on a continuing basis, to match this expenditure. Even Richelieu had recognized the need for economies in the summer of 1642,[1] and as has been seen, a dispute over the war estimates was one reason why Louis XIII dismissed Sublet des Noyers as war minister in April 1643. Richelieu died on 4 December 1642 and Louis XIII the following 14 May without having achieved a peace settlement that would allow a return to more orderly forms of administration and lower levels of taxation. Equally, they had failed to secure sufficient revenues to continue the war indefinitely, although on 16 April 1643 Louis XIII confirmed the fiscal powers recently accorded to the provincial intendants, which ensured that there was a new institution to enforce the levy of taxation in the localities.[2]

In April 1643 the continuing ill health of the king led him to consider measures to ensure a stable form of government during the impending royal minority. Louis XIII was concerned lest his own death would lead to a period of instability and the reversal of his foreign and domestic policies. In particular, the king questioned the competence of Anne of Austria, his wife, to act as Regent, and doubted her commitment to his anti-Habsburg foreign policy: in 1637 he had menaced her with repudiation because of a secret correspondence with her brother, the Cardinal Infante.[3] There was also the permanent problem of Gaston d'Orléans, Louis's disruptive younger brother, who as recently as December 1642 had been debarred from holding public office in France or participating in a Regency government. Louis XIII may have had little understanding of finance, but he must also have feared a collapse of financial confidence following his death such as had occurred in 1559 on the death of Henri II.

The 'déclaration . . . touchant le gouvernement du royaume après sa mort', usually referred to as the last will and testament of Louis XIII, dated 20 April 1643 and duly registered in the *Parlement* of Paris, was an attempt to resolve these issues. It was also, as contemporaries noted with ironic humour, an attempt by Richelieu's ministerial team to secure their position under the Regency.[4] The royal declaration established a form of govern-

---

[1] A.A.E. France 843, fo. 283, 30 Aug. 1642.

[2] The *Cour des Aides* of Paris refused to register this legislation without modification: Bonney, *Political change in France under Richelieu and Mazarin*, pp. 253–6.

[3] Dethan, *Gaston d'Orléans*, pp. 265–6. A.A.E. France 827, fo. 307. Confession of Anne of Austria, 17 Aug. 1637.

[4] Ormesson, *Journal*, ed. Chéruel, i. 32. Talon, *Mémoires*, ed. Michaud and Poujoulat, pp. 86, 299. During the last months of Richelieu's life, Bouthiller displayed anxiety about his

ment which the king hoped would last until 1652, when his elder son would reach the age of 14.[3] It committed the Regency to continue his foreign policy and maintain existing diplomatic alliances. Anne of Austria was to become Regent, and Gaston lieutenant-general of the kingdom, but the powers of both were to be curtailed by a Regency council—comprising, in addition to these two, Condé, Mazarin, Séguier, Bouthillier and Chavigny[2] —which would determine all important issues of foreign and domestic policy, including financial questions and the conduct of the war, by majority decision. Louis envisaged no changes to the composition of the Regency council except through forfeiture (that is to say, if a member committed treason) or death in office, in which case the vacancy would be filled by co-option, again by majority decision. The appointment of a successor to Bouthillier as *surintendant des finances* was mentioned specifically as an appointment to be made by the whole council, and the Queen's powers of patronage were curtailed;[3] doubtless Louis XIII was trying to prevent a repetition of the sort of patronage exercised by Concini and Léonora Galigaï through their hold over his mother between 1610 and 1617.

The declarations of 16 and 20 April 1643 thus have to be viewed together as a serious attempt by the king to assure continuity in foreign and domestic policy after his death. He wanted the war to be brought to fruition, as Richelieu had planned, and the resources to be found for the final struggle against the Habsburgs. Whether or not Louis's actions—which were unprecedented in recent times—conformed to the fundamental laws of the French monarchy as they were understood by contemporaries, is open to question. It is probably true that a dying king could not bind the hands of his successor; equally, however, no new laws could be promulgated during a royal minority, and thus there was some point in Louis XIII's stating what he considered to be current policy at the end of his lifetime. What mattered, of course, was not the theory but the practice, and the most serious objection to

---

own position. Cf. A.A.E. France 843, fo. 272, 24 Aug. 1642: 'les spéculatifz y disposent touiours de toutes choses mesmes des gouvernementz et grandes charges vacantes ou qu'ilz voient proches à vacquer . . .'

[1] Actually 7 Sept. 1651, shortly after Louis XIV had attained his thirteenth birthday.
[2] Le Tellier was not mentioned, probably because he had only recently been appointed and was as yet an untried force.
[3] Moote, *The revolt of the judges*, pp. 64–5. *Chambre des Comptes*, ed. Boislisle, p. 412. A.A.E. France 846, fos. 153–62, [20] Apr. 1643.

Louis XIII's death-bed measures is that instead of possible misunderstanding and conflict under the Regency being resolved,
they were made more probable. Anne of Austria was humiliated
by the twin allegations of incompetence and support for Spain,
and probably had the declaration disavowed before *notaires*.[1] Yet
it was clear that if the terms of Louis XIII's last will and testament were to be renounced publicly, Anne of Austria would need
assistance from the *Parlement* of Paris, and such assistance would
expect the reward of political concessions. The tensions of the
Regency government arose largely from misunderstandings
caused by the events of the first few days after Louis XIII's death
on 14 May 1643.

[1] Omer Talon thought so: Talon, *Mémoires*, ed. Michaud and Poujoulat, p. 86.

Chapter V

Bankruptcy and the Fronde, 1643–1653

The Regency of Anne of Austria was proclaimed officially in the *Parlement* of Paris on 18 May 1643, and at the same time the limitations on the Regent's powers imposed by the last will and testament of Louis XIII were removed. Anne of Austria was thus made president of the council and given those powers of appointment and patronage which her husband had sought to deny her. Almost inevitably, this accretion of power to the Regent made Cardinal Mazarin, her favourite, chief minister and the delicate checks and balances within the proposed regency council were removed at a stroke. The future of the Bouthilliers, father and son, was in doubt from the outset of the Regency. Anne of Austria wanted to appoint her own finance minister, precisely because this power had been denied her under Louis XIII's last will and testament. Bouthillier left office for good in June 1643. Chavigny, Bouthillier's son, was Mazarin's defeated rival for the position of chief minister and could not long survive as secretary of state for foreign affairs after the dismissal of his father. Chavigny was obliged to resign as foreign minister, although he remained in the council 'sans aucun crédit'.[1] Nicolas le Bailleul, baron de Château-Gontier and Claude Mesmes, comte d'Avaux, were appointed as joint *surintendants des finances*. Both were former *maîtres des requêtes* who had served as ambassadors. D'Avaux's role was not particularly significant, since he was made one of the three French plenipotentiaries at the Westphalian peace negotiations and departed thither in the autumn.[2] Except in the years 1649–50, his part in the conduct of financial affairs was minimal.

Bailleul's appointment was much more significant. He was a loyal servant of the Regent, having been *Chancelier de la Reine* since 1630, an office which he attempted to sell in 1644 for 300,000

---

[1] *Mémoires . . . de Montglat*, ed. Michaud and Poujoulat, p. 139. Appointment of Henri-Auguste Loménie de Brienne as secretary of state for foreign affairs, Chavigny's former office: A.A.E. France 846, fo. 210, 23 June 1643. Appendix One, Table I.

[2] Ormesson noted his departure on 11 Oct.: Ormesson, *Journal*, ed. Chéruel, i. 112. Cf. Tallemant des Réaux, *Historiettes*, ed. L. J. N. Monmerqué and P. Paulin (3rd. ed., 1862), iii. 476. In Apr. 1643, before the declaration of the Regency, it had been thought that d'Hémery would accompany d'Avaux: *Chambre des Comptes*, ed. Boislisle, p. 412.

livres.[1] Anne of Austria must have valued his advice, since after his resignation as finance minister in 1647 he remained in the council as minister of state.[2] Bailleul was a *président* in the *Parlement* of Paris and his promotion was partly a reward to that court for its co-operation in May 1643. A more appropriate office, however, would have been that of Keeper of the Seals, a post which was mentioned in his connection in November 1643.[3] Bailleul lacked the strength of character, knowledge, and ability necessary to administer the king's finances. The weakness of central direction in the finance ministry under Bailleul required a counterweight and this was provided by Michel Particelle, sieur d'Hémery (Particelli d'Emeri). Already one of the intendants of finance and joint controller-general, d'Hémery was commissioned as sole *contrôleur-général* on 8 November 1643.[4] By the end of the year most commentators were agreed that d'Hémery was 'le tout puissant' in financial affairs and indeed the second minister in the government after Mazarin.[5] By June 1644 he had a *brevet* to sit in the council of state when financial affairs were discussed.[6] It has been claimed that d'Hémery's career was held in check because Mazarin was afraid of him.[7] This is most unlikely: in fact, d'Hémery was especially trusted by the Cardinal, and a client of his since 1635,[8] and he was promoted above colleagues such as Jacques Tubeuf. However, if the presence of a Mazarini as chief minister was already unpopular, it was unwise to increase hostility by promoting a Particelli from the Italian *émigré* family at Lyon.[9]

[1] Ormesson, *Journal*, ed. Chéruel, i. 192.

[2] A.G. A1 101, no. 344, 18 July 1647.

[3] Although this would have made way for the appointment of d'Hémery as *surintendant* at an earlier date: A.A.E. France 847, fo. 90, 7 Nov. 1643. No Keeper of the Seals was appointed under the Regency until the appointment of Châteauneuf in 1650.

[4] B.N. MS. fr. 18510, fo. 61. Cf. A.A.E. France 847, fo. 90, 7 Nov. 1643. Appendix One, Table II.

[5] Ormesson, *Journal*, ed. Chéruel, i. 130. A.A.E. France 849, fo. 4ᵛ., 2 Jan. 1644: 'Ledit sr. d'Hémery est le tout puissant après M. le Card[inal] Mazarin.'

[6] Cf. A.A.E. France 849, fo. 306ʳ., 25 June 1644.

[7] Dent, *Crisis in finance*, p. 96. However, Véron de Forbonnais's judgement (*Recherches*, i. 252) was quite different. He thought d'Hémery 'l'homme du Cardinal Mazarin qui l'éleva à la surintendance des finances pour mieux en disposer . . .' Mazarin's relationship with d'Hémery is of crucial importance because of the later allegations of peculation levelled against the chief minister during the Fronde.

[8] Dethan, *The young Mazarin*, p. 162. This was in marked contrast to Mazarin's relationship with Bouthillier and Chavigny, who appeared to be dependent politically on Gaston d'Orléans (Chavigny was Gaston's Chancellor): ibid., p. 156. Ranum, *Richelieu and the councillors of Louis XIII*, pp. 86–7.

[9] At least d'Hémery was a second generation Frenchman, since his father had become a naturalized Frenchman in 1595: Bourgeon, *Les Colbert avant Colbert*, pp. 83–4. Mazarin became a naturalized Frenchman only in Apr. 1639: Dethan, op. cit., pp. 113–14.

Even if he was less corrupt than contemporaries thought, d'Hémery was a political liability because he was too much the specialist financier[1] and too reliant on the views, and perhaps business interests, of the intendants of finance. His elevation to the position of *surintendant* on Bailleul's resignation (17 July 1647)[2] thus compounded earlier errors by the Regent and chief minister. It did not alter the political reality: d'Hémery was the effective finance minister from 1643 to 1648. His methods prevailed, just as had Bullion's in the 1630s.

D'Hémery's financial policies were determined very largely by the foreign situation. Although the testament of Louis XIII had been annulled as far as the Regent's powers were concerned, in other matters it was regarded as binding. Thus Anne of Austria and Mazarin were obliged to continue the foreign policy and diplomatic alliances of Louis XIII; the instructions to the French plenipotentiaries at Münster, which were drawn up on 30 September 1643, are generally considered to have been a continuation of Richelieu's foreign policy, perhaps based on a memorandum drawn up by the Cardinal before his death.[3] However, the Regency government had to show caution in its negotiations with the Habsburgs: Anne of Austria was the sister of Philip IV and Mazarin was a foreigner by birth. For these reasons, it would have been political suicide to sign a peace with Spain that could later be criticized as detrimental to French interests.[4] In the heady days after the great victory at Rocroi in 1643 a total defeat of the Habsburgs must have seemed possible—but the deterioration of the French position after 1646 was a more normal state of affairs, the war being essentially a struggle for resources with neither side able to drive home a short-term advantage on the battlefield. After a long war, it was to be expected that the peace negotiations would be protracted and that military pressure would need to be sustained while the conference was in session at Münster. It was therefore unwise to make optimistic statements about the outcome of the negotiations. In April 1644 Mazarin was reported as

---

[1] As *contrôleur-général de l'argenterie*, he had been fined by the *chambre de justice* of 1624–5: Richelieu, *Mémoires*, iv. 286. *Les papiers de Richelieu*, ed. Grillon, i. 140.

[2] Appendix One, Table I.

[3] H. Weber, 'Richelieu et le Rhin', *Revue Historique*, ccxxxix (1968), 268. *Acta pacis Westphalicae*, ed. Dickmann et al., i. 58–138. Mazarin later referred to the 'instruction qui fut dressé du temps du feu Roy par M. le Cardinal de Richelieu (qu'on conserve en original) si on avoit seulement la prétention de retenir un pied de terre en Allemagne': A.A.E. France 874, fo. 186ʳ., n.d. [1651].

[4] A.A.E. France 874, fo. 186ʳ., n.d. [1651].

saying that peace would be signed within three months.[1] These early hopes of peace were dashed, however, and in August 1647 Mazarin argued the need for further war taxes to force Spain to make peace.[2] The foreign policy of Anne of Austria and Mazarin carried risks in the domestic political situation. It was regarded as unusual, even by the ministers themselves,[3] for a Regency government to fight a foreign war. Catherine de Médicis had inherited a country at peace after Cateau-Cambrésis. Marie de Médicis had rapidly withdrawn from the Cleves-Jülich conflict. Contemporaries would thus have found Anne of Austria's tenacity in adhering to the last will and testament of Louis XIII difficult to understand. Quite apart from the unpopularity of the standpoint, it was always questionable whether the government could sustain the war effort in fiscal terms. Already on 29 February 1644, d'Hémery was protesting at the level of royal expenditure and declared that he could not see how expenses for the following year could be met.[4] Certainly the levels of royal expenditure in the early years of the Regency were even higher than in the lifetime of Louis XIII, a fact which after 1648 brought about much criticism of the government.[5]

What was needed above all was a *surintendant* who could reassure the financiers and obtain sufficient funds to keep the war effort going. D'Hémery was successful in his dealings with the financiers up to the end of 1647. The accession of a new king who was not of age to rule might well have led the financiers to panic at the prospect of a royal bankruptcy. On 3 July 1643, however, the financiers were reassured about the security of their investment, and in particular the high interest rates paid on loan and tax contracts.[6] A small amount was levied in fines in both 1643 and

[1] A.A.E. France 849, fo. 169ᵛ., 17 Apr. 1644.

[2] Talon, *Mémoires*, ed. Michaud and Poujoulat, p. 204. R. J. Bonney, 'The French civil war, 1649–53', *European Studies Review*, viii (1978), 79.

[3] Bailleul, Tubeuf and d'Hémery told the *procureur-général* of the *Chambre des Comptes* on 8 Apr. 1644 that it was no use citing precedents from the minority of Louis XIII: 'pendant ceste minorité, il n'y avoit eu guerre . . . et qu'alors la Bastille estoit remplie de finances.' *Chambre des Comptes*, ed. Boislisle, p. 415.

[4] Ormesson, *Journal*, ed. Chéruel, i. 156.

[5] Appendix Two, Table I. The *Requête des Trois États* . . ., a *Mazarinade* from 1648, was particularly critical of the anticipation of revenues, the high level of expenditure through the *comptants*, and the fact that although expenditure had reached 100 or 120 million Mazarin 'n'a payé ny les gens de guerre, ny les pensions . . . ni pourveu les places frontières d'hommes ny de munitions, ny satisfait aux estats de la marine et de l'artillerie . . .': *Choix de Mazarinades*, ed. Moreau, i. 30–1.

[6] The great financier Thomas Bonneau cited the contradictory dates of 3 July and 10 Aug. 1643: cf. E 259a, fo. 336, 13 Aug. 1653. E 263b, fo. 621, 25 Feb. 1654. He appears to have been referring to the amnesty to the financiers from prosecution by a *chambre de justice*.

1645; in return the financiers were amnestied from any investigation by a *chambre de justice*.[1] They responded as d'Hémery had hoped to the climate of confidence. Mallet's figures indicate the continuing importance of the *deniers extraordinaires*, which represented about 46 per cent of total income during the 1640s.[2] Part of this may have been simply paper transactions. There is no doubt at all, however, that while d'Hémery was unable to obtain as much revenue as Bullion from the *affaires extraordinaires*, he succeeded in raising on average 22 million *livres* a year from this source.[3] Rather than rely on *traités*, however, d'Hémery's policy was to increase the royal borrowing requirement.

Bullion and Bouthillier had borrowed as an expedient to cover the budgetary deficit. In contrast, and almost as a precursor of John Law, d'Hémery elevated the search for credit to the level of a financial principle.[4] More money was borrowed in the early years of the Regency than at any time in the previous history of the French monarchy.[5] There were impelling practical reasons, foreign and domestic, for this unprecedented recourse to borrowing. To convince the Spanish negotiators at Münster of French intentions to continue the war if necessary, an enormous military effort had to be sustained on several fronts. To mount this military effort there had to be an assurance of a continuous flow of funds which only credit could ensure.[6] D'Hémery was not the first to anticipate revenues such as the *taille*, but he was the first to do so as far in advance. In 1645 he had borrowed on the revenues of the

---

[1] P 2369, pp. 601–14, July 1643. The taxes were levied initially by Jean Doublet under the *prête-nom* of Denis Esmé: E 186a, fo. 546, 20 Jan. 1644. However, Le Vieux and La Rallière replaced Doublet and entered a new contract under the name of Jean Conçelin with a *forfait* of 2,360,000 *livres* and a remise of 629,333 *livres*. Conçelin complained of difficulty in levying the fines because of fraudulent transfers of property by the financiers: E 191b, fo. 428, 30 June 1644. P 2370, pp. 975–80, Aug. 1645. Véron de Forbonnais, *Recherches*, i. 250, criticized d'Hémery for taxing the financiers at a time when the crown sought further loans. However, the fines were so derisory that the effect, as in 1635, was to reassure the financiers that they were safe from a thorough-going *chambre de justice*.

[2] Appendix Two, Tables IV and V.

[3] Appendix Two, Table VII A. (Average of net amount payable.)

[4] It was said that d'Hémery had an 'aversion contre les affaires à cause de l'incommodité qu'il disoit qu'elles apportoyent au peuple, au lieu desquelles il a estably les prestz . . .': A.A.E. France 853, fo. 164. Cf. also his speech quoted in L. C. de Beaupoil de Sainte-Aulaire, *Histoire de la Fronde* (3 vols., 1827), i. 162–4.

[5] Appendix Two, Table VIII A.

[6] Talon, *Mémoires*, ed. Michaud and Poujoulat, p. 245. B.L. Harleian 4466, fo. 112, [5] July 1648: '. . . pour toutes ces dépenses, il n'y a point de deniers comptans à l'épargne, mais bien des promesses et des billets des hommes d'affaires, qui doivent payer de mois en mois les sommes qu'ils ont promises, sur l'asseurance desquelles promesses les desseins de la guerre ont été entrepris'.

French monarchy up to the end of 1647. By 1648, he had borrowed on those of 1650 and 1651.[1]

For a time, this reliance on borrowing and massive anticipation of revenues obscured the fact that there had been no underlying improvement in the revenue-raising system. The monetary expansion under Bullion and Bouthillier had been so extensive that a period of stability and recuperation was required. Between 1645 and 1648 the issues of coin were relatively small.[2] There was no prospect of extracting more revenue from the office-holders that Bullion had obtained, and indeed the income from the *parties casuelles* declined significantly from over half the ordinary revenue of the French monarchy in the 1630s to less than a quarter in the following decade.[3] The proportion of ordinary royal income derived from the revenue farms and the direct taxes seems to have increased in the 1640s: respectively they provided 26 per cent and 46 per cent of ordinary revenues. Indeed, d'Hémery called the *taille* 'nostre seule ressource asseurée'.[4] However, the payments to the Treasury did not increase because of any great rise in the direct and indirect taxes paid in the provinces, but because d'Hémery systematically revoked salary payments and other types of royal expenses which had formerly been assigned locally on the proceeds of these revenues. (These *retranchements des gages* and *rentes* were desperately unpopular not least because the apparent savings to the government were almost cancelled out by loan contracts with the financiers which carried high rates of interest.)[5] In fact the Regency government was under considerable political pressure to reduce the direct taxes, and did so by sixteen million between 1643 and 1647. The total levy of direct taxes (*taille, taillon, subsistances* and *étapes*) on 23 *généralités* on the eve of the Fronde stood at 56.5 million.[6]

[1] Talon commented (ibid., p. 300) that d'Hémery 'mangeoit par avance en l'année 1648 les années 1650 et 1651'. However, these anticipations were revoked by the crown on 18 July 1648.

[2] Spooner, *The international economy and monetary movements in France*, pp. 338–9.

[3] Appendix Two, Tables IV and V.

[4] A.A.E. France 858, fo. 185ᵛ., 30 June 1647.

[5] Examples of loan contracts anticipating the *retranchements* in certain *généralités*: E 217b, fo. 513, 28 Nov. 1646. E 218a, fo. 249, 5 Dec. 1646. E 219b, fo. 433, 30 Jan. 1647. These interest payments to financiers on revenues which in normal years would have formed part of the income of office-holders were well known (Talon, *Mémoires*, ed. Michaud and Poujoulat, pp. 271, 300) and help explain their hostility to the financiers during the Fronde.

[6] As against 72.6 million in 1643: B.N. MS. fr. 18510, fo. 7. The *Parlement* of Paris had registered a remission of 10 million on the *taille* and certain other taxes on 3 Sept. 1643: X1a 8388.

The need to reduce the direct taxes, and the continuing difficulty of the revenue farmers who sought remissions on their rents or to abandon their leases,[1] led d'Hémery ineluctably towards new fiscal expedients. It is this aspect of his administration which has been criticized most severely both by contemporaries and historians. Several of d'Hémery's expedients were highly controversial, yet produced relatively little revenue compared to the political damage to the Regency government.[2] In this context, it is important to recall that d'Hémery's hands were tied to a considerable extent by the policy of his predecessors. For example, it was impossible to establish a significant number of new *rentes* because Bullion had flooded the market in 1634. Part of the relatively small creation of *rentes* under d'Hémery had to be distributed forcibly in the form of a new *taxe des aisés* which broke a formal pledge by the government in 1640.[3] However, the fundamental difficulty faced by the Regency government was political. During the 1630s, the sovereign tribunals had frequently delayed registration of the fiscal edicts which formed the juridical authority for new tax contracts. Registration helped allay public disquiet and eased the tax contractor's task in levying the new taxes. In the last resort, Louis XIII had enforced registration, either by sending princes of the blood to preside over the sovereign tribunal or else by going in person and presiding over an extraordinary session (*lit de justice*). From 1644, when Gaston was sent to the *Chambre des Comptes* and Condé to the *Cour des Aides* to enforce new fiscal edicts, it became clear that the office-holders were determined to resist the presence of princes of the blood.[4] Two royal *lits de justice* held in the *Parlement* of Paris on 7 September 1645 and 15 January 1648 resulted in the enforced registration of some 26 fiscal edicts, an unprecedented number for a royal minority.

[1] In Oct. 1647, the consortium of farmers of the *gabelles de France* under the name of Jacques Dattin wanted to abandon their lease. However, the government induced them to make a loan of 4,588,000 *livres* in 15 payments from 1 Oct. 1648, anticipating the rents of the farm for 1650, and to accept a further lease from 1650. These arrangements were affected by the revocation of loan contracts in 1648. But cf. E 249a, fo. 322, 19 Oct. 1651. E 249b, fo. 405, 29 Nov. 1651. Evidence of remissions in Bonney, 'The failure of the French revenue farms', 19 n. 3.

[2] Moote, *The revolt of the judges*, pp. 98–106. One of the controversial measures was the Parisian *toisé*. Yet the *traité* for the *toisé* entered upon by François Tardif under the name of Silvan Baillon was for a *forfait* of 1,080,000 *livres* and a *remise* of 360,000 *livres*: E 186b, fo. 181, 27 Jan. 1644. This was a drop in the ocean.

[3] The pledge was made in the edict establishing the sales tax: AD IX 8, Nov. 1640. For the small amount of *rentes* established by d'Hémery: G. Martin and M. Bezançon, *L'histoire du crédit en France sous le règne de Louis XIV* (1914), p. 27.

[4] *Chambre des Comptes*, ed. Boislisle, p. 415.

Nevertheless, d'Hémery's regime was fatally weakened by this open reliance on force. He gained the reputation of an 'ami . . . de la violence et ennemi . . . du Parlement'. In his famous speech on the occasion of the second royal *lit de justice*, Omer Talon denounced the frequency of 'levées extraordinaires de deniers' and declared roundly that Frenchmen were not slaves but freemen who wanted peace and prosperity.[1] The honeymoon between the Regency government and the office-holders was over.

By 1647, Mazarin was convinced that the obstructionism of the sovereign tribunals, and especially the *Parlement* of Paris, towards royal fiscal policies was one of the chief reasons why the Spanish refused to make concessions in the Westphalian negotiations.[2] It is difficult to be sure of the motives of the members of the sovereign tribunals, which were complex and varied from one court to another. There is no doubt at all that the Regency government had raised expectations that it had not been able to fulfil. It is very doubtful whether a majority of Frenchmen understood or supported Mazarin's policy of continuing the war as long as necessary to secure a satisfactory peace settlement. What they wanted was an immediate peace settlement and the reduction of taxation.[3] Doubtless many office-holders objected to the enforced registration of fiscal edicts by means of the *lit de justice* when the king was not of age to rule personally and declare his true intention. In any case, such action was unprecedented: 'pendant la minorité du feu roy (Louis XIII) cela n'avoit esté pratiqué'.[4] As early as 1644–5 voices were raised in the *Parlement* of Paris at the alleged excessive profits made by the financiers and their vast fortunes. There was also an attempt to make the financiers of the past twenty years carry the entire cost of a *taxe des aisés*. Tempers ran high, and Samuel Gaudon de la Rallière, the farmer of the *entrées* of Paris, declared that the *Parlement* of Paris was on the way to becoming a French version of the Long Parliament.[5] Attitudes

---

[1] For Talon's comment on d'Hémery's reputation: Talon, *Mémoires*, ed. Michaud and Poujoulat, p. 126. For his speech: ibid., pp. 209–12. Moote, op. cit., p. 108 n. 36, cites Mailfait's opinion that the speech Talon delivered was more critical of the government than the version in the memoirs. This would explain Laubardemont's comment that 'cet insolent discours fut suivy de l'union des compagnies': A.A.E. France 882, fos. 348ᵛ.–349ᶠ., 21 May 1652.

[2] Talon, op. cit., pp. 126, 204.

[3] Talon commented that 'la plupart des levées ayant pour prétexte la nécessité de la guerre, chacun espéroit que la paix lui donneroit du soulagement': Talon, *Mémoires*, ed. Michaud and Poujoulat, p. 299.

[4] *Chambre des Comptes*, ed. Boislisle, p. 415.

[5] E. H. Kossmann, *La Fronde* (Leiden, 1954), p. 34. Moote, *The revolt of the judges*, p. 107. Ormesson, *Journal*, ed. Chéruel, i. 214,238, 312. A.A.E. France 850, fo. 55, 10 Sept. 1644.

hardened on both sides after 1645, when d'Hémery was forced to cut payments of *rentes* and *gages* by half. The cuts were to be on a permanent basis and were to be even more severe in subsequent years.[1]

The massive anticipation of revenues in 1645 meant that without agreement to new taxes the crown was effectively bankrupt by the end of 1647. The question was whether the bankruptcy would be declared by the government, and manipulated in its interests, or caused by a collapse of confidence among the financiers. At the end of August 1647 there was serious discussion about declaring a royal bankruptcy, but this was ruled out. The ministers felt that the disadvantages of a collapse of confidence that would follow from this action would outweigh any possible budgetary gain.[2] Philip IV's bankruptcy earlier that year had given the French an important psychological advantage in the war of attrition. In addition, d'Hémery had high hopes that two new fiscal measures would bring in a significant amount of additional revenue. On 21 December 1647, municipal revenues (*deniers communs et d'octroi*) were diverted into the crown's empty coffers. This completely undermined municipal finances, and although the towns were authorized to double their *octrois* to make good the loss, many of them were reluctant to increase taxes so drastically and preferred to raise loans.[3] The second fiscal measure was a new forced loan to be paid by the office-holders in return for the renewal of the *droit annuel*, which expired on 31 December. At the very moment the government was seeking to enforce the registration of new fiscal edicts at the *Parlement* of Paris, the office-holders felt their position threatened because the notorious 40-day clause came into operation and disturbed the orderly process of resignation of office.[4] D'Hémery delayed the announcement of the size of the forced

---

A.A.E. France 848, fo. 290. 'Touchant les assemblées du Parlement', n.d., *c.* Apr. 1645. The financiers were extremely worried at the idea of a *taxe des aisés* and purchased exemption from the government by promising to lend 8 million and purchase 300,000 *livres* in *rentes: Arrêts du conseil du roi*, ed. Le Pesant, no. 328.

[1] Ibid., nos. 352, 373. E 203a, fo. 501, 14 June 1645. E 214b, fo. 440, 18 Aug. 1646.

[2] Talon, *Mémoires*, ed. Michaud and Poujoulat, p. 206.

[3] N. Temple, 'The control and exploitation of French towns during the *ancien régime*', *History* clxxi (1966), p. 18. AD + 295, no. 27.

[4] Office-holders had to take out special provisions from the government to guarantee their right of resignation: *Arrêts du conseil du roi*, ed. Le Pesant, nos. 783, 784, 813, 816, 820, 821, 826, 827. Not surprisingly, the three *trésoriers de l'Épargne* were among the first office-holders to come to terms with the government: E 227c, fo. 105, 4 Dec. 1647 (Le Pesant no. 767).

loan until 29 April 1648, well after the conflict over the forced registration of the fiscal edicts had subsided.

By the time the government announced the terms on which the *droit annuel* would be confirmed, the political atmosphere had deteriorated. The difficulties between the crown and its office-holders had already had an adverse effect on the negotiations for the anticipation of the revenues of 1650.[1] The office-holders saw little reason to co-operate with a government which appeared to be acting against their interests, and this attitude had hardened with the news that the Dutch Republic, which had been allied with France since 1624, had made a separate peace with Spain at a time when the prospect of peace between France and the Habsburgs appeared to have receded. Why should the office-holders contribute towards a foreign policy which appeared to have failed? On 29 April 1648, d'Hémery precipitated the crisis by suspending the *gages* of all the tribunals in France with the exception of the *Parlement* of Paris as a *quid pro quo* for the renewal of the *droit annuel*.[2] At a stroke, he united the opposition. The *Parlement* of Paris expected, and had in the past received, most favoured status, but this measure was too crude. Moreover, many of the *parlementaires* had relatives in the other Parisian tribunals who applied pressure on them to stand firm.[3] The result was the *arrêt d'union* of 13 May 1648, by which the Parisian sovereign tribunals declared their intention of meeting in the *Chambre Saint-Louis* to discuss their grievances. Once he had realized his mistake, d'Hémery advocated retreat, for a number of reasons including fear of an investigation of his financial administration.[4] At this point, however, he was overruled by other members of the government who pointed to the unprecedented nature of the *arrêt d'union* and the implications that independent political assemblies such as the proposed meeting at the *Chambre Saint-Louis* would have for the future of absolute monarchy in France. The original proponents of the hard line arguments are not known, but Chancellor Séguier became their chief spokesman during the ensuing

---

[1] Z1a 162, fo. 245, 7 Jan. 1648.

[2] Talon blamed d'Hémery: *Mémoires*, ed. Michaud and Poujoulat, p. 271. So too did a number of contemporary, or near contemporary, memoranda: A.A.E. France 853, fo. 176, n.d., *c.* 1650. A.A.E. France 881, fos. 221, 431, 5 Feb. and 6 Mar. 1652.

[3] The *arrêt d'union* was 'imputé . . . aux alliances et parentèles de la pluspart des officiers': B.L. Harleian 4466, fo. 81ᵛ., 8 June 1648.

[4] Talon, *Mémoires*, ed. Michaud and Poujoulat, pp. 222–3.

six weeks of negotiations.[1] The political temperature was further raised by two intemperate decrees issued by the council of state on 10 and 15 June.[2]

The impasse over the *arrêt d'union* in May and June 1648 led to the collapse of confidence that had been so feared by the ministers the previous year. The financiers refused to make further loans to the government until the struggle between the crown and its office-holders was resolved: 'il y a six sepmaines que le commerce de l'argent a cessé'.[3] What the financiers feared most of all was that the proposed meeting at the *Chambre Saint-Louis* would not limit itself to the grievances of the office-holders, but would discuss royal financial policy in general. This in turn would broaden into 'une occasion de plaincte et douleur générale pour descrier le gouvernement de l'estat'.[4] These fears were well founded. In the end the government had to allow the meeting at the *Chambre Saint-Louis* to take place. When it met in the days after 30 June 1648, the *Chambre Saint-Louis* proposed, among other measures, a reduction in the secret expenses, the revocation of all *traités* and loan contracts, a reduction in direct taxes by 25 per cent (equivalent to the interest rate charged by financiers on loans anticipating the revenues of the *taille*),[5] and the holding of a *chambre de justice*. The sovereign tribunals were to regain all their former powers, following the abolition of the intendants. The power of the crown to issue commissions was also to be curtailed. There were to be no new judicial offices at all, whether in the sovereign or lesser tribunals. New financial offices would be allowed, but only after edicts had been registered in the courts 'avec liberté entière des suffrages'. New taxes were to be raised only in accordance with the proper procedure, that is to say after the registration of edicts in the courts, again after a free vote. The salaries of the office-holders and the payment of *rentes* were to be re-established progressively. The *droit annuel* was to be renewed on advantageous

[1] On the constitutional implications: B.L. Harleian 4466, fos. 79ᵛ., 87ᵛ.–88ᵛ., 28 May and 8 June 1648. On the precedents: U 28, fo. 174, 13 June 1648. Talon also reported these negotiations.

[2] Kossmann, *La Fronde*, pp. 47–8. *Arrêts du conseil du roi*, ed. Le Pesant, nos. 888 and 890.

[3] B.L. Harleian 4466, fos. 106ᵛ.,–107ʳ, 30 June 1648. Cf. Z1a 163, fo. 59ᵛ., 9 July 1648: '. . . les gens d'affaires avoient pris l'alarme, [tiennent] leurs bourses fermées et ne trouvoient plus d'argent'.

[4] B.L. Harleian 4466, fo. 84ᵛ., 8 June 1648.

[5] Mazarin argued correctly that interest rates on loans anticipating the revenues of the *taille* varied according to area, but incorrectly that the rate was higher in the *généralité* of Paris than elsewhere: Z1a 163, fo. 75ᵛ., 11 July 1648. In fact, the interest rate in the *généralité* of Paris was 16.6 per cent; elsehwere it was 25 per cent: B.N. MS. fr. 18510, fo. 236. 'Mémoire pour les prests faicts au Roy par les receveurs', 1648.

terms. It would be very difficult for the government to exploit the system of office-holding for fiscal purposes, or for that matter to finance the war effort at all, if these proposals were fully implemented.

Mazarin recognized that the crisis had broken. Anticipating the demand for d'Hémery's dismissal, he sacked his finance minister on 9 July. The former *surintendant* retired to his estate at Châteauneuf in the knowledge that he was safe from prosecution because the government 'craignait qu'il ne parlast'.[1] Some commentators, such as the maréchal d'Estrées, believed that if d'Hémery had remained in office the royal declaration of bankruptcy could have been staved off for three or four years;[2] but they were thinking in terms of normal conditions of political stability. The mistake had been to allow the meeting of the *Chambre Saint-Louis* to take place. Once the office-holders had voiced their opinion, Mazarin had to concede the essence of the argument. A royal declaration summoning a *chambre de justice* was drawn up on 12 July in an attempt to forestall criticism of the financiers.[3] Six days later, the crown revoked the loan contracts.[4] By acting in this way, Mazarin hoped to anticipate the revenues of 1649–51 once more, but at lower rates of interest.[5] Some financiers, such as Thomas Bonneau and Denis Marin, were willing to renegotiate their loan contracts for fear of worse alternatives.[6] However, it seems doubtful whether the majority were willing or able to do so. The revocation of the loan contracts confirmed publicly the existing state of affairs, namely that the money market had collapsed. The financiers were unable to borrow on the private market in order to re-lend to the crown, and the king's council had to block legal actions against the financiers by their creditors.[7] 1648 was

---

[1] *Journal des guerres civiles de Dubuisson-Aubenay, 1648–1652*, ed. G. Saige (2 vols., 1883, 1885), i. 34.

[2] Quoted by Meuvret, *Études d'histoire économique*, pp. 15–16. According to Dubuisson-Aubenay (i. 35) the maréchal d'Estrées made a loan to the government of 90,000 *livres* 'contre le vouloir de sa femme'.

[3] Talon, *Mémoires*, ed. Michaud and Poujoulat, pp. 249, 252–3. K 117b, nos. 38, 39, 12 and 18 July 1648.

[4] *Arrêts du conseil du roi*, ed. Le Pesant, no. 905.

[5] *Letters du Cardinal Mazarin pendant son ministère*, ed. P. A. Chéruel and G. d'Avenel (9 vols., 1872–1906), iii. 160.

[6] E 231b, fos. 461, 465, 467, 23 July 1648.

[7] For example, the *surséance* of actions by private creditors against the financiers Simon, Pierre, Jean and Étienne Romanet: E 231b, fo. 487, 23 July 1648. There are many decrees in the council of finance records according similar suspensions of actions during and after the Fronde.

thus a *banqueroute universelle*, a large-scale version of the Sabathier bankruptcy seven years earlier, this time affecting dozens of financiers. It is difficult to see how the crown could benefit from this situation, although it is probably true that the nobles and office-holders who were the private creditors of the financiers indirectly paid a heavy tax to the government through the bankruptcy.[1]

The real problem, however, was that bankruptcy paralyzed the government without permanently removing the burden of debt. Mazarin's hope of restoring the financial position of the monarchy was unrealistic in the context of political instability. The deficit on the current account was worsened by the concessions made to the office-holders in the summer and finally implemented in the declaration of 22 October 1648. These concessions reduced the revenues of the crown by about 30 million *livres* (15 million from the cuts in the payment of salaries of office-holders, which were to be restored; 10 million from the reduction in the *taille*; there were remissions of 2 million in the levies of extraordinary taxes on Paris, and three million for other towns).[2] Yet certain expenses had actually increased. If the crown was serious about its intention to restore credit, then a fund had to be established from which to pay current interests to the financiers on outstanding royal debts from the bankruptcy of July. In the autumn of 1648, a fund of 10 million was set up for those financiers who presented their loan contracts to the government for 'settlement' (*liquidation*).[3] According to La Meilleraye's statement at the end of September 1648, the deficit on the current account stood at 24 million.[4] In addition, there were paper debts resulting from the revocation of the loan contracts which were variously estimated at 80, 100, and 120 million. It is impossible to calculate the precise amount, because the treasury bills were reassigned to meet current expenditure.[5] Indeed, one of the most important consequences of the

---

[1] Véron de Forbonnais, *Recherches*, i. 256. Cf. the judgement of Jeannin de Castille that 'bien loing d'apporter de l'argent dans l'Espargne . . . cette révocation tarissoit toutes les sources d'où l'on en pouvoit espérer': B.N. Morel de Thoisy 156, fo. 516ᵛ. *Défenses* of Jeannin de Castille, *c.* 1662.

[2] *Journal des guerres civiles de Dubuisson-Aubenay*, ed. Saige, i. 80.

[3] The fund was mentioned in Talon, *Mémoires*, ed. Michaud and Poujoulat, p. 281. According to Foucquet, this was the first occasion when the term *liquidation* had been used to describe a general procedure of this type in France: *Archives de la Bastille. Documents inédits. Règne de Louis XIV*, ed. F. Ravaisson-Mollien (1886, repr. Geneva, 1975), ii. 281.

[4] Appendix Two, Table IX B. Guéry ('Les finances de la monarchie française', 236) calculates the deficit at 53 million, which rests on no firm contemporary evidence.

[5] B.N. Morel de Thoisy 156, fo. 517 . *Défenses* of Jeannin de Castille, *c.* 1662.

bankruptcy of 1648 was that it made precise accounting of the royal finances virtually impossible during the Fronde.

D'Hémery's replacement as *surintendant* on 9 July 1648[1] was Charles de la Porte, Maréchal de la Meilleraye, Richelieu's cousin and the lieutenant-general in Brittany. Criticized by some as a political extremist and enemy of the office-holders, and by others said to be a better soldier than finance minister,[2] La Meilleraye's appointment was a return to the days of Sully and Schomberg when magnates had held the office with that of *grand maître de l'artillerie*.[3] The war against Spain, after all, was continuing. Mazarin and the Regent appear to have had some doubts about La Meilleraye's abilities, however, for two former *maîtres des requêtes* and intendants—Antoine Barillon de Morangis and Étienne d'Aligre—were appointed as his assistants with the title of *directeurs des finances*. The appointment of assistants in this open way was unprecedented in recent times, yet while they were persons of known integrity, Barillon and Aligre were not financial specialists. In the short term, therefore, a key role remained for Jacques Tubeuf who, as the link with the past, gave a detailed account of the financial situation to the *Parlement* of Paris on 10 July while La Meilleraye spoke only in general terms. The new appointees were in office less than a fortnight before bankruptcy was declared and concessions were made to the *Chambre Saint-Louis*. Their first real task was to limit the concessions as far as possible and end the meetings of the *Chambre Saint-Louis* without which it would be impossible to restore financial confidence. Diplomacy failed, and the meetings had to be ended by a show of force—a royal *lit de justice* held on 31 July.

However, once started public debate could not be stopped so easily.[4] At the *lit de justice*, Mathieu Molé, the *premier président* of the *Parlement*, declared that he was in favour of the wholescale confiscation of the assets of the financiers as the means of solving

---

[1] Appendix One, Table I.

[2] Cf. the contrasting judgements in Talon, *Mémoires*, ed. Michaud and Poujoulat, pp. 248, 273 and Ormesson, *Journal*, ed. Chéruel, i. 738.

[3] Technically, La Meilleraye did not hold the two offices at the same time since on 26 Apr. 1648 the crown accepted the resignation of the office of *grand maître* to his son: P 2373, pp. 407–21. On the other hand, Charles-Armand de la Porte was a youth of only sixteen at the time of the resignation and thus could not control the artillery. As late as 1652, when the government needed cannon, it had recourse to La Meilleraye, who was appointed the royalist commander in Anjou: *Mémoires . . . de Montglat*, ed. Michaud and Poujoulat, p. 262. The *Chambre des Comptes* registered the resignation only on 16 Dec. 1652.

[4] Moote (*The revolt of the judges*, p. 150) considers the *lit de justice* 'a dismal failure'.

the financial problems of the crown.[1] Earlier in the month, Pierre Broussel, one of the most senior and influential *conseillers* in the *Grand'Chambre*, had denounced the vast sums raised by fiscal edicts which had not been registered in the sovereign courts,[2] and on 4 August Broussel pursued the attack by requesting an investigation of corruption in financial administration.[3] Throughout the Fronde, Broussel was an ardent defender of the rights of the *rentiers* and claimed that the financiers diverted funds received from the provinces which should have been used to pay the *rentes*. On 22 August, the *Parlement* ordered an investigation into the conduct of certain financiers, including François Catelan, Martin Tabouret and Martin Lefebvre. Other financiers panicked, and pressure to stand firm was put on the government by a number of nobles at court with investments in loan contracts.[4] The news of Condé's great victory at Lens strengthened the resolve of the ministers to arrest Broussel and five other leading critics of the regime. Ironically, Broussel had not been in favour of the decree of 22 August,[5] but Mazarin considered him a dangerous demagogue. The upshot was as disastrous as Charles I's attempted arrest of the five members in England in 1642.[6] The operation was carried out more successfully, but the mob of the Île de la Cité set up barricades on 26–8 August: by its ineptitude, the government had created an alliance of different social groups, including members of the sovereign courts, *bons bourgeois*, and the Parisian mob.[7] A deputation of the *Parlement* refused to co-operate with the government, arguing that it was impossible to contain the riot

---

[1] U 28, fo. 397, 31 July 1648.

[2] U 28, fo. 392, 16 July 1648. Broussel claimed that 200 million *livres* had been raised in this way, but did not state the period during which this had occurred.

[3] U 28, fo. 399, 4 Aug. 1648.

[4] According to Ormesson, Guillaume Bautru, the commandeur de Jars, and two *maréchaux de France*, La Ferté-Sénectère and d'Estrées. The influence was exercised through Madame de Beauvais, the *première femme de chambre* of Anne of Austria. It should be noted that the financiers singled out for attack were those who held 'le parti du retranchement des gages des officiers': *Journal des guerres civiles de Dubuisson-Aubenay*, ed. Saige, i. 49. To some extent, the motivation of the *parlementaires* could thus be said to be self-interested.

[5] Ormesson, *Journal*, i. 555 is quite explicit, and Mousnier, *La plume*, p. 287, appears in error.

[6] The English comparison is examined in more detail in R. J. Bonney, 'The English and French civil wars', *History*, lxv (1980), 365–82.

[7] Mousnier's argument (*loc. cit.*) that the barricades were the work of the *menu peuple* has been contested by J. L. Bourgeon, 'L'Île de la Cité pendant la Fronde: structure sociale', *Paris et Île de France. Mémoires*, xiii (1962), 127–144. Bourgeon's case (pp. 129–30) that an official version of events was fabricated to obscure the political isolation of the Regent appears to be borne out by A.A.E. France 860, fo. 164, 26 Sept. 1648.

without releasing Broussel;[1] the ministers reluctantly had to concede the point, though not before La Meilleraye had been fired on
by the mob. In Mazarin's words, the populace had joined with
Broussel and the *Parlement* in the hope of being 'délivré des impôts
par leur moyen'.[2]

Thus the government was left at the beginning of September
without a certain financial policy and with less political support
than before. Mazarin was already considering evacuating the
court from Paris and blockading the capital[3] when, on 12 September, Molé and Broussel once more led the *Parlement* to take
measures against the financiers.[4] The following day, the court was
moved to Rueil and ultimately Saint-Germain-en-Laye: it seemed
that the trial of strength was now to begin. However, the criticism
of Mazarin in the *Parlement* on 22 September, the fear that the
nobles would be drawn into the conflict on the side of the Parisian
sovereign courts, and the crucial stage reached by the Westphalian negotiations convinced the ministers of the desirability of
a compromise solution. At the council of state held at Saint-
Germain on 4 October, Mazarin, Gaston, Condé, Conty, Longueville, Séguier, and La Meilleraye advised the Regent to make
concessions provided that the *Parlement* abandoned its more
extreme demands; if not, they were prepared to 'se porter à toute
extrémité contre ledit Parlement'.[5]

The upshot was the declaration of 22 October, registered by the
Parlement two days later, which in some respects extended the
financial concessions extracted from the government by the
Chambre Saint-Louis. As a result of this declaration, the *taille* for
1648 was to be reduced by one-fifth. A variety of indirect taxes
were also to be reduced, and procedures were established for the
administration of revenue farms which were to preclude the anticipation of rents. The salaries of the most important office-holders
were completely restored, although the lesser office-holders received less favourable treatment. Half payment of all *rentes* was to
be guaranteed, and some *rentiers* received better terms than this.
The redemption of *rentes* in wartime was to be abandoned, and
those who had redeemed *rentes* since 1630 were to repay the state,

[1] U 28, fo. 404ᵛ., 27 Aug. 1648.
[2] P. A. Chéruel, 'Les carnets de Mazarin pendant la Fronde (septembre–octobre 1648)',
Revue Historique, iv (1877), 126.
[3] Ibid., 107. Kossmann, *La Fronde*, p. 70.
[4] Martin Tabouret and the financiers Canto, Lombard, and Poulart were ordered to
appear before the *Parlement*: X2b 507, 12 Sept. 1648.
[5] A.A.E. 860, fo. 173.

with a penal clause affecting those who had benefited from the high rate of 18 times the annual interest.[1] An investigation into the extent of the royal lands was announced, and all holders[2] of lands were to present their title deeds before the *Parlement* and the *Chambre des Comptes*. The use of the *comptants* was to be restricted to genuinely secret expenses and not for interest payments to financiers. No new judicial or financial offices were to be established for four years, and after that time limit only by edicts which had been registered in the sovereign courts. The property of tax farmers and contractors and their associates was to be secured by mortgage as a guarantee of their solvency. Five other articles in the declaration covered diverse matters such as recently created offices in Paris, disorders of the troops, trading privileges, special commissions and a French version of *habeas corpus* applying only to office-holders.[3]

It was not necessary to be a financial expert to recognize that although the declaration of October 1648 made significant concessions to the Parisian sovereign courts, it did not by any means resolve all the issues at dispute. For example, while the use of the *comptants* was to be restricted, no ceiling was placed on such expenditure. Predictably both the *Chambre des Comptes* and the *Cour des Aides* presented amendments,[4] and the *Comptes*, for example, insisted on a limit of 3 million *livres* per annum on secret expenditure. In their remonstrances of 14 October, which were not presented until nearly a fortnight later and were thus too late to influence the royal declaration, the *Comptes* attacked the whole basis of financial administration since 1630 in far-reaching terms. They proposed a review of the *comptants* and *traités* since that time and calculated that the redemption of *rentes* had cost the crown 30 million *livres*, while a further 15 million had been lost in mismanaged sales of royal lands. The administration of the revenue farms was severely criticized—the methods by which the leases were marketed, the motives of the farmers, and the cloak of secrecy surrounding the financial consortia all came under scrutiny. The *Comptes* roundly condemned the policy of the council of finance in allowing the farmers to make loans instead of providing a cash payment as surety, and allowing the farmers and contractors to

---

[1] The penal rate was a fine of four times the illicit gain plus the payment of interest for the period during which the illicit gain had been enjoyed.

[2] The *possesseur* of crown lands was not necessarily the legal owner. He might be an *engagiste*.

[3] Talon, *Mémoires*, ed. Michaud and Poujoulat, pp. 293–6. P. R. Doolin, *The Fronde* (Cambridge, Mass., 1935), pp. 20–1.

[4] Talon, op. cit., pp. 307–11, 313–14.

enjoy their leases and *traités* before they had been registered (and thus if necessary amended) by the *Comptes*. Arrangements similar to the ^mortgage clause contained in the royal declaration of 22 October were approved as a means of preventing the fraudulent bankruptcy of financiers and *comptables*. More significant was the opposition of the members of the *Comptes* to the whole idea of the *affaires extraordinaires*. They believed that many of the proposals received in previous years by the council of finance had tended to subvert the laws of the kingdom and should have been rejected. In future, the activity of *donneur d'avis*—the presentation of such proposals to the council—should be made illegal. Indeed, the *Comptes* were critical of much of the day-to-day conduct of the council of finance, which frequently prevented their investigation of accounts, work which they considered to be within their jurisdiction and duty in accordance with earlier royal ordinances. The remonstrances concluded by condemning the process whereby the council of finance had anticipated the revenues of the *taille*. They considered the interest payments and costs of collection much too high as the system had been practised between 1642 and 1648, while the method of employing special brigades under the supervision of provincial intendants was compared to the levy of contributions by an enemy army of occupation. The *Comptes* also commented on the fact that the *receveur-général des finances* had frequently been dispossessed by the financial consortium which had made the loan to the government, with the result that effective accounting had become impossible. The crown thus had compelling reasons, in the view of the *Comptes*, to return to the *status quo ante* 1642.[1]

Yet La Meilleraye and his advisers were proposing exactly the reverse policy—the anticipation of revenues of the *taille*—for equally compelling, if different reasons. It was evident that the crown could not meet current expenditure. Even with expenses drastically pruned, the deficit on the current account stood at 24 million *livres* towards the end of the year, while no further revenues were expected before May 1649.[2] In the hope of securing loans on the revenues of 1649, La Meilleraye offered interests at 15 per cent on the *taille*,[3] and a maximum of 25 per cent interest on

---

[1] A.A.E. France 860, fos. 199–217, 14 Oct. 1648. Presented 27 Oct. 1648.

[2] Talon, op. cit., p. 281. Appendix Two, Table IX B i.

[3] Interest payments were generally reduced to 15 per cent by La Meilleraye well before his announcement on 9 Dec. 1648, although there are some examples of interests at 17.5 per cent: E 232a–233b, *passim*. His proposals were considered ungenerous by the financiers: B.N. MS. fr. 18510, fo. 236, 1648. The Sorbonne considered La Meilleraye's proposals

new *affaires extraordinaires*. His proposals, which were drawn up on 9 December,[1] were presented to the *Chambre des Comptes* presumably in the hope of obtaining its agreement and thus stabilizing the credit market. If this was indeed La Meilleraye's intention, he was politically inept. There was no prospect of obtaining the agreement of the *Comptes*, in view of their policy as outlined in the October remonstrances, and La Meilleraye's proposals had to be withdrawn on 2 January 1649. Even had this court proved more co-operative, there would still have been the attitude of the *Parlement* to consider. When it learnt of La Meilleraye's proposals, there was an explosion of anger, and it was the prospect of combined opposition of the Parisian courts aimed at obtaining concessions beyond the royal declaration of 22 October that steeled Mazarin to a new trial of strength. The court was evacuated from Paris to Saint-Germain on the night of 5–6 January 1649, and the blockade of the capital began almost immediately. The news of Pride's Purge in England, which set Parliament along the path of abolishing the monarchy, may also have strengthened the resolve of the French government.[2] Mazarin was convinced of the parallel between his own position and that of Strafford in England (once Charles I had sacrificed Strafford, so the argument ran, the monarchy itself did not long survive); he also wanted to ensure that France did not follow the trend across the Channel where the independent financial powers of the crown had been drastically curtailed.[3] The position of the government was also somewhat stronger than in the earlier crisis in the autumn of 1648, for although war with Spain continued, a peace treaty had been signed with the Emperor on 24 October.

The surprising fact about the crisis of January 1649 was that it had been so long deferred. Here the crucial factor seems to have been the conservatism of the opposition rather than the moderation of the government. The Parisian sovereign courts were reluctant to resort to armed rebellion, and the vital decision on 9

---

usurious and declared it a mortal sin to lend to the king at an interest rate above 10 per cent: *Journal des guerres civiles de Dubuisson-Aubenay*, ed. Saige, i. 98–9.

[1] A.A.E. France 860, fo. 235.

[2] Kossmann, *La Fronde*, pp. 77–8.

[3] P. A. Knachel, *England and the Fronde. The impact of the English civil war and revolution on France* (Ithaca, N.Y., 1967), pp. 28, 32, 47. Montglat's comment on the declaration of 22 Oct. 1648 had already been that 'les finances étoient aussi réglées, et le pouvoir de lever des deniers si limité, qu'il étoit impossible que le roi pût dorénavant soutenir la guerre': *Mémoires . . . de Montglat*, ed. Michaud and Poujoulat, p. 200.

January—to set up a fund for the levy of troops—came only after the failure of last-minute negotiations at Saint-Germain. Once the break came, two main arguments were deployed to justify resistance. The first was the argument of self-defence, justified by the blockade of the capital and the attempt to starve it into submission. The *Parlement* was therefore entitled to keep the roads open for the arrival of food, prohibit the king's troops from occupying towns within 20 leagues of the capital, and set up its own army to enforce these decisions. Reference to the *taxe de Corbie* of 1636, when northern France had suffered a Spanish invasion, in the decision to set up a war fund of 2.4 million *livres*, added weight to the argument of self-defence.[1] The second justification for resistance centred on the traditional argument that the Parisian courts had no intention other than the good of the king and the state,[2] while the cause of the troubles rested squarely with the king's evil counsellors and above all Cardinal Mazarin. On 8 January, Mazarin was declared a 'perturbateur du repos publicq, ennemy du Roi et de son estat',[3] and on 21 January remonstrances were drawn up for the Parlement by Le Coigneux, Broussel, and Longueil which blamed Mazarin for the conflict and declared the position of chief minister illegal. Mazarin was considered a tyrant, who was responsible for the breakdown of peace negotiations with Spain and the collapse of financial administration. Indeed, the two were believed to be related: Mazarin wanted to continue the war as a pretext for levying vast sums in taxes for self-enrichment. Mazarin's personal control of, and responsibility for, the financial system was stressed: he it was who had caused the excessive reliance on financiers and the anticipation of 150 million *livres* in revenues. Above all, Mazarin was accused of duplicity in the last months leading to the breakdown. He had talked of financial reform, yet had had a declaration sent by La Meilleraye to the *Chambre des Comptes* authorizing loans and interest payments for his *coup d'état* against the Parisian tribunals.[4]

These charges against Mazarin were extremely damaging, because they were at least partially true. The position of chief minister brought with it overall control of patronage and the financial system, even if the day-to-day decisions were taken by

---

[1] For an army of 14,000 infantry and 4000 cavalry: Z1a 163, fos. 173–177ᵛ., 19 Jan. 1649. The original fund was for one million *livres*: Talon, *Mémoires*, ed. Michaud and Poujoulat, p. 321.

[2] U 28, fo. 273, 6 Jan. 1649.

[3] U 28, fo. 278ᵛ.

[4] Talon, *Mémoires*, ed. Michaud and Poujoulat, pp. 323–8.

the *surintendant*. Control of the system also offered enormous financial rewards to the chief minister himself. Mazarin was to die with a fortune of 37 million, most of which was built up after the Fronde. There is not much detailed information on Mazarin's private finances between 1643 and the Fronde. It is clear, however, that the chief minister had become extremely wealthy. His fortune attracted public attention, and it was said in hostile political pamphlets that he had 'pillé et ravi toutes les finances du roy et réduit Sa Majesté en une indigence extrême . . .'[1] There seems little doubt that the profits from office were substantial, and sufficient to enable Mazarin to make covering loans to the crown after the bankruptcy of 18 July 1648.[2] Moreover, the *Parlement* was correct in arguing that Mazarin had a close relationship with the financiers, and this was reinforced by the events of the first civil war. The financiers had much to fear from a victory of the Parisian sovereign tribunals. Already they and their families were subject to special taxes to help pay for the upkeep of the Parisian army of resistance after 21 January 1649.[3] Moreover the political pamphlets which circulated freely in the capital during the blockade led the financiers to fear worse treatment: the *Catalogue des Partisans*, one of the more influential of these pamphlets, enumerated the crimes of the financiers and exaggerated the contrast between their humble social origins and their vast wealth in an attempt to stir up popular resentment.[4] In contrast, La Meilleraye's establishment of a fund to pay interest on royal debts and the inactivity of the *chambre de justice* had given the financiers hope from the present government. When faced with a choice of sides, it is scarcely surprising that they turned to Mazarin. Thomas Bonneau, one of the most important financiers, was one of the first to decide. The morning after the evacuation of the court to Saint-Germain (6 January), he tried to send to Mazarin a cartload of money from the capital which, however, was stopped and pillaged by the mob on the rue Saint-Honoré.[5] Other financiers made less

[1] *Choix de Mazarinades*, ed. Moreau, i. 30.

[2] *Lettres . . . de Colbert*, ed. Clément, i. 176, 274. Mazarin mentioned his loans in a letter to Louis XIV: A.A.E. France 879, fo. 187ᵛ., 23 Dec. 1651.

[3] *Journal des guerres civiles de Dubuisson-Aubenay*, ed. Saige, ii. 314–16.

[4] *Choix de Mazarinades*, ed. Moreau, i. 113–39.

[5] A.A.E. France 864, fo. 6ʳ., 7 Jan. 1649. Cf. E 259a, fo. 337, 13 Aug. 1653. This act of loyalty was rewarded by Mazarin, who wrote to the directors of finance on 30 Apr. 1649 requesting that the interests of Bonneau and Marin be 'particullièrement [*sic*] protegez' and that a speedy *liquidation* of their debts be conducted. The letter, and the *liquidations*, are summarized in Bonneau's probate records: Minutier Central XXX 61, 26 Jan. 1663. Respectively items 370 and items 344–360.

exaggerated gestures of support, but probably co-operated with the transfer of funds to Saint-Germain rather than the capital.[1]

Apart from the assistance of financiers within France, Mazarin also retained international financial connections, one of which was to be of crucial importance in the spring of 1649. Barthélémé Hervart was a banker from Lyon, whose family originated from Augsburg. He had served Bernard of Saxe-Weimar in the 1630s and after Bernard's death in 1639 had thrown in his lot with the king of France. Mazarin had continued to employ him after 1643, and had rewarded him with lands in Alsace. In 1649, this relationship proved its worth. Turenne, the commander of the 'army of Germany' based in Alsace, and the outstanding French general, was poised to march on Paris in support of the rebellion. Had Turenne relieved the blockade of the capital, the outcome of the first civil war might have been very different. Mazarin appreciated the danger, and dispatched Hervart to Alsace on 9 February with instructions to negotiate with Turenne and, if the negotiations failed, to buy off his troops. D'Erlach, the commander of Breisach, Baussan, the intendant of Alsace, and Hervart between them won over the loyalty of the troops: but they would have failed had Hervart not been able to advance 800,000 *livres* to cover the immediate pay of the troops. To the military leaders of the rebellion this was a thunderbolt which crushed their hopes,[2] and Turenne had to take refuge in the Netherlands. Mazarin did not forget Hervart's success and later in the year persuaded Anne of Austria to disregard his Protestantism and allow him to buy a vacant office of *intendant des finances*.[3]

Thanks to Mazarin's financial contacts and good luck, the danger from Turenne had been averted: but there remained grave risks to the government in pursuing the blockade of the capital. The Parisian courts were not isolated in their struggle, but had support in the provinces, particularly Normandy and Provence. Moreover, a motley band of discontented nobles had arrived at Paris and on 18 January signed an alliance among themselves pledging general support to the *Parlement* and resolute hostility to

---

[1] The transfer of funds was ordered by the council of finance: E 234a, fos. 28–59, 14–19 Jan. 1649. Payment of *rentes* and *gages* at Paris was also to be stopped: *Arrêts du conseil du roi*, ed. Le Pesant, no. 980.

[2] Bouillon, Turenne's brother, was reported as calling it 'un coup de foudre': *Oeuvres de Retz*, ed. A. Feillet *et al.*, (10 vols., 1870–96), iii. 418.

[3] On the 1649 incident: Guy Patin, *Lettres au temps de la Fronde*, ed. A. Thérive (1921), pp. 163–4. G. Livet, *L'intendance d'Alsace sous Louis XIV, 1648–1715* (1956), p. 130. On Hervart: Depping, 'Un banquier protestant', *Revue Historique*, x (1879), 303, 309.

Mazarin.[1] The *Parlement* never formally recognized this alliance, but in practice it was forced to establish a working relationship with the nobles, and Conty was appointed the generalissimo of the *Frondeur* army. From the point of view of the conservative leadership of the courts, it was important to put on a show of strength in order to extract the best possible terms from the government; like Conty, they had to speak as men who wanted war yet act as men who wanted peace.[2] They faced a threat to their position on several fronts apart from the government—from the nobles, from Spain, from the populace, and from the spread of radical ideas. There was a serious possibility that these different threats could become linked. Conty was negotiating secretly with the Spanish, and a treaty between them could have resulted in a Spanish invasion of northern France to relieve Paris. The discontented nobles could have manipulated the Parisian mob to coerce the courts to follow their policies. The longer the conflict was drawn out, the more chance there was that radical ideas such as those contained in the *Contrat du mariage du Parlement avec la ville de Paris*[3] would gain acceptance. Some of these ideas would have had profound constitutional and financial implications, as for example the suggestions that the *Parlement* propose to the king names for the post of finance minister, gain the right of dismissing ministers, and take over the powers formerly vested in the office of *contrôleur général des finances* to act as a check on the executive. These, and other dangerous ideas, circulated freely in more than 400 *Mazarinades* published during the blockade of Paris.[4] If the conservative office-holders feared radicalism, their desire for a compromise peace was reinforced by a consideration of self-interest. On 15 February 1649, the council of state had ordered a levy of 523,000 *livres* on the estates of Parisian office-holders who had demonstrated their opposition to the government by remaining in the capital. Once the levy was published, all knew what to expect at the hands of the royal army: from Molé's lands at Le Plessis Vallée down to Broussel's house at Pontoise, all were defenceless before the subsistence requirements of the king's troops.[5] The

[1] *Oeuvres de Retz*, ed. Feillet *et al.*, ii. 636–7. B.N. MS. fr. 3854, fo. 1. B.N. 500 Colbert 3, fo. 44.

[2] Retz's description of Conty: *Oeuvres de Retz*, ed. Feillet *et al.*, ii. 298.

[3] Ibid., v. 438–50. *Choix de Mazarinades*, ed. Moreau, i. 39–50.

[4] B.L. Harleian 4468, fo. 205, gives the total as 401 between 6 Jan. and 31 Mar. 1649. Grand-Mesnil's estimate of 800 appears too high: Grand-Mesnil, *Mazarin, la Fronde et la presse*, p. 122.

[5] *Choix de Mazarinades*, ed. Moreau, i. 207–23. *Arrêts du conseil du roi*, ed. Le Pesant, no. 989.

longer the struggle went on, the greater the damage to the outly-
ing estates of the Parisian *noblesse de robe*. Their willingness to
jettison allies who sought to prolong the conflict by negotiating
with Spain, and to patch up a compromise peace with Mazarin
which included a remission of direct taxes in the Île-de-France,[1] is
therefore scarcely surprising. A preliminary treaty was signed on
11 March 1649 by a Parisian delegation of twenty-two office-
holders and *bourgeois*, led by Molé.

The Peace of Rueil provided for a reciprocal cessation of hostilities, the ending of the blockade of Paris, and a *lit de justice* in the
Parlement to be held at Saint-Germain-en-Laye. (In the event, this
exceptional *lit de justice* at Saint-Germain never took place.) There
were to be no further assemblies of the chambers in the *Parlement*
in 1649, although this clause, too, proved unenforceable. The
royal declarations of 18 July and 22 October 1648 were to be
carried out, thus apparently guaranteeing the survival of the
financial and other measures imposed on the government by the
office-holders. All controversial decrees of the *Parlement* since 6
January 1649 were to be annulled, as were royal *lettres de cachet*
issued against the rebels during the blockade. The rebel army was
to be disbanded in return for the withdrawal of the royal troops
from the environs of Paris. The Bastille was to be handed back to
royal control, and the citizens of Paris undertook not to rebel
again (a promise which was broken in 1652). The ambassador of
the archduke Leopold William, governor of the Spanish Netherlands, who had been sent to negotiate with the rebels, was to be
told to leave the capital without any offer of terms. The crown was
to be allowed to borrow money[2] at 8.33 per cent interest (*denier 12*)
during 1649 and 1650. (This clause was later rejected by the
Parlement.) Conty, Longueville, and the other nobles who had
allied with the Parisian tribunals were guaranteed their offices,
rights, and privileges provided that they laid down their arms
within ten days. The king undertook to return to Paris as soon as
possible. In the meantime, there was an amnesty for illegal seiz-
ures of royal taxes and levies of troops by the rebels. The crown
also undertook to revoke the unpopular second tribunals
(*semestres*) which had been established in the *Parlements* of Aix-en-
Provence and Rouen.

---

[1] *Mémoires de Mathieu Molé*, ed. A. Champollion-Figeac (4 vols., 1855–1857), iii. 370–4
(article 17 at p. 373). *Arrêts du conseil du roi*, ed. Le Pesant, nos. 999–1011.

[2] The phrase used was 'emprunter les deniers'. It was not made explicit whether this
meant the anticipation of revenues, but it is difficult to see how significant sums could have
been borrowed without anticipation.

In essentials, Molé and the conservative leadership forced acceptance of the terms of the peace of Rueil on the *Parlement*, despite violent objections from Conty and the other *Frondeur* nobles. In separate bargaining, Conty tried to force the government to agree to the dismissal of Mazarin and the opening of immediate peace negotiations with Spain. However, Conty's hand was decisively weakened by the publication of his exorbitant private demands and those of his followers without reference to their broader political objectives.[1] The peace of Rueil was thus a crushing defeat for the nobles and a relative success for the *Parlement*. The government was left no stronger than before since it had agreed to uphold the declarations of 1648 and indeed the rejection of clause eleven concerning royal borrowing left it without a financial policy. On 14 April 1649 La Meilleraye resigned.[2] Although his reasons were not made public at the time, it seems probable that as the partisan of royal borrowing and strong-arm measures against the courts, he regarded the peace of Rueil as a rejection of his policies. Three names—René Longueil de Maisons, Claude Mesmes d'Avaux and Abel Servien—were mooted as his successor. Servien was probably offered the *surintendance* as a reward for negotiating peace with the Emperor at Münster, but declined the offer: in the financial chaos of 1649, the post offered few attractions to a career politician who wanted to succeed. Instead, a holding operation was mounted from April until November 1649 by Aligre and Barillon, the *directeurs des finances*, with Le Tellier, the war minister, acting as honest broker. The absence of strong central financial leadership was symptomatic of the general political situation.

After the peace of Rueil, Mazarin tried to proceed as if nothing had happened, and to divert attention from the recent civil disorder he determined on a vigorous military campaign against the Spanish. The siege of Cambrai was decided on, despite the inherent risks in a situation where only 20 million *livres* remained to the crown in net revenues after remissions of taxes, the re-establishment of the *gages* and *rentes*, and the refusal of some provinces to pay their taxes.[3] The weakness of the central finan-

---

[1] *Choix de Mazarinades*, ed. Moreau, i. 431–6. Talon, op. cit., pp. 347–8, 350, *Oeuvres de Retz*, ed. Feillet *et al.*, ii. 454.

[2] Appendix One, Table I. However, there had been speculation about an impending resignation in Dec. 1648 and Jan. 1649: *Journal des guerres civiles de Dubuisson-Aubenay*, ed. Saige, i. 97, 101. A.A.E. France 864, fo. 2ᵛ., 1 Jan. 1649.

[3] Talon, op. cit., p. 360. A.A.E. France 864, fos. 392, 408ᵛ., 4 July and n.d., c. July 1649.

cial leadership was graphically illustrated by its difficulties in dealing with the financiers, who almost to a man refused to lend to the government because of the prevailing political uncertainty.[1] Launay Gravé, La Rallière and their associates, the farmers of the *entrées*, led the way in extracting concessions from Aligre and Barillon. The government was faced with little choice but to concede the financiers' terms with a view to retrospective taxation through a *chambre de justice* at a later date. The disadvantage of this approach, however, was that when retrospective taxation was levied, the financiers would claim that the government had broken faith and confidence would once more be shaken. Le Tellier lamented the 'avantages que les traictans prennent de la nécessité présente' and noted that the financiers would complain of a *manque de parole* if the government sought to 'reprendre sur eux ce qu'ils exigent à contretemps'.[2] Even by conceding interest rates higher than those envisaged in the preliminary terms of the peace of Rueil it was not possible to borrow sufficient money to pay for the siege of Cambrai. In June 1649, the government had recourse to a particularly disastrous expedient that had not been employed since the time of the Catholic League. Four new offices of intendant of finance were created, bringing the number of these officials to eight, and almost a million *livres* was raised from the sales to Le Tillier, Bordier, Foullé and Bordeaux.[3] There was talk of establishing another four offices, taking the number of these officials to twelve,[4] but this decision was deferred until 1654. Instead, further expedients such as pressure on Antoine Le Camus, the controller-general, to lend to the crown, and the sale of a secretaryship of the council to François Catelan, a leading financier, were adopted. These measures had one common feature: they put the short-term requirements of cash advances for the siege of Cambrai before long-term considerations such as the quality of the appointees and a rational allocation of responsibility for financial administration.[5]

By the autumn of 1649, Mazarin's political position was becoming more precarious as it became clear that the gamble of a last attempt to snatch a peace from the Spanish had not worked. The

---

[1] A.A.E. France 864, fo. 385, 2 July 1649.
[2] A.A.E. France 864, fo. 392, 4 July 1649.
[3] Appendix One, Table III.
[4] A.A.E. France 864, fo. 396ᵛ., 4 July 1649.
[5] Dent, *Crisis in finance*, p. 99. Barillon and Aligre divided responsibilities between the *intendants des finances* on 23 June 1649: *Archives curieuses de l'histoire de France*, 2nd ser., vi (1838), 470–1.

power of the leading *Frondeur* nobles had probably increased, yet those who had sided with Mazarin in the spring of 1649 had high expectations. Most notable among the latter was Louis II de Bourbon, prince de Condé, who had been one of Mazarin's most important allies in 1648–9 but was now openly critical of the chief minister. His supporters were talking of ousting Mazarin and replacing him with a regency council drawn from the nobility; they talked also of setting up an investigation of financial administration from 1642 and bringing to task those who allegedly had 'prevented' peace with Spain since 1646.[1] It is not known how seriously this talk was taken, but Mazarin's position was rapidly undermined. On 2 October, Condé virtually made himself chief minister since he gained a veto on appointments and dismissals and on all important decisions of policy. Moreover, since Condé was entitled to propose new appointments, it is likely that he used his powers to suggest the recall to power of d'Hémery and d'Avaux as joint finance ministers, which occurred on 8 November.[2]

Mazarin's friends regarded this decision as a Machiavellian trick of Condé's to discredit the Cardinal and stir up popular resentment,[3] and it was certainly greeted with astonishment because of d'Hémery's general unpopularity, not least with the office-holders. D'Avaux had a reputation as a man of integrity, but only took the position to show that he had been unfairly dismissed in 1647. He would have resigned after two months in office but for d'Hémery's illness which required his taking over the day-to-day conduct of financial affairs, despite his lack of financial acumen.[4] D'Avaux's integrity, however, could not offset criticism of the recall of d'Hémery and the suspicion that he had been brought back at the request of financiers who had suffered in the bankruptcy the previous year and who hoped to obtain reimbursement. There was also the suggestion that other candidates for office had been excluded after the refusal of the financiers to co-operate.[5] These various rumours were apparently confirmed

[1] Patin, op. cit., pp. 156–7.
[2] K 118a, no. 17 [Musée AE II 843], 2 Oct. 1649. Appendix One, Table I.
[3] A.A.E. France 864, fos. 490–1, 494, 31 Oct. and 6 Nov. 1649.
[4] A.A.E. France 868, fo. 230, 28 May 1650.
[5] Ormesson, *Journal*, ed. Chéruel, i. 779, does not make this point, but Patin, op. cit., p. 160, does. Patin commented that the new finance minister was to have been La Vieuville, 'mais les partisans lui ont donné l'exclusion, protestant tout haut qu'ils ne traiteraient jamais d'aucune affaire avec lui . . .' This exclusion of La Vieuville was probably more important than any positive qualities of d'Hémery, who was discredited ('s'il a gâté les

by the first decision of the council of finance over which d'Hémery presided, which set up a committee of five—including the two *directeurs*—to establish a full list of outstanding royal debts with a view to 'settlement' (*liquidation*).[1] However, though d'Hémery promised the financiers reimbursement, unlike La Meilleraye, he did not set up a fund for the purpose. By March 1650, it was clear that he had broken his word: the funds that had been assigned to the financiers were being diverted and they openly showed their dissatisfaction.[2] Their unco-operativeness was reinforced by news of d'Hémery's illness and the suspicion that they would soon have to deal with his successor.[3]

If the recall of d'Hémery and d'Avaux had been forced on Mazarin by Condé, the first prince of the blood gained little political advantage for his pains. In so far as the finance ministers had any clear-cut political allegiance at all,[4] it was to the Regent and through her to Mazarin, while the Cardinal continued to enjoy the support of Gaston d'Orléans who was no friend of Condé. On 16 January 1650 Condé extracted a new declaration of support from Mazarin;[5] but the chief minister had found new and rather surprising allies in some of the former *Frondeurs* and two days later had Condé, Conty, and Longueville arrested. This *coup d'état* was the equivalent of Mazarin crossing his Rubicon. Afterwards, political events rapidly got out of hand. The incarceration of the princes was an acid in the body politic. There would be continual revolts by their supporters until they were released in February 1651. The duchesse de Longueville and Turenne, who were based at Stenay on the north-east frontier of France, signed a treaty with archduke Leopold William on 30 April 1650. The

---

affaires', Patin commented, 'il saura mieux qu'un autre comment il faudra les réformer'). It was probably also more important than the cabal in favour of d'Hémery led by Jacques Le Coigneux, a *président* in the *Parlement* of Paris who was d'Hémery's brother-in-law. In 1616, d'Hémery had married Marie Camus, the daughter of the financier Nicolas Camus or Le Camus (Bourgeon, *Les Colbert avant Colbert*, p. 83). In 1648, Jacques Le Coigneux's son married Marie's younger sister Angelique, who was the widow of the great financier Jean Galland: Y 187, fo. 316 and Minutier Central XIV 65, 11 Jan. 1648. The cabal is mentioned by Martin and Bezançon, *L'histoire du crédit*, p. 35.

[1] E 237b, fo. 179, 13 Nov. 1649. E 238, fo. 232, 11 Dec. 1649. E 241, fo. 102, 10 Mar. 1650.

[2] A.A.E. France 870, fo. 266ʳ., 22 Mar. 1650.

[3] A.A.E. France 870, fos. 244ᵛ., 252ᵛ., 18 and 20 Mar. 1650.

[4] Moote (*The revolt of the judges*, pp. 243, 248) calls d'Hémery a 'Condéan supporter', but it is not clear what this meant in practice: there was no suggestion of d'Hémery's resignation in Jan. 1650 after the arrest of the princes.

[5] B.N. Dupuy 775, fo. 122. On the general question of Mazarin's relations with the princes, cf. R. J. Bonney, 'Cardinal Mazarin and the great nobility during the Fronde', *English Historical Review*, xcvi (1981).

princesse de Condé, Bouillon, La Rochefoucauld, Sauveboeuf, and Lusignan, who were based at Bordeaux, signed a treaty with Philip IV on 26 June 1650. The terms of the treaties were similar, although the Bordelais rebels hoped for greater financial assistance from Philip IV since they were to be given less military support. Both treaties interpreted Mazarin's hostility to peace with Spain as the reason for his having arrested the princes: both treaties envisaged a joint effort to secure the release of the princes and immediate peace negotiations between France and Spain.[1] The weakness of these rebellions was their dependence on Spanish support, which took a long time to organize. In the meantime, Mazarin and the royalist army mopped up resistance in Normandy and Burgundy and after a siege of Bordeaux which recalled the blockade of the capital the previous year, a compromise peace was signed with the rebels there (29 September 1650). The campaigns were not the resounding success that Mazarin later claimed,[2] but the crucial point was that the resistance of the princes' supporters within France was poorly co-ordinated with the planned triple invasion from abroad. When the invasion came, it was much less than had been expected: although the Spanish captured Le Catelet, they abandoned the siege of Guise on 1 July, while Turenne's invasion force was decisively defeated by Plessis Praslin on 15 December[3]—one of only two defeats in Turenne's career.

In the short term, Mazarin was able to exploit the disunity of his new *Frondeur* allies and remained in control of policy and appointments. There seems little reason to doubt that the appointment of René Longueil de Maisons as finance minister on 24 May 1650, after the death of d'Hémery, was Mazarin's decision.[4] What the Cardinal wanted was a finance minister who would find cash as required, keep the financiers happy, and above all pay the chief minister current interest on his debts—and preferably reimburse them. He had no gold mine of his own, Mazarin told Le Tellier.[5] Yet if Mazarin saw only the possible advantages of a tractable finance minister who owed personal advancement to himself, others were much more sceptical about

---

[1] Bonney, 'The French civil war', 80.

[2] A.A.E. France 874, fo. 187, n.d. [1651]: 'toutes les voyages ayans heureusement réussy . . .'

[3] Commandant de Piépape, *Turenne et l'invasion de la Champagne, 1649–1650* (1889).

[4] Patin thought Longueil 'un animal mazarinique' and criticized the appointment: Patin, op. cit., pp. 159, 221–2. Appendix One, Table I.

[5] A.A.E. France 873, fo. 286, 15 Apr. 1650.

the appointment, and a memorandum denouncing the decision was sent to the Cardinal. Apart from his alleged personal defects, particularly his idleness and the fact that he was in debt, Longueil was considered lacking in technical expertise. He was, moreover, a *président à mortier* in the *Parlement* of Paris. It was believed that his office would hinder free debate within the council of state, for there would always be the suspicion that Longueil would reveal council secrets to the *Parlement*. Doubt was also cast on the willingness of the financiers to co-operate with 'un homme de justice' such as Longueil.[1] These doubts would come to the fore again in 1651. In the short-term, Longueil inherited a situation in which the financiers were reluctant to lend to the crown,[2] and in which it was considered a real achievement to find 2 million *livres* to pay current expenses.[3] The new finance minister exuded good intentions. He would try to ensure payment of the *rentes*.[4] He would continue the process of verifying outstanding royal debts with a view to 'settlement', promised to pay the financiers current interest at 5.55 per cent backdated to 1 January 1650, and set up an annual fund of 3 million *livres* for the purpose.[5] The difficulty was in putting these good intentions into effect. There were no revenues to assign over to the financiers: instead, the rents of the revenue farms for 1652 had to be promised.[6] Yet the administration of the three most important revenue farms was in chaos, and the farmers were trying to abandon their leases.[7] Meanwhile, the government lived from hand to mouth, levying forced loans on the leading citizens of Paris[8] and issuing vast sums of coin as a fiscal expedient, particularly in 1651. By May 1651 there was even talk of levying 10 million *livres* by a *chambre de justice* as the 'seul moyen extraordinaire qui reste au Roy'.[9]

If the government's military position remained strong, its

---

[1] A.A.E. France 871, fo. 68. 'Considérations sur la surintendance de M. de Maisons', May 1650.

[2] A.A.E. France 871, fos. 151^v.–152^r., 207^v., 23 June and 15 July 1650.

[3] A.A.E. France 872, fo. 302, 5 Nov. 1650.

[4] *Arrêts du conseil du roi*, ed. Le Pesant, no. 1179.

[5] Ibid., no. 1211. E 243a, fos. 210, 232, 13, and 15 July 1650.

[6] E 243b, fos. 115, 118, 5 Aug. 1650.

[7] The farmers of the *gabelles de France* had tried to give up their lease on 27 Oct. 1649; those holding the *cinq grosses fermes* wanted to give up their lease on 1 Oct. 1650: E 244a, fo. 81. The farmers of the *aides* had to be forced into continuing their lease on 8 July 1651: E 248a, fo. 100. Some of the smaller farms presented equally severe problems. There was a public outcry at the lowering of the rent on the *entrées* of Paris: A.A.E. France 876, fo. 73, 8 July 1651.

[8] A.A.E. France 871, fo. 421, 29 Aug. 1650. A.A.E. France 875, fo. 110, 28 May 1651.

[9] A.A.E. France 875, fo. 110, 28 May 1651.

finances were weak, and Mazarin's unpopularity had been further increased by the arrest of the princes: his position was vulnerable to a sudden shift in alliances or volte-face by former supporters. In the summer of 1650, Mazarin had already run into difficulties with the clergy, which normally supported him, because of the arrest of Conty who was an ecclesiastic. In the autumn, Mazarin gradually lost the support of Gaston d'Orléans, who blamed the Cardinal for the failure of peace negotiations with Spain and for the deterioration of his relations with the Regent. He determined that the king's council should be reorganized on Mazarin's downfall. On 30 December, the *Parlement* of Paris, too, demanded the release of the princes and it was clear that it would not be long before this request had to be conceded. Two other events forced Mazarin's hand. The so-called 'union of the two Frondes' of 30 January 1651, an agreement between Condé's supporters and certain *Frondeur* nobles of 1649, was formed, and pledged to work towards the release of the princes. Gaston's position was strengthened, both by this alliance and by the presence in the capital of a considerable number of lesser nobles—at first 200 or so, but later 800—who flocked there on behalf of the princes and held a special assembly of their own with Gaston's permission. The assembly began on 6 February, and Mazarin withdrew from Paris on the same evening. The following day, the *Parlement* requested the exclusion of Cardinals from the king's council. On 10 February Gaston and the Regent agreed on terms for the release of the princes: but in the event Mazarin went to Le Havre and released the princes after securing meaningless verbal assurances. Condé thus found himself free on 13 February and in a stronger position than before —'l'épée au côté' as Mademoiselle de Montpensier put it.[1] Mazarin rapidly appreciated the gravity of his mistake, and, fearing arrest and prosecution, went into exile. He eventually established himself at Brühl in the archbishopric of Cologne, where he remained until the end of the year.

Condé, Conty, and Longueville were left to fight for political supremacy against two groups—Gaston and his supporters and the clients of Mazarin. The first task was to get rid of the assembly of lesser nobles, which could only be achieved by a promise from

---

[1] *Mémoires de Mademoiselle de Montpensier . . .*, ed. J. F. Michaud and J. J. F. Poujoulat, 3rd ser. iv (1838), p. 79.

the princes,[1] backed by the Regent, that a meeting of the Estates-General would be held on 8 September 1651, the day after the declaration of Louis XIV's majority. The date was chosen deliberately, so that there could be no discussion at the Estates-General of postponing the king's majority and establishing a regency council dominated by the magnates.[2] Nevertheless, the proposed meeting carried considerable risks for the government. During the summer there were election disputes in various parts of the kingdom as the rival factions competed for influence.[3] There was a serious possibility that the Estates-General, if it met, would criticize the conduct of financial administration,[4] and perhaps the failure to secure peace with Spain too. For their part, the princes sent Foucquet de Croissy, one of Condé's clients and a signatory of the so-called 'union of the two Frondes', to Stenay to negotiate with a representative of the archduke Leopold William. The negotiations broke down on 27 April 1651, however. This in turn led to Turenne's breaking his treaty with Spain and his return to France.

Within the government, the first trial of strength between the factions came on 3 April, when Condé imposed Molé as Keeper of the Seals, only to have his decision reversed ten days later when Molé was dismissed at Gaston's insistence. Other changes had been proposed, including the dismissal of Servien, Lionne, and Le Tellier, who were regarded as clients of Mazarin, the bringing into office of Molé's son Champlâtreux, and Longueil's removal from the *surintendance*.[5] Nevertheless, the changes when they came did not amount to much, the Regent was probably left in a stronger position,[6] and certainly she still remained under the influence of Mazarin who continued to send her coded dispatches from his place of exile. At the end of April there was a new threat to Longueil's position when a group of financiers led by Jean Doublet presented fundamental criticisms of his policy, which were debated by the council of state under Gaston's presidency.

---

[1] From Gaston, Condé and Conty: A.A.E. France 874, fo. 184, 24 Mar. 1651. The promise was of great importance as a legal pretext for assemblies of the lesser nobles in the 1650s.
[2] Le Tellier thought that this would be proposed: A.A.E. France 874, fo. 286ᵛ., 21 Apr. 1651.
[3] A.A.E. France 875, fo. 132, 2 June 1651. Several cases of election disputes came before the council of state.
[4] A.A.E. France 875, fo. 110ᵛ., 28 May 1651.
[5] A.A.E. France 874, fos. 240, 243, 263ᵛ., 13, 14 and 15 Apr. 1651.
[6] A.A.E. France 874, fo. 286, 21 Apr. 1651.

Doublet and his supporters declared their willingness to lend the king 4.5 million *livres* during the next four months but on one condition: the dismissal of Longueil and the appointment of La Vieuville, 'le seul capable de restaurer les finances'.[1]

After much haggling over details, there was general agreement in the council of state that direct taxes were being levied in the *pays d'élections* at 40 million a year, but that the net payment to the crown was only 23 million.[2] The interest payment to the existing financiers was thus 17 million a year (42.5 per cent). This colossal interest charge was explained by two factors. Much of the revenue from the direct taxes became payable to the Treasury in 16 or 18 monthly instalments beginning in June 1651. The result was that a substantial proportion of the money was consumed in interest payments to financiers who anticipated revenues which would normally have become payable in 1652. A second problem was the payment of troops during the winter quarter in 1650–1. The *subsistances* to the troops had been estimated at 7 or 8 million *livres*, but had actually cost 24 million. These payments to the army levied locally where troops were billeted rendered difficult the subsequent levy of the direct taxes. There were other criticisms of the revenue-raising system. Doublet and his supporters argued that the revenue farms should be leased out to new consortia which would lead to an increase in rents of at least 3 million a year to 14 or 15 million *livres*.[3] There was general agreement that a review should be undertaken of revenues assigned over the previous three years. Doublet maintained that assignments to the value of 34 million had been 'extorquées par la nécessité du temps' and should be revoked. Longueil retorted that this was tantamount to a new declaration of bankruptcy. The king's household expenses, for which the *trésoriers de l'Épargne* had advanced over 11 million between 1647 and 1651, could not be paid if the *assignations* were

---

[1] A.A.E. France 875, fos. 15ᵛ.–16ʳ., 115–16, 6 May and n.d., 1651. The financiers did not request La Vieuville's appointment in their meetings with the council on 27 and 30 Apr., but may well have done so in a private meeting with the Regent on 1 May. The printed *factum* which reports these meetings is of great interest: B.N. MS. fr. 16626, fos. 165–78. The Regent, Gaston, Condé, Séguier, Villeroy, Bailleul, Servien, Chavigny, Longueil, and the four secretaries of state were present at the first council meeting. The second meeting was before a smaller group comprising Gaston, Condé, Longueville, Séguier, Schomberg, Chavigny, and Longueil.

[2] Mallet's figure for the yield from the *pays d'élections* in 1651 was 23.7 million: Appendix Two, Table IV.

[3] Mallet's figure for the yield from the revenue farms was just under 10.2 million: Appendix Two, Table IV.

revoked.[1] Neither the Swiss guards nor the *rentes* could be paid if this policy were adopted, and in the view of the finance minister if the *rentes* went unpaid there would be rioting in Paris. Longueil also contended that a new declaration of bankruptcy would prevent the crown from borrowing on the money market since 'personne ne voudroit plus . . . rien prester'.

The meetings of Doublet's group of financiers with the council of state on 27 and 30 April 1651 are of great importance. They demonstrate a concerted, though ultimately unsuccessful, attempt of one group of financiers to oust a *surintendant* by offering to lend the crown money and increase the yield from the direct and indirect taxes. The financiers were well informed, because much to Longueil's chagrin they had undertaken 'une exacte et diligente recherche de tous les revenus et de toutes les dépenses du royaume'. Some of their proposals were of great significance, such as the argument that the disorders of the troops in the provinces could be contained if they were billeted on the towns and paid 16 or 17 million in *subsistances*, double the official rate during the winter quarter of 1650–1. Above all, the meetings show that the financiers did not all have common interests. The crown had the whip-hand in the relationship. It could divide and rule, offering different treatment to various groups of financiers, who competed against each other more assiduously than they united against the monarchy. Doublet and his group represented creditors of the French crown who had not been paid current interest on outstanding debts from the bankruptcy of 1648. They had undertaken their review of financial policy to demonstrate that there was sufficient public revenue in France to meet all expenses and leave a fund of 5 or 6 million a year to pay current interest on their debt until they were fully reimbursed after a peace treaty had been signed with Spain. Their great grievance was that they had not been treated fairly since the crown had made substantial interest payments to a preferred group of revenue farmers and *receveurs-généraux des finances* whose continued service the government had regarded as essential after 1648. Doublet and his supporters were in a weaker negotiating position, since they represented financiers who had 'point de maniement',[2] that is to say, did not directly handle royal revenues as did the *receveurs généraux des finances* and

---

[1] Cf. B.N. Morel de Thoisy 156, fo. 77. Loans for the *maisons royales* were *liquidés* by the council on 9 Dec. 1651 at 11,198,996 *livres*. Eventually the *assignations* to the *trésoriers de l'Épargne* were delayed until 1652–9.

[2] A.A.E. France 875, fo. 115, n.d. (May 1651).

revenue farmers. They had thus not received new assignments to replace the loan contracts revoked in 1648.

This debate at the end of April 1651 fully revealed the gravity of the financial position of the crown. All the revenues of 1651 had been assigned, as had most of those of 1652 and part of those for 1653. There was general agreement on the need for a review of royal policy,[1] even if Doublet's proposals were unacceptable to the council of state. The king's revenues had been over-assigned: in some cases, two or three financiers held treasury bills which authorized reimbursement against the same revenue. Such over-assignment detracted from the value of the treasury bill as a royal security. As Doublet said, 'les billets de l'Épargne . . . sont si fort décréditez que personne n'ose plus s'y asseurer . . .'[2] The underlying reason for this vast over-assignment was the bankruptcy of 1648. After the revocation of the loan contracts, the *assignations* to the value of between 80 and 120 million which had previously acted as the security to the financiers were not destroyed. Successive finance ministers reissued them, and these *assignations* were transferred from one accounting year to the next during the Fronde. This explains Mallet's high income figures for the *deniers extraordinaires* at a time when it was very difficult for the government to secure new loans or tax contracts. Indeed, according to Mallet, the *deniers extraordinaires* represented 63 per cent of total revenues between 1650 and 1654.[3]

The difficulties of the finance minister had been made much worse by the declaration of the *Chambre des Comptes* on 27 November 1648 imposing a limit of three million *livres* per annum on the secret expenses (*comptants*). Such legislation was not binding on the government, but as with so many of the decrees of the sovereign courts issued in 1648–9, political weakness forced the ministers to adopt a conciliatory standpoint: on 22 December 1648, a royal declaration was issued which appeared to accept the

---

[1] Chancellor Séguier commented that there was 'un règlement à faire, mais qu'il estoit périlleux de rien innover avant que d'estre asseuré des moyens de faire subsister l'estat': B.N. MS. fr. 16626, fo. 173ᵛ.

[2] B.N. MS. fr. 16626, fo. 175ᵛ.

[3] Appendix Two, Tables IV and V B. Mazarin's comment to Chanut on the bankruptcy of 1648 is worth recalling. The king, he said, 'a reculé leurs assignations et leur remboursement . . . on avoit mangé toute l'année courante et les deux suivantes et on a trouvé moyen de les remanger une seconde fois, Sa Majesté rentrant dans tous ses revenus et ne donnant à ceux à qui elle doit que l'intérest de leur argent à six pour cent': *Lettres du Cardinal Mazarin*, ed. Chéruel and d'Avenel, iii. 159–60.

restriction imposed by the *Comptes*.[1] The totals of the *acquits de comptants* presented to the *Chambre des Comptes* for registration in the years 1649–52 show that the government tried to implement its pledge. With the exception of the year 1651, the average was below three million a year. Even with the high figure for 1651 included, the average was less than 5.25 million, an enormous reduction on the annual average of over 39 million in the years 1645–9.[2] On the other hand, all the finance ministers from La Meilleraye in 1648 to La Vieuville in 1652 recognized that in a period of civil and foreign war 'les dépenses secrettes devoient nécessairement excéder les trois millions'. Their solution to the problem was similar to their approach to the assignment of revenues. The *comptants* serving as interest payments to the financiers on loan contracts revoked in 1648 had already been presented in the form of *acquits* to the *Chambre des Comptes* for registration. These money orders were not destroyed after the revocation of the loan contracts in July 1648. Instead, they were reissued to financiers as interest payments on new loans or to cover other types of secret expenditure. This procedure explains the discrepancy between the official figures of the *comptants* and Mallet's totals, which were much higher, although it should be noted that Mallet's figures almost certainly reflect the fact that such expenditure was carried over from one accounting year to the next.[3]

It thus becomes apparent that, chiefly for political reasons (the desire to avoid the consequences of the bankruptcy of 1648 and the limitation on secret expenditure), the totals of expenditure and income were greatly inflated during the Fronde.[4] However, it was not because of any ability to resolve such problems, or any great financial expertise, that Longueil retained his position in the months from May 1651, but because of secret promises to pay

[1] Dent, *Crisis in finance*, p. 100. Moote, *The revolt of the judges*, pp. 166, 181. The hostility of the *Comptes* was made apparent by a speech of the *premier président* as early as 3 Aug. 1648: *Chambre des Comptes*, ed. Boislisle, pp. 426–7.

[2] Appendix Two, Table III. There is an error in the figures in Bonney, 'The secret expenses of Richelieu and Mazarin', 829. The quinquennial total for 1645–9 should read 196,363,614 *livres* and the average per annum 39,272,723 *livres*.

[3] Appendix Two, Table II. Jeannin de Castille, the *trésorier de l'Épargne* who held the fund both in 1648 and 1652, noted hat the finance minister simply reissued the *comptants* with the note 'cette ordonnance vaudra pour telle ou telle somme'. He also commented that 'on les fit passer de [16]48 en [16]51 et de [16]51 en [16]52': B.N. Morel de Thoisy 156, fos. 505ʳ–ᵛ, 518ᵛ. *Défenses* of Jeannin, *c.* 1662.

[4] The carrying over of important items both of expenditure and income from one accounting year to the next make it virtually impossible to calculate a precise annual deficit. This appears to be a compelling argument against the method adopted by Guéry, 'Les finances de la monarchie française', 236.

Mazarin interest on his debts, promises which do not seem to have been fulfilled.[1] This was of vital importance to the Cardinal, who was effectively bankrupt. Once he had left for exile at Brühl, the income from his benefices had been stopped, and the *syndicat* of his creditors had obtained the backing of Broussel and the *Parlement* of Paris. It would need all the industry of Colbert, Mazarin's recently appointed *intendant de la maison*, the appointment of a finance minister who was more favourably disposed towards the Cardinal, and Mazarin's return from exile, to sort out the chief minister's personal affairs. From the end of July 1651, Mazarin wanted the appointment of La Vieuville as finance minister and the dismissal of Longueil. La Vieuville had secretly promised to pay off the government's debts to Mazarin and in the meantime had made a personal gift (*pot de vin*) of 400,000 *livres*.[2] From this moment, Longueil's position was precarious because of Mazarin's continuing influence over the Regent from his place of exile. From May 1651, Doublet's group of financiers wanted La Vieuville as the man to restore financial confidence and settle the royal debts outstanding from the bankruptcy of 1648. The coincidence of interests became complete when, as the financiers recalled, Mazarin wrote to La Vieuville advocating the repayment of principal to *all* financiers ('véritables créanciers du roy') or at least current interest on outstanding royal debts.[3] The dismissal of Longueil was probably delayed until September 1651 for two reasons. There was little point in bringing in a new finance minister before the autumn, when it was hoped that new revenues would begin to flow into the Treasury.[4] It was also the case that the formal end of the Regency and the declaration of Louis XIV's majority on 7 September 1651 would provide the opportunity for more general ministerial changes.

Until the declaration of the king's majority it was difficult to co-ordinate action against Condé. The first prince of the blood saw conspiracies for his arrest everywhere and was convinced of the need to break once and for all the secret influence over the Regent exercised by Mazarin from Brühl. On 6 July, Condé left

---

[1] A.A.E. France 875, fo. 109ᵛ., 28 May 1651: 'le duc d'Orléans a dit qu'il s'estoit bien remis dans l'esprit de la Reyne, fournissant de l'argent pour M. le Cardal'. Longueil could not have satisfied all Mazarin's requirements, however, or the Cardinal would not have turned to La Vieuville. It was said that Longueil 'ne fait rien pour vous (i.e. Mazarin) que par force . . .': A.A.E. France 876, fo. 182, 28 July 1651.

[2] A.A.E. France 876, fo. 182, 28 July 1651.

[3] A.A.E. France 890, fo. 240, *c.* Feb. 1653.

[4] A.A.E. France 876, fo. 185ᵛ., 29 July 1651.

the capital and went to Saint-Maur, where he was joined in what looked like, but never became, a full-scale rebellion by Conty, Madame de Longueville, Bouillon, Turenne, and La Rochefoucauld. A letter was sent by the princes to the *Parlement* of Paris, denouncing Mazarin's secret influence and the power exercised by his clients in office, and warning of the need to prevent his return from exile.[1] Later in the month, Condé obtained his principal demand—the dismissal of Servien, Lionne, and Le Tellier in a ministerial reshuffle unprecedented since 1616–17. The break between Condé and the Regent remained permanent, however, despite this concession. Anne of Austria never forgave Condé for his recourse to violence. In the *Parlement* of Paris, Molé, the *premier président* who was shortly to be appointed Keeper of the Seals, denounced his actions and recalled the examples of other princes of the blood including princes of Condé who had started civil wars.[2] Nevertheless, Condé's appeals to the *Parlement* played on its fear of Mazarin's restoration and the office-holders' dissatisfaction with the Cardinal's continuing influence on the Regent. On 6 September 1651, the day after Louis XIV attained his thirteenth birthday, the Regent was forced to issue a declaration sanctioning Mazarin's exile, although it was drafted in fairly bland terms. Once Mazarin returned to France he had it explained officially that the measure had been conceded by the Regent to prevent any attempt to postpone the declaration of the king's majority which occurred on 7 September.

The opposition had now shot its bolt. On 8 September, the day after the formal end of the Regency and the declaration of Louis XIV's majority—when, under constitutional theory, the king had entered his *plenitudo potestatis*—the long heralded ministerial changes were announced: La Vieuville was appointed finance minister[3] and Molé Keeper of the Seals. Although still in exile, Mazarin had to a considerable extent established a council of his choosing,[4] outside the control of the princes. It would not be long before first Servien and Lionne and later Le Tellier[5] would be recalled. The deputies who had met at Tours to participate in the

---

[1] A.A.E. France 876, fos. 2, 70, 6 and 8 July 1651.

[2] Talon, *Mémoires*, ed. Michaud and Poujoulat, p. 434. A.A.E. France 876, fos. 56, 72ᵛ., 8 July 1651.

[3] Appendix One, Table I.

[4] Not entirely of his choosing, because of the presence of Châteauneuf as interim head of the council: Moote, *The revolt of the judges*, p. 318.

[5] Le Tellier's recall was delayed by La Vieuville, who accused him of preventing his appointment as finance minister in 1650: *Lettres . . . de Colbert*, ed. Clément, i. 156.

Estates-General were told unceremoniously to return home with little real likelihood of a meeting at a later date. Condé's worst fears had come to pass, but he had already left the capital for Guyenne and rebellion. Gaston took less resolute action, but withheld his support from the new government.[1] Once the court left Paris in mid-October, first for Bourges, later for Poitiers, so as to be able to conduct the campaign against Condé more effectively, Gaston was left in virtual control of the capital—control which was left unchallenged after the departure of La Vieuville and Molé for Poitiers at the end of December.[2]

Only two previous finance ministers in the seventeenth century (Jeannin and d'Hémery) had regained office after demotion or dismissal. None had done so after a period of twenty-seven years, which prompts the question why Mazarin, apart from the *pot de vin*, saw in La Vieuville the qualities necessary to help restore the fortunes of the monarchy in a period of renewed civil war. There is little doubt that an extraordinary change in public attitudes towards La Vieuville had taken place since his arrest in 1624. He was now considered to have exercised the *surintendance* with integrity,[3] and his reputation was enhanced by his persecution during Richelieu's ministry, the amnesty of 1643, the restoration of his property and the payment of interest on lost revenues during his period of exile abroad.[4] It was also true that the range of talent available to fill the post of finance minister in seventeenth-century France was never very great. La Vieuville was at least a known quantity who commanded a certain degree of support from the financiers, even though he had failed in each attempt to gain reappointment between 1648 and 1651. From Mazarin's point of view, however, the political factors probably outweighed other considerations. In 1643, La Vieuville had been restored to the position of lieutenant-general in Champagne,[5] and had remained loyal to the Regent and her chief minister throughout the Fronde. (Indeed, he was created a duke and peer in December 1651 largely as a reward for his loyalty.)[6] The continued support of the

---

[1] A.A.E. France 876, fo. 391, 8 Sept. 1651.

[2] Moote, op. cit., pp. 326–7. A.A.E. France 877, fo. 475, 23 Dec. 1651.

[3] Talon, *Mémoires*, ed. Michaud and Poujoulat, p. 248.

[4] *Arrêts du conseil du roi*, ed. Le Pesant, no. 343. La Vieuville had creditors at the beginning of the Regency: E 182b, fo. 445, 29 Aug. 1643.

[5] Cf. E 185b, fo. 389, 23 Dec. 1643. A.A.E. France 860, fo. 79, 18 May 1648.

[6] Bonney, 'Cardinal Mazarin and the great nobility during the Fronde'. Anselme, *Histoire généalogique et chronologique de la maison royale . . .*, v. 867–70. The *brevet* was issued at Poitiers on 26 Dec. 1651, four days after La Vieuville left Paris to follow the court, rather than remain in the capital which was dominated by Gaston and supporters of the princes

lieutenant-general of Champagne was worth having during the rebellion of Conty, its governor. La Vieuville owed his return to public life, and now high office, entirely to Anne of Austria and Mazarin, from whom he had gained more in eight years than he had from the eighteen years of Richelieu's ministry. As Brienne told Mazarin, he was a 'surintendant des finances disposé de vous servir et de faire justice . . .'[1]

La Vieuville would not be likely to forget where his first loyalties lay in a period of civil war, especially since the princes of the blood and their supporters were determined to secure his dismissal—implicitly from the time of his secret appointment and openly from the signing of the treaty between Gaston and Condé on 24 January 1652.[2] La Vieuville was inevitably committed to the return of Mazarin, his protector, from exile and to financial measures that would enable the crown to defeat Condé's rebellion. Among the earliest of his decisions was the suspension of all previously assigned payments on 15 September,[3] thus freeing the few revenues that remained to the crown. At the end of September, the momentous decision was taken to anticipate one-third of the revenues of the *taille* for 1652—13.3 million *livres* out of a total of 40 million—to pay for the military campaign against Condé during the winter and early spring.[4] The crown now had some hope of pursuing the struggle successfully, especially since further revenues were freed on 7 October by La Vieuville's decision to suspend all payments of *gages* and *rentes* except those at Paris,[5] where a breakdown of public order would have followed such a decision. The stage was now set for Mazarin's return. The chief minister, who had been mortified by the royal declaration of 6 September 1651 endorsing his first exile, naturally had been

---

(cf. A.A.E. France 877, fo. 475, 23 Dec. 1651). Anselme included La Vieuville's letters patent among 'duchez non enregistrez' by the sovereign courts. Cf. Labatut, *Les duc et pairs de France*, pp. 77 (where the elevation is misdated 1650, before he was reappointed finance minister) and pp. 95–6 (where it is correctly dated). La Vieuville was attacked by the mob at Reims in the spring of 1649 because of his loyalty to Mazarin: *Mémoires . . . de Montglat*, ed. Michaud and Poujoulat, p. 211.

[1] A.A.E. France 876, fo. 395ᵛ., 8 Sept. 1651. The *acte de justice* was presumably to pay Mazarin interest on his loans.

[2] On 19 Nov. 1651 there were 'billets imprimés jetés par la rue' in Paris which demanded 'un autre surintendant . . . qui soit hors du mazarinisme': *Journal des guerres civiles de Dubuisson-Aubenay*, ed. Saige, ii. 130. The princes emphasized La Vieuville's having bought his position with 'une notable somme d'argent': A.A.E. France 881, fo. 137ᵛ., 24 Jan. 1652.

[3] *Arrêts du conseil du roi*, ed. Le Pesant, no. 1500.

[4] Ibid., nos. 1523, 1528. E 249a, fo. 5, 30 Sept. 1651.

[5] E 249a, fo. 124, 7 Oct. 1651.

awaiting the opportunity with impatience. It has been argued that he deliberately provoked Condé into rebellion in the autumn of 1651;[1] at any rate there were certainly advantages in a new civil war since this justified his return for military reasons. Condé's prestige in the army was high, his patronage connections were enormous, and his talents as a commander were second to none but Turenne (whose attitude at this time was equivocal). The dangers of a military takeover by Condé must have seemed very real, especially after 6 November 1651 when he had negotiated military and financial support from Spain on similar terms to those agreed in 1650 and proposed in 1649. Mazarin—presumably with the proceeds from La Vieuville's *pot de vin*—hired at his own expense a force of between 5000 and 6000 German mercenaries, mostly from the elector of Brandenburg, and marched across France at the end of the year, reaching the court at Poitiers on 28 January 1652. He had to be discouraged from marching straight at the army of the princes. However useful his additional forces, Mazarin's presence was needed less as a general than as chief minister: 'c'est par ce caractère', it was said, 'qu'on donne la loy aux généraux d'armées . . .'[2] Without the chief minister to impose a co-ordinated strategy and clear command structure on the generals, and to lure Turenne from neutrality to the acceptance of overall command,[3] it would have been difficult to mount an effective campaign against the princes.

Mazarin's return acted as a focus of discontent, and on 29 December 1651, in 'the most partisan and intemperate *arrêt* of the entire Fronde',[4] the *Parlement* of Paris declared the chief minister guilty of *lèse-majesté* and placed a price of 150,000 *livres* on his head, which was to be paid from the sale of his confiscated library. Gaston now openly declared his hand, and arguing that the king was not of age to rule personally and that in effect he was held in captivity by Mazarin[5]—a convenient if inaccurate rationalization of the situation at Poitiers—accepted the alliance offered by

---

[1] Kossmann, *La Fronde*, p. 210. Cf. Moote, op. cit., p. 321.

[2] A.A.E. France 877, fo. 379, 9 Dec. 1651.

[3] The central issue dividing Mazarin from Turenne was compensation to Bouillon, his elder brother, for the expropriation of Sedan in 1642. A settlement required amending laws passed by Louis XIII, and could not be undertaken until the proclamation of Louis XIV's majority. For a more detailed examination of this question: Bonney, 'Cardinal Mazarin and the great nobility during the Fronde'.

[4] Moote, op. cit., p. 329.

[5] 'Un journal inédit du Parlement de Paris pendant la Fronde (1 déc. 1651–12 avril 1652', ed. H. Courteault, *Annuaire-Bulletin de la Société de l'Histoire de France*, no vol. [année 1916] (1917), 228.

Condé. Their agreement on 24 January envisaged the continuation of the armed struggle until Mazarin was exiled permanently from France, a meeting of the Estates-General had been held and peace negotiations with Spain had been opened; among its other provisions were the full implementation of the declaration of 22 October 1648 and the dismissal of La Vieuville.[1] Perhaps the princes overestimated the support they could hope to receive for this programme. Their commitment to a meeting of the Estates-General was a mistake since it tended to alienate the *parlementaires* of Paris, who in any case would find it difficult to take to arms against a king they so recently had declared to be of age to rule. There were considerable differences between the crisis of 1649, when the future of the Parisian sovereign courts had appeared to be threatened, and that of 1652 when it did not. When the princes sought the voluntary support of the *Parlement*, in January 1652, the alliance was rejected—despite the unpopularity of the decree of the council of state on 8 January, by which La Vieuville had diverted all assigned payments for 1652, including payment of the Parisian *rentes* and *gages*.[2] Mazarin appreciated the political danger of withholding the Parisian *rentes* at such a time, and ordered La Vieuville to withdraw the measure.[3]

The changes in royal policy left the *Parlement* confused. On 13 March, it decided to summon a new meeting of the *Chambre Saint-Louis* with the objective of setting up a permanent fund for the payment of the crown's contractual obligations that was independent of royal control[4]—in effect a return to the *conseil de bon ordre* proposed in 1596. Yet nothing came of the idea, and the *Parlement* turned its attention to criticism of Mazarin in the remonstrances of 23 March.[5] The remonstrances contained a wide-ranging indictment of Mazarin's conduct of government and asserted that there could be no permanent solution to the Fronde without his dismissal and prosecution on charges of peculation. It was claimed that Mazarin had diverted payment of the *rentes* and created a personal fortune on the back of the French tax-payer. He had become reliant on the financiers, 'ses

---

[1] A.A.E. France 881, fo. 136, 24 Jan. 1652.

[2] *Arrêts du conseil du roi*, ed. Le Pesant, no. 1593.

[3] Ibid., nos. 1642, 1671. A.A.E. France 887, fo. 23, 18 Jan. 1652.

[4] 'Un journal inédit . . .', ed. Courteault, pp. 261, 289–90. A.A.E. France 882, fo. 46, 13 Mar. 1652.

[5] R. J. Bonney, 'Cardinal Mazarin and his critics: the remonstrances of 1652', *Journal of European Studies*, x, (1980), 15–31. Dubuisson-Aubenay reported allegations in Feb. 1649 that Mazarin had pillaged funds sent both to Italy and Germany for the war effort in the 1640s: *Journal des guerres civiles de Dubuisson-Aubenay*, ed. Saige, i. 171.

tributaires', who charged excessively high rates of interest for their services, and who made such gains during his ministry that they were 'les plus ardentz solliciteurs du retour de leur protecteur'. Mazarin, it was claimed, was guilty of peculation on an enormous scale, and there was a pressing need to examine the accounts of Thomas Cantarini who had handled some 36 million *livres* destined to pay for the war in Italy. As a summary of accusations against Mazarin the remonstrances of 23 March 1652 were extremely significant, but their practical impact was small. It seems doubtful whether the charge of peculation could ever have been proven against the chief minister, because it would have been very difficult to elucidate charges in the financial chaos of the Fronde.[1] Besides, while Mazarin continued to enjoy royal favour he had nothing to fear from a financial inquiry—ultimately all monies which he had received could be said to have been voluntary gifts from the king to his most loyal servant.

In the last resort, the war of words mattered less than the actual fighting, and despite their assistance from Spain and Lorraine, the army of the princes suffered a series of setbacks, notably at the faubourg Saint Antoine, the gates of the capital, on 2 July. The princes found it increasingly difficult to levy their war taxes and feared the collapse of support within the capital. On 4 July, their supporters organized a show of strength, the so-called 'massacre' at the *hôtel de ville*, which was followed by the establishment of a puppet municipal government, with Broussel as mayor. On 20 July, the *Parlement* of Paris was coerced into joining a military alliance with the princes, whose chief aim now was to release Louis XIV from the captivity in which he was allegedly held by Mazarin. These actions were essentially counter-productive. It was doubtful whether many feared Mazarin's continuation in office more than dictatorship of the princes; indeed, royalist propaganda suggested that fifty years of Mazarin as chief minister

---

[1] The preliminary trial papers are in B.N. MS. fr. 6888. The evidence was circumstantial, the charges not fully thought out. (Mazarin was accused of 'la déprédation . . . sur les vaisseaux estrangers, dissipation des finances, transport des deniers hors le royaulme, empeschement à la paix et mauvaises impressions par luy données au Roy'.) There was a third-hand accusation that Mazarin had received a pension from abroad to encourage him to continue war against Spain (fo. 255ᵛ). There was also a claim by one of Cantarini's associates (fo. 257) that Mazarin had used an agent to draw between 30 and 40 million *livres* from the secret expenses (*comptants*). It is interesting to note that Foucquet claimed at his trial over a decade later that Mazarin had indeed sent money abroad, though presumably he was referring to the years after the Fronde: 144 a.p. 66, Dr. 1, fo. 5 [156 mi. 15]. Foucquet criticized 'un estranger seul [qui] met des millions à couvert dedans et dehors le Royaume abusant de son autorité absolue . . .'

could do less harm than four more days of civil war.[1] Moreover, the government now felt free to play on the fears of specific interest groups by selected retaliatory measures: the funds for the payment of Parisian *rentes* and *gages* were diverted once again on 23 July,[2] and a rival *Parlement* was established at Pontoise eight days later. The continued absence of the court from Paris was also taking its toll, for on this depended 'l'abondance dans la ville, le commerce chez les gens de négoce et le repos dans les familles'.[3] A winter blockade, reviving memories of 1649, was unacceptable. After careful preparation and secret assistance from the government, facilitated by Mazarin's self-imposed second exile, a royalist *coup* occurred in Paris on 14 October. Condé had already left the capital earlier in the month to secure his control in north-east France. Gaston, always the weak link in the alliance of the princes, announced his intention of retiring to his estate at Limoux on 21 October,[4] and the court returned to Paris the same day.

At the *lit de justice* of 22 October, the *Parlements* of Paris and Pontoise were united, and a royal declaration imposed which, among other provisions, prohibited the *Parlement* from interfering in affairs of state, in financial questions, and in the work of the ministers of the crown. Previous interventions in such matters were annulled retrospectively. In the short term, the action was taken to protect the jurisdiction of the *Chambre des Comptes* and *Cour des Aides* of Paris[5] quite as much as to assist Mazarin and La Vieuville. In the longer term, the financial sovereign courts had always been more amenable to royal control than the *Parlement*. Mazarin, meanwhile, was able to concentrate his forces on chasing the Spanish beyond the French border and reducing Condé, the most dangerous of his opponents, to the status of a Spanish generalissimo. Time worked on Mazarin's side, as did the resumption of payment of the Parisian *rentes* and *gages* (they had never been stopped for those who had followed the government from the capital to Pontoise).[6] After a respectable absence from the capital, Mazarin's return to Paris could be orchestrated by the

[1] University of London, Add. MSS. 247, fo. 7.
[2] *Arrêts du conseil du roi*, ed. Le Pesant, nos. 1734, 1740.
[3] University of London, Add. MSS. 247, fo. 6'.
[4] He said he would leave the following day: A.A.E. France 885, fo. 244.
[5] A.A.E. France 885, fo. 226, 20 Oct. 1652.
[6] E 252b, fo. 274, 17 Aug. 1652. Claude Chatelain recalled 'le plus hardy traicté qui ayt esté faict de nos jours' in a letter to Mazarin *c.* 1659: A.A.E. France 908, fo. 160.

ministers and 'doucement insinué dans les espritz . . .'[1] Indeed, when he returned in February 1653, Mazarin was hailed ironically as the hero of the *rentiers*, an attribute which the ministers had been planning during the previous year.[2]

La Vieuville did not see Mazarin's return, for he died on 2 January 1653 after a short illness,[3] leaving a fortune of just under 2 million *livres*.[4] Whether he would have adapted as finance minister to the new conditions of civil peace is a matter of conjecture. He certainly had a clear idea of the seriousness of the financial plight of the French monarchy: in January and February 1652 he had talked darkly of the collapse of the state and warned Mazarin that the royal finances could scarcely be in a worse position.[5] Encouraged by Guillaume de Bordeaux, one of the *intendants des finances*, La Vieuville had argued the case for a new bankruptcy.[6] The unpopular decree of 8 January 1652 which suspended payment of the *rentes* and *gages* was intended, more importantly, as a means of avoiding paying current interest on outstanding royal debts which La Vieuville argued it was unrealistic to pay in a period of foreign and civil war. Just as with d'Hémery in 1649–50, La Vieuville had been recalled at the suggestion of financiers who had suffered in the royal bankruptcy of 1648, only to dash their hopes of reimbursement once he had come to power. Ironically, Mazarin suffered a similar fate. He had wanted a pliant *surintendant* to re-establish his personal fortune, but in March 1652 complained that La Vieuville was still not paying off his debts.[7] The reason is not difficult to find. La Vieuville was unable to meet current expenditure which would have saved Barcelona, Casale, Dunkirk, and Gravelines from falling into Spanish hands.[8] The budget could not be balanced without domestic expenditure cuts which were politically unacceptable. At the end of November 1652, La Vieuville warned Mazarin that there were insufficient funds to pay the *rentes* in full.[9]

[1] A.A.E. France 885, fo. 388, 1652.
[2] Martin and Bezançon, *L'histoire du crédit*, pp. 21–2, 37. Le Tellier had planned this in Jan. 1652: A.A.E. France 881, fo. 73ᵛ., 11 Jan. 1652.
[3] A.A.E. France 886, fo. 333, 28 Dec. 1652. A.A.E. France 892, fo. 36, 2 Jan. 1653.
[4] Labatut, *Les ducs et pairs de France*, p. 264.
[5] *Lettres . . . de Colbert*, ed. Clément, i. 192. A.A.E. France 881, fos. 71, 347, 11 Jan. and 22 Feb. 1652.
[6] A.A.E. France 881, fo. 30, 8 Jan. 1652.
[7] A.A.E. France 889, fo. 161, 15 Mar. 1652.
[8] A.A.E. France 891, fo. 73, anon. memorandum (1653).
[9] A.A.E. France 886, fo. 107, 30 Nov. 1652. Shortly after Mazarin's return to Paris (3 Feb. 1653) an order was issued cutting payment of the *rentes* on the *taille* by half: P 2373, pp. 895–914, 8 Feb. 1653.

All the contemporary evidence demonstrates that 1652 was a crisis year for the French monarchy. For the oppressed peasant tax-payers in the Île-de-France it was the worst ordeal since the horrors of the 1590s.[1] The crisis was equally serious from the point of view of the king's finances, for without money the army of the princes could not be defeated.[2] The rival armies were forced to live off the land and to a certain extent became self-financing. The social cost was enormous: La Vieuville's successors denounced its consequences to Mazarin, talked of the king's subjects being treated as *peuples conquis*, and claimed that the royalist army in Guyenne had levied 11 million *livres* in fifteen months.[3] Such figures belie the original estimate of 13.3 million for the winter quarter of 17,000 cavalry and 35,000 infantry in 1652–3, a figure which Le Tellier had criticized as excessive.[4] They also take no account of the 'contributions' levied by the army of the princes. It may well be the case that increased amounts of currency in circulation assisted the payment of taxes. There were substantial issues of coin during the Fronde, amounting to 22.7 million *livres* in 1651, 39.4 million in 1652, and 22.7 million in 1653. The figure for 1652 was a record in the history of the French monarchy, exceeding even the large issues during the ministry of Bullion and Bouthillier.[5]

Yet if increased amounts of coin in circulation facilitated the payment of the troops in the provinces, it did not greatly assist the treasury. According to Mallet's figures, the ordinary revenues of the crown amounted to only 37 million,[6] of which the *taille* from the *pays d'élections* comprised 23.6 million (nearly 64 per cent). Royal income from the *parties casuelles* produced a derisory 2.8 million. The total payment from the revenue farms to the treasury was a mere 9.5 million.[7] Indeed, the administration of the indirect taxes was on the verge of collapse in 1652, with some of the

---

[1] Jacquart, *La crise rurale en Île-de-France*, pp. 660–76.

[2] Graphically described by Jeannin de Castille in his *défenses* (B.N. Morel de Thoisy, 156 fo. 521ᵛ., c. 1662): 'qui ne se souvient des étranges et incroyables extrémitez où estoit alors toute la France, par la fureur des guerres civiles? Qui ne sçait que Paris estoit investy, le feu allumé de tous costez, toutes les sources des finances ou détournées ou taries et la disette [d'argent] si extrême . . . que les officiers de la maison du roy furent quelques jours sans pouvoir sortir de quartier, faute d'avoir de quoy leur payer leurs gages?'

[3] A.A.E. France 892, fo. 427, 29 Oct. 1653.

[4] A.A.E. France 886, fo. 361, 31 Dec. 1652.

[5] Spooner, *The international economy and monetary movements in France*, p. 339.

[6] The figure was 37,065,549 *livres*, not 34,198,059 *livres*, the figure cited by Guéry, 'Les finances de la monarchie française', 236. The discrepancy is not large for 1652, because the income from the *parties casuelles* was so derisory.

[7] Appendix Two, Table IV.

farmers having abandoned their leases and other farms leased out cheaply in order to find takers. At his trial, Foucquet cited the example of the lease of the *cinq grosses fermes* signed by Cardinal Mazarin. The consortium of revenue farmers, comprising François Jacquier, Claude Boylesve and Claude Gruyn, undoubtedly exploited their opportunity and made substantial profits. A comparison between the rents payable by the revenue farmers in 1660 (4.4 million) and the amount demanded eight years earlier (1.9 million) would suggest that Mazarin's conduct was one of criminal negligence until the circumstances surrounding the negotiations are recalled. On 13 May 1652, the government had had to resort to direct administration (*régie*) of the *cinq grosses fermes* in view of the abandonment (*délaissement*) of the revenue farm by the previous consortium. The government was lucky to find any takers at all, although it did ensure that the rent would be increased to 2.3 million a year once the civil disturbances had ceased and 2.5 million once peace was signed with Spain. It also secured a loan from the new consortium anticipating the rents of the revenue farm by nearly 1.4 million.[1]

The loan anticipating rents of the *cinq grosses fermes* illustrates perhaps the most important reason why the crown survived the financial crisis of 1652: expectation among the public at large, and among the financiers in particular, that the conflict would result ultimately in a royalist victory. It is an open question whether Mazarin's opponents could have formed a credible and enduring government. There were fundamental obstacles to the operation of a successful government dominated by the upper nobility, quite apart from short-term factors in 1652, such as the failure of noble leadership, faltering assistance to the rebels from Spain, loss of support among the office-holders, and war-weariness among the population at large. In April 1652, the resistance of the capital to Mazarin could be compared to other glorious moments in the past, such as 1588 and 1597, when the municipality of Paris had joined in the demands for financial reform.[2] After the 'massacre' at the *hôtel de ville* on 4 July, few believed that the nobles could

---

[1] Foucquet, *Défenses*, v. 291–2; vi. 92; vii. 264. Cf. E 251b, fos. 12, 386, 1 and 26 June 1652. P 2373, pp. 1101–1110, 18 June 1653. The payments of the revenue farmers were later increased to 2.4 million: Appendix Two, Table VI. The idea of the variable rent was also adopted for the farm of the *aides* in 1653. Both the *aides* and the *gabelles de France* were effectively under *régie* in the summer and autumn of 1652: E 252a, fo. 88, 13 July 1652. E 252b, fo. 176, 14 Aug. 1652. E 252c, fo. 132, 11 Sept. 1652. E 253c, fo. 557, 30 Dec. 1652. E 254b, fos. 326, 398, 27 and 29 Jan. 1653.

[2] *Journal des guerres civiles de Dubuisson-Aubenay*, ed. Saige, ii. 207.

achieve reform (if reform was what the nobles really intended) without coercion, and coercion might well prevent the objectives of the nobles from being achieved. The nobles claimed that what they wanted was to re-establish peace and peacetime forms of administration, in effect the *status quo ante* 1635, perhaps *ante* 1630 or even 1624. What they succeeded in doing was worsening the effect of wartime government. Civil war thus destroyed their ideal as expressed in their propaganda, the essential justification for their resistance. If a war government was what was needed, there was no reason why Mazarin should not continue in office and no reason why wartime forms of government, abolished in 1648, should not be restored. Those who had most to fear from a victory of Mazarin's opponents knew where their interests lay. Despite the severe financial problems of the crown in 1652, it was still able to anticipate revenues: 'la cour ne subsista encore la pluspart de cette année-là', commented one of the *trésoriers de l'Épargne*, 'que sur son crédit . . .'[1]

The most enduring legacy of La Vieuville's administration was to establish firmly in power a group of financiers to whom the crown, and Mazarin in particular, owed a debt of gratitude for their help in defeating the princes. By the autumn of 1652, most of the direct taxes for the following year had been anticipated. Loans from financiers such as Pierre Monnerot (*généralité* of Orléans), Martin Tabouret (Moulins and Limoges), Claude Boylesve (Poitiers), Claude Girardin (Caen), and Philippe Gruyn (Alençon) had been raised on these revenues. The problem with debts of gratitude is that they tend to become extremely expensive. Already in 1652, not all of the loan contractors had fulfilled their promises or acted with moderation.[2] Yet Mazarin supported the same group of financiers throughout the 1650s, when they dominated financial administration. It was not until the *chambre de justice* of 1661–5 that their profiteering was finally checked.[3] These men had made loans at a time of political crisis in the firm expectation, which was ultimately correct, that a royalist victory in the Fronde would bring them rich pickings during the years of civil peace. The limitation on the secret expenses, imposed by the *Chambre des Comptes* at the end of 1648, was lifted by a decree of the

---

[1] B.N. Morel de Thoisy 156, fo. 521ᵛ. *Défenses* of Jeannin, n.d., *c.* 1662.
[2] A.A.E. France 891, fos. 73–76. 1653, 'une année qui avoit esté mangée par avance . . .': A.A.E. France 892, fo. 402ᵛ., 2 Oct. 1653.
[3] D. Dessert, 'Finances et société au xviiᵉ siècle: à propos de la chambre de justice de 1661', *Annales, E.S.C.*, xxix (1974), 864–6. Cf. Dent, *Crisis in finance*, p. 89.

council of state on 16 November 1652.[1] From this time on, La Vieuville and his successors were in a position to resume interest payments to the financiers without recourse to the dubious accounting methods of the Fronde: the *comptants* rose dramatically from 3.8 million in 1652 to 20.9 million in 1653 and continued to rise each year until the Peace of the Pyrenees.[2] The prosecution of the financiers by the *chambre de justice* established in 1648 (which had in practice been stalled by the government) was now halted officially, although fines were still to be levied.[3] The taxes abolished in 1648 were restored at the *lit de justice* held in the *Parlement* of Paris on 31 December 1652.[4] Some of the crucial groundwork had thus been laid for a serious resumption of hostilities with Spain under Mazarin and new financial leadership.[5]

[1] *Arrêts du conseil du roi*, ed. Le Pesant, nos. 1800, 1812. The *Chambre des Comptes* tried to resist on 12 Dec. 1652: B.N. MS. fr. 18510, fo. 248.

[2] Appendix Two, Table III.

[3] P 2373, pp. 535–47, Dec. 1652. The taxes were very unpopular with certain financiers, such as Thomas Bonneau: E 259a, fo. 336, 13 Aug. 1653.

[4] X1b 8857, 31 Dec. 1652.

[5] It seems that Mazarin had seriously contemplated appointing the duc de Bouillon as finance minister shortly before his death in July 1652. According to Montglat, when Bouillon died 'il avoit plus de part qu'aucun dans le gouvernement de l'état': *Mémoires . . . de Montglat*, ed. Michaud and Poujoulat, p. 273.

Chapter VI

Mazarin's system, 1653–1661

Mazarin returned from his second exile a much more confident and determined politician than the rather callow figure who had sought refuge in the electorate of Cologne two years earlier. He had never really gone abroad on the second occasion, but had led the royalist armies in their successful campaign against Condé.[1] He now meant to lead the armies of France in a renewed offensive against Spain. The winter campaign of 1652–3 had in one respect set the pattern for subsequent years: during the campaigning season (approximately early April to late October) there were effectively two French governments. One, comprising the Chancellor, the ministers, and the council, was established usually at Paris or one of the royal residences outside the capital. The other, the court of Mazarin, sometimes joined by Anne of Austria and the young Louis XIV—who as early as 1654, to Mazarin's consternation because of the personal danger involved, was showing an ominous enthusiasm for war[2]—was established farther north, at Sedan, or more usually at La Fère. Here Mazarin personally supervised the details of war administration, sending back general letters to Paris requesting provisions and funds for the army.

Financial policy in the 1650s was thus determined by the Fronde in the immediate past, and the present campaign against Spain. Success was far from certain or inevitable. The French forces met with disaster at Valenciennes in July 1656, and two years later there was considerable domestic political agitation, which could have assumed dramatic importance had it been compounded by a further military defeat.[3] What Mazarin wanted was a team which would work together to produce military vic-

---

[1] Mazarin was at Sedan in early Sept., Bouillon in mid-Sept., and Saint-Dizier on 29 Nov. 1652. The main royal commander was of course Turenne, but he was a 'bon serviteur du roy' and Mazarin's 'amy particulier' since their reconciliation earlier in the year: cf. A.A.E. France 893/1, fo. 66, 15 July 1654.

[2] A.A.E. France 893/1, fos. 49ᵛ., 53, 8 and 9 July 1654.

[3] Cf. Servien's comment on the danger of 'un soulèvement général' had the Battle of the Dunes been lost: A.A.E. France 905, fo. 228ᵛ., 3 July 1658. Foucquet recalled the military and political dangers of 1658 during his trial, and stated that one would have needed to be 'un grand prophète' to foresee the rapid conclusion of peace the following year: *Archives de la Bastille*, ed. Ravaisson-Mollien, ii. 253.

tory. There were to be no more concessions to his domestic critics, as in 1649. He would be firmly in charge, not just of the conduct of general policy but of financial decisions too. Mazarin was not prepared to consider a repetition of the personal bankruptcy he had suffered in 1651–2. He did not draw the same conclusions on the need for moderation and economy as some of his advisers,[1] but fully appreciated that there was no point in his taking the blame for decisions taken independently by a successor to d'Hémery and La Vieuville. Mazarin was determined to promote clients who would do his bidding and leave him the reality of power.[2]

It took just over a month (2 January–8 February 1653) for Mazarin to make up his mind which candidates to promote and what type of financial structure to adopt. While the letters of solicitation arrived and were perused by the chief minister, Aligre and Barillon de Morangis, the directors of finance, were left in charge on an interim basis. They could not do much with their opportunity, since their powers were restricted and the financiers refused to work with them, preferring instead to await the appointment of a successor to La Vieuville.[3] But would Mazarin take this course of action? One possible financial structure, which he may have seriously contemplated, was to establish a commission of the council comprising perhaps six directors of finance.[4] However, there were two objections to this idea. Firstly, it smacked of political compromise. In 1652, there had been *projets d'accommodement* which had envisaged reconciliation with Gaston and Condé. The establishment of such a finance commission would have given the princes 'tout ce qu'on leur a osté . . . tout ce qu'ilz ont perdu . . .'[5] By the following year Mazarin no longer needed a compromise formula of this type. The second objection to this idea was that such arrangements tended not to work: 'tels conseils', it was said, 'estoient la ruine des affaires et jamais n'ont subsisté plus de six semaines . . .' The choice of members for the commission would be particularly difficult, since expectations would be raised among members of the various sovereign courts,

---

[1] A.A.E. France 881, fos. 30, 221, 313ᵛ., 8 Jan., 5 Feb. and 19 Feb. 1652.

[2] On Mazarin's patronage in the 1650s: Dent, 'The role of *clientèles*', 51, 53–5. Foucquet claimed that Mazarin's 's'[était] rendu luy-mesme ministre et exécuteur du détail de plus de trois quarts de la fonction de la surintendance . . .': 144 a.p. 60, Dr. 3 [156 mi. 7], fo. 38. It should be noted that the prosecution during the Foucquet trial tried to present him as 'le maistre absolu des finances' during the 1650s, but the former minister denied the allegation: 144 a.p. 62, no. 60 [156 mi. 11], fo. 6.

[3] A.A.E. France 892, fo. 94ᵛ., 10 Jan. 1653.

[4] *Lettres . . . de Colbert*, ed. Clément, i. 199 n. 1. A.A.E. France 892, fo. 65, 7 Jan. 1653.

[5] A.A.E. France 890, fo. 144, 1652.

not all of which could be satisfied. The commission would not lead to either speed or secrecy in decision-making.[1]

The alternative policy—for Mazarin to appoint one or two of his clients as finance minister—avoided these difficulties, although the political problem of choosing the right candidates remained. The obvious financial specialist was Guillaume Bordeaux, one of the *intendants des finances*, and La Vieuville's trusted aide. Bordeaux held the register for expenses and had 'un merveilleux talent pour embarquer les hommes d'affaires'.[2] His claim was supported in January 1653 by Colbert, Mazarin's *intendant de la maison*. In his later years, the chief minister richly rewarded Colbert and his dynasty for services rendered: but at this date Colbert's abilities were not fully tested and it would have been a risk for Mazarin to have handed over to one individual not just his personal fortune but the finances of the state. Besides, the claims of two other candidates, Nicolas Foucquet and Abel Servien, could not easily be ignored. Foucquet, the *procureur-général* of the *Parlement* of Paris since 1650, had displayed outstanding personal loyalty to Mazarin and support for the royalist cause during the Fronde. He presented himself in the guise of a new broom, who would correct financial maladministration which he saw as a principal reason for the unpopularity of the government. He also had close family ties with the world of finance. He was the grandson of Gilles Maupeou, who had been controller-general at the time of Sully. His wife, Marie Madeleine de Castille, was the granddaughter of Jeannin, and the Castille family of financiers were his relatives as a result of the marriage.[3] But there were two objections to giving Foucquet sole control. He was young, only 38 years old at the time of appointment,[4] and thus the youngest finance minister in the first half of the seventeenth century. Moreover, there was the risk of a conflict of interest between the position of *surintendant* and the office of *procureur-général*. Foucquet denied that there was any incompatibility,[5] and was proved correct in the 1650s. But Molé had refused appointment as finance

[1] A.A.E. France 892, fo. 139, 21 Jan. 1653. It should be noted that these arguments were put forward by a specialist—Jacques Le Tillier, an *intendant des finances*—and were expressed personally to Mazarin.

[2] *Lettres . . . de Colbert*, ed. Clément, i. 200, note.

[3] *Lettres du Cardinal Mazarin*, ed. Chéruel and d'Avenel, v. 107. Lair, *Foucquet*, i. 191, 266–71.

[4] Foucquet was baptized on 27 Jan. 1615. The age difference was an important factor in the conflict with Servien, who as late as 22 Dec. 1654 described Foucquet as only 37 years old: A.A.E. France 893/2, fo. 384.

[5] A.A.E. France 892, fo. 39, 2 Jan. 1653.

minister in 1624 precisely because he had envisaged the difficulty of dual loyalties, and conflict between Mazarin and the *Parlement* of Paris was so recent that the chief minister would naturally tend towards caution.

Abel Servien, the former French plenipotentiary at the Westphalian peace negotiations in the 1640s, was an obvious choice as Foucquet's senior colleague. The family ties with the world of finance were less marked in his case, although they certainly existed.[1] More important, perhaps, was the fact that Servien asked for the post as a reward for his services during the Fronde; since he had probably been offered the *surintendance* as early as 1649, he could scarcely be refused four years later. The claim was backed by La Meilleraye, another recent finance minister, who emphasized Servien's integrity.[2] In his letter soliciting the appointment, Servien castigated previous finance ministers, especially Bullion: competent though he had been, 'une des principales parties luy manquast, qui est la probité'.[3] Servien had never lost his resentment that Bullion had forced his resignation as war minister in 1636. Indeed, the sixty-year-old former minister was a stubborn and difficult man, who was prepared to accuse as important a politician and potential ally as Le Tellier of blocking his application for the finance ministry. Perhaps because of fears concerning Servien's suitability, perhaps from motives of personal gain, Mazarin combined the appointment of Servien and Foucquet with a third choice. Barthélémé Hervart, an *intendant des finances* since 1650, was given 'la commission de l'Épargne'.[4] It is doubtful if anyone knew precisely what this title meant. Servien regarded the appointment as a limitation on his power, and in August 1655 denounced Hervart's negligence and ineptitude (and in passing his Lutheran faith).[5] Mazarin, however, defended

---

[1] Antoine Servien, his father, had participated in financial transactions during and after his tenure of the office of *procureur syndic* of the Estates of the Dauphiné: E 30, fo. 203, 30 Apr. 1611. E 42b, fo. 263, 19 Dec. 1613.

[2] A.A.E. France 892, fos. 103, 185, 11 Jan. and 15 Feb. 1653.

[3] A.A.E. France 891, fo. 55 and A.A.E. France 892 fo. 148, 25 Jan. 1653.

[4] 144 a.p. 74, Dr. 7, no. 4 [156 mi 30]. Extract from the list of *comptants*, 1656. Sometimes called *commis à l'enregistrement des fonds*, Hervart was not controller-general until 1657: Depping, 'Un banquier protestant', 316–18. Badalo-Dulong, *Banquier du roi*, pp. 109–10. Dent, *Crisis in finance*, pp. 97–8. Foucquet noted that Hervart occupied the position formerly enjoyed by Bordeaux and defined his powers: Foucquet, *Défenses*, v. 57–9. Dent talks of Hervart's 'illegal role . . . to prevent the *contrôle-général* from operating. In this he was carrying out Mazarin's wishes.' Hervart declared to the *chambre de justice* of 1661–5 that 'il 'n'avoit point calculé les rôles pendant qu'il a été premier commis de la surintendance', but Guénégaud, one of the *trésoriers de l'Épargne*, produced evidence to show that he did: B.N. Morel de Thoisy 156, fos. 194, 203ᵛ., *c*. 1664.

[5] A.A.E. France 894, fo. 272, 16 Aug. 1655.

his agent and recalled his great services during the Fronde;[1] Hervart was too useful to the chief minister to be sacrificed in the interests of good financial management.

The chain of command established by Mazarin to ensure his personal control suffered from crucial weaknesses: it fragmented control over financial policy, and in order to work it required a high degree of co-operation between colleagues, which was most unlikely given the great differences in their age, experience, and temperament. Throughout 1653 and 1654 Servien was unquestionably the senior finance minister, although the precise division of responsibility with Foucquet is not clear.[2] Mazarin, however, began to hold Servien responsible for the continuing financial difficulties of the French crown and the failure to secure the full co-operation of the financiers. On 24 December 1654, Servien was demoted and given charge of expenditure while Foucquet was given the much more difficult task of procuring funds. It was now Foucquet who negotiated the loan contracts, and the financiers ceased visiting Servien's quarters and went to Foucquet's instead. From 1655, whatever the theory of a joint *surintendance*, Foucquet was the real finance minister.[3] Nevertheless, the new arrangements were no more permanent than the old. On at least three occasions—after the disaster at Valenciennes in July 1656, after the failure of the siege of Courtrai in May 1657, and after the death of Servien in February 1659—Mazarin seriously contemplated dismissing Foucquet. This evidence was later used at Foucquet's trial in an attempt to prove that Mazarin had regarded his finance minister as corrupt. Foucquet retorted that Mazarin had deliberately sowed discord between himself and his brother, the abbé Basile Foucquet, and that there had been an almost permanent conspiracy between Colbert and Hervart to oust him from power, again encouraged by the chief minister. On the other hand, Mazarin had had the power and the opportunity to rid himself of Foucquet, but had chosen not to do so: the inference was that the

---

[1] A.A.E. France 896, fo. 210, 17 Aug. 1655.

[2] Foucquet asserted that in 1653 Servien 'par l'ordre de M. le Cardinal agissoit seul, régloit les affaires de toutes natures . . .': Foucquet, *Défenses*, v. 59. Servien 'avoit le crédit et l'authorité' until the ruling of 24 Dec. 1654: B.L. Add. MSS. 39673, fo. 73ᵛ., n.d. [1661].

[3] Lair, *Foucquet*, i. 352–3. Dent, *Crisis in finance*, p. 68. For Servien's bitterness and sense of humiliation: A.A.E. France 893/2, fos. 383, 387, 22 and 25 Dec. 1654. The ruling of 24 Dec. 1654 is in A.A.E. France 893/2, fo. 410; E 272b, fo. 565 and B.N. MS. fr. 4222, fo. 195. When Colbert denounced Foucquet's corruption, he dated his advent to power from the moment that 'par le partage que Vostre Éminence fit en 1655 [*sic*] toute l'autorité des finances fut tombée entre [ses] mains . . .': *Lettres . . . de Colbert*, ed. Clément, i. 390. Foucquet's statement that Servien was pleased to be 'soulagé d'un fardeau qu'il ne pouvoit porter' is scarcely to be believed: Foucquet, *Défenses*, v. 68.

services provided by the *surintendant* had been too valuable.[1] It is not easy to disentangle fact from fiction in the charges and countercharges. The atmosphere of intrigue and suspicion does much to explain—though not to excuse—Foucquet's treasonable *projet de Saint-Mandé*, a plan for his restoration to power if arrested, which went through successive drafts after 1657 and was to provide a powerful case for the prosecution at his trial.[2] Mazarin's attitude to Foucquet was ambivalent and inconsistent. Perhaps he indulged in duplicity for its own sake; he certainly failed to give Foucquet clear guarantees of support for his policies and his continuance in office. The background of intrigue can scarcely have assisted the cause of sound financial administration in the 1650s.

The financial problems of the French monarchy in 1653 arose essentially from two causes. The high levels of expenditure during the Fronde, necessary to defeat the twin perils of Habsburg invasion and magnate insurrection, had left a massive burden of debt. Total royal expenditure in 1653 stood at between 109 and 113 million *livres*, and included about 59 million carried over from the two previous years.[3] It is true that some of this expenditure was the result of the peculiar accounting during the Fronde. The recourse to over-assignment had resulted in an excessive number of treasury bills (*billets de l'Épargne*) in circulation, and this remained true in the later 1650s. The second grave difficulty arose from the near collapse of the normal revenue raising process during the last stages of the civil war. In theory just under 110 million *livres* in revenues were available; in practice it is doubtful whether one-sixth of this figure was left to the crown once the troops had consumed the proceeds from the *taille*, and given the low yield from the revenue farms and the small number of new tax contracts (*traités*) being negotiated.[4] The most important farms were under direct royal administration (*régie*) in 1652–3, while the claims and counter-claims of the farmers were examined. For example, it was suggested that the farmers of the *aides* owed the crown 9.8 million from the years of the Fronde. They responded

---

[1] 144 a.p. 60, Dr. 1 [156 mi. 6], fos. 80, 140ᵛ. 144 a.p. 66, Dr. 3 [156 mi. 15], fos. 130, 138ᵛ–139ᶠ. 144 a.p. 67, Dr. 1 [156 mi. 17], fo. 21.

[2] Lair, *Foucquet*, i. 411–16, 471–4. Dent, 'The role of *clientèles*', 64–6.

[3] Appendix Two, Table I. Nearly 40 million from 1651, and over 19 million from 1652: B.N. n.a.f. 169, fo. 218. Foucquet stated at his trial that in 1653–4 Mazarin demanded enormous sums for 'despenses nécessaires et privillegiées [*sic*] des quatre ou cinq années précédentes', i.e. back to 1648–9: 144 a.p. 66, Dr. 1 [156 mi. 15], fo. 5.

[4] The theoretical figure was given by Bertrand, the *trésorier de l'Épargne*: 144 a.p. 60, Dr. 9 [156 mi. 7], fo. 1ᵛ. The lower estimate was Foucquet's: 144 a.p. 66, Dr. 1 [156 mi. 15], fo. 5.

that the king owed them 5.9 million for loan contracts which had been abrogated in 1648.[1] Despite their misgivings, Servien and Foucquet thought it safer to renegotiate leases with the previous farmers who at least were experienced rather than risk new and untried financial consortia in a very difficult situation.[2] However, the farmers refused to increase rents significantly. The continuing war with Spain played its part.[3] So too did the economic dislocation at the end of the Fronde, and the plight of the peasantry resulting from the subsistence crisis of 1652. The government appeared to be willing to grant compensation to the farmers for their losses in the royal bankruptcy of 1648 and the difficult years which followed by allowing relatively low rents in the 1650s. It also kept rents relatively low in order to attract loans from the farmers: by 1655 rents were being anticipated two years in advance once again.[4]

The administration of the direct taxes in the aftermath of the Fronde proved equally difficult. On 23 July 1653 a loan contract had been negotiated with a consortium of financiers acting under the name of Richard Richer who had undertaken to anticipate 9 million *livres* of the *taille* in eight monthly instalments commencing on 13 October. The chief purpose of the loan was to ensure in advance that the government would be able to pay for the troops during the winter. The provinces were still required to carry the cost of the winter quarter, but the amount due on the *taille* was reduced accordingly. The successful implementation of the scheme required a disciplined army in the provinces. By the end of November, it was already clear to Servien and Foucquet that the scheme was in danger of failing because of indiscipline in the army. The financiers regarded the Richer contract as a test case of the government's intent and its willingness to keep its word. Without action to contain the troops, the financiers would cease to co-operate.[5] Mazarin, however, replied to the *surintendants* in uncompromising language. Indiscipline must be stamped out; but there could be no sympathy with the plight of the peasant

[1] Cf. E 301a, fo. 3, 2 May 1657.

[2] A.A.E. France 892, fo. 352^r.–^{v}., 19 Sept. 1653.

[3] The lease of Jacques André on the *aides* envisaged a variable rent in accordance with the state of civil and foreign war or peace. The highest rent—2.9 million—would be paid once there was general peace, and the council of finance did not enforce this rent until 1 Jan. 1659: E 258a, fo. 371, 12 July 1653. E 317a, fo. 355, 18 Sept. 1658.

[4] For example, loan of 1.9 million *livres* in 1655, anticipating the rents of the *gabelles de France* for 1656–7: E 276a, fo. 157, 8 Apr. 1655. Loan of 3.2 million in 1658, anticipating the rents of the same farm for 1659–61: E 318a, fo. 246, 6 Nov. 1658.

[5] A.A.E. France 892, fos. 445–6, 24 Nov. 1653.

tax-payer, no lamenting that Frenchmen were treated as *peuples conquis*. Mazarin refused point blank to change his plans for the winter quarter and the forthcoming campaign.[1] Unlike the indirect taxes, the yield from the *taille* remained constant during the early 1650s,[2] and rose after 1655. A fresh outbreak of rural disturbances after 1655 confirms the impression that the crown had by then increased direct taxes, and enforced the levy by the use of provincial intendants and troops—a dangerous and unpopular policy, though one necessary to fight the war against Spain.[3]

However, the increase in direct taxation did not keep pace with the rapid growth in expenditure. This seems clear from the emphasis placed on royal borrowing as early as 1653–4. In these years it was Servien's responsibility to secure loans, and he pointed out to Mazarin the difficulty of attracting investors because of the high rates of interest— 15 per cent in 1654—prevailing on the private market.[4] An equally important factor was that public confidence had been badly shaken by the bankruptcy of 1648 and the failure of the crown to honour all its debts. The king of France, unlike the Dutch and Venetian republics, did not repay his creditors, or so it was said.[5] Financiers had to be attracted to invest: this meant high rates of interest, and reimbursement for losses incurred in 1648.[6] Monetary policy might have a marginal influence on the situation, encouraging investment in loan contracts by reducing the value of coin hoarded.[7] But security of investment was much more important. There could be no talk of thoroughgoing investigation of corruption by a *chambre de justice*. La Vieuville had presided over the abolition of the

[1] A.A.E. France 891, fo. 360, 3 Dec. 1653.

[2] Whereas Mallet's figures for the yield from the indirect revenues show a distinct fall (48 million in 1650–4 as against 67 million in 1645–9), the yield from the *taille* in the *pays d'élections* remained constant at 125 million: Appendix Two, Table IV.

[3] Bonney, *Political change in France under Richelieu and Mazarin*, pp. 174–5, 200–3, 229–33.

[4] A.A.E. France 893/2, fo. 121, 4 July 1654.

[5] By the financiers: A.A.E. France 890, fos. 240–1, c. Feb. 1653. A.A.E. France 893/2, fo. 419, n.d., c. 1654.

[6] At his trial, Foucquet stressed the lack of credit resulting from the bankruptcy of 1648, and the need for 'proffits [*sic*] extraordinaires': 144 a.p. 60, Dr. 1 [156 mi. 6], fo. 138. The financiers, he said, were willing to invest only on certain conditions, 'passer un billet de vieille debte ou . . . donner une remise un peu plus forte': 144 a.p. 66, Dr. 1 [156 mi. 15], fo. 6.

[7] Véron de Forbonnais, *Recherches*, i. 265. Lair, *Foucquet*, i. 343, 373–4. A.A.E. France 892, fo. 352ᵛ., 19 Sept. 1653. Foucquet argued that royal borrowing was greatly facilitated in 1653–4 by '[le] rabais des monnoyes', but once the monetary changes stopped loans became difficult to find: Foucquet, *Défenses*, v. 61, 63. For the relative monetary stability after the Fronde, and the low issues of coin after 1656: Spooner, *The international economy and monetary movements in France*, pp. 192–3, 339.

tribunal established during the Fronde but never allowed to do its job. None was actually set up during the 1650s. Instead, from time to time the financiers were required to pay supplementary taxes instead of undergoing trial by *chambre de justice*. The taxes were collected by a consortium of financiers who contracted with the government.[1]

The difficulty with a financial policy reliant on short and medium-term borrowing, apart from the inherent risk of bankruptcy, was that it was subject to the vagaries of the money market. In November 1653 loans were readily forthcoming; by June of the following year they were not.[2] This state of affairs was quite unacceptable to Mazarin, who wanted his finance ministers to guarantee him 25 or 30 million *livres* at the outset of a campaigning season, with payment at specified dates, which would allow him complete freedom to arrange for the pay and logistical support for the army as he saw fit.[3] It seems unlikely that Servien was sufficiently adept to secure loans from the financiers on this scale,[4] or that he possessed sufficient wealth and credit to assume personal responsibility for meeting Mazarin's deadlines. Indeed, Servien called Foucquet disloyal, and thought this 'la cause de la froideur des traitants'; he also asked the chief minister to assist with personal loans.[5] By December 1654, the revenues for 1655 and 1656 had been anticipated and Servien's ingenuity at finding new expedients appeared exhausted.[6] Mazarin seriously contemplated declaring bankruptcy as in 1648. The only alternative was a change of leadership which might encourage the financiers to anticipate the revenues of 1657. Perhaps unfairly Mazarin

---

[1] P 2374, pp. 799–802, Mar. 1655. E 266b, fo. 111, 17 June 1654. E 289b, fo. 314, 20 May 1656. E 296b, fo. 388, 20 Dec. 1656. E 317b, fo. 171, 19 Oct. 1658. E 328b, fo. 345, 18 Sept. 1659. Three of the contracts were—Claude St. Lau (21 Apr. 1655) with a *forfait* of 4.4 million and *remise* of 1.4 million (later increased respectively to 6.3 million and 2.1 million): E 276b, fo. 118; Jean Raguin (20 Dec. 1656), with a *forfait* of 3 million and a *remise* of 1 million: E 296b, fo. 390; and Claude Boisel (19 Oct. 1658) with a *forfait* of 7.2 million and *remise* of 1.92 million, both subsequently reduced: E 317b, fo. 205. Cf. E 320b/321a, fo. 545, 12 Feb. 1659.

[2] A.A.E. France 892, fo. 444, 24 Nov. 1653. A.A.E. France 893/2, fo. 73, 19 June 1654.

[3] Véron de Forbonnais, *Recherches*, i. 267, states 23 million, the management of which was 'contre les loix et ordonnances du royaume'. Dent, *Crisis in finance*, p. 79, gives the same figure. Foucquet at his trial stated 25 or 30 million: 144 a.p. 66, Dr. 3 [156 mi. 16], fo. 367ᵛ. Foucquet, *Défenses*, v. 165, vii. 258, 260.

[4] The figure for 1654 suggests an annual total that was somewhat lower than Mazarin's requirement, and was certainly not available in a lump sum: Appendix Two, Table VIII A. Foucquet acknowledged 'les grands prests faits par M. Servien en 1654 à la prière de M. le Cardinal': Foucquet, *Défenses*, v. 141.

[5] A.A.E. France 893/2, fos. 121, 385, 4 July and 22 Dec. 1654.

[6] 144 a.p. 66, no. 1 [156 mi. 15], fo. 2.

blamed Servien for the financial crisis which imperilled the French war effort, and in a private interview he invited Foucquet to take charge. The *procureur-général* accepted, but made it clear that there would be a change in emphasis in royal policy: in his view, Servien had not always kept his word to the financiers, and this was one of the reasons why it had become so difficult to obtain loans.[1]

The ruling of 24 December 1654 gave Foucquet charge of securing funds in Servien's place. He immediately set to work negotiating new loan contracts, keeping Mazarin informed of the details.[2] Foucquet's task was made easier by the new political climate after the *lit de justice* of 20 March 1655, followed up by Louis XIV's order to the *Parlement* of Paris on 13 April to cease its political deliberations. Throughout 1654 Servien especially had advocated the need for a show of royal power to enforce the registration of fiscal edicts that would provide much needed new revenues for the war effort.[3] In a sense March 1655 was a replay of January 1648. Instead of seven fiscal edicts, there were seventeen with an estimated tax yield of 15 million *livres*. This time the government won, partly because its position was stronger after the failure of the Fronde, and partly because Foucquet as *procureur-général* was regarded as a friend of the *Parlement*—seven years earlier there had been much personal opposition to d'Hémery and his methods. In 1653–4 there had been relatively few new *traités* on which loans could be secured, but the situation improved rapidly after the *lit de justice* had been held.[4]

Foucquet thus assumed personal control at a less difficult time than Servien two years earlier, which explains partially his success in securing new loans. Yet he also offered the financiers what they wanted: security of investment and high profits.[5] One of the most important ways in which high profits were conferred on the financiers was by reassigning old treasury bills (*billets de l'Épargne*) on new revenues. The bankruptcy of 1648 had left many treasury bills in circulation which had become worthless because the revenues on which they were assigned had been diverted to other

---

[1] Foucquet, *Défenses*, v. 65–7.
[2] Copies of loan contracts for 1655 are to be found in Mazarin's papers: A.A.E. France 894 and 895, *passim*.
[3] A.A.E. France 893/2, fos. 95ᵛ., 203ᵛ., 358ᵛ., 26 June, 4 Aug. and 11 Oct. 1654.
[4] 14.8 million *livres* in 1654, but 47.2 million in 1655: Appendix Two, Table VII A. The estimated yield from the 17 fiscal edicts is provided by Lair, *Foucquet*, i. 356.
[5] Foucquet, *Défenses*, v. 66–7, and Lair, *Foucquet*, i. 350–1: 'ne menacer jamais de banqueroute . . . le principal secret en un mot estoit de leur donner à gagner . . .'

purposes. These bills had been a great object of speculation among financiers, who bought them cheaply from weaker royal creditors who could not afford to wait and hope. The risk was that the bills would remain worthless. The speculation for the financier was that a bill bought for a price at somewhere between 5 and 10 per cent of its face value would suddenly be reassigned on new royal revenues as part of the conditions of a loan or tax contract.[1] Gourville, an adventurer brought in by Mazarin to manage the loan contracts on the revenues of Guyenne,[2] was just one of those who, in his own words, drew enormous profits from this speculation in treasury bills. The rapid increase in the secret expenses under Foucquet—from 41 million *livres* in 1655 to 86 million in 1658[3]—is explained by the high interest rates paid on loan and tax contracts and by the policy of reassigning treasury bills. In 1655 Mazarin began to grow uneasy about the cost of this policy;[4] two years later he thought it overgenerous to the financiers. At least 25 million *livres* in old treasury bills had been reassigned by 1657.[5]

The climate of business confidence was greatly assisted by Foucquet's participation in the borrowing of the French monarchy. Foucquet's wealth and ability to secure credit were an important part of Mazarin's decision to reallocate financial responsibilities in December 1654. Whatever was later said by the prosecution at his trial, Foucquet was undoubtedly already rich by the time he was appointed *surintendant*, and in 1653–4 was borrowing for the crown.[6] From 1655, Foucquet undertook to supply whatever sum Mazarin required and then sought to subcontract to the main financiers. The relationship between Maza-

---

[1] Dent, *Crisis in finance*, pp. 83, 87. 144 a.p. 69, Dr. 4 [156 mi. 21], fo. 50. About 5 per cent according to Foucquet: 144 a.p. 69, Dr. 6 [156 mi. 22], fo. 59ᵛ. About 10 per cent according to Gourville: *Mémoires de Jean Hérault de Gourville*, ed. J. F. Michaud and J. J. F. Poujoulat, 3rd ser., v (1838), p. 524. F. R. Freudmann, *L'étonnant Gourville, 1625–1703* (Geneva-Paris, 1960), p. 77.

[2] Gourville's account, op. cit., pp. 522–3, and Freudmann, op. cit., pp. 75–6, are substantiated by Foucquet: A.A.E. France 902, fo. 340, n.d. [1657].

[3] Appendix Two, Table III.

[4] A.A.E. France 894, fo. 285ᵛ., 23 [?] Aug. 1655. A.A.E. France 896, fos. 97ᵛ.–98ʳ., 12 July 1655.

[5] *Lettres . . . de Colbert*, ed. Clément, i. 501–2. A.A.E. France 902, fo. 119, 26 June 1657.

[6] Though Foucquet's personal accounts were confused: Appendix Two, Table X. It is clear that Foucquet did not deliver a statement of his properties and revenues at the time of his appointment. The list entitled 'lors que j'ay esté surintendant au commancemt. de 1653 mon bien consistoit' (B.A. MS. 7167, fo. 163) has the values left blank, indicating that it was drawn up at the time of his trial in the expectation that Foucquet would complete and sign it. For Foucquet's claim that he was wealthy in 1653: 144 a.p. 66, Dr. 1 [156 mi. 15], fo. 4. For Talon's retort that Foucquet regarded the administration of finance 'comme un bien de nouvelle conqueste': 144 a.p. 68, Dr. 1 [156 mi. 18], fo. 78.

rin and his finance minister was much like that of a financier to his subcontractor. Mazarin, too, advanced his own money to the crown and charged interest for his services,[1] but—encouraged by Colbert—naturally sought to keep his commitments to a minimum while involving Foucquet as completely as possible. The system appears to have worked reasonably well in 1655 and the first half of 1656 but began to run into difficulties once the government had to find new financial expedients on which to secure loans. The royal decree of 19 October 1656, confirming the supremacy of the council of state over the *Parlement* of Paris, is in part explained by the need to register new fiscal edicts at that court.[2] The government began to consider cutting back on the payment of salaries and *rentes*, which had been regarded as sacrosanct since the end of the Fronde, and other fiscal measures with serious political repercussions such as a *recherche de noblesse*: this was one of the most important causes of the assemblies of lesser nobles which became particularly serious by 1657–8.[3]

As the government ran into new financial difficulties, so the recriminations began. In June 1656 Mazarin accused Foucquet of not providing the full 13.5 million he had promised: two royal armies were owed over 700,000 *livres*.[4] The French army met with disaster at Valenciennes the following month, and Foucquet responded to the crisis by advancing just under a million and contemplated a forced loan payable by members of the king's council and the financiers.[5] In September 1656 Mazarin was once more criticizing Foucquet's conduct, especially his apparent financial pessimism. The abbé Basile Foucquet actually reported to his brother that the chief minister had demanded his resignation, but this seems to have exaggerated Mazarin's displeasure.

---

[1] Foucquet's verdict (144 a.p. 60, Dr. 2 [156 mi. 6], fo. 38) is borne out by Le Tellier, a more impartial observer: Ormesson, *Journal*, ed. Chéruel, ii. 134. For Mazarin's desire to keep his commitments to a minimum: Foucquet, *Défenses*, xii. 118.

[2] *Arrêts du conseil du roi*, ed. Le Pesant, no. 2366. The financial implications were spelt out by Chancellor Séguier in a letter to Mazarin: A.A.E. France 900, fo. 324, 23 Aug. 1656.

[3] Foucquet regarded the *gages* and *rentes* as sacrosanct (144 a.p. 60, Dr. 1 [156 mi. 6], fo. 138, 144 a.p. 69, Dr. 4 [156 mi. 21], fo. 253) and advised Mazarin against tampering with the *rentes* in 1657: A.A.E. France 902, fo. 110ᵛ., 12 June 1657. For the *retranchement des gages*, cf. E 314a, fo. 371, 6 June 1658. For the *recherche de noblesse*: E 301a, fo. 496, 19 May 1657. E 312b, fo. 309, 10 Apr. 1658. Note the small amount raised from *traités* in 1656: Appendix Two, Table VII A.

[4] A.A.E. France 901, fo. 48, 6 June 1656.

[5] Lair, *Foucquet*, i. 380–1. A.A.E. France 900, fos. 180, 186, 199ᵛ., 19 July and 22 July 1656. Mazarin recognized Foucquet's services in a letter from La Fère written on 24 July 1656, which the former minister was able to quote at his trial: Foucquet, *Défenses*, xiv. 379–82 and 144 a.p. 69, Dr. 3 [156 mi. 20], fos. 172ᵛ.–174ᵛ.

Foucquet denied that he had kept the state of the king's finances to himself, although it appears that a secret budgetary review had been postponed. More important, perhaps, was that Mazarin was awaiting the outcome of Lionne's peace mission to Madrid before determining on another round of expenditure and the anticipation of revenues for 1659.[1] Further difficulties arose after the failure of the siege of Courtrai in May 1657, when Foucquet made it clear that he could not make any further loans on his own account.[2] Perhaps unwisely, the finance minister had called in some of his loans to the crown to pay his private debts and the marriage costs of his daughter Marie to Armand de Béthune, marquis and later duc de Charost, who was Sully's grand-nephew.[3] Matters were made much worse by the fact that Foucquet had not recently paid any interest to Mazarin on his loans to the crown. For his part, Colbert deliberately excited criticism of the *surintendant* by warning Mazarin that as in 1648 he was now the chief financier of the state.[4]

Foucquet offered to resign but his offer was not taken up. Instead, Mazarin acknowledged Foucquet's past services and encouraged him to participate in a massive new loan in November 1657. Four contracts were signed, totalling 11.8 million *livres*, to anticipate the revenues of the winter quarter for 1657–8. The effective loan was 10.2 million once the interest charge of 1.6 million had been deducted. Foucquet held approximately a one-third share (4.3 million gross; a net loan of 3.7 million once the interest payment of 0.6 million had been deducted). His partners, Hervart, the new controller-general, and Jeannin, the *trésorier de l'Épargne*, were able to borrow at lower rates of interest due to Foucquet's personal guarantee; his own borrowing was not covered by a third party and on one transaction he had to pay a 20 per cent interest charge. The overall interest rate on the loan was about 14 per cent, however.[5] This loan was successfully floated, but the underlying problems remained, and the following year it proved much more difficult to borrow money with the situation reaching crisis proportions in July 1658 at the time of Louis XIV's

[1] *Lettres . . . de Colbert*, ed. Clément, i. 497–501. A.A.E. France 900, fo. 354, 12 Sept. 1656.

[2] Foucquet stated that it was 'impossible d'y estre plus absolument engagé': A.A.E. France 902, fo. 85, 20 May 1657.

[3] *Lettres . . . de Colbert*, ed. Clément, i. 501–3. A.A.E. France 902, fos. 119–25, 26 June 1657.

[4] *Lettres du Cardinal Mazarin*, ed. Chéruel and d'Avenel, vii. 529–30. *Lettres . . . de Colbert*, ed. Clément, i. 274. Lair, *Foucquet*, i. 407–10.

[5] Foucquet, *Défenses*, viii. 249–64. Cf. ibid., v. 247, 287. 144 a.p. 69, Dr. 3 [156 mi. 20], fo. 175. *Archives de la Bastille*, ed. Ravaisson-Mollien, ii. 337.

serious illness. Had the king died, the separate bankruptcies of several financiers which had already occurred could well have developed into a *banqueroute générale*[1] comparable to 1648. As in that year, Mazarin contemplated revoking the loan contracts which would have forced Foucquet's resignation since it undermined the basis of his financial policy, namely security of investment and high profits. After some hesitation at the end of June, when during a period of illness he contemplated winding up his credit operations and resigning from office, Foucquet decided to weather the storm. With a gambler's instinct[2] he borrowed a further 400,000 *livres* from Bertrand de la Bazinière and the Monnerot brothers. As late as March 1659 Foucquet was still a creditor of the French monarchy to the extent of at least 5 million,[3] but his ability to secure credit had been imperilled by the intrigue of Colbert and Hervart to oust him from office after Servien's death the previous month. After four days' hesitation in which he considered becoming joint *surintendant*, Mazarin confirmed Foucquet's powers.[4] But the intrigues of Colbert and Hervart had not ended: in July 1659, when the revenues of 1660 were anticipated, they redoubled their efforts.[5]

The position of Foucquet was particularly vulnerable because it appeared that the long war against Spain was about to end. A truce had been signed on 8 May, followed by the treaty of Paris on

---

[1] Foucquet used this term in a letter of 14 July 1658 (A.A.E. France 905, fo. 262ᵛ.) quoted by Lair, *Foucquet*, i. 445–6.

[2] Lair, *Foucquet*, i. 446–7, transcribes Foucquet's letter of 28 July 1658 (A.A.E. France 905, fos. 294–5) with a crucial misreading 'honneur' instead of 'humeur'. Foucquet stated that he had 'fait chose peut-être imprudente mais . . . conforme à mon humeur' by further committing himself. Lair's conclusion that this was a letter of resignation is incorrect; if Foucquet was seeking to leave office, he would hardly have lent more money to the crown. Lair (op. cit., i. 470) suggested that Foucquet again offered his resignation on 17 Dec. 1658. The document (A.A.E. France 905, fo. 535), which is incorrectly cited, contains no allusion to resignation. At his trial, Foucquet claimed that he had offered his resignation at the end of 1658 (Foucquet, *Défenses*, vi. 250) but his memory for dates was rather vague.

[3] Lair, *Foucquet*, i. 479. *État* of 7 Mar. 1659 cited by Foucquet, *Défenses*, v. 152; viii. 269 (5,012,939 *livres*).

[4] Foucquet asserted that the scheme of a joint *surintendance* was a ploy of Colbert, who knew that the chief minister had insufficient time and detailed knowledge to exercise the position, and would delegate his authority to his *intendant de la maison*: Foucquet, *Défenses*, v. 80–1.

[5] On the conflict between Foucquet and Colbert: Gourville, *Mémoires*, ed. Michaud and Poujoulat, pp. 525–7. Depping, 'Un banquier protestant', 326–35. Lair, *Foucquet*, i. 486–95. Badalo-Dulong, *Banquier du roi*, pp. 138–46. In a letter to Mazarin on 28 Oct. 1659, Colbert denied any close association with Hervart (*Lettres . . . de Colbert*, ed. Clément, i. 392–3) but this does not disprove Foucquet's contention that they both sought his dismissal.

4 June 1659. Mazarin had then moved south to Saint-Jean-de-Luz to oversee the final negotiations that would lead to the signing of the peace of the Pyrenees on 7 November. Foucquet stayed at Paris after the departure of the chief minister and then joined the court, first at Bordeaux and later Toulouse. Colbert, however, remained at or near the capital throughout the crisis, which explains the *surintendant*'s difficulties in stamping out rumours of his impending dismissal which had a serious effect on financial confidence.[1] The struggle between Foucquet and Colbert fully revealed Mazarin's cynicism and duplicity:[2] he it was who had started off the trouble by asking for a review of the royal finances by Colbert (which was strictly speaking outside his area of responsibility); the chief minister prolonged the crisis by revealing to Colbert his secret conversations with Foucquet. For their part, Foucquet and Gourville acted with dubious legality by stopping the post and copying out Colbert's secret memorandum to the chief minister. If none of the participants emerges from the crisis with any credit, it is clear that vital issues of political power and financial principle were at stake. Colbert wanted to oust Foucquet from office and become *surintendant* in his place: he also wanted to hold a *chambre de justice*, partly as a means of dealing with his rival but also in a clean sweep against financial corruption. Far from worrying about maintaining financial confidence, he saw positive advantages in a royal declaration of bankruptcy that would result chiefly in losses to the financiers.[3]

Foucquet's views were diametrically opposed. The loss of credit following the royal bankruptcy of 1648 had taught him to view sudden gains from the revocation of loan contracts as largely illusory, while the long term effect on interest rates was disastrous. He wanted to 'laiss[er] aller les affaires'[4] and reform financial

---

[1] At his trial, Foucquet cited a letter he had received from Bruant, his clerk, in November 1659. The letter denounced the Colbert–Hervart conspiracy 'à dessein d'allienner [*sic*] les gens d'affaires et leur oster la confiance qu'ils ont pour Monsieur [Foucquet]: 144 a.p. 66, Dr. 3 [156 mi. 15], fos. 138ᵛ.–139ʳ.

[2] *Lettres . . . de Colbert*, ed. Clément, i. 515: '. . . je mettray toutes pièces en oeuvre', wrote Mazarin, 'pour renvoyer le surintendant persuadé que vous [i.e. Colbert] ne m'aviez rien mandé . . .'

[3] Colbert proposed a *chambre de justice* on 31 Aug. 1659, but Mazarin rejected the idea, crossing out the relevant section of the letter: *Lettres . . . de Colbert*, ed. Clément, i. 361. In his memorandum of 1 Oct. 1659, Colbert wrote: 'je ne prétends pas que l'on fasse banqueroute, quoy qu'il n'y eust pas un grand inconvénient . . .': ibid., vii. 181.

[4] 144 a.p. 60, Dr. 1 [156 mi. 6], fo. 115. On Foucquet's reluctance to 'dépouiller' the financiers: 144 a.p. 69, Dr. 8 [156 mi. 23], fo. 163ᵛ. On his view of the disastrous effects of the bankruptcy of 1648: 144 a.p. 66, Dr. 3 [156 mi. 16], fo. 328. On his preference for taxes rather than a *chambre de justice*: 144 a.p. 66, Dr. 1 [156 mi. 15], fo. 6ᵛ.

administration gradually as the conditions of peace permitted. Moreover, Foucquet was still the leading creditor of the French monarchy. In an allusion to Colbert, Foucquet denounced to Mazarin 'des gens . . . bien zelez et prompts à censurer les actions des autres' who would not have lent money to the crown freely and without guarantees as he had done.[1] Perhaps Foucquet may be regarded as naïve for failing to respond to the criticisms of Colbert by seeking specific written assurances from Mazarin. He returned to Paris with kind words of support from the chief minister and nothing more. Colbert's memorandum remained in the archives unanswered, ready to be brought out and dusted off at a later date. There was no public defence of Foucquet's financial administration, no formal guarantee of his position as leading royal creditor.[2] All that happened was that Mazarin instructed Foucquet and Colbert to cease their bickering and co-operate. It is an open question whether Mazarin was simply biding his time before dismissing Foucquet and adopting Colbert's solution. Alternatively, he may have sided with Foucquet and politely ignored Colbert, whom he could not do without[3] but who was not promoted in Mazarin's lifetime.

What is clear is that Foucquet, far from resting on his laurels, had been attempting to persuade Mazarin throughout the autumn of 1659 to take new policy decisions in the context of peace.[4] The positive outcome of the power struggle between Foucquet and Colbert was that it forced the chief minister to decide on a reduction of royal expenditure and an attempt to expand revenues.[5] Foucquet returned to Paris, tried to patch up the quarrel with Colbert, and set to the task of reallocating the leases on the revenue farms which had been declared vacant since November. The policy of seeking to amalgamate the revenue farms into the largest units possible, and increase the yield of indirect taxes by this and other means—a policy later brought to

---

[1] A.A.E. France 908, fo. 26, 3 Sept. 1659.

[2] However, Foucquet could scarcely insist on this, because to do so would question Mazarin's word of honour: Foucquet, *Défenses*, xiii. 241–2; xvi. 245. 144 a.p. 60, Dr. 1 [156 mi. 6], fo. 139. 144 a.p. 69, Dr. 4 [156 mi. 21], fo. 348ᵛ.

[3] Foucquet thought that Mazarin could not dismiss Colbert, since he had made himself 'maistre de tout son domestique et de tous ses effets': Foucquet, *Défenses*, viii. 286; 144 a.p. 66, Dr. 3 [156 mi. 15], fo. 131.

[4] Foucquet asked for 'une règle certaine qui paroisse stable': A.A.E. France 908, fo. 31ᵛ., 3 Sept. 1659.

[5] *Arrêts du conseil du roi*, ed. Le Pesant, no. 3004.

fruition by Colbert—thus originates with Foucquet.[1] Before 1660 the achievement was slight: but in that year a considerable start was made. The rent payable by the farmers of the *gabelles de France* was increased from 8.6 to 14.8 million *livres*; that of the farmers of the *aides* from 3.2 to 4.5 million; and that of the farmers of the *cinq grosses fermes* from 2.4 to 4.4 million.[2] Colbert still argued that Foucquet's administration of the revenue farms left much to be desired, and on 24 September 1661, shortly after his arrest, the farms were reallocated yet again and rents substantially increased.[3] Another new direction pursued by Foucquet in the spring of 1660 was to reduce royal expenditure on *rentes*. Over nine million *livres* in new *rentes* had been established between 1653 and 1659 as part of the fiscal expedients of wartime.[4] Foucquet's reduction of 2 million in the annual payments to *rentiers* was the first serious attempt to reverse the trend, and was a considerable achievement given the intense political opposition to any reductions at all.[5] When Colbert made his much more significant reductions in the *rentes* after 1664, there were similar political difficulties, but his position was much stronger since Louis XIV had declared his personal rule and assumed control of his financial affairs.[6]

If Foucquet had some solid achievements by the end of 1660, there were still areas of financial policy where his record was vulnerable. The level of secret expenditure remained high: at 30.7 million, it was considerably in excess of the figure when Servien was still in command, even if an improvement on the levels of 1657–9.[7] After Mazarin's death, Colbert denounced the level of

---

[1] The policy was linked with the remission of arrears of the direct taxes: Lair, *Foucquet*, i. 506 and A.A.E. France 910, fo. 152, 2 Apr. 1660. For Foucquet's desire to amalgamate the farms: Foucquet, *Défenses*, xvi. 87 and 144 a.p. 60, Dr. 1 [156 mi. 6], fo. 49. However, as late as 1660 some leases tended to fragment rather than consolidate. For example, the administration of the *gabelles* of the Lyonnais and Languedoc was still divided: E 332a, fo. 90, 11 Feb. 1660.

[2] Appendix Two, Table VI.

[3] E 384b, fos. 365, 369, 24 Sept. 1661.

[4] Dent, *Crisis in finance*, p. 50. The policy of Servien and Foucquet on *rentes* is fully discussed by Martin and Bezançon, *L'histoire du crédit*, pp. 54–62.

[5] Lair, *Foucquet*, i. 503, talks of Foucquet's 'politique modérée' yet in his transcription of the letter to Mazarin of 11 Mar. 1660 (A.A.E. 910, fo. 93) omits an important passage which alters the tone of the *surintendant*'s comments. Foucquet wrote: 'il la faut exécuter comme une affaire *de la volonté expresse du Roy et non pas comme une affaire* ordinaire des finances à laquelle on puisse espérer changement ou modération, ny faire exception de personne . . .' (The passage omitted by Lair is italicized.)

[6] For the political troubles: Ormesson, *Journal*, ed. Chéruel, ii. 149, 158. Foucquet's and Colbert's reductions are mentioned by Dent, op. cit., pp. 51, 54.

[7] Appendix Two, Table III.

secret expenditure to Louis XIV and argued that 'sous couleur de ce secret se cachent tout les abus et tous les malversations qui se commettent dans les finances'.[1] On 24 December 1661, after Foucquet's arrest, the council of state ordered an investigation into the secret expenses since 1635; ironically, it was of great importance that Foucquet, unlike his predecessors in the 1630s, had not burnt the detailed records.[2] A further source of weakness in Foucquet's position was the extent of royal borrowing—at over 40 million in 1660, the level of borrowing remained high despite the return to peacetime conditions—and the excessive rates of interest still being paid on loans. He had sought to reduce the rate to 12.5 per cent, it is true;[3] but this was still a high rate to pay in peacetime. After Foucquet's arrest in the autumn of 1661, Colbert abrogated the loan contracts and reduced the rate of interest to a maximum of 7.5 per cent.[4] Foucquet did little to reduce his position as a principal royal creditor, which left him open to the charge that he was a direct beneficiary of high interest rates paid to the financiers. Foucquet did not hold a *chambre de justice*: instead, he publicly proclaimed the policy of gradualism and social peace. Condé and his supporters had been allowed to return to France and take up their offices after the signing of the Peace of the Pyrenees. If rebellious nobles who had acted treasonably could benefit from an amnesty so too could financiers who had loyally supported the crown in its long war against the Habsburgs. The families of financiers should not be harassed by retrospective taxation: instead they should lend to the crown at unusually low rates of interest (5.55 per cent) and on revenues that would not fall due until 1662–5.[5]

Foucquet's policy of gradualism was thrown into confusion by the death of Mazarin on 9 March 1661. The circumstances surrounding his death are shrouded in mystery. It appears that Mazarin's confessor[6] denounced the chief minister's corruption

[1] *Lettres . . . de Colbert*, ed. Clément, ii. pt. i. 28–9.

[2] 144 a.p. 70, Dr. 6 [156 mi. 24], no. 7, copy of decree of 24 Dec. 1661. Mazarin and Séguier had suggested that Foucquet burn the records: Foucquet, *Défenses*, xiii., 96–7 and 144 a.p. 69, Dr. 4 [156 mi. 21], fos. 258ᵛ.–259ᶠ.

[3] A.A.E. France 910, fo. 72, 20 Feb. 1660.

[4] E 350, *passim*.

[5] E 338a, fo. 337, 4 Sept. 1660. E 339c, fo. 362, 27 Nov. 1660. The argument about Condé and his supporters is found in Foucquet's letter to Le Tellier after his arrest: B.L. Add. MSS. 39673, fo. 73, n.d. [1661]. Cf. also Foucquet, *Défenses*, xvi. 156. The amnesty to the financiers was discussed 'sur le chemin d'Orléans' by Mazarin, Foucquet, Villeroy, and Le Tellier, and decided by Louis XIV and Mazarin at Fontainebleau: ibid., vi. 38–9 and 144 a.p. 66, Dr. 1 [156 mi. 15], fo. 6ᵛ.

[6] In Foucquet's account, simply 'quelques gens d'église': Foucquet, *Défenses*, v. 93.

and urged him to return all monies he had acquired illegally. In a remark which may be apocryphal, but is nevertheless significant, Mazarin is alleged to have said 'si cela est, il faut tout restituer.'[1] This is precisely what he did on 3 March 1661. For three days he heard nothing from the king and began to panic: 'ma pauvre famille n'aura pas de pain', he is alleged to have said in despair. However, there was never any serious risk that Louis XIV would confiscate Mazarin's fortune: this would have amounted to a public disavowal of the chief minister's achievements in domestic and, above all, foreign policy at a time when his international prestige was at its height after the Peace of the Pyrenees. Colbert returned on 6 March with Louis XIV's donation. Mazarin was allowed to bequeath his wealth as he saw fit and to keep the details secret, thus implying that there would be no investigation or confiscation after his death.[2] In the event, Louis XIV ordered the drawing up of probate records on 30 March despite Mazarin's instructions, which revealed total assets of about 37 million *livres*. This amounted to probably the largest personal fortune bequeathed under the *ancien régime*, and was considerably larger than that left by Richelieu. It was also a fortune recently acquired. With the exception of the Palais Mazarin, bought from Jacques Tubeuf in 1649, all the Cardinal's property had been acquired after the Fronde: the duchy of Mayenne in 1654, that of the Nivernais in 1659; Belfort and other lands in Alsace were donated by the king in 1658–9. Yet Mazarin's landed property, which was valued in 1661 at 6.7 million,[3] was matched by his vast accumulation of money orders from the Treasury: he held 5.9 million in *billets de l'Épargne*, almost certainly from revenues assigned to him by Foucquet, and he had also acquired 2.6 million in alienated royal revenues. His 21 abbeys were farmed out to the great financier Pierre Girardin and yielded an annual income of nearly 2 million. Mazarin had also built up an impressive collection of paintings and jewellery (including the 18 *Mazarins*, the best diamonds in Europe, which were worth nearly 2 million).

What was most striking about Mazarin's fortune, however,

[1] *Mémoires pour servir à l'histoire de Louis XIV par l'abbé de Choisy*, ed. J. F. Michaud and J. J. F. Poujoulat, 3rd ser., vi (1839), pp. 569–70, who states that the question had been posed by Mazarin's confessor.

[2] D. Dessert, 'Pouvoir et finance au xviiᵉ siècle: la fortune de Mazarin', *Revue d'Histoire Moderne et Contemporaine*, xxiii (1976), 161–81, is a contribution of fundamental importance. Dessert (162–3) confirms the chronology; the abbé de Choisy provides the gloss on Mazarin's panic.

[3] 5.2 million (*terres*) plus 1.5 million (*palais et maisons*): ibid., 166.

were the vast cash deposits: his was perhaps the largest personal cash bequest under the *ancien régime*. At nearly 9 million *livres*, his private store of cash was considerably larger than that much more famous public store deposited by Sully in the Bastille. He had kept the cash either near his place of residence (4.2 million at Paris, nearly 1.5 million at Vincennes) or else prudently stored near the border in case of another enforced departure from the kingdom as in 1651: 1.2 million was stored at Brouage (not far from La Rochelle, of which he was governor), 1.1 million at Sedan, and over half a million at La Fère; 400,000 *livres* were deposited in Italy. Perhaps the cash deposits at the time of Mazarin's death were even larger than those officially recorded in the probate records.[1] The speed with which his wealth had been acquired—in 1658 his total assets were only 8 million[2] —and the size of the cash deposits and treasury bills provide convincing evidence that the fortune had been acquired corruptly. There were few outright gifts from the king—Belfort and the other lands in Alsace being the exception. Almost all the allegations of corruption later levelled against Foucquet[3] could be made with equal, if not greater, validity against the chief minister and his agents. Indeed, Foucquet did not hesitate to assert that whereas he left office poorer than when he entered, Mazarin, Colbert, and Berryer—Colbert's agent and business associate—had made immense gains since 1653;[4] but the *surintendant* asked in vain for Mazarin's probate records to be used as evidence at his trial.

Colbert outmanoeuvred Foucquet at the time of Mazarin's death. Although one of the five executors of the chief minister's last will and testament,[5] Foucquet was never involved in the secret dealings between Louis XIV and Colbert: he was named as executor because of the office he held as *procureur-général* in the

---

[1] Dessert, (ibid., 171) notes the cash deposits, and at p. 176 cites Foucquet's view that Mazarin had transferred money abroad. The abbé de Choisy asserted that Colbert revealed cash deposits of 18 or 19 million to Louis XIV: 'ce fut là le commencement de la fortune de Colbert'. This could be hearsay; on the other hand, there was plenty of time between 9 Mar. and 30 Mar. to remove some of the cash deposits.

[2] According to Colbert, 8,052,165 *livres: Lettres . . . de Colbert*, ed. Clément, i. 520–30.

[3] For example, Talon's assertion that 'le seul excès des biens qu'il possède et des profusions qu'il a faictes le rendent criminel': 144 a.p. 68, Dr. 1 [156 mi. 18], fo. 67ʳ.–ᵛ. Talon accused Foucquet of disloyalty to Mazarin's memory, but did not counter the fundamental point concerning Mazarin's fortune: 144 a.p. 67, Dr. 1 [156 mi. 17], fo. 21ᵛ.

[4] Foucquet, *Défenses*, vi. 136–7 and vii. 242 (where he includes Hervart in the denunciation). On Berryer's rapid rise: F. Dornic, *Une ascension sociale au xviiᵉ siècle. Louis Berryer, agent de Mazarin et Colbert* (Caen, 1968). Dornic (p. 99) quotes Foucquet's comment.

[5] The others were Colbert, Le Tellier, Lamoignon, *premier président* of the *Parlement* of Paris, and Mazarin's old friend Ondedei, bishop of Fréjus.

Parlement of Paris, in order to forestall criticism from that quarter.[1] In contrast, Colbert had dominated the negotiations with the king and the beneficiaries of Mazarin's estate, exploiting to the full his detailed knowledge and the trust of his patron. Mazarin recognized that most of his orders to Colbert had been given orally; as a result, he requested that Colbert's word be accepted without question.[2] Yet most of Mazarin's orders to Foucquet had also been given orally. If Foucquet and Colbert disagreed, as they already had, which version of events would be accepted by the king? There was no written request that Foucquet's word be accepted without question. This was of crucial importance to the *surintendant*, who had lent money to the king on Mazarin's instructions. If the king refused to honour his debts, Foucquet could conceivably have taken civil action for redress against Mazarin during his lifetime. Indeed, Foucquet had retained a letter from the chief minister—which had been written on 20 October 1659 and authorized a loan of one million—precisely for this purpose.[3] With Mazarin dead, and his probate records covered with a cloak of secrecy and immunity, this course of action was no longer open. Sooner or later, Louis XIV would have to make a choice between Foucquet and Colbert—and there could be no doubt which would prove the cheaper solution. By protecting Mazarin's fortune from the claims of the legions of his financial agents, and eliminating all traces of a somewhat compromising political past as *intendant de la maison*, Colbert had won the decisive first round in the struggle for the king's confidence.[4]

On his death-bed, Mazarin held a private interview with Louis XIV. Exactly what passed between them is not known.[5] According to some versions, the chief minister commented on the abilities of Louis's advisers, praising Foucquet more than Lionne or Le Tellier;[6] in other accounts, particularly Colbert's, Mazarin is said

---

[1] '. . . dans la pensée que j'en faciliterois l'exécution . . .': Foucquet, *Défenses*, xi. 134–5.

[2] Dessert, 'Pouvoir et finance au xviiᵉ siècle', 179.

[3] Foucquet, *Défenses*, viii. 290.

[4] Foucquet commented that during the secret negotiations he treated Colbert with deference 'comme s'il eût été mon supérieur . . .': ibid., v. 94.

[5] Louis XIV's account was left incomplete because of 'certaines intrigues': *Lettres . . . de Colbert*, ed. Clément, i. 535–6.

[6] Foucquet, *Défenses*, xi. 134. A rather less favourable version to Foucquet is given by R. Darricau and M. Laurain-Portemer, 'La mort du Cardinal Mazarin', *Annuaire-Bulletin de la Société de l'Histoire de France* (1958–9, published 1960), 120 note. Foucquet was warned on 4 Mar. 1661 that Mazarin had told the king that 'si l'on vous pouvait ôter les bâtiments et les femmes de la tête vous étiez capable de grandes choses, mais surtout il fallait prendre garde

to have warned the king against Foucquet, but suggested that his dismissal be deferred because of the risk of 'quelque fascheux mouvement à l'estat'.[1] What is clear is that Foucquet met the king and made damaging revelations about the conduct of financial administration in the 1650s. Foucquet's attitude was that he had only done what was necessary in the circumstances and what the Cardinal had ordered. Perhaps what he had done was wrong; certainly it was 'contre l'ordre'. On the other hand, Mazarin never gave precise instructions on financial matters, 'il blasmoit et permettoit'. Foucquet claimed to be poorer in 1661 than when he had entered office and as a result asked for the king's pardon. Louis XIV is supposed to have replied 'oui, je vous pardonne . . .'[2] The *surintendant* then presented the king with an account of royal expenditure, which remained high despite the signing of the Peace of the Pyrenees,[3] and a list of revenues which had been anticipated. It was clear that it would prove difficult, if not impossible, to borrow the necessary sums on the public market because of the political uncertainty following Mazarin's death.[4] Foucquet thus undertook personally to fund the deficit: he lent the crown nearly 20 million *livres*, much of it borrowed with the assistance of Pierre Girardin; he paid 10 per cent interest, five per cent less than the current rate.[5] At the time of his arrest, Foucquet claimed that his personal debts, resulting from his loans to the crown, amounted to 12 million, with interest payments at 10 per cent amounting to 1.2 million a year.[6] If Foucquet was telling the truth, then all his assets with the exception of his *châteaux* at Vaux-le-Vicomte and Saint-Mandé were offset by his debts.

à votre ambition': E. Spanheim, *Relation de la cour de France en 1690*, ed. Bourgeois (1900), p. 304 n. 2.

[1] *Lettres . . . de Colbert*, ed. Clément, ii. pt. i. 33. The abbé de Choisy thought that Foucquet did not know 'tout ce que ce cardinal mourant avoit dit au Roi sur son chapitre . . .': *Mémoires*, ed. Michaud and Poujoulat, p. 574.

[2] Foucquet was consistent on the king's verbal pardon: Foucquet, *Défenses*, v. 95: xiii. 130; xvi. 156. 144 a.p. 60, Dr. 1 [156 mi. 6], fo. 82ᵛ. B.L. Add. MSS. 39673, fo. 75ᵛ.: '. . . sa parole doibt avoir quelque éffect, donnée à un subject dans un temps de paix, sans contrainte . . .' But did Louis XIV fear Foucquet?

[3] Because of the 'licentiement des troupes, gratiffica[tij]ons et autres despences qu'il auroit pleu au Roy commander': Foucquet, *Défenses*, xvi, 104. 144 a.p. 60, Dr. 1 [156 mi. 6], fo. 59.

[4] In Foucquet's expression, 'les bourses se trouvoient ordinairement fermées dans les grands changemens'. The financiers feared that Louis XIV would declare bankruptcy; Foucquet's participation in the market was a guarantee against this.

[5] Foucquet, *Défenses*, v. 96, 142; viii. 297–8. 144 a.p. 66, Dr. 3 [156 mi. 15], fo. 137.

[6] Foucquet, *Défenses*, xvi. 250. 144 a.p. 60, Dr. 1 [156 mi. 6], fo. 142. B.L. Add. MSS 39673, fo. 77.

Foucquet's assets were much more extensive than those of Bullion in 1640, but Bullion's debts had been negligible. Can a finance minister be called corrupt if his liabilities to the crown cancelled out his assets?[1] Louis XIV had certainly encouraged Foucquet to make these loans. Outwardly, the prestige of the *surintendant* was immense. In the afternoons, he met with the king alone to discuss the state of the royal finances. In the mornings he was the leading light in the king's sessions on foreign and secret affairs in which Le Tellier and Lionne also participated.[2] Yet some of Mazarin's Machiavellian tendencies may have rubbed off on his political disciple. Was Louis simply giving Foucquet enough rope to hang himself?[3] Both Lionne and Le Tellier were considerably older than Foucquet, would naturally resent his claim to seniority, and might decide to unite against him.[4] Moreover, Foucquet's control of financial policy was now restricted by the need to inform the king, and by Colbert who brought the register of revenues and expenses to the afternoon sessions. At Le Tellier's request, Colbert, his former clerk, had been made *intendant des finances* in March 1661, without having to buy the office,[5] and the register of the *surintendance* was

---

[1] At his interrogation on 8 Mar. 1662, Foucquet contended that his total assets did not reach 12 million, the total of his debts: Foucquet, *Défenses*, xvi. 38–9. 144 a.p. 60, Dr. 1, fo. 21ᵛ. His assets, with the exception of the two *châteaux*, reach 12 million only by including the dowry paid to Marie Foucquet in 1657: Appendix Two, Table X E. The 'estat des biens de Monsieur Foucquet au mois de septembre 1661' (B.A. MS. 7167, fos. 169–173) is incomplete, although it contains the interesting comment that 'ce qui estoit à Bellisle et à Paris en très grand nombre a esté diverty'. The 'estat de(s) sommes que Mons. Foucquet a déclaré debvoir à divers particuliers par son interrogatoire' (B.A. MS. 7167, fo. 165) contains an official total of 9,043,000 *livres* in debts and an actual total of 8,586,000 *livres*: it seems incomplete, in view of Foucquet's assertion of 12 million. The recent estimate of Foucquet's fortune by Dessert is somewhat higher (15.5 million—but N.B.: including Vaux-le-Vicomte and St. Mandé) but so too is the estimate for his debts (15.5 million), and the author comments 'son patrimonie est en fait largement compensé par des dettes . . . l'actif équilibre tout juste le passif'. The author also notes that his calculations of Foucquet's fortune are indeed estimates: D. Dessert, 'L'affaire Fou(c)quet', *L'histoire*, xxxii (1981), 39–47.

[2] Foucquet, *Défenses*, xi. 136, 138–9.

[3] Louis XIV told the archbishop of Embrun on 16 Sept. 1661 that he had begun to see the necessity of Foucquet's arrest four months previously, i.e. by the middle of May 1661: *Archives de la Bastille*, ed. Ravaisson-Mollien, i. 363. The crucial decisions do not appear to have been taken until mid-July, however. It was then that Foucquet's influence with Anne of Austria collapsed, and that the decisions to sell his office of *procureur-général* and for the court to visit Brittany were taken: P. A. Chéruel, *Mémoires sur la vie publique et privée de Foucquet . . .* (2 vols., 1862), ii. 167, 180. N.B.: if this view is correct, it places the decision to arrest Foucquet *before* the famous *fête* at Vaux-le-Vicomte on 17 Aug: ibid., ii. 222.

[4] The abbé de Choisy commented that 'les autres ministres . . . furent offensés et se réunirent contre lui . . .': *Mémoires*, loc. cit.

[5] Foucquet, *Défenses*, v. 27–8.

transferred from Hervart's to his custody. Foucquet may have hoped that his severest critic would thus be implicated in his financial policies: but at a stroke, the weapons at Colbert's disposal, and the power base from which to strike at his rival were vastly strengthened. The sale of Foucquet's office of *procureur-général* in the *Parlement* of Paris on 12 August 1661 marked a decisive step towards the collapse of his position. Louis XIV asked for a cash fund of one million *livres* at Vincennes, which could only be raised from this source.[1] Foucquet thought he had secured the king's favour by offering to sell his office; at the same time, he offered the king his *châteaux* at Vaux-le-Vicomte and Belle-Île and to resign as *surintendant*—none of which were accepted. Yet in reality, the king had a deeper purpose. The office would have given Foucquet an automatic right to trial before the *Parlement* of Paris, and almost certain acquittal.[2] If Louis XIV was determined to arrest Foucquet, and keep him imprisoned at all costs, Foucquet had to be induced to sell his office first, after which he could be put on trial before royal commissioners especially selected for their compliance. Foucquet was thus duped. He sold his office 'comme un innocent, se mettant par là la corde au cou ...'[3] In less than a month Foucquet was arrested, significantly at Nantes rather than Paris or Fontainebleau since Louis wanted an army at hand to occupy the fortress of Belle-Île.[4]

The arrest of Foucquet on 5 September 1661 was followed shortly afterwards by other measures bringing Mazarin's system to an end: the establishment of the *conseil royal des finances* on 15 September, and the revocation of the loan contracts on 16 November.[5] The king had thus assumed personal control of his finances, and declared the bankruptcy that had been feared by the financiers since the end of the war and particularly since the death of Mazarin. The *chambre de justice* set up in November 1661—composed of twenty-nine members, nineteen drawn from the Parisian courts and ten from the provinces[6]—was designed to prosecute Foucquet and the many financiers who had participated in tax contracts, leases on the revenue farms, and loans to the king since

[1] The sale produced 1.4 million: Lair, *Foucquet*, ii. 36–7, 45. Foucquet, *Défenses*, xvi. 96.
[2] Dent, 'The role of *clientèles*', 67. A. N. Hamscher, *The Parlement of Paris after the Fronde, 1653–1673* (Pittsburgh, Pa., 1976), p. 124.
[3] As the abbé de Choisy commented: *Mémoires, loc. cit.*
[4] J. B. Wolf, *Louis XIV* (1968), p. 140. Wolf comments at p. 139 that 'Louis was clearly afraid of him'.
[5] E 349b, fo. 91, 16 Nov. 1661. Cf. E 349c, fo. 163, 15 Dec. 1661.
[6] Bosher, '*Chambres de justice* in the French monarchy', 21.

1635.[1] However, the procedure became quite unworkable. From 1662 the two trials—that of Foucquet on the one hand and the financiers on the other—proceeded separately. This was demonstrated more clearly on 11 December 1663 when, after the dismissal of Denis Talon as *procureur-général* of the *chambre de justice*, Chamillart was appointed his successor for the Foucquet trial, and Hotman de Fontenay for the cases of the financiers.[2] Nevertheless, the two trials were clearly related. In prosecuting Foucquet along with the financiers, Louis XIV and Colbert sought to conceal their true political purpose and keep public sympathy for the principal victim to a minimum.[3] Even the trial of the financiers may have had a political purpose, however, namely the substitution of one dominant group under Colbert's control, in place of the group of financiers established by Mazarin and Foucquet.[4] The trial of the financiers was a relatively straightforward affair. 494 individuals were taxed for a total of nearly 157 million *livres*; these fines were moderated in October 1665 to 110 million.[5] Compared to all its predecessors, and even in comparison with its successor in 1716–17, the *chambre de justice* of 1661–5 was severe to the financiers. However, the terms on which the fines were paid were rather less severe than the amount demanded. Colbert wanted to bring about considerable savings in royal expenditure and to reduce the mass of treasury bills and *rentes* in circulation. Since the financiers had substantial holdings of both,[6] it was natural that the collection of fines should be facilitated by a severe redemption both of treasury bills and *rentes*. There were protests,[7] but on the whole the financiers accepted their fate tamely because they had no choice.

Foucquet, on the other hand, deployed all his skills as a former *procureur-général* to mobilize the arguments for his defence. It is clear from the protracted trial proceedings, and from the disorganized way in which the prosecution presented its case, that

[1] The edict is published in *Lettres . . . de Colbert*, ed. Clément, ii. 751–3. On 12 Sept. 1661, those who had made loans since 1 Jan. 1659 were ordered to account to the council; on 25 Oct., the investigation was extended back to May 1643: E 349a, fo. 354.
[2] *Archives de la Bastille*, ed. Ravaisson-Mollien, ii. 162–3.
[3] Bosher, '*Chambres de justice* in the French monarchy', 32.
[4] D. Dessert and J. L. Journet, 'Le lobby Colbert: un royaume ou une affaire de famille?', *Annales E.S.C.*, xxx (1975), 1310–11.
[5] 248 individuals were fined more than 100,000 *livres* each. Dent, *Crisis in finance*, pp. 107, 151. Dessert, 'Finances et société au xviiᵉ siècle', 850, 872–81. Appendix Two, Table IX C.
[6] As the decree of 9 Sept. 1665 recognized with regard to the *rentes*: E 381a, fo. 334.
[7] Protests of the *héritiers* Bonneau to the king, Aug. 1665: *Archives de la Bastille*, ed. Ravaisson-Mollien, ii. 448–9.

Foucquet's resolve, technical knowledge, and skill in argument took the government by surprise. The man who would best have led the prosecution case—Colbert, whom Foucquet consistently referred to as his true accuser[1]—could not do so without risk of alienating the less partisan judges; Talon and Chamillart bungled the task. From the outset, there were both political and financial charges against Foucquet.[2] Under the heading of *crimes d'état*, Foucquet was accused of having written a plan for a political conspiracy or rebellion in the event of his arrest (the so-called *projet de Saint-Mandé*).[3] He was also accused of fortifying his fortress on the island of Belle-Île off the coast of Brittany; of acting in a similar way with his other Breton fortress, Concarneau; finally it was alleged that he had established a clientage network with individuals providing written undertakings to serve his cause. The *malversations au fait des finances* of which Foucquet was accused were more numerous. It was said that he had authorized unnecessary royal borrowing and while *ordonnateur* he had lent the king money, which he should not have done. It was claimed that he had made no distinction between his own and the king's money, and had drawn up the royal accounts at his private residence. He was accused of participating in the revenue farms and tax contracts under assumed names and of taking pensions and other illicit payments from the tax farmers and contractors. Finally, Foucquet was blamed for, and alleged to have profited from, the abuse of treasury bills. The entire period of his financial administration was denounced as contrary to the king's interests. Most of these charges were apparent in the early interrogations of Foucquet by royal commissioners in March 1662. There is some evidence that greater emphasis was placed on the political charges in the later stages of the trial. This is scarcely surprising since the *projet de Saint-Mandé* was the one piece of testimony that Foucquet did not contest—though, of course, he denied the charge of treason which the prosecution sought to prove from this evidence. On all the financial charges, however, Foucquet was better informed than his prosecutors. It is doubtful whether the materials used by the prosecution could have revealed conclusive evidence of the type they were seeking. Moreover, Foucquet's private papers had been removed in September 1661 and carefully edited

---

[1] *Archives de la Bastille*, ed. Ravaisson-Mollien, i. 59. 144 a.p. 66, Dr. 1 [156 mi. 15], fo. 3.

[2] These are conveniently summarized in Foucquet, *Défenses*, v. 2–4.

[3] Published by Chéruel, *Mémoires sur la vie publique et privée de Foucquet*, i. 489–501. Manuscript version acknowledged by Foucquet: 144 a.p. 71, Dr. 5 [156 mi. 25]. Plan summarized by Dent, 'The role of *clientèles*', 64–6.

by Colbert and Berryer, his agent. The less partisan judges were offended by this manipulation of the evidence, a point to which the accused frequently returned in his defence.[1]

Foucquet professed that he could not understand the reason for his arrest, or the need for a trial. In financial affairs, 'tout [était] en bon estat'. He had already offered to resign as *surintendant*; if the king was no longer satisfied with this offer, he would live under house arrest in Brittany.[2] He thus dismissed the arguments levelled against him as a political conspiracy master-minded by Colbert, and argued that the paucity of evidence produced against him after nine years in office revealed the difficulties of the prosecution in substantiating a case.[3] In answer to the argument that a finance minister as *ordonnateur* should never lend personally to the crown, Foucquet replied that he had been asked to do so by Mazarin and the king, and that the interest he had charged for his services was lower than the rate usually charged by financiers who in any case had been unwilling to lend.[4] He specifically denied the allegations concerning participation in the revenue farms and tax contracts.[5] Nor had he taken pensions or other gifts from the tax farmers and contractors: the time to have done so would have been in 1660, when the rents paid by the revenue farmers were greatly increased and he could have profited by several million had he so chosen.[6] Foucquet made a damaging admission that he had taken insufficient 'exactitude et précaution' in keeping the registers of the royal finances,[7] but the attempt to prove from his personal accounts that he had stolen the king's money appears to have broken down.[8] Nevertheless, the investigation of his personal finances served to confirm the contemporary verdict on Foucquet's extravagance and conspicuous consumption, particularly in regard to the cost of building work and decorations at Vaux-le-Vicomte and Saint-Mandé. If he had lived in an 'honneste parcimonie', it was said, he would not have needed to steal

---

[1] Foucquet, *Défenses*, xv, *passim*. The 'fautes importantes dans les inventaires' were noted by Lefèvre d'Ormesson as one of the reasons why there was no death sentence: Ormesson, *Journal*, ed. Chéruel, ii. 289.

[2] Chéruel, *Mémoires sur la vie publique et privée de Foucquet*, ii. 263–70. B.L. Add. MSS. 39673, fos. 75ᵛ.–76ʳ.

[3] Foucquet, *Défenses*, v. 202.

[4] Ibid., vii. 196–8.

[5] 'Je [n]'aye jamais joint la qualité de traitant à celle d'ordonnateur': 144 a.p. 69, Dr. 6 [156 mi. 22], fo. 29ᵛ.

[6] Foucquet, *Defenses*, xvi. 85–6. 144 a.p. 60, Dr. 1 [156 mi. 6], fos. 47ᵛ.–48ʳ.

[7] Ibid., xvi. 210–11. 144 a.p. 60, Dr. 1 [156 mi. 6], fo. 118. The prosecution placed great emphasis on this point: 144 a.p. 67, Dr. 1 [156 mi. 17], fo. 18ᵛ.

[8] Appendix Two, Table X. Cf. B.A. MS. 7167, fo. 175.

from the king. Foucquet was his own worst enemy: the moral of the story was that his ambition and extravagance had contributed to his downfall.[1] With disarming frankness, Foucquet accepted that he had been extravagant, but denied the charge of peculation.[2] On he general charge of financial maladministration, he stated simply that his objective had been to satisfy Cardinal Mazarin and ensure that there were revenues to meet royal expenditure.[3] Certainly, much money had been borrowed—this had been his principal task when in office—but the loans were necessary and justified and had been authorized either by Mazarin or the king.[4] Though it is doubtful whether the prosecution proved the case of corruption,[5] the *chambre de justice* found Foucquet guilty on this charge. On 20 December 1664, his property was ordered to be confiscated, and he was sentenced to exile abroad for life.[6]

Although its verdict may well have been influenced by the charge of treason, the *chambre de justice* did not pronounce on the *crime d'état*. However, and very unusually in French judicial procedure, the crown immediately intervened to make the sentence more severe. Foucquet's punishment was converted from life exile to life imprisonment, 'veu la connaissance particulière qu'il avoit des affaires les plus importantes de l'estat'.[7] This was the last of the *coups d'autorité* which had marked successive stages in the trial.[8] What had determined this course of action was the suspicion, which Foucquet vigorously denied, that he had been prepared to force his continuance in office as finance minister, if necessary by armed rebellion.[9] It is certainly true that Foucquet had a strong power base in Brittany, his native province. The terms on which

[1] 144 a.p. 68, Dr. 1 [156 mi. 18], fo. 43ᵛ. 144 a.p. 72, Dr. 3, no. 1 [156 mi. 27]. fo. 2.

[2] Foucquet, *Défenses*, vi. 157: 'il faut prouver que j'ay pris au roy, c'est ce qui ne se peut [faire]'.

[3] Ibid., xiii. 240.

[4] Ibid., viii. 299; xvi. 71. 144 a.p. 60, Dr. 1 [156 mi. 6], fos. 39ᵛ.–40ʳ.

[5] F. Cherchève, 'Le procès de Nicolas Foucquet', *Quelques procès criminels des xviiᵉ siècles*, ed. J. Imbert (1964), pp. 115–17.

[6] Lair, *Foucquet*, ii. 403–4. *Archives de la Bastille*, ed. Ravaisson-Mollien, ii. 390. 144 a.p. 74, Dr. 10 [156 mi. 30], no. 2.

[7] Lair, *Foucquet*, ii. 407.

[8] Royal intervention in the trial was quite blatant on 23 Aug. 1663, when Lefèvre d'Ormesson was summoned to see Louis XIV, and 3 May 1664, when Colbert met Ormesson's father: Ormesson, *Journal*, ed. Chéruel, ii. 45–6, 136–8. He later recalled the 'coups de haine et d'autorité': ibid. ii. 289.

[9] *Archives de la Bastille*, ed. Ravaisson-Mollien, ii. 377. The charge was made in the interrogation of 16 Mar. 1662: Foucquet, *Defenses*, xvi. 147. 144 a.p. 60, Dr. 1 [156 mi. 6], fo. 78ᵛ. Though an *homme de robe*, it was said that Foucquet was prepared to act as a rebellious magnate: ibid., vii. 354.

Deslandes, his client, held the fortress of Concarneau excluded loyalty to a third party which might be interpreted as meaning the king.[1] Moreover the island fortress of Belle-Île could equally have been mobilized against the king since it was held for Foucquet by another client, the sieur de la Haye. Foucquet claimed that since la Haye was a relative of the great French ambassador Pierre Chanut, his loyalty was above suspicion, but this argument was not accepted by the king.[2] Foucquet's power in Brittany was not undisputed, since he was a political rival of La Meilleraye, the lieutenant-general and former finance minister.[3] His fortress, Belle-Île, had formerly belonged to the Retz family, and had become a security risk during the exile abroad of Cardinal de Retz from 1654 to 1662. Thus Foucquet had been asked by Mazarin to purchase the fortress in 1658, and had subsequently been empowered to repair the fortifications.[4] Foucquet maintained that his possession of Belle-Île and Concarneau was a temporary service to the chief minister, who intended them ultimately to form part of the inheritance of the duc Mazarin, La Meilleraye's son, who married Hortense Mancini, the Cardinal's niece, in 1661.[5]

All this may have been true, but Louis XIV felt threatened. He told the archbishop of Embrun that Belle-Île was capable of greater resistance than Sedan.[6] The comparison with Sedan was particularly damaging, for the ducs de Bouillon had based their numerous conspiracies in the seventeenth century on possession of this *place de sûreté*, indeed this was why it had been expropriated by the crown in 1642. Had Bouillon not agreed to the confiscation of his fortress, he would have lost his head for his part in the

---

[1] Chéruel, *Mémoires sur la vie publique et privée de Foucquet*, i. 396–7.

[2] Foucquet, *Défenses*, x. 139–40, 194.

[3] Ibid., x. 149–50, 197. However, La Meilleraye was named in an earlier draft of the *projet de Saint-Mandé*, a mistake to which Gourville drew Foucquet's attention: Gourville, *Mémoires*, ed. Michaud and Poujoulat, p. 530.

[4] Respectively by letters patent of 20 Aug. 1658 and 20 Jan. 1660: Foucquet, *Défenses*, v. 359–65. 144 a.p. 68, Dr. 2 [156 mi. 19], fos. 198ᵛ.–199ᶠ. There was a long-standing concern of the French monarchy with the security of Belle-Île. Henri IV considered buying it from the duc de Retz in 1594: *Lettres . . . de Henri IV*, iv. 146. Vendôme tried to obtain it through a marriage alliance for his son, but Louis XIII stopped his plans, and in 1626–7 the idea of purchase came up again: *Les papiers de Richelieu*, ed. Grillon, i. 108–9; ii. 35, 37. Petit, *L'assemblée des notables de 1626–1627*, p. 83.

[5] Charles-Armand de la Porte had sought the marriage of Hortense Mancini, according to Foucquet, for four or five years, and Cardinal Mazarin had considered in what ways he could make him 'très puissant': Foucquet, *Défenses*, xi. 12, 20. 144 a.p. 68, Dr. 2 [156 mi. 19], fos. 208, 216. The marriage contract was dated 28 Feb. 1661: G. Livet, *Le duc Mazarin. Gouverneur d'Alsace, 1661–1713* (Strasbourg-Paris, 1954), p. 15.

[6] *Archives de la Bastille*, ed. Ravaisson-Mollien, i. 364.

Cinq-Mars conspiracy. Was Foucquet planning a similar conspiracy, a Fronde led by an ousted finance minister?[1] The *projet de Saint-Mandé* appeared to provide the evidence, for in this memorandum in Foucquet's handwriting, a number of aristocrats were named who were to take action to secure their patron's release in the event of his arrest and the government showing no willingness to release him within three months. The measures to be taken included several features of aristocratic rebellions such as those in 1650 after the arrest of the three princes: the publication of a manifesto against the government, the attempt to seize fortresses and raise provinces in rebellion, to capture royal revenues at the local *caisses*, and to suborn regiments from the royal army. There would also be an attempt to kidnap Foucquet's rivals in office, particularly Le Tellier. What made the scheme credible was Foucquet's possession of Belle-Île and Concarneau; his son-in-law, the comte de Charost, was governor of Calais; certain provincial governors and lieutenants-general may also have been favourable to his cause. At his trial, Foucquet dismissed the plan as a chimera: he had never meant it to be taken seriously, nor had there been an actual conspiracy.[2] Clearly, the three-month delay before any action was taken was crucial. The government would have been well-prepared to crush any attempts to force the release of Foucquet. It is also the case that Foucquet had fewer aristocratic supporters than he thought.[3] All this suggests that the finance minister's rivals were probably correct, and that he lacked judgement. The *projet de Saint-Mandé* document should have been destroyed, or better still, never written; it should certainly not have been left behind a mirror in Foucquet's *château*. Foucquet paid dearly for the atmosphere of intrigue and mutual suspicion prevailing under Mazarin's system: he remained imprisoned at Pinerolo until his death in 1680. Foucquet's incarceration was perhaps Louis XIV's most dramatic break with the past and served as the clearest warning to potential conspirators.

---

[1] Freudmann (*L'étonnant Gourville*, p. 88 n. 3) talks of a *Fronde des financiers*, but the expression rests on a misconception. Foucquet's clientage network was much broader than the financiers and encompassed other social groups. Perhaps, indeed, it was too diversified: Dent, 'The role of *clientèles*', 64–6.

[2] Foucquet, *Défenses*, ii. 57; iii. 257, 263.

[3] Dent's verdict is that Foucquet 'over-estimated his own importance; to the court he was just an agreeable official who gave away money . . . [his] *clientèle* was amorphous and had no solid base'. Dent, *loc. cit.* N.B. The delay before the operation of the plan is incorrectly stated as six months by Dent, which would make it appear even less realistic.

Conclusion

The fundamental financial problem of the French monarchy in the seventeenth century was the inefficiency of its revenue raising system, which was not overhauled effectively after 1589 to meet new requirements that were qualitatively different from the period of the Renaissance. The weakness of the system resulted from a tax base that was too narrow combined with an ineffective machinery for the collection of taxes. There were attempts, particularly in the 1630s, to improve the administration of the *taille*, the chief direct tax: but it continued to burden disproportionately the poorer peasants. Those better off tended to escape lightly, while the clergy and nobles were largely exempt. Until Colbert's establishment of the *ferme-générale* in 1681, there was little attempt to reform the indirect taxes which—so the theory ran—spread the fiscal burden more widely over the nation. The rich, it was argued, consumed more than the poor and therefore paid more in indirect taxes. Yet the theory underlying the indirect taxes was clearly incorrect unless the chief items of popular consumption, particularly foodstuffs and wine, were scarcely to be taxed at all. In fact, the reverse was true, since salt, an important item of popular consumption, was heavily taxed by the various farms of the *gabelles* in most of France, as was wine by the farm of the *aides*.

Even when the reform of the indirect taxes came in 1681, it took the form of administrative improvement—basically the amalgamation of several leases and revenue raising systems into one general lease and revenue system—without a change in the social and economic basis of the taxes themselves. Yet the fundamental underlying principle, the belief that indirect taxes were equitable, was a chimera. It was true only in comparison with the *taille*, since for political reasons it was impossible to tax the clergy[1] and nobility effectively. Although Richelieu and Buillon may have laid plans for financial reform in the event of peace with Spain in their lifetime, there is little suggestion that they envisaged a

---

[1] A financial memorandum of 1656 argued that since 1610 the third estate had contributed 2,400 million *livres* in taxes whereas the clergy had contributed just 80 million. It claimed, moreover, that the clergy held over half the wealth of the kingdom: A.A.E. France 899, fo. 237.

fundamental redistribution of taxation between privileged and non-privileged. Indeed, in the *Testament Politique* attributed to Richelieu, the peasant taxpayers of France were likened to mules, beasts of burden deserving only the consideration which an intelligent farmer gives to his animals. Moreover, in Richelieu's view, the maintenance of the social order required that this state of affairs continue.[1] The failure of the second sales tax experiment in 1640–3 marks the end of attempts to overhaul the revenue raising system. Thereafter, the emphasis was largely on the enforcement of existing taxes and on fiscal expedients which were in reality concealed forms of debt.

All the early Bourbon kings were in debt, although at first sight their debts are hidden from view by the procedure of single-entry book-keeping, which required that the separate lists of royal expenditure and income should tally.[2] The debt grew as royal expenditure outpaced revenues in an attempt to pay for what contemporaries called 'les nécessités', that is to say the political and military objectives of the French monarchy at home and abroad. Colbert, who was reasonably successful in reducing royal expenditure until Louis XIV brought down a European coalition on France after 1673,[3] argued that much of the increase in royal expenditure before the fall of Foucquet had been fictitious. Foucquet, too, accepted that the accounts had been overburdened by paper debts which had been transferred from one accounting year to the next.[4] Paper debts they may have been, but it left unredeemed, they earned interest to the creditors of the French monarchy. Once incurred, a public or private debt was difficult to pay off in the circumstances of the seventeenth century.[5] In 1592, a list had been drawn up of Henri IV's debts to Christian of Anhalt, commander of a force of German *reitern* and *landsknechts* in the king's service. By 1624, part of the debt had been paid off; but in 1818, Anhalt's heirs demanded from Louis XVIII immediate repayment of capital and 193 years' interest.[6] The example is of

---

[1] Richelieu, *Testament politique*, ed. André, pp. 253–4.

[2] Appendix Two, Table I.

[3] Appendix Two, Table XI.

[4] 'Ce ne soit que du papier pour conserver le titre aux créanciers': Foucquet, *Défenses*, vi. 104–5. The transfer of debts from one accounting year to the next was by the procedure known as the *ordonnance de remise en d'autre Épargne* and was made worse by the fact that in most years the chief treasurer changed too: Appendix One, Table IV. Bad debts could easily become confused with good ones, since the finance minister could not keep track of all the money orders: Foucquet, *Défenses*, v. 107; xii. 195; xvi. 100.

[5] 'Les dettes au xviie siècle ont la vie dure': Leroy-Ladurie, *Les paysans de Languedoc*, i. 596.

[6] Appendix Two, Table IX, sources A iii (l).

course untypical. Some debts were settled, wholly or in part, much nearer the date they were contracted. Others were not settled at all. Kings tended to renegue on their debts, as in 1589[1] when there was a change of dynasty, and in 1661 after a long royal minority and period when the king had not been of age to rule personally. Monarchical absolutism rationalized default on repayment to its creditors. It was an irresponsible political power whose contractual word was not its bond. Agreements with creditors were kept so long as it was in the crown's interest to do so. If the interest rate paid to creditors was later considered too high, the contract could be broken and the financier taxed retrospectively: 'ce doit estre présumé avoir été dans l'intention de ceux qui ont passé les clauses des traitez en ceux-temps là . . .'[2] Only when the crown had no choice, as in the 1650s when it would not have been able to contract new loans without repaying its debts from the bankruptcy of 1648,[3] did it keep faith with its creditors. Even then the policy was later reversed. Colbert criticized Foucquet's policy of borrowing: 'le roy n'a aucun crédit,' he stated, '. . . on ne traite avec luy que dans la croyance qu'il doit faire banqueroute.'[4] The bankruptcy of 1661 was designed to offset the gains to the financiers in the 1650s, which in turn had offset the bankruptcy of the Fronde.

It was scarcely surprising that the French financiers placed a heavy emphasis on 'la foy publique gardée'. In the Venetian and Dutch Republics, they told Mazarin in February 1653, state creditors were repaid 'à banque ouverte.' They were in no doubt that interest rates would have been as low in France as they were, for example, in the Netherlands but for the fear that the crown would default on its debts, either directly through a declaration of bankruptcy as in 1648, or indirectly through a *chambre de justice* as in 1661. What the financiers hated above all was any change in the terms of their contracts, particularly after a long period of time had elapsed, when the accounts of the consortium had been finalized and the profits distributed among the partners. The *chambre de justice* came close to an attack on property. How could a financier dispose of his property to his heirs, and consider himself

---

[1] Strictly speaking, Henri IV did not finally renounce Henri III's debts until 1608. His bankruptcy was in 1598: but his parlous financial state on his accession in 1589 made a renunciation of all previous debts only a matter of time.

[2] The words were Foucquet's who perhaps, of all the finance ministers of the seventeenth century, was the most inclined to keep his agreements: Foucquet, *Défenses*, v. 136.

[3] Ibid., v. 118–19.

[4] *Lettres . . . de Colbert*, ed. Clément, vii. 180–1.

'maître de ses effets' if the government could order a 10 per cent tax on profits twenty years later?[1] The regularity of the *chambre de justice*, its retrospective character, and its outcome—the taxing of profits, giving the financiers incentive to 'voler de nouveau dans l'espérance d'une nouvelle grâce'[2]—tended to force up interest rates and drive honest financiers from the king's service. The absence of private accounts of financiers makes it difficult to ascertain how often transactions with the government could be loss-making, but there is no doubt that they could.[3] The 'hasard de perte ou gain'[4] was graphically illustrated during Richelieu's ministry by the bankruptcies of Antoine Feydeau, Pierre Payen, Claude Charlot, and François Sabathier, and these examples were not lost on their contemporaries.[5] One could scarcely expect financiers experiencing the consequences of the royal bankruptcy of 1648 to agree with the verdict of one historian that the crown was their 'vassal and tributary'.[6]

If it is misleading to suggest that all financiers were equally successful, it is equally clear that enormous gains could be made very quickly in the king's financial service. A distinction needs to be drawn between the political pressure of financiers, the consequences of which the crown was usually able to evade, and the strength of market forces. It was surprisingly rare for financiers to act as a unified group imposing political terms on the government. When such pressure occurred, it was not always successful and tended to be the pressure of one or two consortia, not all financiers. The crown thus usually had the whip-hand in the relationship: it could divide and rule, offering different treatment to various groups of financiers, who competed against each other more often than they united against the monarchy. On the other hand, the crown could do very little faced with the harsh realities of the money market: the interest rate paid by the crown on royal borrowing fluctuated according to political circumstances, the

---

[1] E 312a, fo. 386, 3 Apr. 1658.

[2] Richelieu, *Testament politique*, ed. André, p. 252.

[3] For example, the *traité* of 9 Jan. 1630 contracted by Montauglon, Le Ragois de Bretonvilliers, Jean Le Vasseur, and Étienne Brioys under the name of Jean Baudoin. A loss of 322,233 *livres* was recorded 'à cause des grands intérests et fraiz payez et soufferts'. The council of finance refused compensation: Minutier Central LI 279. Cf. E 103a, fo. 97, 18 Apr. 1630.

[4] E 62c, fo. 215, 30 Dec. 1619.

[5] Cf. Foucquet, *Défenses*, vi. 118.

[6] Dent, 'An aspect of the crisis', 256. Dent quotes Isaac Bourgoin's view in 1617. But since Bourgoin wanted to hang all financiers, the propaganda purpose of his pamphlet is clear.

rate paid by borrowers on the private market, and the amount demanded by the crown. If the political position of monarchy was uncertain as in 1647–8, if it was difficult to borrow on the private market as in 1654, or if the sums required by the king were very large as in 1645, then the rate of interest payable on loans was accordingly high. Similar rules applied in the negotiation of tax contracts and leases on the revenue farms.

It is extremely difficult, but nevertheless important, to distinguish these fluctuations of the money market from the more permanent problems of administrative weakness and the inherent corruption within the system. Contemporaries talked of the need to make a 'distinction des temps'.[1] At his trial, Foucquet cited the example of the lease on the *cinq grosses fermes* signed by Cardinal Mazarin in 1652. A comparison between the rents payable by the farmers in 1660 and the amount demanded eight years earlier would suggest that Mazarin's conduct was one of criminal negligence until the circumstances surrounding the negotiations are recalled: the administration of the revenue farms had collapsed at the end of the Fronde. Much more needs to be known about the speed and methods by which the fortunes of financiers were created, and the duration or dissipation of their wealth, before it can be stated with confidence that the profiteering of financiers was the most significant factor in creating the debts of the French monarchy. If the humble social origins of financiers were sometimes exaggerated, so too was the size of their fortunes. There were sound business reasons why a financier would be quite happy to have it said that he enjoyed vast wealth—for wealth was an obvious sign of the successful entrepreneur, a crucial element in establishing confidence among those who 'vouldront . . . confyer leurs bourses et leurs moyens'[2] in his activities. Yet when the evidence permits a closer examination, the estimated wealth of a financier may be found to be greatly exaggerated.[3] It is not surprising that such contrasts between real and estimated wealth could exist: the paper transactions of financiers were covered with a cloak of secrecy which even contemporaries found it difficult to

---

[1] Foucquet, *Défenses*, v. 291–2.

[2] A.A.E. France 801, fo. 304, anon. memorandum, 1631. Bouthillier thought in this way: A.A.E. France 839, fo. 173, 17 Aug. 1641.

[3] Thus Nicolas Camus, who was rumoured to have left 9 million *livres* on his death in 1648, in fact left, nearer 2.7 million: Bourgeon, *Les Colbert avant Colbert*, p. 253. Another obvious example—though not, strictly speaking, of a financier—is Mazarin, whose wealth at his death was rumoured to be 100 million: Dent, 'The role of *clientèles*', 61.

penetrate[1] and which aroused deep suspicion. Thus the financier François Sabathier borrowed widely on the private market, offering as security letters of change or simple written promises. When he went bankrupt in 1641, the royal commissioners adjudicating the extent of his debts found that the names of his creditors had been left blank in the letters of change and promises. Moreover, Sabathier's wealth had been dispersed into the acquisition of property by agents acting on his behalf, but again without there being conclusive proof. Thus the size of the debts and assets of the financier were subject to an enormous range of variables: the assets could be doubled or halved, depending on whether his creditors were prepared to moderate their claims in the hope of regaining part of their investment.[2]

Why were the dealings of the crown with its financiers, and those of the financiers with their creditors, kept so secret? Why did both ministers[3] and financiers use nominees (*prête-noms*), dealers (*courtiers de change*), and other intermediaries, and a variety of *écrits*–some witnessed before notaries, others simply *sous seing privé*–to hide their transactions? Clearly, in the case of ministers it was because it was considered best to keep the interrelationship of public and private finance at the centre of government hidden from public eye. Concini, Luynes, Richelieu, and Mazarin had all controlled the patronage system, lent money to the crown, and received interest payments on their loans. A finance minister such as Foucquet managed the loan contracts of others yet also lent the king money. How could interest payments in general be distinguished from interest payments he received in his own right? It was not easy to do so. Colbert denounced the whole system before 1661 as corrupt and argued that a 'maxime de la confusion' was deliberately followed by *surintendants* to protect their political position and their illicit profits.[4] Even Foucquet recognized that the system was *potentially* corrupt, but thought that it needed the actions of men to make it so.[5] In this respect, there is a qualitative difference between one the one hand the regimes of Sully, Schomberg, and d'Effiat, and on the other those of Bullion, d'Hémery, and Foucquet (even if, in Foucquet's case, the evidence is

---

[1] Cf. Foucquet's comments on the fortunes of his *commis*: Foucquet, *Défenses*, xvi. 13 and 144 a.p. 60, Dr. 1 [156 mi. 6], fo. 7.

[2] A.A.E. France 845, fo. 175, *c.* 1641–2.

[3] Foucquet used a *courtier de change* and a blank contract witnessed before a *notaire* for his borrowing in 1657–8: Foucquet, *Défenses*, viii. 252.

[4] *Lettres . . . de Colbert*, ed. Clément, vii. 170–1.

[5] Foucquet, *Défenses*, vii. 198.

rendered suspect by Colbert's editing of the trial papers). While a minister enjoyed royal favour he had nothing to fear: ultimately all monies could be said to have been voluntary gifts from the king to his loyal servant. Once he had fallen from grace, however, the secret conduct of business would make it almost impossible to prove a charge of peculation—this was true even in the case of Foucquet, although Louis XIV felt there were nevertheless compelling political reasons to incarcerate his former minister. Some contemporaries were prepared to draw a sharp distinction between the illegal gain of the entrepreneur and that of the minister: the former at least had to run huge risks; the latter did not, and it was against the families of successive finance ministers and other functionaries in the council of finance that a thorough-going *chambre de justice* should be directed.[1] The observation was accurate, but the proposal was unsound politically.

The financiers kept their dealings secret precisely because of the fear of retrospective taxation through the *chambre de justice*. If the valuation of wealth, especially property, was rendered difficult, time-consuming, and expensive to the government, such taxation would be ineffective. The financier would pay a fine proportionate to the scale of his past transactions, not a tax on his actual wealth or even on the property gained as a result of his business ventures. However, the crucial reason for the all-pervasive secrecy—and indeed for the existence of financiers acting as intermediaries on such a widespread scale in France—is to be found elsewhere, in prevailing social attitudes. The capital raised through the Parisian money market was essentially provided by the wealthy and privileged social groups, that is to say broadly speaking the nobles, office-holders and *rentiers*: contemporaries talked of the ruin of 10,000 families of whom 'il y a a très grand nombre de personnes de condition' if there was a royal bankruptcy.[2] Those who either had recently attained or aspired to noble status nevertheless avoided open participation in financial transactions,[3] although this sometimes occurred.[4] The rule of

---

[1] A.A.E. France 875, fo. 110ᵛ., 28 May 1651.

[2] B.N. MS. fr. 18510, fo. 237, 1648. A.A.E. France 890, fo. 241, Feb. 1653.

[3] Cf. Foucquet's comment that 'il y a des gens qui avoient appréhension de passer pour traitan[t]s et qui ne vouloient pas que leur nom parust dans les affaires . . .': Foucquet, *Défenses*, xii. 147.

[4] As in the case of nobles who presented financial proposals (*avis*) to the king's council. Duc de Ventadour: E 39b, fo. 49, 7 Mar. 1613. Maréchal de Vitry: E 63b, fo. 271, 27 May 1620. Maréchal de Créquy: E 79b, fo. 91, 17 July 1624. Princesse de Conty: E 89, fo. 425, 23 Dec. 1626. Duchesse d'Ornano et maréchal de Bassompierre: E 90b, fo. 229, 13 Feb. 1627. Duc de Vaudemont: E 91a, fo. 10, 3 Mar. 1627. Marquis de Notz: E 106a, fo. 63 , 15

dérogeance prohibited the nobleman from participating directly in business enterprises, although he might do so secretly under an assumed name. Strictly speaking, financial activity was not in itself a demeaning act: the service was provided to the king, and was therefore honourable.[1] Nevertheless, there were obvious dangers in open participation in financial activity. The unpopularity of royal fiscal policies and the agents of those policies attracted public attention and opprobrium: the stigma of direct association could be avoided if intermediaries were used and secrecy maintained. Another obvious danger was that the taking of profit at usurious rates of interest[2] might be viewed as incompatible with the lifestyle of a nobleman. The *Chambre des Comptes* of Paris voiced contemporary attitudes in 1648 when it denounced the financier's alleged 'avidité insatiable de devenir riche . . . en peu de temps'.[3] Landed society was patrimonial in outlook: what was gained by the father was handed down to the son with only a few additions. All that was expected in this *rentier* mentality was to retain one's patrimony and live off the small but steady income it produced. Rapid capital accumulation was thus regarded by contemporaries as a sin, and in certain circumstances a crime.[4] Secrecy and the use of financiers as intermediaries thus brought great advantages to the investor:[5] if the financier was regarded as a

May 1631. The widow of the maréchal de la Châtre: E 249c, fo. 360, 16 Dec. 1651. The duchesse de Guise and Joyeuse: E 249c, fo. 506, 20 Dec. 1651.

[1] R. É. Mousnier, *Les institutions de la France sous la monarchie absolue, 1598–1715. I. Société et état* (1974), p. 110. Leases of revenue farms sometimes included a clause allowing the farmer to include nobles and office-holders in the consortium: *Cahiers des États de Normandie sous les règnes de Louis XIII et de Louis XIV . . .*, ed. C. de Robillard de Beaurepaire (5 vols., Rouen, 1876–8, 1883, 1891), iii. 152. P 2352, p. 931, 13 Dec. 1623. The royal declaration of 9 Dec. 1648, outlining terms on which loans would be negotiated in the future, made it clear that to lend to the king was not an *acte dérogeante*: A.A.E. France 860, fo. 236.

[2] At the end of Dec. 1648, the archbishop of Paris and the Sorbonne appeared committed to the view that to lend to the king even at the low rate of 10 per cent was a mortal sin: *Journal des guerres civiles de Dubuisson-Aubenay*, ed. Saige, i. 98–9. In 1678, when Colbert proposed setting up provincial *caisses de prêt* on the Dutch model, he received some support from the Jesuits. Louis XIV felt obliged to consult the Sorbonne, however, which denounced the scheme and declared that pastors and preachers would be obliged to preach against it. Colbert had to abandon the scheme. Though the Jansenists were in the avant-garde of the opposition to 'usury', they received wide clerical support on this matter: R. Taveneaux, *Jansénisme et prêt à intérêt . . .* (1977), p. 44.

[3] A.A.E. France 860, fo. 200, 14 Oct. 1648.

[4] D'Effiat was prepared to regard rapid capital accumulation by a financier without other known sources of wealth as a 'juste présomption du péculat': Petit, *L'assemblée des notables*, p. 285. This was also part of the prosecution case against Foucquet.

[5] Cf. J. Dewald, *The formation of a provincial nobility. The magistrates of the Parlement of Rouen, 1499–1610* (Princeton, N.J., 1980), p. 233: 'aristocratic resistance to the publicity of debts was based on the advantage . . . which secrecy was thought to offer the borrower.'

pariah, this served to deflect public attention away from criticism of the privileged few who enjoyed wide social and fiscal privileges and secretly placed their investments with the financier as middleman.

Many investors and financiers had an interest in the survival of the French fiscal system, with all its defects. Yet the profits drawn by these vested interests do not alone account for the financial problems of the crown. A less ambitious foreign policy, more closely related to the true revenue-raising capacity of the French state, would have permitted retrenchment and reform. It is significant that the periods of reform occurred in the first and sixth decades of the seventeenth century, when France enjoyed relative peace. Bullion and Richelieu considered reforms in the later 1630s, but had to abandon them; Foucquet suggested reforms in accounting procedures to Mazarin, but the chief minister refused to consider them in wartime.[1] The timing of payments to the army became critical to the success of the war effort. Since revenues tended to arrive at Paris sporadically and after long delays, short-term borrowing was inevitable to meet the fixed timing of payments on the army.[2] Even among critics of royal fiscal policies in the *Parlement* of Paris there was recognition of the fact that the crown had in certain circumstances to borrow in order to prevent the collapse of the war effort.[3] The great failure of the French finance ministers of the seventeenth century was to find an acceptable means of regularizing the public debt, attracting the necessary investment without overburdening the resources of the state in future generations. The lottery scheme known as the *Tontine*, which was introduced in 1653 on a small scale, would have had disastrous long-term implications if applied more widely. Colbert's *caisse des emprunts* was an improvement, but it was not introduced until 1674, the return on investment was low compared to the profits made by a tax contractor, and it required the government to keep faith with its creditors over several generations: after Colbert's death, the scheme was rapidly wound down.[4] Despite many proposals to set up a public bank in France,[5]

---

[1] Foucquet, *Défenses*, v. 113.

[2] Cf. A.A.E. France 883, fo. 334, anon. memorandum, *c*. 1649–52.

[3] Ormesson, *Journal*, ed. Chéruel, i. 599–600.

[4] Both schemes are discussed in Martin and Bezançon, *L'histoire du crédit*, pp. 59–60, 92–4.

[5] It was, for example, suggested on 21 May 1615 and reconsidered on 11 July 1618: E 59a, fo. 21. Richelieu's papers contain a plan for a 'société de banque' with 10 million *livres* in capital: A.A.E. France 769, fo. 327.

none was established because of fiscal conservatism prevailing in ministerial circles and the unwillingness of the public at large to place deposits with any institution dependent on the government. The crown thus became reliant on short-term borrowing, as at the time of d'Hémery and Foucquet, and permanently reliant on an extremely inefficient source of income from the consolidated debt in offices and *rentes*. The crown received a capital sum from each new office or annuity sold at a longer term cost of paying an annual interest, respectively the *gages* and *rentes*. The capital raised from sales is difficult to estimate because the market in offices and annuities was rapidly glutted. This caused a wide variation between the theoretical value of the office or annuity and the actual price obtained on sale. The value of offices rose in the course of the later sixteenth and earlier seventeenth centuries, it is true: but the crown scarcely benefited from this rise in values, the main beneficiary being the individual who resold his office on the private market.[1] Yet if the crown gained much less than it had hoped from this source, it had to pay substantial sums to service the debt. It proved impossible to carry this burden in wartime, and thus from 1588 until 1598 and from 1639 until 1648 revenues normally assigned to pay the *gages* and *rentes* were diverted to the war effort. However, both office-holders and *rentiers*—and the two groups overlapped in social terms[2]—were vocal in their opposition to cuts, and it is significant that the call for institutional checks on royal financial administration arose from these aggrieved vested interests in 1597 and 1652.

From the point of view of the government, the great advantages of continuing the system were political and social. The fortunes of a substantial group of office-holders and *rentiers* were linked with the regime, 'leur intérest estoit inséparable de celle du roy, du repos et de la tranquillité de l'estat'.[3] In 1594, after the collapse of the Catholic League at Paris, and again in 1652, after the collapse

[1] On the other hand, the crown would have had to pay the inflated values to buy out the office-holders, which would have been impossible financially. To have attempted to buy them out on reduced values would have been impossible politically. The crown had obtained mutation fees at each subsequent change of owner after the first sale of the office. It had also, from the period of d'Effiat's ministry onwards, sought to extract a forced loan from office-holders equivalent to a percentage of the value of the office. The crown was nevertheless much less successful in raising revenue from this source before 1661 than in the later years of Louis XIV.

[2] The farmers of the *aides* claimed that more than three-quarters of the members of the *Parlement* of Paris were *rentiers*: E 252c, fo. 132, 11 Sept. 1652.

[3] Ormesson, *Journal*, ed. Chéruel, ii. 158 (on the *rentiers*). Cf. the comment of one of Torcy's pamphleteers, quoted by J. Klaits, *Printed propaganda under Louis XIV. Absolute monarchy and public opinion* (Princeton, N.J., 1976), pp. 265–6.

of the Fronde, despite grave misgivings the office-holders and *rentiers* returned to their traditional allegiance to the crown as the lesser evil than civil war. In normal years, this political and social support carried a heavy cost. The consolidated debt was necessarily inefficient, and largely incapable of structural reform, since it was not managed purely in terms of financial gain. Yet its very existence was an enormous hindrance to the development of a sound and firmly-based financial system. Frenchmen preferred to buy offices rather than invest in commercial and industrial activities—or for that matter make short-term loans to the king.[1] Contrary to the experience of some other European countries, the extension of financial investment in France in the seventeenth century brought in its wake little economic activity or enterprise of a more general type. It follows that the general benefit to the economy of the financial system was slight, indeed that it was in large measure parasitic on it. Loans to the government were almost invariably employed in non-productive uses—that is, unless one considers warfare and its consequences a productive use—and the growth of taxation outstripped the growth of the economy. By 1661 the total burden of taxation in France was much heavier, and its debilitating consequences, especially on French agriculture, were much more serious than sixty years earlier.[2]

---

[1] '. . . l'argent est réservé par les meilleures bourses pour l'achapt des offices . . .': quoted by Ranum, *Richelieu and the councillors of Louis XIII*, p. 155.

[2] Colbert considered that the French traditionally paid about 45 million in taxes, nearer one-third than half the total money stock, but that the traditional proportion had fallen out of balance by the 1660s: 'il n'y a plus de 120 millions de livres dans le commerce public. En observant la mesme proportion, les revenus du roy ne doivent estre que de 40 millions; mais . . . ils sont constamment de 70 millions . . .': *Lettres . . . de Colbert*, ed. Clément, vii. 237. Cf. Meuvret, *Études d'histoire économique*, p. 137. Spooner's estimates suggest that between one-third and a half the money stock was absorbed by the revenues of the state in the sixteenth century and after 1650, with a higher proportion in the first four decades of the seventeenth century: Spooner, *The international economy and monetary movements in France*, p. 316. Cf. also his comparative graph (31) which shows estimates of 'national income', money stock and royal revenues in France, 1500–1750: ibid., p. 306. However, his estimates are vitiated by his reliance on Clamagéran's figures.

Appendices

Appendix One

Table I
The French finance ministers (*surintendants des finances*), 1589–1661

1578–24 Oct. 1594 (d).	François d'O, seigneur de Fresnes and de Maillebois[1]
25 Nov. 1594; renewed 20 May 1596	[interim with finance commission][2]
1598–26 Jan. 1611	Maximilien de Béthune, baron de Rosny, later duc de Sully[3]
5 Feb. 1611– 6 Sept. 1619	Pierre Jeannin, baron de Montjeu[4] [Controller-general with finance commission, 1611–14; finance minister, 1614–July 1615; controller-general, July 1615–19 May 1616; finance minister while Barbin was controller-general, 19 May 1616–24 Apr. 1617; thereafter undisputed power as finance minister]
6/7 Sept. 1619– 20/21 Jan. 1623	Henri de Schomberg, comte de Nanteuil[5]
23 Jan. 1623– 12 Aug. 1624	Charles, marquis de la Vieuville[6]
27 Aug. 1624– Feb. 1626	Jean Bochart, seigneur de Champigny[7] Michel Marillac, seigneur de Fayet
20 Feb. 1626– 1 June 1626	Michel Marillac seigneur de Fayet[8]
9 June 1626– 27 July 1632 (d.)	Antoine Coiffier de Ruzé, marquis d'Effiat[9]
4 Aug. 1632– 23 Dec. 1640 (d.)	Claude Bullion, seigneur de Bonnelles[10] Claude le Bouthillier
22 Dec. 1640– 6 June 1643	Claude le Bouthillier[11]
13 June 1643– 17 July 1647	Nicolas le Bailleul, baron de Château-Gontier[12] Claude Mesmes, comte d'Avaux

17 July 1647– 9 July 1648	Michel Particelle, sieur d'Hémery[13]
9 July 1648– 14 Apr. 1649	Charles de la Porte, Maréchal de la Meilleraye[14]
	[interim with two directors of finance, Barillon de Morangis and Aligre]
8 Nov. 1649– 23 May 1650 (d.)	Michel Particelle, sieur d'Hémery[15] Claude Mesmes, comte d'Avaux
24 May 1650– 8 Sept. 1651	René Longueil, marquis de Maisons[16]
8 Sept. 1651– 2 Jan. 1653 (d.)	Charles duc de la Vieuville[17]
	[interim with two directors of finance, Barillon de Morangis and Aligre]
8 Feb. 1653– 17 Feb. 1659 (d.)	Abel Servien, marquis de Sablé[18] Nicolas Foucquet, vicomte de Melun
21 Feb. 1659– 5 Sept. 1661	Nicolas Foucquet, vicomte de Melun[19]

[No other *surintendant* during the *ancien régime* with the exception of John Law in 1720][20]

Comments There are two introductions to the problem, neither of which are entirely accurate: André Lefèvre d'Ormesson, 'Les surintendants des finances que j'ai vus et connus' [BM. Rouen, MS. Léber 5767 (3252), t.i., fo. 9, published by P. A. Chéruel, *Histoire de l'administration monarchique en France depuis l'avènement de Philippe-Auguste jusqu'à la mort de Louis XIV* (2 vols., 1855), ii. 389–91.] The second introduction is the list compiled by Boislisle, 'Semblançay et la surintendance des finances', 265–70.

Sources

[1] *Inventaire des arrêts du conseil d'état*, ed. Valois, i. p. lxvi. Sully, *Oeconomies royales*, ed. Barbiche and Buisseret, i. 530–1.

[2] Valois, op. cit., p. lxx–lxxi. Sully, *Oeconomies royales*, ed. Barbiche and Buisseret, i. 556–8. 120 a.p. 29, fo. 1. B.N. MS. fr. 16218, fo. 225.

[3] The problem of the apparent absence of a *brevet* of appointment is discussed by Barbiche and Buisseret, 'Sully et la surintendance des finances'. For his resignation: ibid., 543 and B.N. Dupuy 90, fo. 204.

[4] In Jeannin's words, Marie de Médicis gave him 'l'emploi des finances sous le nom de contrôleur-général avec pareil pouvoir que si elle m'eût donné le titre de surintendant....': *Les négociations du président Jeannin*, ed. Michaud and Poujoulat, p. 714. The office of *surintendant* had been abolished on 5 Feb. 1611, and Jeannin was called controller-general from 1611 to 1614: A.A.E. France 768, fo. 235 (1612); A.A.E. France 769, fo. 94 (1613).

However, in 1614–15 he was *surintendant*: A.A.E. France 769, fo. 315; A.A.E. France 770, fo. 79. For his next period as controller-general: cf. E 59a, fo. 10, 11 July 1618 (which gives the terminal date as 19 May 1616, when Barbin took over). Jeannin was given the *surintendance* while Barbin was controller-general 'en apparence' and 'pour quelque sorte d'honneur et de récompense . . .': P. Phélypeaux de Pontchartrain, *Mémoires* . . ., ed. J. F. Michaud and J. J. F. Poujoulat, 2nd ser. v (1839), p. 363. However, it was reported on 26 Nov. 1616 that Barbin wanted to become *surintendant* in Jeannin's place: Griselle, *Louis XIII et Richelieu*, p. 152. For Jeannin's undisputed power as *surintendant* after the arrest of Barbin: E 61b, fo. 343, 27 Mar. 1619. A.A.E. France 772, fo. 22, 1618. He was explicitly called *surintendant* in Schomberg's *brevet* of 7 Sept. 1619.

[5] B.N. MS. fr. 18152, fo. 77, 6 Sept. 1619. A.A.E. France 772, fo. 127, 7 Sept. 1619. Different dates for his dismissal in Arnauld d'Andilly, *Mémoires*, ed. Michaud and Poujoulat, p. 441 and A.A.E. France 772, fo. 126.

[6] O1 9, fos. 128–9 and B.N. MS. fr. 16626, fos. 227–8, 6 [*sic*—for 23 or 26] Jan. and 31 Jan. 1623. For the date of La Vieuville's arrest: A.A.E. France 778, fo. 195.

[7] A.A.E. France 778, fo. 194.

[8] B.N. MS. fr. 16626, fo. 235.

[9] A.A.E. France 780, fo. 37.

[10] A.A.E. France 802, fo. 324.

[11] Bouthillier last attended the council of finance on 6 June 1643: E 180a.

[12] There was no signature of a *surintendant* in the council of finance of 10 June, but Bailleul and d'Avaux both signed on 13 June 1643: E 180a, fo. 268. D'Avaux was sent to the Westphalian peace negotiations on 11 Oct. (Ormesson, *Journal*, ed. Chéruel, i. 112), but had not sat in the council of finance after 1 July 1643.

[13] O1 1, fo. 65, 17 July 1647. Cf. A.A.E. France 857, fo. 141, 18 July 1647. Technically, d'Hémery became joint *surintendant* with d'Avaux, since it was only Bailleul who resigned and became a minister of state. However, d'Avaux was still abroad, and d'Hémery opposed his recall. When d'Avaux returned, he was in disgrace, and it was not until 18 Sept. 1648—that is, after the dismissal of d'Hémery—that d'Avaux was appointed minister of state: cf. A.A.E. France 860, fo. 239, 15 Dec. 1648.

[14] Ormesson, *Journal*, ed. Chéruel, i. 540. B.N. MS. fr. 4222, fo. 206, 9 July 1648. For his resignation: Ormesson, *Journal*, ed. Chéruel, i. 736, 738. Patin, *Lettres au temps de la Fronde*, ed. Thérive, pp. 90, 92. La Meilleraye was not elevated to the status of duke and peer until 1663.

[15] Ormesson, *Journal*, ed. Chéruel, i. 779. D'Avaux sat in the council of finance for the first time on 10 Nov., and D'Hémery on 13 Nov. 1649: E 237b, fos. 87, 179. Their powers were renewed on 17 Mar. 1650: B.N. MS. fr. 4222, fo. 212. D'Hémery died on 23 May 1650: Patin, op. cit., p. 218.

[16] Patin, op. cit., p. 221.

[17] *Journal des guerres civiles de Dubuisson-Aubenay*, ed. Saige, ii. 115. La Vieuville first sat in the council of finance on 16 Sept. 1651: E 248c, fo. 15. He last sat there on 30 Dec. 1652 (E 253c, fo. 559) and on 8 Jan. 1653 only the directors signed (E 254a, fo. 70).

[18] A.A.E. France 890, fo. 239, 8 Feb. 1653. O1 7, fo. 44, 10 Feb. 1653. 144 a.p. 74, Dr. 7 [156 mi. 30], no. 1, 8 Feb. 1653. They first sat in the council of finance on 12 Feb. 1653: E 254c, fo. 297.

[19] O1 7, fo. 45, 21 Feb. 1659. 144 a.p. 74, Dr. 7 [156 mi. 30], no. 3, 21 Feb. 1659.

[20] J. Buvat, *Journal de la régence, 1715–1723* . . ., ed. E. Campardon, 2 vols., (1865), ii. 73. According to Buvat, letters patent to this effect were issued in Jan. 1720, and were registered by the *Parlement* of Paris on 15 Apr. 1720. Cf. E. Faure, *17 juillet 1720. La Banqueroute de Law* (1977), p. 316.

Table II
The French controllers-general (*contrôleurs-généraux des finances*)
before Colbert

Jan. 1594–Feb. 1596	Eight intendants of finance acting as controllers-general, only four operative in the council at any one time
11 Feb. 1596–1599 (d.)	Charles Saldaigne, seigneur d'Incarville
1599–1608 (d.)	Jean Vienne
1608–1611	Gilles Maupeou, seigneur d'Ableiges
5 Feb. 1611–1616	Pierre Jeannin, baron de Montjeu
19 May 1616– 24 Apr. 1617	Claude Barbin, seigneur de Broyes
1617–1619	Gilles Maupeou, seigneur d'Ableiges
1619–1623	Pierre Castille
23 Jan. 1623–1626	Jean Bochart, seigneur de Champigny
1 Mar. 1626–1628 (d.)	Simon Marion, baron de Druy
7 Dec. 1628–1629	François Sublet, seigneur des Noyers
1629–1634	Three, later four, intendants of finance as controllers-general
12 Jan. 1634–1636 (d.)	Charles Duret, seigneur de Chevry
1637–1643	Three or four intendants of finance as controllers-general
8 Nov. 1643–1648	Michel Particelle, seigneur d'Hémery
21 Apr. 1648–1657	Antoine Le Camus (with Claude Ménardeau, seigneur de Champré after 14 May 1655)
5 Sept. 1657	Jacques Le Tillier
24 Oct. 1657– 12 Dec. 1665	Louis Le Tonnelier, seigneur de Breteuil, and Barthélémé Hervart

Comments   The fragmented nature of the documentation makes this list somewhat tentative, although this serves to illustrate the general weakness of the *contrôle-général* before Colbert. Further research into the families of the intendants of finance may modify the detailed picture somewhat. The list provided by Jouvencel, *Le contrôleur-général des finances sous l'ancien régime*, pp. 420–1, is clearly inaccurate and incomplete.

Table III
The French intendants of finance (*intendants des finances*), 1594–1661

Jan. 1594–1596	Eight intendants of finance, certain of whom were already in office before 1594: Michel Sublet, seigneur d'Heudicourt Claude Marcel Charles Saldaigne, seigneur d'Incarville Jacques Vallée, seigneur des Barreaux Louis Picot, seigneur de Santeny Louis Guibert, seigneur de Bussy Jean Vienne Louis-Gilbert Gombault (d. by Aug. 1594); replaced by Octavien Dony, seigneur d'Attichy (Commissions of Sublet, Saldaigne, and Vienne subsequently renewed after 1596)
1600–1619	Gilles Maupeou, seigneur d'Ableiges
21 Oct. 1605– 14 Oct. 1617 (d.)	Isaac Arnauld
1614–30 Mar. 1616 (d.)	Louis Dollé, seigneur de Vivier en Brie
1615–1634	Charles Duret, seigneur de Chevry
1616–24 June 1629 (d.)	Pierre Castille
17 May 1617– 2 May 1618	Guichard Déageant, seigneur de Saint-Marcellin
2 May 1618–1628 (d.)	Pierre Baudoyn, seigneur de Soupire (known as Desportes-Baudoyn)
1618–1619	Guy Chansy, seigneur des Portes
1621–1641 (d.)	Claude Mallier, seigneur du Houssay
1621–1624	Thomas Le Clerc
24 Jan. 1623– 7 Feb. 1624	Charles le Beauclerc
1624–1626	Louis Tronson, seigneur du Coudray
14 July 1629– 16 Feb. 1636	François Sublet, seigneur des Noyers
25 May 1631– 8 Nov. 1643	Michel Particelle, seigneur d'Hémery
12 Jan. 1634– Sept. 1638 (d.)	Claude Cornuel
12 Nov. 1638–1650	Jacques Tubeuf
26 Dec. 1640–1658	Séraphin Mauroy, seigneur de Saint-Ouin-sur-Seine

1643–16 Nov. 1649	François Le Charron
3 July 1643–1649	Pierre Mallier, seigneur de Moncharville
10 June 1649– Sept. 1662	Jacques Le Tillier, seigneur de la Chapelle
10 June 1649– 12 Oct. 1660	Jacques Bordier
18 June 1649– 12 Oct. 1660	Guillaume Bordeaux, seigneur de Génitoy
18 June 1649– 5 Oct. 1658	Étienne Foullé, seigneur de Prunevaux
8 Jan. 1650– 24 Oct. 1657	Barthélémé Hervart
1650–1657 (d.)	Pierre Gargan
1650–27 June 1678 (d.)	Denis Marin
12 July 1654– 5 Oct. 1658	Guillaume Brisacier

July 1654–5 Oct. 1658 Jacques Paget, seigneur de Villemomble
July 1654–5 Oct. 1658 Claude Boylesve
July 1654–5 Oct. 1658 Claude Housset
Sept. 1657–5 Oct. 1658 Jacques Amproux, baron de Lorme (known as
Delorme)
1657–5 Oct. 1658 (?) Fieubet, seigneur de Caumont

16 Mar. 1661– 12 Dec. 1665	Jean-Baptiste Colbert

Comments Further research is required on the complicated subject of the early intendants of finance. This list does not claim to be definitive, but is a considerable improvement on that provided by Mosser, *Les intendants des finances au xviiie siècle*, pp. 291–2. Apart from general vagueness on dates of appointment, Mosser includes individuals who did not exist (e.g. Macré, 1637) or who were not intendants of finance (Denis Amelot, after 1623–1655?).

Table IV
The French chief treasurers (*trésoriers de l'Épargne*), 1589–1661

1589 Pierre Molan, seigneur de St-Ouen
      Balthazar Gobelin
1590 François Hotman

1591	Balthazar Gobelin
1592	François Hotman
1593	Balthazar Gobelin
1594	François Hotman
1595	Balthazar Gobelin
1596	François Hotman
1597	Balthazar Gobelin
1598	Étienne Puget
1599	Vincent Bouhier, seigneur de Beaumarchais
1600	Balthazar Gobelin
1601	Étienne Puget
1602	Vincent Bouhier, seigneur de Beaumarchais
1603	Raymond Phélypeaux, seigneur d'Herbault
1604	Étienne Puget
1605	Vincent Bouhier, seigneur de Beaumarchais
1606	Raymond Phélypeaux, seigneur d'Herbault
1607	Étienne Puget
1608	Vincent Bouhier, seigneur de Beaumarchais
1609	Raymond Phélypeaux, seigneur d'Herbault
1610	Étienne Puget
1611	Vincent Bouhier, seigneur de Beaumarchais
1612	Raymond Phélypeaux, seigneur d'Herbault
1613	Étienne Puget
1614	Vincent Bouhier, seigneur de Beaumarchais
1615	Raymond Phélypeaux, seigneur d'Herbault
1616	Thomas Morant, baron du Mesnil-Garnier
1617	Vincent Bouhier, seigneur de Beaumarchais
1618	Raymond Phélypeaux, seigneur d'Herbault
1619	Thomas Morant, baron du Mesnil-Garnier
1620	Vincent Bouhier, seigneur de Beaumarchais
1621	Balthazar Phélypeaux
1622	Thomas Morant, baron du Mesnil-Garnier
1623	Vincent Bouhier, seigneur de Beaumarchais
1624	Balthazar Phélypeaux
1625	Guillaume Sève, seigneur de Saint-Julien
	Thomas Morant, baron du Mesnil-Garnier
	Antoine Feydeau, seigneur des Bois-le-Vicomte
1626	Thomas Morant, baron du Mesnil-Garnier
	Pierre Payen
	Gabriel Guénégaud, seigneur du Plessis Belleville
1627	Paul Ardier, seigneur de Beauregard
1628	Macé I Bertrand, seigneur de la Bazinière
1629	Gabriel Guénégaud, seigneur du Plessis Belleville
1630	Gaspard Fieubet
1631	Macé I Bertrand, seigneur de la Bazinière

1632 Gabriel Guénégaud, seigneur du Plessis Belleville
1633 Gaspard Fieubet
1634 Macé I Bertrand, seigneur de la Bazinière (?)
1635 Gabriel Guénégaud, seigneur du Plessis Belleville
1636 Gaspard Fieubet
1637 Macé I Bertrand, seigneur de la Bazinière
1638 Henri Guénégaud, seigneur du Plessis Belleville
1639 Gaspard Fieubet
1640 Macé I Bertrand, seigneur de la Bazinière
1641 Henri Guénégaud, seigneur du Plessis Belleville
1642 Gaspard Fieubet
1643 Denis Gedoyn [for Macé II Bertrand, seigneur de la Bazinière]
1644 Claude Guénégaud
1645 Nicolas Jeannin, seigneur de Castille
1646 Macé II Bertrand, seigneur de la Bazinière
1647 Claude Guénégaud
1648 Nicolas Jeannin, seigneur de Castille
1649 Nicolas Jeannin, seigneur de Castille*
1650 Macé II Bertrand, seigneur de la Bazinière
1651 Claude Guénégaud
1652 Nicolas Jeannin, seigneur de Castille
1653 Macé II Bertrand, seigneur de la Bazinière
1654 Claude Guénégaud
1655 Nicolas Jeannin, seigneur de Castille
1656 Macé II Bertrand, seigneur de la Bazinière
1657 Claude Guénégaud
1658 Nicolas Jeannin, seigneur de Castille
1659 Macé II Bertrand, seigneur de la Bazinière
1660 Claude Guénégaud
1661 Nicolas Jeannin, seigneur de Castille
1662 Nicolas Jeannin, seigneur de Castille*
        (imprisoned May 1662)

Comments In the 1590s, the chief treasurer administered his fund (*caisse*) only one year in two, and thereafter only one year in three. The list establishes which chief treasurers administered the fund in a given year. The asterisk indicates the years in which the fourth office, established in October 1645, was exercised by one of the chief treasurers with the agreement of the other two. The administration of the fund was divided in 1625–6 partly due to sales of the office of chief treasurer, partly to bankruptcies, and partly one suspects to the attempt by the government to change the administration every four months.

Table V
The French revenue raising system under the early Bourbons

A. Indirect taxes

King
↓
Council of finance and finance minister
↓
Council of finance, or appropriate specialist committee, decides to increase rent of existing revenue farm, to establish a new farm, or to lease out to a new consortium
↓
Auction of lease. New bid accepted, or council of finance confirms existing arrangements
↓
Lease sent by council of finance to *Chambre des Comptes* for registration
↓
Revenue farmer empowered by council of finance to collect revenues for set number of years without awaiting registration of lease
↓
Revenue farmer negotiates leases with sub-farmers who collect indirect taxes locally
↓
Revenue farmer may anticipate rent of farm by making a loan to the king
↓
Revenue farmer submits accounts to the council of finance or specialist committee
↓
Chambre des Comptes audits accounts

Statistics for this source of revenue: Appendix Two, Table VI.

B. The *affaires extraordinaries* (*traités*)

King

↓

Council of finance and finance minister

↓

Council of finance receives a financial proposal (*avis*) from a dealer (*donneur d'avis*) acting on behalf of a financial consortium. A percentage of the proposed tax (*droit d'avis*) is accorded to the dealer

↓

Council of finance or specialist committee examines proposal, and, if acceptable, a *traité* is accorded to the agent (*prête-nom*) acting on behalf of a financial consortium. [This may or may not be the same consortium making the original proposal.] The interest payment (*remise*) is specified

↓

If a new tax is established by the *traité*, a fiscal edict (*édit bursal*) is drawn up by the council of finance and sent to the *Chambre des Comptes* or other sovereign court for registration

↓

Council of finance may empower the contractor to levy the tax without awaiting registration

↓

Contractor sub-contracts at fixed rate of interest (*remise*)

↓

Contractor may anticipate levy of tax by making a loan to the king

↓

Tax levied. Contractor submits accounts to council of finance or specialist committee

↓

Chambre des Comptes audits accounts

Statistics for this source of revenue: Appendix Two, Table VII.

C. The direct taxes in the *pays d'élections*

King

↓

Council of finance and finance minister

↓

Council of finance decides to levy the same amount of direct tax as the previous year or to increase taxes

↓

Brevet establishes amount of direct taxes for each *généralité*. Sent to the *bureau des finances*, where the *trésoriers de France* ratify the amount (by adding their *attache*) and distribute the tax between the *elections* (*département général*). After 1642 the *trésoriers* are subordinated to the authority of the provincial intendants

↓

Élus distribute the tax between parishes within each *élection* (*département particulier*). After 1642 the *élus* are subordinated to the authority of the provincial intendants. The *élus* exercise a civil and criminal jurisdiction in fiscal cases arising from the levy of the *taille*, with appeal to the local *Cour des Aides*

↓

Assessors in each parish distribute the tax between parishoners

↓

Collectors collect the tax at parish level and pay it to the *receveur particulier* in each *élection*

↓

The *receveurs particuliers* pass over the funds collected to the *receveur-général* of each *généralité* and submit accounts to him

↓

The *receveur-général* pays the funds to the *Trésorier de l'Épargne* at Paris. The *receveur-général* may anticipate the levy of the tax by making a loan to the king

↓

A financier or financial consortium at Paris may anticipate the levy of the tax by making a loan to the king. The financier or consortium may sub-contract to the *receveur-général* or other agents

↓

The *receveur-général* submits accounts to the *trésoriers de France* (after 1642 to the provincial intendants) acting as delegates of the council of finance

↓

Chambre des Comptes audits accounts

Statistics for this source of revenue: Appendix Two, Table IV (yield of the *taille* in the *pays d'élections*).

Appendix Two

Introduction

Table I. Single-entry book-keeping: Mallet's totals for expenses and revenues of the French monarchy compared with other sources, 1600–56. The figures are presented in the way in which the accounts were kept, that is to say separate lists of royal expenditure and income which were required to tally and thus adjusted where necessary by the clerks of the treasury. Some states in seventeenth-century Europe employed modern (i.e. double-entry) accounting techniques: the Dutch Republic did so, and so did Sweden after the appointment of the Dutchman Abraham Cabeliau as Auditor-General in 1624. The French monarchy did not. Simon Stevin is said to have offered to demonstrate the system of double-entry accounting to Sully, who refused to take it up.[1] In the view of this author it is impossible to recast the figures from single-entry into double-entry, and thus to calculate the true annual surplus or deficit. Guéry has recently attempted this task,[2] but apart from errors in his figures, his method of calculation rests on the assumption that all expenses were 'genuine' but some royal income (the *deniers extraordinaires*) was 'fictitious'. In fact, as both Foucquet and Mallet pointed out, there were paper transactions underlying both sets of figures, not simply the figures for income but also those for expenditure. Moreover, while some adjustment was made to the figures of the *deniers extraordinaires* to keep the separate accounts for income and expenditure in balance, it is certain that the crown enjoyed real revenues from this source as is demonstrated by the contemporary accounts for 1632. Overall, Guéry's method of calculation produces some very odd results (for example, a deficit rather than a surplus for Sully's ministry) and tends to exaggerate the current account deficit. It becomes almost impossible to see how the French monarchy escaped with only three bankruptcies in 1598, 1648, and 1661.

Table II. Mallet's figures for certain expenses payable by the French Treasury, 1600–56. This list does not include all the items of expenditure listed by Mallet, but provides totals of the most important elements. Hayden's figures have been checked for the years 1600–30,[3] but this list is somewhat different from his in that it includes expenditure on royal buildings

---

[1] Buisseret, *Sully*, p. 85. Roberts, *Gustavus Adolphus*, i. 271.

[2] Guéry, 'Les finances de la monarchie française'. Guéry does not cite any manuscript reference for the period 1598–1661.

[3] Hayden, *France and the Estates-General of 1614*, p. 220.

within the item 'household and royal buildings'. The most difficult
elements of expenditure to interpret are Mallet's figures for the *comptants*,
or extraordinary expenses. He gives no detailed explanation of his
distinction between ordinary and extraordinary expenditure, and his
figures differ from the contemporary figures for the *comptants* listed in
Table III. The most important discrepancy is for the years of the
Fronde, which is the easiest problem to resolve. The finance ministers
felt unable to honour the limit of three million *livres* placed on the
comptants in 1648. They therefore reissued the money orders representing
interest payments to financiers which had been agreed before the revocation of loan contracts in 1648, and which had not been destroyed
subsequently. This procedure explains the discrepancy between the
official figures for the *comptants* and Mallet's totals, which were much
higher, although it should be noted that Mallet's figures almost certainly
reflect the fact that such expenditure was carried over from one accounting year to the next.

*Table III. The secret expenses (comptants) of the French monarchy, 1594–
1681.*   This list represents the most complete surviving contemporary
statistical series, although the figures have been compiled from different
archival sources. The secret expenses were payments made on the orders
of the finance minister which in theory concerned matters so secret that
public knowledge of them would endanger the state. In practice, the
types of payment made in this way were often not of a secret nature at all
(in the sense of affecting affairs of state) but payments which for political
reasons it was convenient to keep from public scrutiny. They offered the
finance minister a procedure whereby high interest rates could be paid to
the financiers without public knowledge (because the separate items
were not specified in detail) and without the risk that the *Chambre des
Comptes* would withhold approval of these payments in the final audit of
accounts.[1] The trend of the secret expenses thus reflects several different
tendencies such as the overall level of expenditure, reliance on financiers,
and the extent to which the government sought to circumvent the
vigilance of the *Chambre des Comptes*.

*Table IV. Mallet's figures for certain revenues payable to the French Treasury,
1600–56.*   This list does not include all the items of revenue listed by
Mallet, but provides totals of the most important elements. The criteria
used by Mallet for the inclusion of particular kinds of revenue in the
deniers extraordinaires are vague. The figures for the 1630s seem to reflect
royal income from the *traités*, including the establishment of offices and
rentes. Those for the 1640s appear to include the anticipation of revenues
in the form of loans. The figures for the years of the Fronde reflect the
policy of finance ministers in reissuing assignments after the bankruptcy

---

[1] Bonney, 'The secret expenses of Richelieu and Mazarin', 825–7.

of 1648, and transferring these paper credits from one accounting year to the next. The Fronde was undoubtedly a period when it was very difficult for the government to secure new loans or tax contracts on the scale indicated by Mallet's figures for the *deniers extraordinaires*. The recent study by Collins[1] makes an important cautionary point with regard to the interpretation placed on the figures for the *taille* and income from the revenue farms. Based on a study of local tax records in Champagne before 1635, Collins's article argues that Mallet's figures provide an incomplete picture of the total burden of taxation in that province. However, it is important to distinguish between the total levy of taxation in the provinces and the net receipts paid into the Treasury. Mallet makes it perfectly clear that it is impossible to provide national figures for the total burden of taxation in the provinces because before 1661 the accounts were not kept in this way.[2]

Table V. Relative importance of certain types of royal revenue, 1600–54. This table recapitulates material in tables I and IV. Table V A provides quinquennial totals in millions of *livres tournois*. The miscellaneous items of revenue include income from the *bois*, the *pays d'états*, the *taillon*, etc., but is arrived at by the deduction of the totals from columns i–iv from total income as in column vi. Table V B provides the calculation of specific revenues as a proportion of total income on the basis of the preceding table. Where necessary, the miscellaneous revenues have been slightly adjusted to arrive at a total of 100 per cent. Table V C provides the calculation of specific revenues as a proportion of ordinary revenue (i.e. with the *deniers extraordinaires* deducted from total revenues). The miscellaneous revenues have been slightly adjusted where necessary to arrive at a total of 100 per cent.

Table VI. Rents payable by certain revenue farmers to the French monarchy, 1603–64. The revenue farms were leases of taxes by the crown to private contractors for a set number of years in return for a fixed annual rent, any additional profits of the farm accruing to the contractor. The three most important revenue farms, which according to Mallet's figures produced over 80 per cent of royal income from the revenue farms in the years 1600–30, were the *gabelles de France*, the *aides* and the *cinq grosses fermes*. Virtually all the leases of these three revenue farms survive in manuscript form,[3] and the figures in Table VI represent annual rents payable by the revenue farmers according to the terms of their leases. The rent is recorded in the year in which the lease was negotiated, although it should be noted that some leases envisaged the payment of rent back to an earlier date, others the commencement of payments at a

[1] Collins, 'Sur l'histoire fiscale du xviie siècle'.
[2] Mallet, p. 212. The quotation is cited by Chartier in his comments on Collins's article: Collins, art. cit., 343.
[3] Bonney, 'The failure of the French revenue farms', 26–8.

later date. Increases in rents envisaged in the leases are given in italics. The table covers the years when a new lease was negotiated or a change occurred in the rents payable by one or other of the farmers. Where there is no figure, no change is discernible in the payment of rent. It should not be assumed that the revenue farmers always paid the full rent: remissions were very important after the 1630s.

Table VII. Royal income from the affaires extraordinaires (traités). Table VII A provides annual totals for the years 1623 to 1661 with the exception of the years 1642 and 1649–52, when the evidence is much less complete. The sources for the 1620s are also incomplete, and the figures for these years should be regarded as an underestimate. The table is compiled from 1049 surviving *traités* and represents the total amount contracted by the finance minister in a given year. The interest charge is included in the gross amount (*forfait*) but is usually specified in the contract. Mallet's figures for the *deniers extraordinaires* differ from the totals of the *traités* in two important respects. There was a crucial time lag between the signing of a contract and the first payment under the terms of the agreement. Mallet's figures include income from the *traités* within a given year, not the amount for which contracts were signed. Secondly, Mallet's figures include some anticipation of revenues. It was perfectly possible for the revenues from *traités* to be anticipated: but these were negotiated in separate loan contracts and form part of the figures listed in Table VIII. For this reason, the totals of Tables VII and VIII should not be added together. Tables VII B and VII C provide a perspective on the period of Richelieu and Mazarin. The heavy recourse to *affaires extraordinaires* during the two great wars of 1689–97 and 1702–13 emerges clearly from the figures. As the peace negotiations at Utrecht got under way, the reliance on this income declined. These figures may well be an underestimate: there are probably contracts in the records of the council of finance not to be found in the register used as the source.[1] Table VII C compares royal income from the *affaires extraordinaires* in three different periods. The comparison is shrouded in uncertainty, since the type of financial transaction may have changed between the different periods. Moreover, the figures for 1631–41 may include some transactions which were not fulfilled, while those after 1691 are probably an underestimate. Nevertheless, the rate of price increase was slowing down by the later period and the value of the *livre tournois* as expressed in its theoretical silver content had certainly fallen: the very high figures for 1631–41 are therefore significant. The figures for the 1640s and 1650s are incomplete: but the surviving contracts provide totals of around 230 million for the gross amount in the years 1641–51 and 1651–61.

Table VIII. Loans contracted by the French monarchy, 1613–61. The evidence before the 1630s and for the years of the Fronde is incomplete. The

[1] B.N. MS. fr. 7734.

statistics in Table VIII A are drawn from 1798 surviving loan contracts, the annual totals representing the addition of the contracts signed within a given year. There are some problems in this approach, because there was a crucial time lag between the signing of the contract and the first payment under the terms of the agreement. Thus Étienne Macquart anticipated the revenues of the *recette générale* of Toulouse for 1648 by a loan contract signed on 5 July 1646. His first payment, however, did not begin until 1 October 1646 and the total loan was payable in 12 monthly instalments.[1] Not all the loan contracts envisaged payments at the same intervals. Two smaller loans were later contracted on the *recette générale* of Toulouse for 1648, the second on 30 March 1647.[2] Sometimes 'loans upon loans' (*prêts sur prêts*) were negotiated which speeded up payments under an existing loan contract. Nevertheless, the surviving evidence does not permit an accurate or complete picture of the timing of payments or of the anticipation of revenues. The gross amount includes the interest charge on the loan contract. In Table VIII B the interest charge is calculated on 464 of the 633 loan contracts from the years 1656–61. The calculations suggest that the interest rate on loans fell somewhat in the last years of Foucquet's ministry.

Table IX. The bankruptcies of the French monarchy (1598, 1648, 1661). The procedure of single-entry book-keeping and the incomplete evidence on the anticipation of revenues makes estimates of the scale of the royal bankruptcies extremely hazardous. For the bankruptcy of 1598, the size of the deficit on the current account in 1596 is available from the statement made to the assembly of notables in that year,[3] although the situation had probably worsened since 1596. The figures of the debts not repaid or only partially repaid after 1598 are Sully's.[4] For the bankruptcy of 1648, La Meilleraye's statement[5] is partially borne out by other contemporary evidence.[6] The variations in the estimate of the value of the revoked loan contracts is explained by the policy of over-assignment: in some cases two or three financiers held treasury bills which authorized

---

[1] Details of the payments from E 232a, fo. 285, 12 Aug. 1648. The loan was contracted under the name of Jean Baudinet: E 213a, fo. 236, 5 July 1646.

[2] For the second of the two loans:·E 221b, fo. 373, 30 Mar. 1647.

[3] A. Chamberland, *Un plan de restauration financière en 1596. . . .* (1904), pp. 6–8. Charlier-Meniolle, *L'assemblée des notables*, pp. 25–7.

[4] Sully, *Oeconomies royales*, ed. Michaud and Poujoulat, ii. 28–30. B.N. MS. fr. 10311, fos. 64–7. Sully gives the figures at the date of 1605, and Véron de Forbonnais (*Recherches*, i. 28) at the date of 1595. Few historians, however, have doubted that they attempt to depict the situation in 1598, at the beginning of Sully's ministry. Poirson inflated the figures by adding the arrears of *rentes* in 1605, thus arriving at the total of nearly 349 million: Poirson, *Histoire du règne de Henri IV*, i. 91–2. Mariéjol considered that Sully exaggerated the problems at the outset of his ministry in order to emphasize his own achievement: *Histoire de France . . .*, ed. E. Lavisse (9 vols., 1911), vi. pt. ii., 53 n. 2.

[5] Talon, *Mémoires*, ed. Michaud and Poujoulat, p. 281.

[6] B.N. n.a.f. 64, fo. 143. 144 a.p. 74, Dr. 5 [156 mi. 30]. Cf. also Véron de Forbonnais, *Recherches*, i. 257. U 28, fo. 389ᵛ., 11 July 1648.

reimbursement on the same revenues. For the bankruptcy of 1661, the deficit on the current account and the value of revoked loan contracts are drawn from the figures given by Mallet.[1] (However, Mallet exaggerates the deficit by including the figure of 384.8 million in *comptants* from the years 1655–60, which have been removed from the calculations since much of this expenditure must have been met on actual revenues at the time.) The estimate is made more hazardous by the fact that the figure for royal expenditure in 1661 is not known.[2] Mallet's figure for 1662 has been adopted instead. Since the size of the fines levied on the financiers was tantamount to a second declaration of bankruptcy, the contract for the collection of the fines is also listed.[3]

Table X. Foucquet's personal accounts.   Table X A, the totals of income and expenditure in the years 1653–6 summarize 38 accounts kept by Charles Bernard, Foucquet's clerk. Foucquet doubted whether Bernard had in fact clearly separated income from expenditure. He also claimed that he had kept the accounts among his papers in order to check them at a later date, but had not had time to do so.[4] In Foucquet's first interrogation, the royal commissioners argued that this extensive income demonstrated that the finance minister 's'est servy des deniers publics pour ses usages particulières'. Foucquet replied that Bernard had not distinguished between different types of income, private and public, and that this inference was invalid. He agreed that the figures for income included assignments made over to him by his colleague Servien (who had responsibility for assigning revenues both before and after the ruling of 24 December 1654) as reimbursement for loans to the crown. Once the revenues had been assigned to Foucquet, they became his private property. The growth of expenditure, Foucquet asserted, was due to the increasing cost of his private borrowing and lending to the crown.[5] Table X B shows that the annual income of Foucquet is reduced to less than 4 million once the assigned revenues are deducted, although this is still an enormous figure, presumably explained by the scale of his private borrowing. The royal commissioners appear to have been unable to re-establish Foucquet's complete private accounts after 1656 because his five clerks (Bernard, Taffus, Pelisson, Vatel, and Lespine) kept their registers in different ways. The discrepancy between the total expendi-

---

[1] Mallet, p. 97. These figures are presented uncritically by Dent, *Crisis in finance*, p. 43 ('the total indebtedness of the crown amounted to just over 451 million *livres*').

[2] The figure given by Guéry, 'Les finances de la monarchie française', 237, is in fact the figure for net revenues (viz. Mallet, p. 101, who calls it the *trésor royal*). Véron de Forbonnais, *Recherches*, i. 291. *Lettres . . . de Colbert*, ed. Clément, ii. pt. i. 41. The figure for the *comptants* alone in 1661 was 20.4 million, and thus Guéry's figure for total expenditure of 31.8 million must be too low.

[3] Ormesson, *Journal*, ed. Chéruel, ii. 400–1. Dessert and Journet, 'Le lobby Colbert', 1308, 1330.

[4] Foucquet, *Défenses*, xvi. 14, 178.

[5] ibid., xvi. 182–3.

ture for 1653–6 in Tables X A and X B is accounted for by the second being the official and not the actual total. Table X E enumerates certain of Foucquet's assets seized by the crown in 1661, and listed by his creditors *c*. 1675.[1] The creditors placed a valuation of one million on the office of *procureur-général*, the amount Foucquet deposited at Vincennes, but the figure of 1.4 million was the sale price. Three items have been added to the list (the value of Belle-Île, the residence at Paris, and the dowry to Marie Foucquet)[2] from figures mentioned in Foucquet's interrogation. There is no valuation on Vaux-le-Vicomte or Saint-Mandé in the trial papers.

Table XI. Total royal expenditure during the ministry of Colbert, 1662–83. This table serves as comparison with the expenditure totals in Table I. There is an almost complete series of expenditure accounts for these years (the figures for 1678, 1680, and 1681 are incomplete and no accounts survive for the years 1682–3).[3] There is also a manuscript register[4] which supplements Mallet's figures. The conclusion would seem to be that Colbert was successful in reducing expenditure until the widening of the Dutch war into a general European conflict in 1673–4. After this date, he was unable to reduce expenditure to the peacetime levels of the 1660s.

[1] B.N. Morel de Thoisy 158, fos. 592–6. The list was drawn up in about 1675, and Foucquet's creditors demanded interest payments up to that date: these sums have been removed from the calculations as have one or two items such as the garrison costs at Belle-Île.

[2] The dowry was paid in 1657. However, notarial practice included dowries to daughters in the total value of the inheritance: cf. Labatut, 'Aspects de la fortune de Bullion', 25.

[3] B.N. Mélanges Colbert 264–310, *passim*.

[4] KK 355. This register provides the figures listed under 'other contemporary sources'.

Table I

Single-entry book-keeping: Mallet's totals for expenses and revenues
of the French monarchy compared with other sources, 1600–1656
(*livres tournois*)

| Date | Total revenues | | Total expenses | |
	Mallet	Other sources	Mallet	Other sources
1600	20,542,817	—	20,446,819	—
1601	16,118,526	—	16,189,333	—
1602	19,365,429	—	20,011,606	—
1603	21,041,340	—	21,041,347	—
1604	21,574,460	—	21,474,462	—
1605	26,879,068	27,029,238	26,873,375	27,029,238
1606	28,378,359	28,419,071	28,434,556	28,419,071
1607	29,842,059	29,926,864	29,930,018	29,670,732
1608	32,787,296	32,259,938	32,172,624	32,259,938
1609	32,463,438	32,569,706	32,573,449	32,569,706
1610	33,339,336	33,666,835	33,580,066	—
1611	27,636,008	27,622,005	26,631,258	27,612,574
1612	26,746,800	26,951,472	27,156,808	26,915,002
1613	28,184,497	28,761,027	28,760,669	28,760,674
1614	29,454,299	29,423,740	29,425,067	29,423,740
1615	24,299,554	24,551,601	24,592,890	24,572,901
1616	33,073,195	34,487,169	34,336,150	34,388,039
1617	34,084,640	34,407,452	34,297,915	34,411,615
1618	27,637,812	27,321,911	27,814,213	27,817,981
1619	39,288,725	40,057,832	39,676,500	40,057,695
1620	38,955,778	37,235,467	36,727,625	37,235,467
1621	42,811,119	43,082,584	43,152,717	43,070,594
1622	49,933,819	49,612,817	49,297,147	49,502,808
1623	37,304,145	36,415,068	32,596,326	36,331,381
1624	34,049,415	34,315,583	33,335,868	34,295,586
1625	51,016,111	—	49,524,557	47,247,801
1626	44,130,616	—	44,657,161	44,818,797
1627	39,388,849	38,387,706	38,476,477	38,728,857
1628	41,715,983	—	41,851,630	41,924,636
1629	55,419,762	54,804,580	54,641,354	54,804,580
1630	42,805,928	42,018,417	41,912,677	41,912,795
1631	40,874,771	39,505,279	39,469,407	—
1632	57,504,923	57,450,336	57,069,390	57,510,336
1633	72,005,958	71,378,435	65,429,424	65,314,435
1634	120,270,853	—	120,561,596	—
1635	208,309,671	208,391,521	(208,251,089)[a]	—
1636	108,717,257	108,880,845	108,256,236	108,854,243

Date	Total revenues		Total expenses	
	Mallet	Other sources	Mallet	Other sources
1637	85,178,677	86,768,540	85,960,384	—
1638	96,791,276	97,477,593	98,090,257	—
1639	89,140,746	89,413,620	89,352,496	89,412,510
1640	90,659,417	92,277,630	92,214,814	—
1641	115,967,272	108,604,050	118,356,100	—
1642	86,607,219	(88,838,209)ᵇ	89,220,501	88,838,209
1643	123,113,237	—	124,216,107	120,187,622
1644	140,671,913	—	142,177,447	—
1645	134,558,822	136,186,279	134,782,314	136,181,222
1646	133,129,029	—	131,267,603	—
1647	142,744,020	—	142,267,833	—
1648	85,087,533	—	85,335,195	—
1649	93,821,939	—	95,953,941	—
1650	95,954,643	—	95,972,062	—
1651	142,554,958	—	143,363,739	—
1652	111,667,256	—	112,232,615	—
1653	108,868,079	109,515,996	109,833,202	113,535,651
1654	148,111,962	—	147,334,778	—
1655	139,656,905	—	139,071,089	—
1656	140,730,226	142,332,826	142,682,713	—

ᵃ Mallet's total for expenses in 1635 is certainly too low, and this figure has been taken from the manuscript version of his table [B.N. MS. fr. 7750, fo. 56ᵛ–57ʳ.]

ᵇ Cf. B.N. MS. fr. 10410, fo. 168: '[dépense] pareille à la recepte'.

Sources (i) Total revenues. 1605–9: 120 a.p. 2. 1610: B.N. MS. fr. 4518, fo. 127. 1611: A.A.E. France 768, fo. 188. 1612: 768, fo. 235. 1613: 769, fo. 94. 1614: 769, fo. 315. 1615: B.N. MS. fr. 16627, fo. 103ᵛ. 1616: A.A.E. France 770, fo. 208. 1617: 771, fo. 350. 1618: 772, fo. 22. 1619: 772, fo. 126. 1620: 773, fo. 191. 1621: 774, fo. 224. 1622: 777, fo. 223. 1623: 778, fo. 145. 1624: 779, fo. 219. 1627: 787, fo. 213. 1629: 795, fo. 313. 1630: 797, fo. 221. 1631: 797, fo. 217. 1632: B.I. Godefroy 144, fo. 259. 1633: B.N. MS. fr. 10410. 1635: A.A.E. France 819, fo. 153. 1636: 823, fo. 116. 1637: 828, fo. 368. 1638: 832, fo. 250. 1639: 834, fo. 317. 1640: 837, fo. 58. 1641: 844, fo. 128. 1642 and 1645: B.N. MS. fr. 10410. 1653 and 1656: 144 a.p. 60, Dr. 9 [156 mi. 7], fos. 1ᵛ.–2ʳ.

(ii) Total expenses. Where a figure is indicated, sources as for total revenues, with the exception of the following years. 1615: A.A.E. France 770, fo. 79. 1625: 780, fo. 313. 1626: 783, fo. 200. 1628: 797, fo. 208 (a list of totals, 1621–30). 1630, 1633 and 1639: B.N. MS. fr. 10410. 1653: B.N. n.a.f. 169. For several dates there are other sources which give slightly different readings, both for total expenses and total revenues. Considerations of space preclude a detailed enumeration of these variants.

Note: Mallet's figures for total expenses are compiled from his sub-totals of ordinary and extraordinary expenditure. The figures for total income are more difficult to compile, and have proved a minefield to the unwary. For 1600–10, Mallet gives the total for ordinary income with the *parties casuelles* included. The *deniers extraordinaires* have been added to reach the total revenues. For 1611–56, however, Mallet's figures for ordinary income exclude the *parties casuelles*. These figures, together with the *deniers extraordinaires*, have to be added to reach the total revenues. Guéry ('Les finances de la monarchie française', 238) failed to notice this change in Mallet's method of keeping the accounts, with the result that his figures for total revenues are consistently too low after 1611. In this book, the *parties casuelles* has been counted as ordinary income for the whole period.

Table II

Mallet's figures for certain expenses payable by the French Treasury, 1600–1656

(*livres tournois*)

Date	Pensions and gifts[a]	Household and royal buildings[b]	War[c]	Extraordinary[d]
1600	2,283,942	2,927,251	6,568,235	7,067,685
1601	2,326,920	3,090,683	3,791,838	3,940,935
1602	2,318,683	3,057,004	4,001,164	7,688,426
1603	2,689,543	3,119,887	3,802,086	9,144,529
1604	2,645,659	2,981,500	1,898,942	11,331,207
1605	3,281,340	2,752,644	4,805,018	13,614,346
1606	3,549,717	3,317,304	5,106,956	13,960,894
1607	3,019,746	2,872,354	4,148,434	15,551,230
1608	3,323,534	3,134,377	4,966,329	18,383,208
1609	3,869,282	3,196,921	4,332,469	18,396,956
1610	4,690,829	4,327,515	8,974,025	12,814,536
1611	6,739,904	2,763,809	4,065,559	10,400,401
1612	7,216,881	3,409,480	5,089,865	8,731,806
1613	7,313,040	3,241,305	5,765,139	9,849,933
1614	6,608,341	4,879,838	7,550,224	7,660,295
1615	5,224,231	4,348,798	8,923,336	3,197,281
1616	5,959,643	4,782,622	11,759,252	10,751,335
1617	6,137,238	5,413,454	12,544,791	8,704,677
1618	6,770,765	4,946,572	8,017,934	5,958,158
1619	7,289,781	7,564,361	11,209,791	11,552,567
1620	6,431,475	6,494,620	12,972,380	8,758,566
1621	6,693,806	5,786,948	18,842,672	10,053,341
1622	5,182,246	5,028,609	22,433,466	15,601,079
1623	3,614,945	4,567,000	11,891,393	11,523,382
1624	4,631,512	6,240,878	11,483,683	8,920,122
1625	1,903,891	5,361,454	17,167,279	21,616,350
1626	5,104,756	6,597,728	12,109,122	17,402,986
1627	3,989,551	5,773,469	14,136,955	12,935,056
1628	4,655,401	5,404,633	19,368,753	11,040,220
1629	4,171,052	5,942,533	18,324,513	24,434,778
1630	3,267,054	5,002,269	22,977,243	8,637,296

Date	Pensions and gifts[a]	Household and royal buildings[b]	War[c]	Extraordinary[d]
1631	3,383,104	4,712,821	15,064,851	14,649,936
1632	3,362,924	3,418,977	18,613,021	29,752,935
1633	3,392,569	3,813,287	16,838,676	39,426,994
1634	3,374,338	5,357,666	24,800,919	84,376,898
1635	3,716,806	4,838,624	41,308,486	15,535,449
1636	3,513,250	4,216,483	33,677,965	65,767,781
1637	3,555,533	4,073,924	27,314,639	49,432,950
1638	3,508,531	4,789,720	31,494,331	56,885,175
1639	3,275,644	4,126,811	32,089,459	48,043,010
1640	3,312,252	4,493,644	31,308,794	51,497,999
1641	2,818,266	4,683,074	33,407,146	75,492,096
1642	2,761,968	5,264,375	32,542,143	46,970,146
1643	3,091,426	6,920,833	48,550,314	64,132,918
1644	3,264,018	6,812,000	47,335,684	83,156,297
1645	4,357,148	6,649,685	44,922,354	77,304,696
1646	2,582,251	6,021,822	38,521,977	81,429,361
1647	2,190,060	4,892,493	39,642,937	93,523,591
1648	2,741,952	5,287,621	32,456,102	43,313,775
1649	2,928,029	4,704,335	24,078,693	62,473,679
1650	2,835,829	4,668,573	18,693,240	68,747,078
1651	3,045,293	4,457,404	20,625,384	113,435,088
1652	2,836,893	3,960,678	23,454,400	80,540,616
1653	2,971,653	4,241,154	27,109,414	74,085,775
1654	3,932,203	4,455,841	30,283,131	107,049,526
1655	3,431,941	5,476,936	29,105,553	99,601,733
1656	3,662,238	6,114,353	29,697,273	101,395,984

Note: Certain types of expenditure (for example, the *Ligues Suisses*, the *ponts et chaussées*, *ambassades* and *menus dons et voyages*) have been excluded from these lists.

[a] Includes pensions and *acquits patents*.

[b] Includes *Maison du Roi, chambre aux deniers, argenterie, menus, écuries, offrandes et aumônes, troupes de la maison du roi, prévôté de l'hôtel, cent suisses, venerie et fauconnerie, maison de la Reine, maison de la Reine mère, maison de Monseigneur* (Gaston, and later Philippe, d'Orléans) as Mallet gives figures from time to time. Finally, the *bâtiments* are included.

[c] Includes *ordinaire et extraordinaire des guerres, artillerie, fortifications, marine et galères*.

[d] Mallet variously calls this type of expenditure 'remboursements, intérêts d'avance, etc.' or *comptants*.

Table III
The secret expenses (*comptants*) of the French monarchy, 1594–1681
(*livres tournois*)

Date	Various contemporary sources	Chambre des Comptes (*list compiled in 1648*)
1594	12,907,299	
1595	5,002,625	
1596	3,325,095	
1597	1,207,060	
1598	4,094,130	
1599	2,626,483	
1600	2,145,342	
1601	1,609,002	
1602	2,135,058	
1603	2,674,664	
1604	2,510,501	
1605	3,062,568	
1606	3,446,080	
1607	3,345,193	
1608	2,939,176	2,951,175
1609	2,246,956	2,999,426
1610	—	1,685,853
1611	1,896,502	1,886,210
1612	1,714,517	1,747,477
1613	1,900,015	1,914,999
1614	1,936,958	1,936,958
1615	1,937,103	1,936,421
1616	6,070,637	6,070,636
1617	4,151,231	4,237,080
1618	3,790,681	3,786,080
1619	6,149,673	6,150,173
1620	5,577,820	5,000,538
1621	7,448,916	7,469,416
1622	11,647,058	10,647,154
1623	9,193,649	9,193,689
1624	6,768,868	6,769,670
1625	4,084,073	7,988,049
1626	12,408,048[a]	13,796,100
1627	6,093,707[b]	9,535,217
1628	8,655,809	8,820,522
1629	11,961,408	12,276,908
1630	6,311,336	6,427,636
1631	10,816,107	10,980,807

Date	Various contemporary sources	Chambre des Comptes (list compiled in 1648)
1632	19,127,444	19,349,157
1633	22,686,604	22,886,603
1634	—	39,494,037
1635	61,933,682	61,183,682
1636	31,486,840	31,726,839
1637	36,158,067	36,408,066
1638	29,808,841	39,990,400
1639	37,559,849	37,571,849
1640	29,587,521	27,593,200
1641	44,253,787	48,121,956
1642	32,978,120	32,990,119
1643	48,453,125	48,287,125
1644	53,843,208	59,457,354
1645	57,707,991	
1646	48,369,465	
1647	57,023,353	
1648	30,397,235	
1649	2,865,570	
1650	1,979,119	
1651	12,274,456	
1652	3,848,236	
1653	20,946,006	
1654	23,950,716	
1655	41,150,088	
1656	51,105,669	
1657	66,922,351	
1658	86,392,303	
1659	88,439,475	
1660	30,663,091	
1661	20,378,043	
1662	22,180,376	
1663	5,307,172	
1664	4,033,791	
1665	7,918,918	
1666	7,391,421	
1667	8,566,410	
1668	7,208,741	
1669	7,033,674	
1670	4,747,007	
1671	13,705,711	
1672	10,202,907	
1673	13,885,737	

Table III—*continued*

Date	Various contemporary sources
1674	16,708,900
1675	12,614,581
1676	9,254,259
1677	11,303,862
1678	9,902,332
1679	11,163,370
1680	7,899,257
1681	9,630,427

[a] An alternative reading is 13,574,831 *livres*.
[b] An alternative reading is 9,529,280 *livres*.
Source for alternative readings: A.A.E. France 797, fo. 115. Considerations of space preclude the enumeration of all the alternative readings.

Sources   Chambre des Comptes. A.A.E. France 861, fo. 226.

Various contemporary sources:
1594–1608: 120 a.p. 10, 11. 1609: 120 a.p. 2, fo. 253.
1611–43: as income and expenditure lists in Table I.
1644–61: B.L. Harleian 4472b, fos. 413–17 ('Inventaire des Estatz de comptant qui sont ès mains de Monseigneur le Chancelier'). These figures are more or less complete from 1639 to 1661, thus demonstrating that the agreement between Richelieu and Bullion in 1639 to keep detailed records of the *comptants* was implemented.
1662–81: B.N. Mélanges Colbert 264–310, *passim*.

Table IV
Mallet's figures for certain revenues payable to the French Treasury,
1600–1656
(*livres tournois*)

Date	Taille (pays d'élections)[a]	Parties casuelles	*Revenue farms*	Deniers extraordinaires
1600	9,949,999	1,644,046	3,097,344	4,333,994
1601	10,191,031	625,006	2,554,368	1,003,059
1602	9,394,647	1,314,312	3,297,656	3,370,903
1603	9,666,235	1,967,530	3,940,379	3,566,519
1604	9,665,645	1,551,674	3,446,918	4,897,987
1605	9,863,995	2,324,394	4,818,065	7,892,643
1606	9,650,692	1,918,067	6,105,678	8,587,688
1607	9,626,083	1,842,638	5,589,711	10,656,470
1608	9,274,105	3,479,592	6,088,102	12,065,665

Date	Taille (pays d'élections)[a]	Parties casuelles	Revenue farms	Deniers extraordinaires
1609	9,004,643	2,263,751	6,138,391	13,086,864
1610	9,169,759	1,668,108	5,524,198	15,515,008
1611	8,967,293	1,868,082	6,469,741	8,877,398
1612	9,019,954	2,421,746	6,464,492	7,188,716
1613	9,225,176	4,797,286	6,623,975	6,023,934
1614	9,268,511	3,766,285	7,054,379	7,641,693
1615	9,510,137	2,183,795	7,268,213	3,380,865
1616	9,950,648	10,717,400	6,676,535	4,013,579
1617	9,096,891	6,067,975	7,655,130	9,465,552
1618	8,942,532	2,569,016	6,726,948	7,455,239
1619	9,209,649	3,771,836	12,882,468	11,862,414
1620	10,073,733	13,267,639	7,013,301	6,812,593
1621	8,878,776	14,295,607	6,543,470	11,146,918
1622	8,681,546	20,052,155	8,145,621	11,415,506
1623	8,450,094	17,419,025	5,214,943	4,260,733
1624	8,942,424	10,260,198	5,742,907	7,087,534
1625	5,762,973	16,264,263	6,059,095	21,715,302
1626	8,664,640	15,692,951	7,515,600	10,194,620
1627	4,853,096	17,329,473	6,649,934	8,773,237
1628	4,989,933	11,303,490	9,824,242	12,969,026
1629	7,188,531	17,090,690	8,072,973	19,527,404
1630	7,463,943	18,917,005	6,513,379	5,606,147
1631	7,323,571	17,227,609	7,331,364	5,710,163
1632	6,721,215	28,231,028	8,744,247	10,418,987
1633	8,300,649	36,854,510	9,896,540	10,655,798
1634	7,183,504	28,370,919	11,239,612	66,687,431
1635	5,733,143	33,450,996	7,193,274	156,759,915
1636	7,758,964	28,847,000	10,658,742	56,399,003
1637	12,680,893	20,396,735	13,426,796	35,620,545
1638	17,675,139	27,789,056	10,814,016	35,818,265
1639	15,734,606	33,334,194	11,545,062	23,630,387
1640	22,505,262	18,262,239	15,651,276	28,943,012
1641	32,457,282	18,133,251	15,318,277	43,935,291
1642	18,312,306	8,671,924	20,536,567	36,870,508
1643	48,162,454	9,594,440	17,149,380	42,788,872
1644	36,179,654	27,444,296	23,950,965	47,099,455
1645	37,244,818	20,088,759	22,021,692	51,326,253
1646	31,639,679	13,498,609	14,393,811	68,791,386
1647	18,957,546	6,482,907	12,218,573	101,687,677
1648	20,377,021	5,304,332	7,507,172	48,138,199
1649	17,103,171	2,292,516	11,313,465	61,912,012
1650	18,656,413	3,412,806	4,515,059	67,059,797

Table IV—*continued*

Date	Taille (pays d'élections)[a]	Parties casuelles	*Revenue farms*	Deniers extraordinaires
1651	23,691,022	6,296,430	10,191,719	97,399,066
1652	23,629,369	2,867,490	9,501,669	74,601,707
1653	30,378,923	9,552,425	9,321,554	56,546,498
1654	29,362,945	11,266,887	14,484,897	88,158,753
1655	38,103,713	10,102,416	15,837,292	71,405,626
1656	36,185, 322	6,523,612	8,408,123	83,569,969

[a] Excludes certain other direct taxes, such as the *taillon*, which Mallet lists separately.

Table V
Relative importance of certain types of royal revenue, 1600–1654
A. Quinquennial totals in millions of *livres tournois*

	i deniers extraordinaires	ii parties casuelles	iii revenue farms	iv taille (pays d'élections)	v miscellaneous	vi total income
1600–4	17.2	7.1	16.3	48.9	9.1	98.6
1605–9	52.3	11.8	28.7	47.4	10.2	150.4
1610–14	45.3	14.5	32.1	45.7	7.8	145.4
1615–19	36.2	25.3	41.2	46.7	9.0	158.4
1620–4	40.7	75.3	32.7	45.0	9.4	203.1
1625–9	73.2	77.7	38.1	31.5	11.2	231.7
1630–4	99.1	129.6	43.7	37.0	24.1	333.5
1635–9	308.2	143.8	53.6	59.6	22.9	588.1
1640–4	199.6	82.1	92.6	157.6	25.1	557.0
1645–9	331.9	47.7	67.5	125.3	16.9	589.3
1650–4	383.8	33.4	48.0	125.7	16.3	607.2

Table V B. Certain revenues expressed as a proportion of total
income of the French monarchy

| | (per cent) | | | | |
	deniers *extraordinaires*	*parties* *casuelles*	revenue farms	*taille (pays* *d'élections)*	miscel- laneous
1600–4	17.4	7.2	16.5	49.6	9.3
1605–9	34.8	7.8	19.1	31.5	6.8
1610–14	31.2	10.0	22.1	31.4	5.3
1615–19	22.9	16.0	26.0	29.5	5.6
1620–4	20.0	37.1	16.1	22.2	4.6
1625–9	31.6	33.5	16.4	13.6	4.9
1630–4	29.7	38.9	13.1	11.1	7.2
1635–9	52.4	24.5	9.1	10.1	3.9
1640–4	35.8	14.7	16.6	28.3	4.6
1645–9	56.3	8.1	11.5	21.3	2.8
1650–4	63.2	5.5	7.9	20.7	2.7

Table V C. Certain revenues expressed as a proportion of ordinary
revenue of the French monarchy

| | (per cent) | | | |
	parties *casuelles*	revenue farms	*taille (pays* *d'élections)*	miscellaneous
1600–4	8.7	20.0	60.0	11.3
1605–9	12.0	29.3	48.3	10.4
1610–14	14.5	32.1	45.7	7.7
1615–19	20.7	33.7	38.2	7.4
1620–4	46.4	20.1	27.7	5.8
1625–9	49.0	24.0	19.9	7.1
1630–4	55.3	18.6	15.8	10.3
1635–9	51.4	19.2	21.3	8.1
1640–4	23.0	25.9	44.1	7.0
1645–9	18.5	26.2	48.7	6.6
1650–4	15.0	21.5	56.3	7.2

Table VI

Rents payable by certain revenue farmers to the French monarchy,
1603–1664

(annual rent payable in *livres tournois*)

Date	gabelles de France	aides	cinq grosses fermes
1603		*610,000*	
1604			*670,000*
1605	4,621,000		
1611	4,621,000	*900,000*	995,000
1613			880,000
1616	6,345,140		
1619		*1,400,000*	880,000
1622	5,988,312		
1623		2,300,000	
1624			1,650,000
1625		1,900,000	
1626		2,200,000	
1627	8,500,000	2,485,000	
1632	*12,490,600*	3,135,000	
1633			2,450,000
1634		3,985,630	
1641	13,424,200		
1642		3,846,571	
1643			2,800,000
1644	13,624,200		
1647	13,443,200		
1648		4,250,000	
1650	8,200,000		
1652			*2,440,000*
1653		*3,175,000*	
1656	8,600,000		
1660	14,750,000	4,520,000	4,430,000
1662	13,500,000		5,650,000
1663	13,800,000	13,720,000	
1664			*5,750,000*

Table VII
Royal income from the *affaires extraordinaires* (*traités*)

A. Royal income from the *affaires extraordinaires* (*traités*), 1623–1661
(annual totals in *livres tournois*)

Date	Gross amount (*forfait*)	Interest payable to financiers (*remise*)	Net amount payable to crown	Interest rate per cent
1623	26,028,688			
1624	8,355,000			
1625	10,226,052			
1626	3,011,500			
1627	7,484,726			
1628	6,960,250			
1629	9,645,718			
1630	4,947,860			
1631	16,916,355	2,787,856	14,128,499	16.5
1632	43,998,158	10,086,141	33,912,017	22.9
1633	68,933,189	13,734,833	55,198,356	19.9
1634	51,709,719	14,028,614	37,681,105	27.1
1635	78,986,390	18,883,982	60,102,408	23.9
1636	28,989,609	8,096,861	20,892,748	27.9
1637	43,238,159	9,859,535	33,378,624	22.8
1638	51,887,916	13,444,671	38,443,245	25.4
1639	65,883,235	15,701,361	50,181,874	23.8
1640	55,218,260	14,219,192	40,999,068	25.8
1641	45,752,800	12,744,348	33,008,452	· 27.9

1643	24,465,000	5,493,263	18,971,737	22.5
1644	46,752,350	12,847,774	33,904,576	27.5
1645	41,041,688	11,191,838	29,849,850	27.3
1646	42,722,079	11,824,348	30,897,731	27.7
1647	21,716,556	6,347,728	15,368,828	29.2
1648	6,373,600	1,864,933	4,508,667	29.3

1653	18,237,312	4,711,002	15,526,310	25.8
1654	14,820,000	3,118,333	11,701,667	21.0
1655	47,168,472	14,330,933	32,837,539	30.4
1656	16,774,000	4,199,899	12,574,101	25.0
1657	57,109,600	18,759,195	38,350,405	32.8
1658	30,275,000	9,712,497	20,562,503	32.1

Table VII A.—*continued*

A. Royal income from the *affaires extraordinaires* (*traités*), 1623–1661
(annual totals in *livres tournois*)

Date	Gross amount (*forfait*)	Interest payable to financiers (*remise*)	Net amount payable to crown	Interest rate per cent
1659	34,030,000	9,148,534	24,881,466	26.9
1660	12,290,000	3,212,000	9,078,000	26.1
1661	9,658,000	2,465,667	7,192,333	25.5

Sources B.N. MS. fr. 18205–18, 18221–2, 18224–7, supplemented by B.N. MS. fr. 4524 and E 73–349c as necessary. Note that *subrogations* to *traités*, *traités de bâtiments*, *traités de munitions* and *traités* with variable interest rates have been removed from the calculations. The criteria for inclusion may differ from Mlle F. Bayard ('Fermes et traités en France dans la première moitié du xviie siècle', *Bulletin du Centre d'Histoire Économique et Sociale de la Région Lyonnaise*, iv (1975), graphs 5 and 6 at p. 78) and the calculations were carried out independently.

Table VII B. Royal income from the *affaires extraordinaires* (*traités*),
1689–1715
(quinquennial totals in *livres tournois*)

Date	Gross amount (*forfait*)	Interest payable to financiers (*remise*)	Net amount payable to crown	Interest rate per cent
1690–4	213,277,075	50,530,916	162,746,159	23.7
1695–9	100,980,850	24,276,910	76,703,940	24.0
1700–4	177,402,697	41,356,845	136,045,852	23.3
1705–9	175,822,157	39,852,301	135,969,856	22.7
1710–14	52,456,975	9,782,104	42,674,871	18.6
Total 1689–1715[a]	758,125,488	173,778,110	584,347,388	22.9

[a] The official totals show some variation from these figures, which are the actual totals of the annual figures. The total includes two years not included in the quinquennial totals above.

Table VII C. Selected comparison of royal income from the *affaires*
extraordinaires
(eleven-year totals in *livres tournois*)

Date	Gross amount (*forfait*)	Interest payable to financiers (*remise*)	Net amount payable to crown	Interest rate per cent
1631–41	551,513,790	133,587,394	417,926,396	24.2
1691–1701	328,885,114	76,979,363	251,905,751	23.4
1701–11	375,555,581	84,378,202	291,177,379	22.5

Table VIII
Loans contracted by the French monarchy, 1613–1661

A. Royal borrowing, 1613–1661
(annual totals in *livres tournois*)

Date	Gross amount of loans with interest recorded	Date	Gross amount of loans with interest recorded
1613	415,000	1636	5,109,152
1614	910,000	1637	9,970,140
1615	2,299,800	1638	13,538,850
1616	2,033,000	1639	15,944,464
1617	4,551,700	1640	37,622,933
1618	200,000	1641	41,594,603
1619	9,128,500	1642	26,057,662
1620	6,148,500	1643	63,206,051
1621	5,822,218	1644	51,128,630
1622	10,162,357	1645	123,676,265
1623	3,600,000	1646	83,669,828
1624	4,976,876	1647	51,482,872
1625	12,439,500	1648	8,492,772[a]
1626	9,022,516		
1627	3,844,039	– – – – – – – – –	
1628	304,000	1654	23,893,200
1629	2,095,510	1655	48,041,503
1630	2,431,241	1656	78,569,657
1631	5,113,046	1657	74,722,320
1632	1,920,880	1658	35,281,905
1633	2,207,925	1659	54,164,892
1634	6,426,400	1660	40,553,297
1635	7,410,450	1661	44,500,039

[a] Before the revocation of loan contracts on 18 July 1648.

Table VIII B. Interest rates on certain loans contracted by the
French monarchy, 1656–1661
Annual totals in *livres tournois*

Date	Gross amount of loans with interest recorded	Interest paid to financiers	Net amount paid to crown	Interest rate per cent
1656	75,774,525	12,824,256	62,950,269	16.9
1657	70,360,962	12,051,419	58,309,543	17.1
1658	32,211,905	4,284,955	27,926,950	13.3
1659	50,227,525	5,769,816	44,457,709	11.5
1660	28,591,513	3,824,663	24,766,850	13.4
1661	33,758,690	3,524,823	30,233,867	10.4
Total 1656–61	290,925,120	42,279,932	248,645,188	14.5

Sources   For 1613–48: E 40b/41a–231b, *passim*, supplemented where necessary by *Arrêts du conseil du roi*, ed. Le Pesant, nos. 29, 32, 136, 328; AD IX 413 no. 105, 27 Oct. 1634 (loan of Philippe Hamel) and E 392, fo. 5, 7 Oct. 1666 (reference to loan of Jean Levesque of 2 July 1639). B.N. n.a.f. 201, *traités* excluded.

For 1654–5: E 263a–284b, *passim*, supplemented by B.N. MS. fr. 18221, fos. 165–8 and A.A.E. France 894 and 895, *passim*. For 1656–61, the source is B.N. MS. fr. 18221–7, with *traités* excluded from the calculations. The figures have to be viewed with caution since the copies of the loan contracts sent to Séguier were not dated precisely. Moreover, whereas in the records of the council of finance the loan contracts were filed according to the date of negotiation, Séguier filed them according to the year on which the revenues were anticipated. This obstacle is not insuperable, however, since in 1661 revenues were anticipated one year in advance. For 1661, the contracts on the revenues of 1662 were abrogated by Colbert and are to be found in E 350, *passim*. The contracts for the same revenues in the volume for 1661 were negotiated in 1660 and are thus transposed back to the earlier date (B.N. MS. fr. 18227, fos. 111–45). A similar procedure has been adopted by working backwards through the evidence to 1656. The figures cited earlier by Bonney, 'The secret expenses of Richelieu and Mazarin', 830 ns. 3 and 5 and 832 n. 5, have been revised upwards somewhat by the subsequent discovery of a small number of contracts.

Table IX
The bankruptcies of the French monarchy (1598, 1648, 1661)

A. Bankruptcy of 1598 (not declared officially)
(figures in millions of *livres tournois*)

i. *Deficit on the current account (in 1596)*

Revenues	30.9
Charges and alienated revenues	24.0 −
Net revenues	6.9
Expenses	24.9 −
Deficit on the current account	18.0

ii. *Debts not repaid or only partially repaid (in 1598)*

England	7.4
Swiss Cantons	35.8
German princes (including *reitern*)	14.7
United Provinces	9.3
Arrears of troop payments	6.5
Arrears of *rentes* and payments to amortize the *grand parti de Lyon*	28.5
Debts of Henri III	12.2
Treaties of pacification in the 1590s	32.2
Total excluding alienated royal demesne and revenues (estimated at 150.0)	146.6

iii. *Unsatisfied creditors of the French monarchy at the time of the death of Henri IV and after*

Name of creditor	Amount in claims (livres tournois)
a. Duc de Nevers	100,000
b. Duc de Lorraine	6,500
c. Heirs of Sublet d'Heudicourt	35,532
d. Heirs of Louis Gilbert Gombaud	52,127
e. Barthélémy and Pierre d'Elbène	1.2 million
f. Baron d'Ompmartin, colonel of the *reitern*	583,098
g. German towns of Herford and Northouzan	49,680
h. The sieur de Tavannes	57,547
i. The sieurs de la Buisse and de Bellière	149,307
j. The sieur d'Arpajon	36,000

Table IX A.—*continued*

iii. *Unsatisfied creditors of the French monarchy at the time of the death of Henri IV and after*

Name of creditor	Amount in claims (livres tournois)
k. Scipion Balbany	147,000
l. Christian of Anhalt	873,411
m. John George of Saxony	208,333
n. Duc de Bouillon	400,000
o. Pierre Le Grand	860,193 (excluding interest)
p. Gilbert II Coiffier d'Effiat	12,000

Table IX B. Bankruptcy of 1648 (Revocation of loan contracts, 18 July 1648)

Figures in millions of *livres tournois*

i. *Deficit on the current account (La Meilleraye's statement, end of September 1648)*

Revenues	92.0
Charges	57.0 −
Net revenues	35.0
Expenses	59.0 −
Deficit on the current account	24.0

ii. *Value of revoked loan contracts*

According to the financiers, 1654	80.0
According to Cardinal Mazarin, 1648	100.0
According to La Meilleraye, 1648	120.0

iii. *Certain creditors of the French monarchy during the Fronde*

	Amount in claims
a. Simon Alix, Jacques Forcoal, Ogier de Marcillac and Isaac Monceau, farmers of the *aides*	6.0
b. Jean-Pierre Robier, Jean-François Pradel and Autherin Robier	1.6
c. Simon, Pierre, Jean and Étienne Romanet	1.6
d. Jacques Kerver	2.4
e. Martin Tabouret	2.0
f. Jean Frarin	2.0
g. Thomas Bonneau	6.4

Table IX C. Bankruptcy of 1661 (Revocation of loan contracts, 16
November 1661)
Figures in millions of *livres tournois*

i.	*Deficit on the current account*	
	Revenues	84.2
	Alienated revenues and other debts	40.2 −
	Net revenues	44.0
	Expenses for 1661, approximately	65.2 −
	Deficit on current account	21.2
ii.	*Value of revoked loan contracts*	
	Revenues of 1662 anticipated by 5 Sept. 1661 (arrest of Foucquet)	26.4
iii.	*Taxes on financiers (Contract of 18 October 1665)*	
	Immediate cash payment	2.0
	Cash payment over 5 years	20.0
	Redemption of Treasury bills	38.0
	Rentes, droits et autres bons effets	50.0 +
		110.0

Sources A iii

  a. E 32a, fo. 194, 18 Aug. 1611.
  b. E 32b, fo. 84, 6 Sept. 1611.
  c. E 38b, fo. 157, 15 Dec. 1612.
  d. E 38b, fo. 161, 15 Dec. 1612. Gombaud's heirs were still claiming 88,000 *livres* in principal and interest as compensation in 1636: A.A.E. France 823, fo. 206.
  e. E 41b, fo. 215, 27 Aug. 1613.
  f. E 42a, fo. 391, 24 Oct. 1613.
  g. E 42b, fo. 372, 31 Dec. 1613.
  h. E 43a, fo. 158, 25 Jan. 1614.
  i. E 51, fo. 285, 14 Nov. 1615.
  j. E 52a, fo. 28, 18 Jan. 1616.
  k. E 58b, fo. 372, 16 June 1618.
  l. E 59a, fo. 254, 26 July 1618. In 1592, Henri IV had bound his heirs to pay off the Anhalt debt, and by 1624 only 283,259 *livres* remained to be paid. However, this had still not been paid in 1818, when Anhalt's heirs presented a demand to Louis XVIII for the repayment of capital and 193 years' interest! Cf. Anquez, *Henri IV et l'Allemagne*, pp. 65, 223–4.
  m. E 62b, fo. 402, 14 Sept. 1619.
  n. E 37b, fo. 110, 11 Sept. 1612.
  o. Cf. E 122c, fo. 395, 10 Mar. 1635. This was a loan to Henri III partly secured on three rubies which were valued in 1633 at 347,000 *livres*.
  p. E 38b, fo. 268, 20 Dec. 1612.

Sources B ii
The financiers' estimate is in A.A.E. France 893/2, fo. 419. Mazarin's estimate
was made in a letter to Chanut on 31 July 1648: *Lettres du Cardinal Mazarin*, ed.
Chéruel and d'Avenel, iii. 160. This figure was also given by Denis Talon at
Foucquet's trial: Foucquet, *Défenses*, vi. 220. La Meilleraye's estimate was given in
his financial statement: Talon, *Mémoires*, ed. Michaud and Poujoulat, p. 281.

Sources B iii
a. V6 233 no. 6, 14 May 1649.
b. E 233a, fo. 50, 7 Oct. 1648.
c. E 233a, fo. 52, 7 Oct. 1648.
d. E 250a, fo. 261, 24 Feb. 1652. E 272a, fo. 430, 10 Dec. 1654.
e. E 282a, fo. 204, 13 Oct. 1655.
f. E 256b, fo. 177, 21 May 1653.
g. E 259a, fo. 336, 13 Aug. 1653.

Table X
Foucquet's personal accounts

A. Income and expenditure (including assigned revenues), 1653–1656
(annual totals in *livres tournois*)

	Income (including private borrowing)	Expenditure (including repayments on loans)
25 Feb.1653– end of 1653	5,202,374	891,497
1654	12,175,960	3,483,014
1655	13,287,999	4,243,649
1656	8,735,776	4,510,859
Total	39,402,109	13,129,019
	= 26,273,090 net	

Table X B. Private income and expenditure (excluding assigned
revenues), 1653–1661
(totals in *livres tournois*)

	Income	Expenditure
25 Feb. 1653–end of 1656	13,240,415	13,175,452
25 Feb 1653–14 Aug. 1661	35,916,169	36,922,926

Table X C. Distribution of personal expenditure, 1653–1656
(totals in *livres tournois*)

Total personal expenditure	13,175,452	

Total of itemized expenditure	13,046,064	(99 per cent)
		Proportion of total of itemized expenditure
Repayment of interest on loans	5,147,783	39.5 per cent
Repayments to financiers with cause explained	1,512,050	11.6
Payments to individuals e.g. at court without cause explained	2,977,241	22.8
Payments on the orders of Foucquet and wife	1,393,175	10.7
Building costs and domestic expenditure	804,628	6.2
Payments on Vaux-le-Vicomte	693,621	5.3
Payments on Saint-Mandé	327,607	2.5
Purchases	189,959	1.4

Table X D. Distribution of personal expenditure, 1653–1661
(totals in *livres tournois*)

Total personal expenditure	36,922,926	

Total of itemized expenditure	28,973,345	(78 per cent)
		Proportion of total of itemized expenditure
Repayment of interest on loans	5,674,298	19.6 per cent
Payments on orders of Foucquet and Bruant, his clerk	10,680,736	36.9
Expenses without any cause explained	3,474,826	12.0
Domestic expenditure	2,511,376	8.7
Payments on Vaux-le-Vicomte	1,414,598	4.9
Payments on Saint-Mandé	487,228	1.7
Payments to Bruant (including repayment of loans to Foucquet)	3,444,383	11.8

Table X D.—*continued*

Payments on *billets de l'Épargne*	404,092	1.4
Payments to individuals e.g.		
courtiers	881,808	3.0

Sources *Table A* Summaries of 38 accounts kept by Charles Bernard, Foucquet's clerk: Foucquet, *Défenses*, xvi. 167–76 and 144 a.p. 60, Dr. 1 [156 mi. 6], fos. 89–96. 48 of the 76 separate items are identical in the two sources. The discrepancies are not very large, and in the printed source two items are missing and a third is almost certainly misprinted. For this reason, the manuscript version has been accepted *in toto*.

Tables B to D. 144 a.p. 71, Dr. 9 [156 mi. 25], fo. 11. The figures in Foucquet, *Défenses*, vi. 174–5 (important for Table C but corrected where necessary), 186, 189, 197 and *Archives de la Bastille*, ed. Ravaisson-Mollien, ii. 364–5 and 369 show some variation. Dent, *Crisis in Finance*, pp. 68–9 gives a version of the figures in Table D which is somewhat incomplete.

Table X E. Enumeration of Foucquet's assets in 1661 by his creditors
(totals in *livres tournois*)

Furniture	188,964
Tapestries, fabrics, etc.	40,000
Contents of Vaux-le-Vicomte	33,916
Money order of Clément and Chanut	393,996
Sale of office of *procureur-général* in the *Parlement* of Paris	(1,400,000)[a]
Demesne of the *comté* of Melun	187,558
Alienated rights of Melun	310,413
Impôts et billots of Brittany	185,688
Demesne of Rosporden	60,000
Marc d'or	660,000
Notifications of Champagne	88,950
Rentes	19,000
Revenues of Belle-Île	15,370[b]
Billets de l'Épargne ('pour des avances par luy faictes pour le Roy')	5,330,000
Ships in Brittany	300,000
Office of *greffier extraordinaire* in the council	6,000
Office of Chancellor and Keeper of the Seals *de l'Ordre*	450,000
Governorship of Concarneau, America and St-Michel	216,000
Estimated value of Belle-Île	(1,300,000)[c]
Maison de Paris, formerly belonging to de Thoré	(350,000)[d]
Dowry to Marie Foucquet	(600,000)[e]

Estimated total of Foucquet's assets excluding Vaux-
le-Vicomte and St-Mandé   12,135,855

Estimated total of Foucquet's assets including Vaux-
le-Vicomte and St-Mandé   15,460,350[f]

Note: The items below the broken line were not enumerated by Foucquet's creditors.
 [a] Foucquet, *Défenses*, xvi. 96.
 [b] This item may include revenues after 1661.
 [c] Foucquet, *Défenses*, xvi. 22.
 [d] Ibid., xvi. 26.
 [e] Ibid., xvi. 191.
 [f] Dessert, 'L'affaire Fou(c)quet', 40.

Table XI
Total royal expenditure during the ministry of Colbert, 1662–1683
(livres tournois)

Date	Mallet	Conseil Royal des Finances	Other contemporary sources
1662	65,169,011	76,132,346	72,801,468
1663	46,545,737	42,017,738	46,831,605
1664	63,067,766	63,492,355	63,081,864
1665	82,870,839	77,305,847	90,871,856
1666	56,566,890	66,347,009	66,611,895
1667	72,138,507	70,855,046	72,090,744
1668	64,864,415	67,744,957	70,875,386
1669	76,281,559	74,477,796	76,283,149
1670	77,307,798	77,240,235	77,209,820
1671	83,875,707	85,260,431	83,875,723
1672	87,928,540	91,213,058	87,928,561
1673	98,187,758	99,099,087	98,242,781
1674	107,253,540	113,676,401	107,280,917
1675	111,860,416	115,783,007	111,860,435
1676	110,071,449	106,093,801	110,071,473
1677	115,718,954	111,812,091	115,702,460
1678	109,930,506	(97,781,328)	106,910,322
1679	128,235,624	133,186,898	130,708,165
1680	95,967,860	(82,770,450)	95,885,389
1681	141,040,073	(131,579,495)	141,040,090
1682	199,624,654	—	199,108,189
1683	115,098,507	—	115,133,523

Selected Bibliography

I. MANUSCRIPT SOURCES

Note: This is not a definitive list of all sources consulted or cited in the references to the text.

A. *Archives Nationales*

Conseil d'état et des finances.
Over 600 volumes were systematically reworked for the purpose of this study, viz.: E 26b/27a–349c (June 1610–Dec. 1661). Also E 375a–395a (2 Dec. 1664–17 Mar. 1667), *liquidations* for the redemption of *rentes* following the declaration of 4 Dec. 1664.

Ormesson papers.
144 a.p. 60–74, 25 rolls of microfilm representing 14 cartons of documentary evidence from the *chambre de justice* of 1661–5.

Sully papers.
120 a.p. 2–10, 12, 27–9, 33–4.

Chambre des Comptes.
P 2330–78, about 48 volumes of *mémoriaux*, copies of registers covering the years 1588–1662.

Minutier Central (notarial sources).
XIV 36–46, 49, 52–61, 64–5, 75. About 25 *liasses*, chiefly useful for Jean Galland, although containing material on Claude Cornuel, Denis Marin, Thomas Bonneau, and the sale of *rentes*.
XXI 91–8, 101, 104–6, 109–11, 113, 116, 121, 124–8, 141–6, 148. About 28 *liasses*, chiefly useful for Antoine Feydeau, François Chandonnay, Samuel Gaudon de la Rallière, and Jean Doublet.
XXX 56, 61, chiefly for Thomas Bonneau.
LI 124, 129, 134–47, chiefly for Antoine Feydeau.

Other series. Occasional reference to other series where necessary, for example AD IX 413–15 (leases on the revenue farms), KK 96, 109, 127, 132, 133a, 140–1, 146, 201a, 208 (incomplete accounts), O1 9 (*brevets* of appointment), U 22–4 (Le Nain registers).

B. *Archives des Affaires Etrangères*

About 160 volumes in the series *Mémoires et Documents, France* were systematically reworked for the purpose of this study, viz.: 762–913 (1590s–1661/5).

C. *Bibliothèque Nationale*

Manuscrits Français.

3645, 3947, 4518, 4520, 4524, 4559, 4589, 4680, 6888, 7750, 8182, 10407, 10410, 11165, 15893, 16623, 16627, 17486–7, 18205–27 (21 volumes of *traités* and *prêts, c.* 1633–61), 18489–91, 18494, 18510, 23026.

Other series.
500 Colbert 106, 223–4, 485.
Clairambault 654.
Dupuy 824–7.
Mélanges Colbert 264–310 (expenditure accounts 1662–81).
Morel de Thoisy 148, 150, 155–8, 160, 400
nouvelles acquisitions françaises 164–70 (expenditure accounts), 200.

II. PRINTED SOURCES

Note. All printed works in French are published in Paris unless otherwise stated. All printed works in English are published in London unless otherwise stated. This is not a definitive list of all works consulted or cited in the references to the text.

ANDRÉ, L. (ed.), A. J. du Plessis, Cardinal de Richelieu [?], *Testament politique* (1947).

ANQUEZ, L., *Henri IV et l'Allemagne d'après les mémoires et la correspondance de Jacques Bongars* (1887).

ANSELME DE SAINTE MARIE, P. de GUIBOURS, le Père, *Histoire généalogique et chronologique de la maison royale de France, des pairs, grands officiers de la couronne* . . . 3rd ed., 9 vols. (1726–33).

AVENEL, D. L. M. (ed.), *Lettres, instructions diplomatiques et papiers d'état du Cardinal de Richelieu*, 8 vols. (1853–77).

BADALO-DULONG C., *Banquier du roi. Barthélémy Hervart, 160[7]–76* (1951).

BARBICHE, B., *Sully* (1978).

BARBICHE, B., and BUISSERET, D. J., 'Sully et la surintendance des finances', *Bibliothèque de l'École des Chartes*, cxxiii (1965), 538–43.

BARBICHE, B., and BUISSERET, D. J., *Les oeconomies royales de Sully*, i (1970).

BATIFFOL, L., 'Le coup d'état du 24 avril 1617', *Revue Historique*, xcv (1907), 292–308; xcvii (1908), 27–77, 264–86.

BATIFFOL, L., 'Louis XIII et le duc de Luynes', *Revue Historique*, cii (1909), 241–64; ciii (1910), 32–62, 248–77.

BATIFFOL, L., 'Le trésor de la Bastille de 1605 à 1611', *Revue Henri IV*, iii (1909–12), 200–9.

BATIFFOL, L., 'La fortune du Cardinal de Richelieu', *Revue des Deux-Mondes*, 8th ser., xxvii (1935), 873–96.

BAYARD, F., 'Étude des comptants ès mains du roi sous Henri IV', *Bulletin du Centre d'Histoire Économique et Sociale de la Région Lyonnaise*, iii (1974), 1–27.

BAYARD, F., 'Fermes et traités en France dans la première moitié du xviiᵉ siècle', *Bulletin du Centre d'Histoire Économique et Sociale de la Région Lyonnaise*, iv (1975), 45–80.

BERCÉ, Y. M., *Histoire des croquants. Étude des soulèvements populaires au xviiᵉ siècle dans le sud-ouest de la France*, 2 vols. (Paris-Geneva, 1974).

BERCÉ, Y. M., 'La mobilité sociale, argument de révolte', *XVIIᵉ Siècle*, cxxii (1979), 61–71.

BERGER de XIVREY, M. and GUADET, J. (eds.), *Recueil des lettres missives de Henri IV*, 9 vols. (1843–76).

BLET, P., *Le clergé de France et la monarchie. Étude sur les assemblées générales du clergé de 1615 à 1666*, 2 vols. (Rome, 1959).

BOISLISLE, A. M. de (ed.), *Histoire de la maison de Nicolay. Pièces justificatives. II. Chambre des Comptes* (Nogent-le-Rotrou, 1873).

BOISLISLE, A. M. de, 'Semblançay et la surintendance des finances', *Annuaire-Bulletin de la Société de l'Histoire de France*, xviii (1881), 225–74.

BONNARDOT, F. (ed.), *Registres des délibérations du bureau de la ville de Paris. IX. 1586–1590* (1902).

BONNEY, R. J., 'The secret expenses of Richelieu and Mazarin, 1624–1661', *English Historical Review*, xci (1976), 825–36.

BONNEY, R. J., 'The French civil war, 1649–53', *European Studies Review*, viii (1978), 71–100.

BONNEY, R. J., *Political change in France under Richelieu and Mazarin, 1624–1661* (Oxford, 1978).

BONNEY, R. J., 'The failure of the French revenue farms, 1600–60', *Economic History Review*, 2nd ser., xxxii (1979), 11–32.

BONNEY, R. J., 'Cardinal Mazarin and his critics: the remonstrances of 1652', *Journal of European Studies*, x (1980), 15–31.

BONNEY, R. J., 'The English and French civil wars', *History*, lxv (1980), 365–82.

BONNEY, R. J., 'Cardinal Mazarin and the great nobility during the Fronde', *English Historical Review*, xcvi (1981).

BOSHER, J. F., 'Chambres de justice in the French monarchy', *French government and society, 1500–1850. Essays in memory of Alfred Cobban*, ed. Bosher (1973), 19–40.

BOUCHITTÉ, L. F. H. (ed.), *Négociations, lettres et pièces relatives à la conférence de Loudun* (1862).

BOURGEON, J. L., *Les Colbert avant Colbert. Destin d'une famille marchande* (1973).
BRUNET, G., CHAMPOLLION, A., HALPHEN, E. *et al.* (eds.), *Mémoires-Journaux de Pierre L'Estoile*, 12 vols. (1875–96).
BUISSERET, D. J., *Sully and the growth of centralized government in France, 1598–1610* (1968).

CAREW, Sir George, 'A relation of the state of France', *An historical view of the negotiations between the courts of England, France and Brussels, 1592–1617*, ed. T. Birch (1749).
CHAMBERLAND, A., *Un plan de restauration financière en 1596 attribué à Pierre Forget de Fresne* (1904).
CHAMBERLAND, A., *Le conflit de 1597 entre Henri IV et le Parlement de Paris* (1904).
CHAMBERLAND, A., 'Le budget de 1597. Exposé du projet de l'assemblée de Rouen ...', *Revue Henri IV*, i (1905), 15–20.
CHAMBERLAND, A., 'Le conseil des finances en 1596 et 1597 et les *Économies royales*', *Revue Henri IV*, i (1905–6), 21–32, 152–63, 250–60, 274–84.
CHAMBERLAND, A., 'Le budget de l'Épargne en 1607 d'après des documents inédits', *Revue Henri IV*, ii (1908), 312–26.
CHAMBERLAND, A., 'La comptabilité imaginaire des deniers des coffres du roi et les dettes suisses', *Revue Henri IV*, ii (1908), 50–60.
CHAMPION, P., 'La légende des mignons', *Humanisme et Renaissance*, vi (1939), 494–528.
CHANTÉRAC, marquis Audoin de la Cropte de (ed.), *Journal de ma vie. Mémoires du maréchal de Bassompierre*, 4 vols. (1870–7).
CHARLIER-MENIOLLE, R., *L'assemblée des notables tenue à Rouen en 1596* (1911).
CHAULEUR, A., 'Le rôle des traitants dans l'administration financière de la France de 1643 à 1653', *XVIIᵉ Siècle*, lxv (1964), 16–49.
CHÉRUEL, P. A. (ed.), *Journal d'Olivier Lefèvre d'Ormesson et extrait des mémoires d'André Lefèvre d'Ormesson*, 2 vols. (1860–1).
CHÉRUEL, P. A., *Mémoires sur la vie publique et privée de Foucquet ...*, 2 vols. (1862).
CHÉRUEL, P. A., and AVENEL, G. d' (eds.), *Lettres du Cardinal Mazarin pendant son ministère*, 9 vols. (1872–1906).
CHURCH, W. F., *Richelieu and reason of state* (Princeton, N. J., 1972).
CLAMAGÉRAN, J. J., *Histoire de l'impôt en France*, 3 vols. (1867–76).
CLARKE, J. A., *Huguenot warrior. The life and times of Henri de Rohan, 1579–1638* (The Hague, 1966).
CLÉMENT, P. (ed.), *Lettres, instructions et mémoires de Colbert ...*, 10 vols. (1861–82).
COLLINS, J. B., 'Sur l'histoire fiscale du xviiᵉ siècle: les impôts directs en Champagne entre 1595 et 1635', *Annales E.S.C.*, xxxiv (1979), 325–47.

COUSIN, V., 'Le duc et connétable de Luynes', *Journal des savants* (1861–3), *passim*.

CRÈVECOEUR, R. de, *Un document nouveau sur la succession des Concini* (1891).

DALLINGTON, R., *The view of Fraunce* (1604).

DENT, J., 'An aspect of the crisis of the seventeenth century. The collapse of the financial administration of the French monarchy, 1653–1661', *Economic History Review*, 2nd ser., xx (1967), 241–56.

DENT, J., *Crisis in finance. Crown, financiers and society in seventeenth-century France* (Newton Abbot, 1973).

DENT, J., 'The role of *clientèles* in the financial élite of France under Cardinal Mazarin', *French government and society, 1500–1850. Essays in memory of Alfred Cobban*, ed. J. F. Bosher (1973), 41–69.

DEPPING, G. B., 'Un banquier protestant en France au xviiᵉ siècle. Barthélémy Herwarth . . .', *Revue Historique*, x (1879), 285–338; xi (1879), 63–80.

DESCILLEULS, A., 'Henri IV et la chambre de justice de 1607', *Comptes rendus de l'académie des sciences morales et politiques*, lxv (1906), 276–91.

DESJONQUÈRES, L., *Le garde des sceaux Michel de Marillac et son oeuvre législative* (1908).

DESSERT, D., 'Finances et société au xviiᵉ siècle: à propos de la chambre de justice de 1661', *Annales E.S.C.*, xxix (1974), 847–81.

DESSERT, D. and JOURNET, J. L., 'Le lobby Colbert: un royaume ou une affaire de famille?', *Annales E.S.C.*, xxx (1975), 1303–36.

DESSERT, D., 'Pouvoir et finance au xviiᵉ siècle: la fortune de Mazarin', *Revue d'Histoire Moderne et Contemporaine*, xxiii (1976), 161–81.

DESSERT, D., 'Le "laquais-financier" au grand siècle: mythe ou réalité?', *XVIIᵉ Siècle*, cxxii (1979), 21–36.

DESSERT, D., 'L'affaire Fou(c)quet', *L'histoire*, xxxii (1981), 39–47.

DETHAN, G., *The young Mazarin*, trans. S. Baron (1977).

DEVYVER, A., *Le sang épuré. Les préjugés de race chez les gentilshommes français de l'ancien régime, 1560–1720* (Brussels, 1973).

DEYON, P., *Amiens. Capitale provinciale. Étude sur la société urbaine au xviiᵉ siècle* (Paris and The Hague, 1967).

DORNIC, F., *Une ascension sociale au xviiᵉ siècle. Louis Berryer, agent de Mazarin et de Colbert* (Caen, 1968).

DOUCET, R., 'Les finances de France en 1614 d'après le "traicté du revenu et despense des finances"', *Revue d'Histoire Économique et Sociale*, xviii (1930), 133–63.

DROUOT, H., *Mayenne et la Bourgogne, 1587–1596. Contribution à l'histoire des provinces françaises pendant la Ligue*, 2 vols. (1937).

FEILLET, A., *et al.* (eds.), *Oeuvres de Retz*, 10 vols. (1870–96).

FOUCQUET, N., *Les oeuvres de Mʳ Foucquet, ministre d'estat, contenant son accusation, son procez et ses défenses contre Louis XIV, roy de France*, 16 vols. (1696).

FREUDMANN, F. R., *L'étonnant Gourville, 1625–1703* (Paris and Geneva, 1960).

GIRARD, G., *Histoire de la vie du duc d'Espernon* (1655).
GRILLON, P. (eds.), *Les papiers de Richelieu. Section politique intérieure. Correspondance et papiers d'état* (in progress; volume i, 1975).
GRISELLE, E., *Louis XIII et Richelieu. Lettres et pièces diplomatiques* (1911, repr. Geneva, 1974).
GUÉRIN, P. (ed.), *Registres des délibérations du bureau de la ville de Paris. VIII. 1576–1586* (1896).
GUÉRIN, P. (ed.), *Registres des délibérations du bureau de la ville de Paris, X. 1590–1594* (1902).
GUÉRY, A., 'Les finances de la monarchie française sous l'ancien régime', *Annales E.S.C.*, xxxiii (1978), 216–39.

HALPHEN, E. (ed.), *Journal inédit d'Arnauld d'Andilly, 1614–1620* (1857).
HARDING, R. R., *Anatomy of a power elite. The provincial governors of early modern France* (New Haven and London, 1978).
HAUSER, H., *La pensée et l'action économiques du Cardinal de Richelieu* (1944).
HAYDEN, J. M., *France and the Estates-General of 1614* (Cambridge, 1974).
HAYEM, F., *Le maréchal d'Ancre et Léonora Galigaï* (1910).
HENRARD, P., *Henri IV et la princesse de Condé, 1609–10* ... (Brussels, Ghent and Leipzig, 1870).
HEUMANN, P., 'Un traitant sous Louis XIII: Antoine Feydeau', *Études sur l'histoire administrative et sociale de l'ancien régime*, ed. G. Pagès (1938), 183–223.

JACQUART, J., 'Le marquis d'Effiat, lieutenant-général à l'armée d'Italie (été 1630)', *XVIIᵉ Siècle*, xlv (1959), 298–313.
JACQUART, J., *La crise rurale en Île-de-France, 1550–1670* (1974).
JACQUART, J., 'La rente foncière, indice conjoncturel?', *Revue Historique*, ccliii (1975), 355–76.
JOURDAN, A. J. L., DECRUSY, and ISAMBERT, F. A. (eds.), *Recueil général des anciennes lois françaises depuis l'an 420 jusqu'à la révolution de 1789*, 28 vols. (1821–33).
JOUVENCEL, H. de, *Le contrôleur-général des finances sous l'ancien régime* (1901).

KARCHER, A., 'L'assemblée des notables de St-Germain-en-Laye (1583)', *Bibliothèque de l'École des Chartes*, cxiv (1956), 115–62.
KIERSTEAD, R. F., *Pomponne de Bellièvre. A study of the king's men in the age of Henri IV* (Evanston, Ill., 1968).

KIERSTEAD, R. F. (ed.), *State and society in seventeenth-century France* (New York, 1975).

KOSSMANN, E. H., *La Fronde* (Leiden, 1954).

LABATUT, J. P., 'Aspects de la fortune de Bullion', *XVIIe Siècle*, lx (1963), 11–39.

LABATUT, J. P., *Les ducs et pairs de France au xviie siècle. Étude sociale* (1972).

LAIR, J., *Nicolas Foucquet. Procureur-général, surintendant des finances, ministre d'état de Louis XIV*, 2 vols. (1890).

LAVOLLÉE, R. *et al.* (eds.), A. J. du Plessis, Cardinal de Richelieu, *Mémoires*, 10 vols. (1907–31).

LE PESANT, M. (ed.), *Arrêts du conseil du roi. Règne de Louis XIV. Inventaire analytique des arrêts en commandement. I. 20 mai 1643–8 mars 1661* (1976).

LEROY-LADURIE, E., *Les paysans de Languedoc*, 2 vols. (1966).

LLOYD, H. A., *The Rouen campaign, 1590–1592. Politics, warfare and the early modern state* (Oxford, 1973).

LUBLINSKAYA, A. D., *French absolutism: the crucial phase, 1620–1629* (Cambridge, 1968).

MAJOR, J. R., 'Henry IV and Guyenne. A study concerning origins of royal absolutism', *French Historical Studies*, iv (1966), 363–83.

MAJOR, J. R., 'Bellièvre, Sully and the assembly of notables of 1596', *Transactions of the American Philosophical Society*, new ser., lxiv (1974), 3–34.

MAJOR, J. R., *Representative government in early modern France* (New Haven and London, 1980).

MALLET, J. R., *Comptes rendus de l'administration des finances du royaume de France* . . . (London, 1789).

MARTIN, G. and BEZANÇON, M., *L'histoire du crédit en France sous le règne de Louis XIV* . . . (1913).

MAYER, C. J., *Des États Généraux et autres assemblées nationales*, 18 vols. (The Hague, 1788–9).

MEUVRET, J., *Études d'histoire économique. Recueil d'articles* . . . (1971).

MICHAUD, H., 'L'ordonnancement des dépenses et le budget de la monarchie, 1587–1589', *Annuaire-Bulletin de la Société de l'Histoire de France* [1970–1] (1972), 87–150.

MICHAUD, J. F. and POUJOULAT, J. J. F. (eds.), Sully, *Mémoires des sages et royales oeconomies d'estat* . . ., 2nd ser., ii and iii (1837).

MICHAUD, J. F. and POUJOULAT, J. J. F. (eds.), *Les négociations du président Jeannin*, 2nd ser., iv (1838).

MICHAUD, J. F. and POUJOULAT, J. J. F. (eds.), Fontenay-Mareuil, *Mémoires* . . ., 2nd ser. v (1838).

MICHAUD, J. F. and POUJOULAT, J. J. F. (eds.), P. Phélypeaux de Pontchartrain, *Mémoires* . . ., 2nd ser., v (1838).

MICHAUD, J. F. and POUJOULAT, J. J. F. (eds.), A. J. du Plessis, Cardinal de Richelieu, *Mémoires* . . ., 2nd ser. vii–ix (1837–9).

MICHAUD, J. F. and POUJOULAT, J. J. F. (eds.), R. d'Arnauld d'Andilly, *Mémoires* . . ., 2nd ser. ix (1838).

MICHAUD, J. F. and POUJOULAT, J. J. F. (eds.), Jean Hérault de Gourville, *Mémoires* . . . 3rd ser. v (1838).

MICHAUD, J. F. and POUJOULAT, J. J. F. (eds.), Montglat, *Mémoires* . . ., 3rd ser. v (1838).

MICHAUD, J. F. and POUJOULAT, J. J. F. (eds.), Omer Talon, *Mémoires* . . ., 3rd ser. vi (1839).

MICHAUD, J. F. and POUJOULAT, J. J. F. (eds.), abbé de Choisy, *Mémoires* . . ., 3rd ser. vi (1839).

MONGRÉDIEN, G., *L'affaire Foucquet* (1956).

MONGRÉDIEN, G., *Léonora Galigaï. Un procès de sorcellerie sous Louis XIII* (1968).

MOOTE, A. L., *The revolt of the judges. The Parlement of Paris and the Fronde, 1643–1652* (Princeton, N. J., 1971).

MOREAU, C. (ed.), *Choix de Mazarinades*, 2 vols. (1853).

MOSSER, F., *Les intendants des finances au xviiie siècle. Les Lefèvre d'Ormesson et le 'département des impositions', 1715–1777* (Geneva and Paris, 1978).

MOUSNIER, R. É., 'Sully et le conseil d'état et des finances', *Revue Historique*, cxcii (1941), 68–86.

MOUSNIER, R. É., 'Les règlements du conseil du roi sous Louis XIII', *Annuaire-Bulletin de la Société de l'Histoire de France* (1948), 93–211.

MOUSNIER, R. É., *L'assassinat de Henri IV. 14 mai 1610* (1964).

MOUSNIER, R. É., *La plume, la faucille et le marteau. Institutions et société en France du moyen âge à la Révolution* (1970).

MOUSNIER, R. É., *La vénalité des offices sous Henri IV et Louis XIII*, 2nd ed. (1971).

PAGÈS, G., 'La vénalité des offices dans l'ancienne France', *Revue Historique*, clxix (1932), 477–95.

PAGÈS, G., 'Autour du "grand orage". Richelieu et Marillac. Deux politiques', *Revue Historique*, clxxix (1937), 63–97.

PAGÈS, G., 'Le conseil du roi et la vénalité des offices pendant les premières années du ministère de Richelieu', *Revue Historique*, clxxxii (1938), 245–82.

PARKER, D., 'The social foundation of French absolutism, 1610–1630', *Past and Present*, liii (1971), 67–89.

PARKER, D., *La Rochelle and the French monarchy: conflict and order in seventeenth-century France* (1980).

PARKER, N. G., *The Dutch Revolt* (1977).

PATRY, R., *Philippe du Plessis-Mornay. Un huguenot homme d'état, 1549–1623* (1933).

PETIT, J., *L'assemblée des notables de 1626–1627* (1936).

PICOT, G., *Histoire des États Généraux* . . ., 2nd ed., 5 vols. (1888).

POIRSON, A., *Histoire du règne de Henri IV*, 2nd ed., 4 vols. (1862–7).

RANUM, O. A., *Richelieu and the councillors of Louis XIII. A study of the secretaries of state and superintendents of finance in the ministry of Richelieu, 1635–1642* (Oxford, 1963).
RAVAISSON-MOLLIEN, F. (ed.), *Archives de la Bastille. Documents inédits. Règne de Louis XIV*, vols. i–ii (1866, repr. Geneva, 1975).
REINHARD, M., *La légende de Henri IV* (Saint-Brieuc, 1935).
RICHARD, P., *La papauté et la Ligue française. Pierre d'Épinac. Archevêque de Lyon, 1573–1599* (Paris and Lyon, 1901).
ROTT, E., *Henri IV, Les Suisses et la Haute Italie. La lutte pour les Alpes, 1598–1610 . . .* (1882).

SAIGE, G. (ed.), *Journal des guerres civiles de Dubuisson-Aubenay, 1648–1652*, 2 vols. (1883, 1885).
SAULNIER, E., *Le rôle politique du Cardinal de Bourbon (Charles X), 1523–1590* (1912).
SCHNAPPER, B., *Les rentes au xvie siècle. Histoire d'un instrument de crédit* (1957).
SPOONER, F. C., *The international economy and monetary movements in France, 1493–1725* (Cambridge, Mass., 1972).

TAPIÉ, V. L., *La politique étrangère de la France et le début de la guerre de Trente Ans, 1616–1621* (1934).
TAPIÉ, V. L., *La France de Louis XIII et de Richelieu*, 2nd ed. (1967).
THÉRIVE, A. (ed.), Guy Patin, *Lettres pendant la Fronde* (1921).
THUAU, E., *Raison d'état et pensée politique à l'époque de Richelieu* (1966).
TUETEY, A. (ed.), *Registres des délibérations du bureau de la ville de Paris. XI. 1594–1598* (1902).

VALOIS, N. (ed.), *Inventaire des arrêts du conseil d'état. Règne de Henri IV*, 2 vols. (1886, 1893).
VÉRON DE FORBONNAIS, F., *Recherches et considérations sur les finances de France depuis 1595 jusqu'à l'année 1721*, 2 vols. (Basle, 1758).

WOLFE, M., *The fiscal system of renaissance France* (New Haven and London, 1972).

ZELLER, B., *Le connétable de Luynes. Montauban et la Valteline* (1879).
ZELLER, B., *Richelieu et les ministres de Louis XIII de 1621 à 1624* (1880).
ZELLER, B., *La minorité de Louis XIII: Marie de Médicis et Sully, 1610–12* (1892).
ZELLER, B., *La minorité de Louis XIII. Marie de Médicis et Villeroy . . .* (1897).

ZELLER, B., *Louis XIII. Marie de Médicis, chef du conseil* . . . *1614–1616* (1898).

ZELLER, B., *Louis XIII. Marie de Médicis. Richelieu ministre. Chute et mort de Concini, 1616–1617* (1899).

INDEX